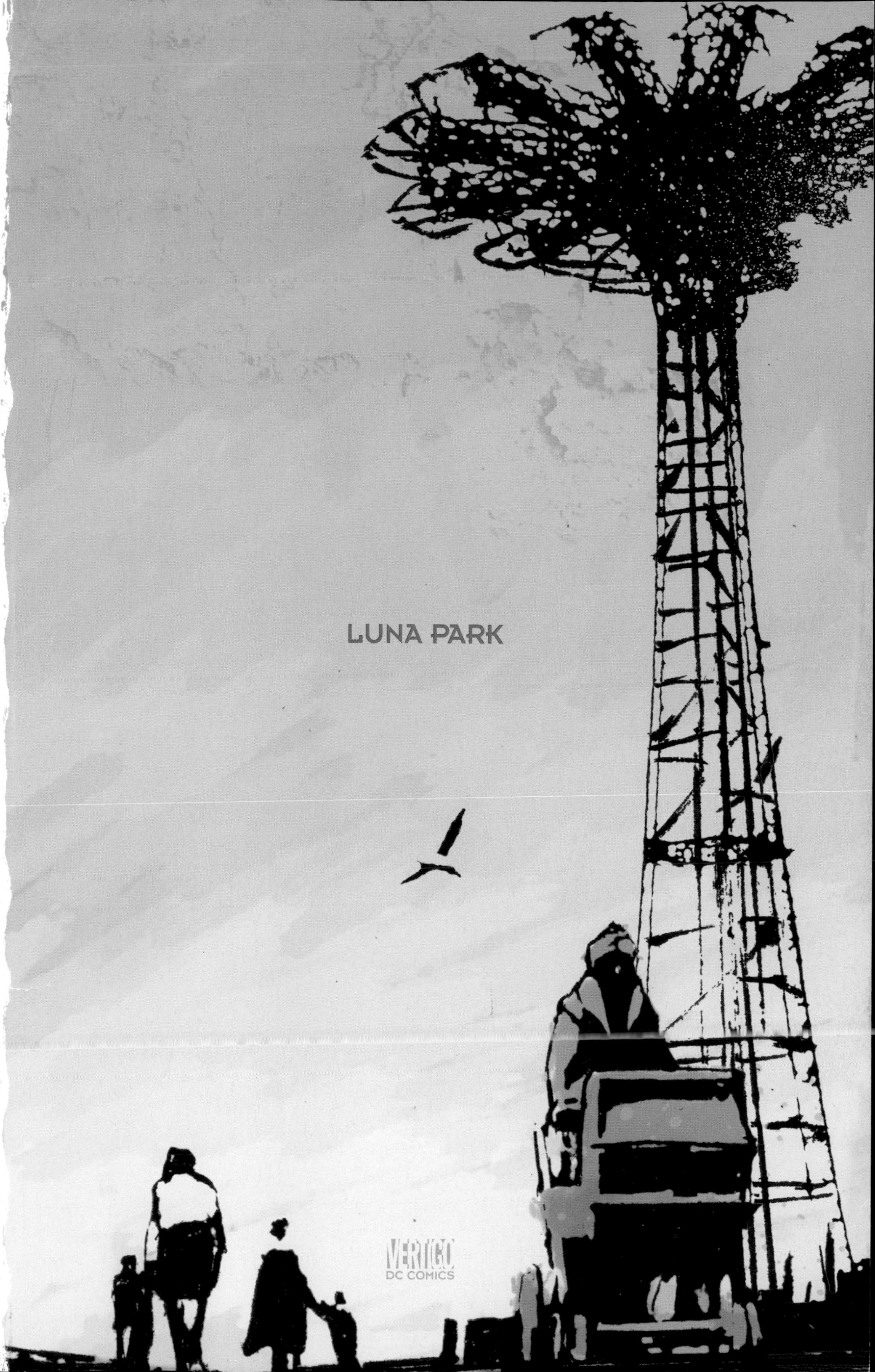
LUNA PARK
VERTIGO
DC COMICS

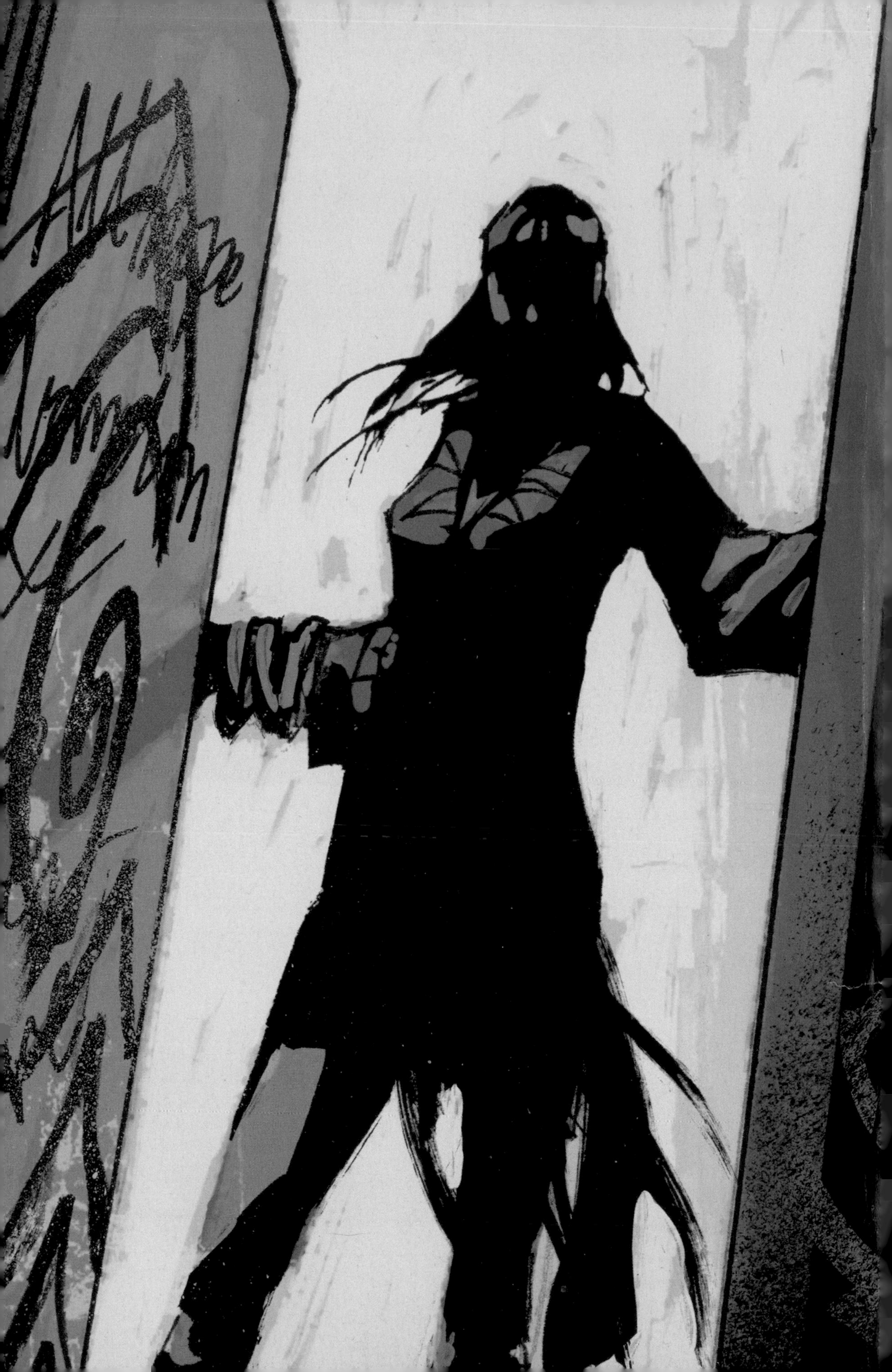

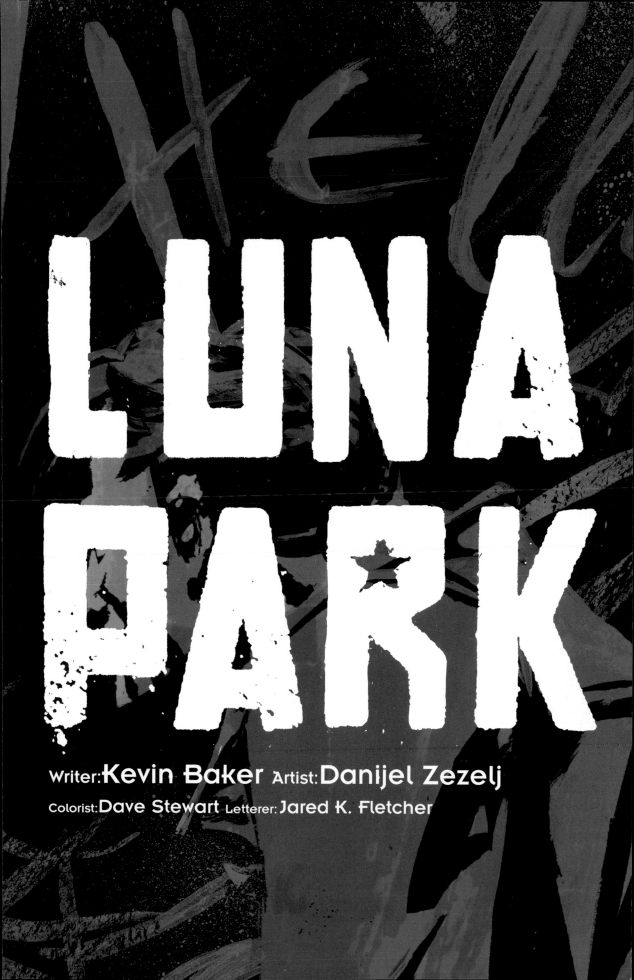

# LUNA PARK

Writer: **Kevin Baker**  Artist: **Danijel Zezelj**

Colorist: **Dave Stewart**  Letterer: **Jared K. Fletcher**

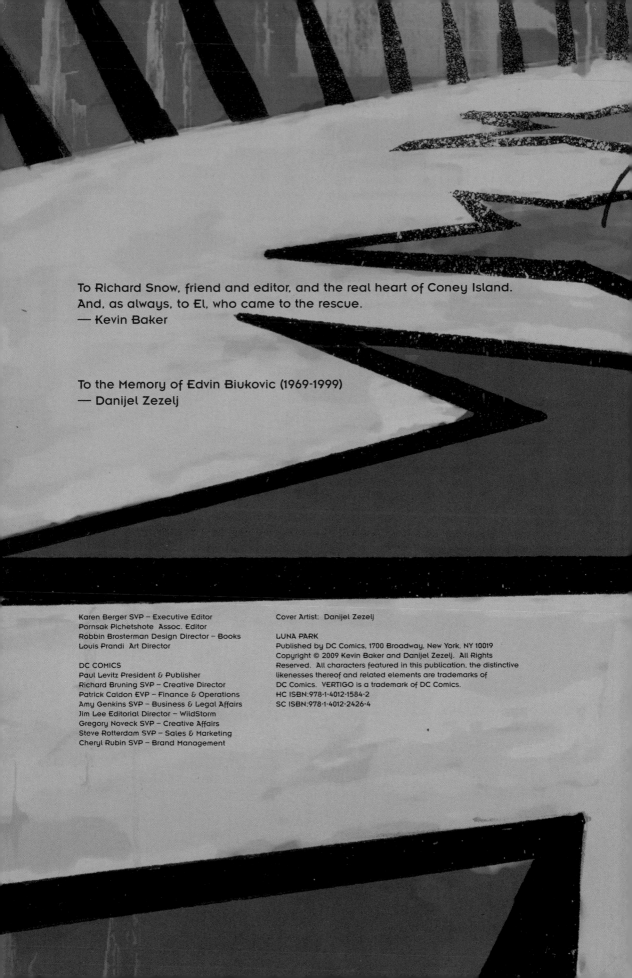

To Richard Snow, friend and editor, and the real heart of Coney Island.
And, as always, to El, who came to the rescue.
— Kevin Baker

To the Memory of Edvin Biukovic (1969-1999)
— Danijel Zezelj

Karen Berger SVP – Executive Editor
Pornsak Pichetshote  Assoc. Editor
Robbin Brosterman Design Director – Books
Louis Prandi  Art Director

DC COMICS
Paul Levitz President & Publisher
Richard Bruning SVP – Creative Director
Patrick Caldon EVP – Finance & Operations
Amy Genkins SVP – Business & Legal Affairs
Jim Lee Editorial Director – WildStorm
Gregory Noveck SVP – Creative Affairs
Steve Rotterdam SVP – Sales & Marketing
Cheryl Rubin SVP – Brand Management

Cover Artist:  Danijel Zezelj

LUNA PARK
Published by DC Comics, 1700 Broadway, New York, NY 10019
Copyright © 2009 Kevin Baker and Danijel Zezelj.  All Rights
Reserved.  All characters featured in this publication, the distinctive
likenesses thereof and related elements are trademarks of
DC Comics.  VERTIGO is a trademark of DC Comics.
HC ISBN:978-1-4012-1584-2
SC ISBN:978-1-4012-2426-4

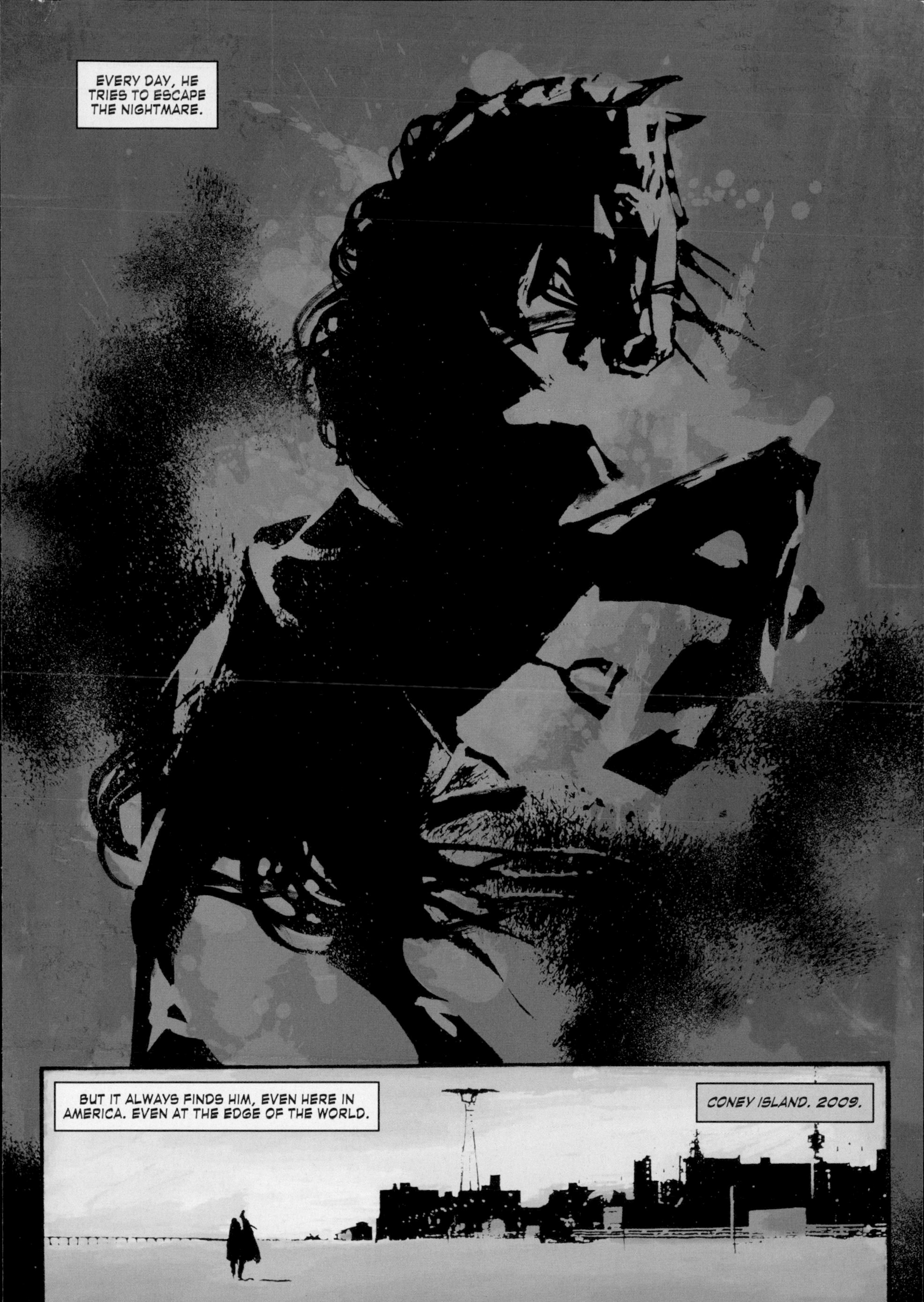
EVERY DAY, HE TRIES TO ESCAPE THE NIGHTMARE.
BUT IT ALWAYS FINDS HIM, EVEN HERE IN AMERICA. EVEN AT THE EDGE OF THE WORLD.
CONEY ISLAND. 2009.

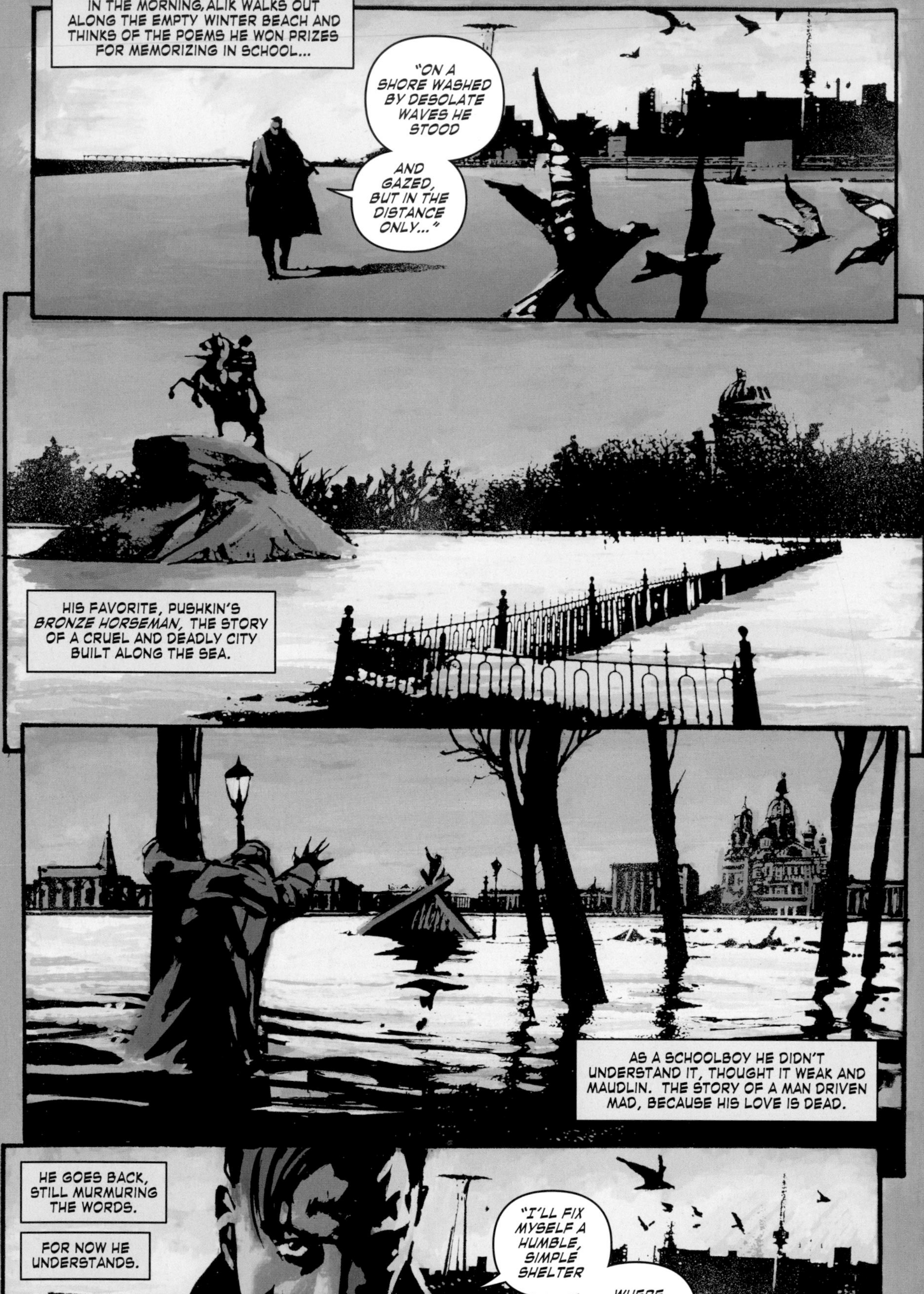

IN THE MORNING, ALIK WALKS OUT ALONG THE EMPTY WINTER BEACH AND THINKS OF THE POEMS HE WON PRIZES FOR MEMORIZING IN SCHOOL...
"ON A SHORE WASHED BY DESOLATE WAVES HE STOOD
AND GAZED, BUT IN THE DISTANCE ONLY..."
HIS FAVORITE, PUSHKIN'S *BRONZE HORSEMAN*, THE STORY OF A CRUEL AND DEADLY CITY BUILT ALONG THE SEA.
AS A SCHOOLBOY HE DIDN'T UNDERSTAND IT, THOUGHT IT WEAK AND MAUDLIN. THE STORY OF A MAN DRIVEN MAD, BECAUSE HIS LOVE IS DEAD.
HE GOES BACK, STILL MURMURING THE WORDS.
FOR NOW HE UNDERSTANDS.
"I'LL FIX MYSELF A HUMBLE, SIMPLE SHELTER
WHERE PARASHA AND I CAN LIVE IN QUIET..."

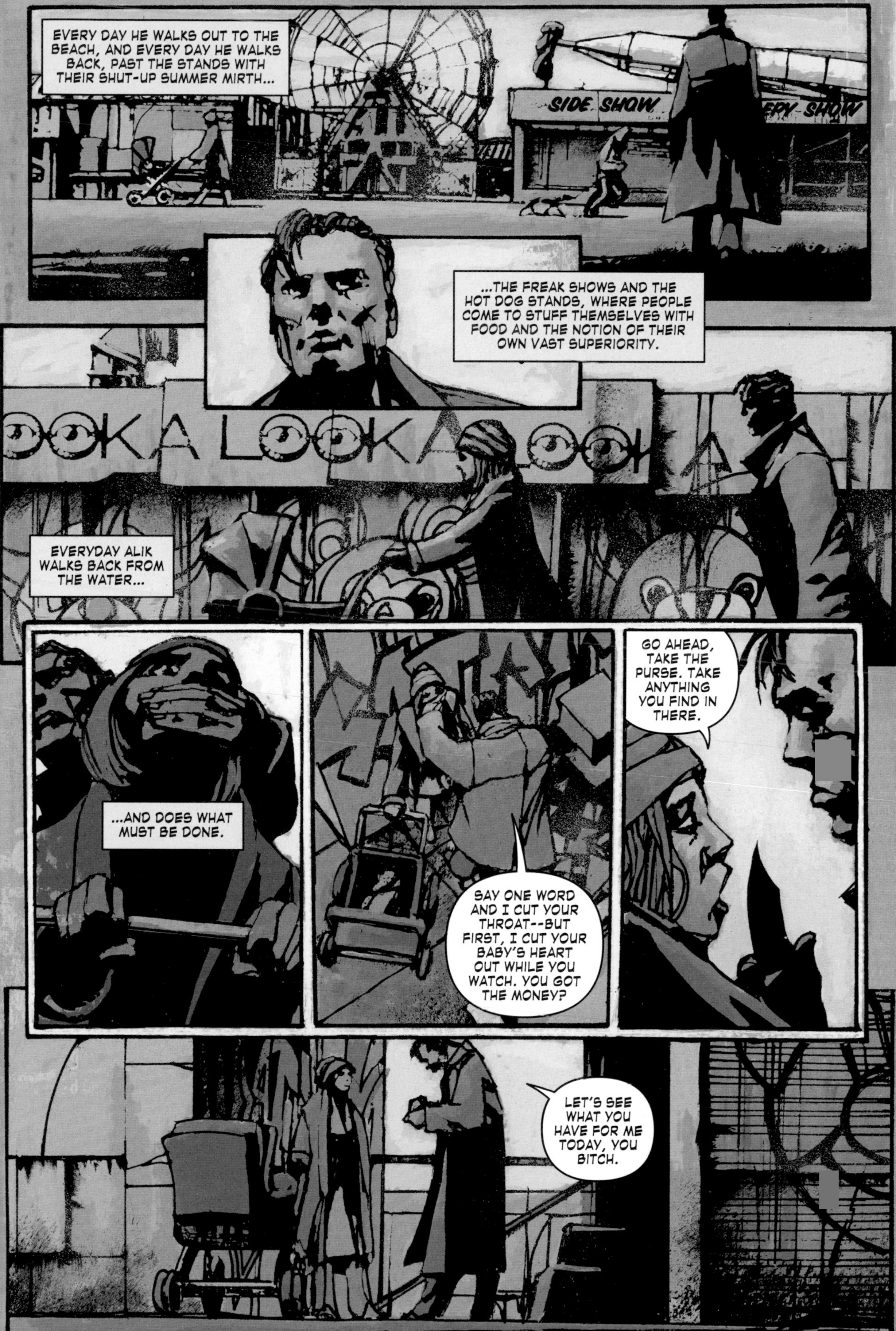
EVERY DAY HE WALKS OUT TO THE BEACH, AND EVERY DAY HE WALKS BACK, PAST THE STANDS WITH THEIR SHUT-UP SUMMER MIRTH...
SIDE SHOW
...THE FREAK SHOWS AND THE HOT DOG STANDS, WHERE PEOPLE COME TO STUFF THEMSELVES WITH FOOD AND THE NOTION OF THEIR OWN VAST SUPERIORITY.
EVERYDAY ALIK WALKS BACK FROM THE WATER...
...AND DOES WHAT MUST BE DONE.
SAY ONE WORD AND I CUT YOUR THROAT--BUT FIRST, I CUT YOUR BABY'S HEART OUT WHILE YOU WATCH. YOU GOT THE MONEY?
GO AHEAD, TAKE THE PURSE. TAKE ANYTHING YOU FIND IN THERE.
LET'S SEE WHAT YOU HAVE FOR ME TODAY, YOU BITCH.

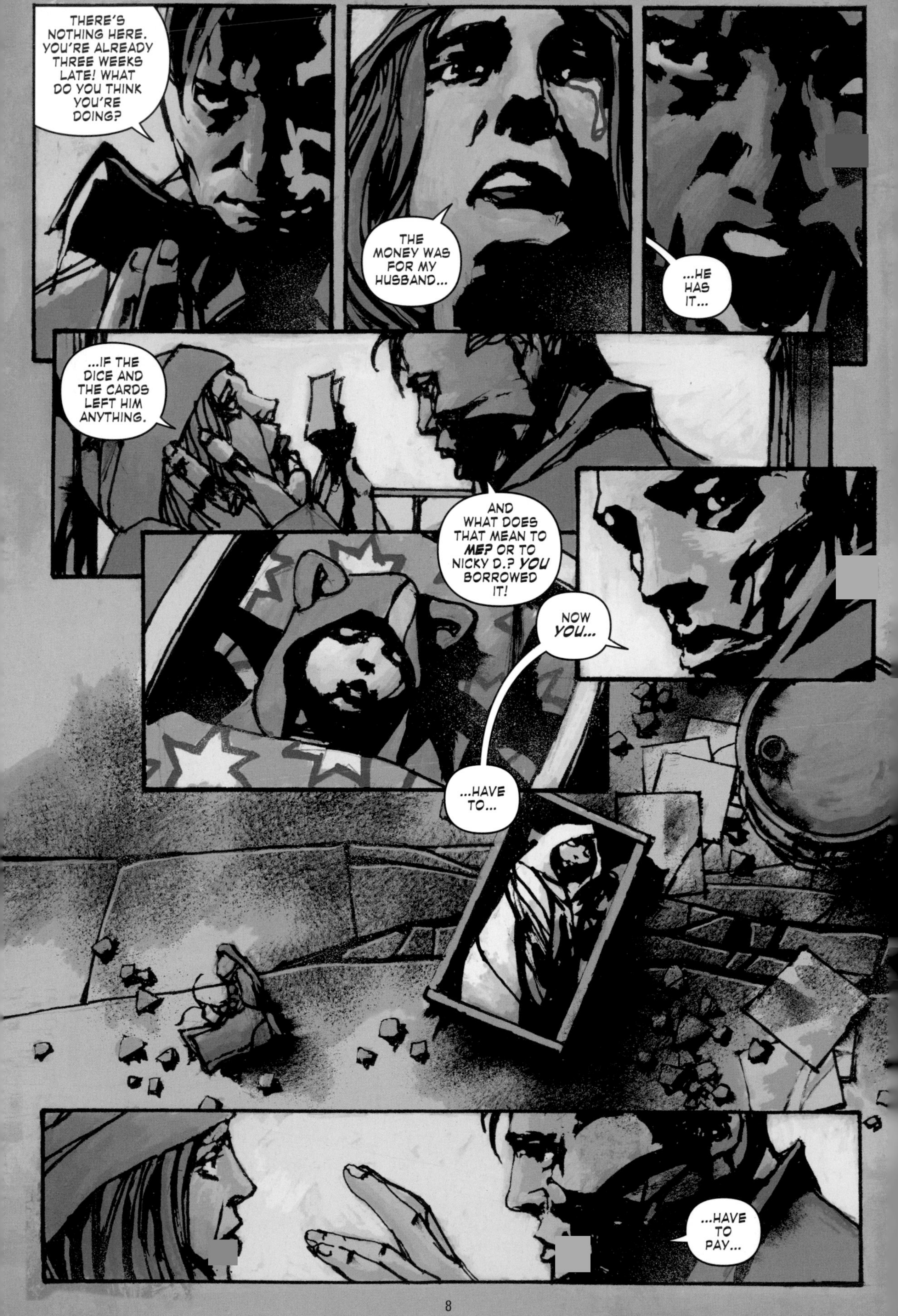
THERE'S NOTHING HERE. YOU'RE ALREADY THREE WEEKS LATE! WHAT DO YOU THINK YOU'RE DOING?
THE MONEY WAS FOR MY HUSBAND...
...HE HAS IT...
...IF THE DICE AND THE CARDS LEFT HIM ANYTHING.
AND WHAT DOES THAT MEAN TO *ME?* OR TO NICKY D.? *YOU* BORROWED IT!
NOW *YOU*...
...HAVE TO...
...HAVE TO PAY...

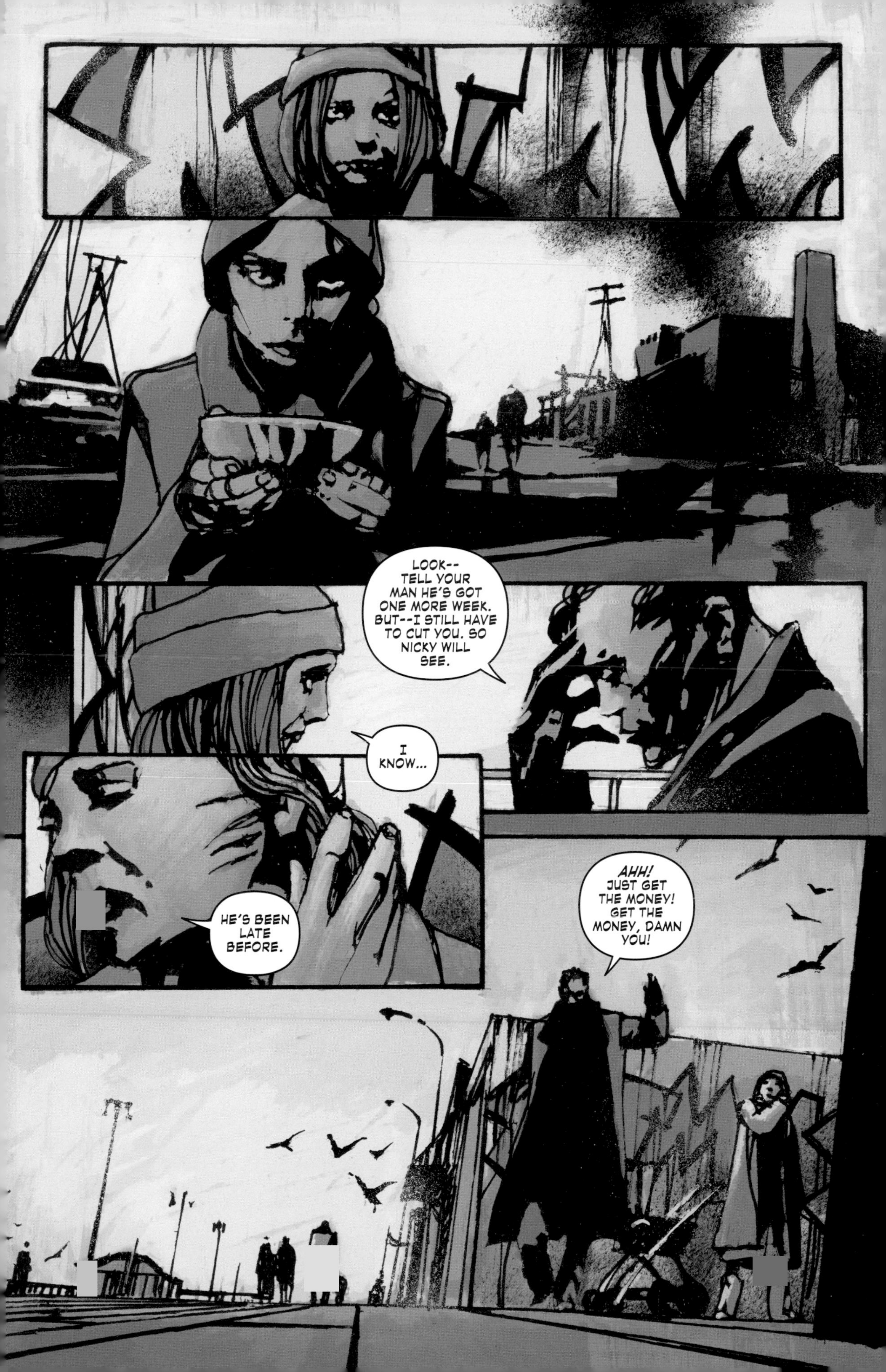
LOOK-- TELL YOUR MAN HE'S GOT ONE MORE WEEK. BUT--I STILL HAVE TO CUT YOU. SO NICKY WILL SEE.
I KNOW...
HE'S BEEN LATE BEFORE.
AHH! JUST GET THE MONEY! GET THE MONEY, DAMN YOU!

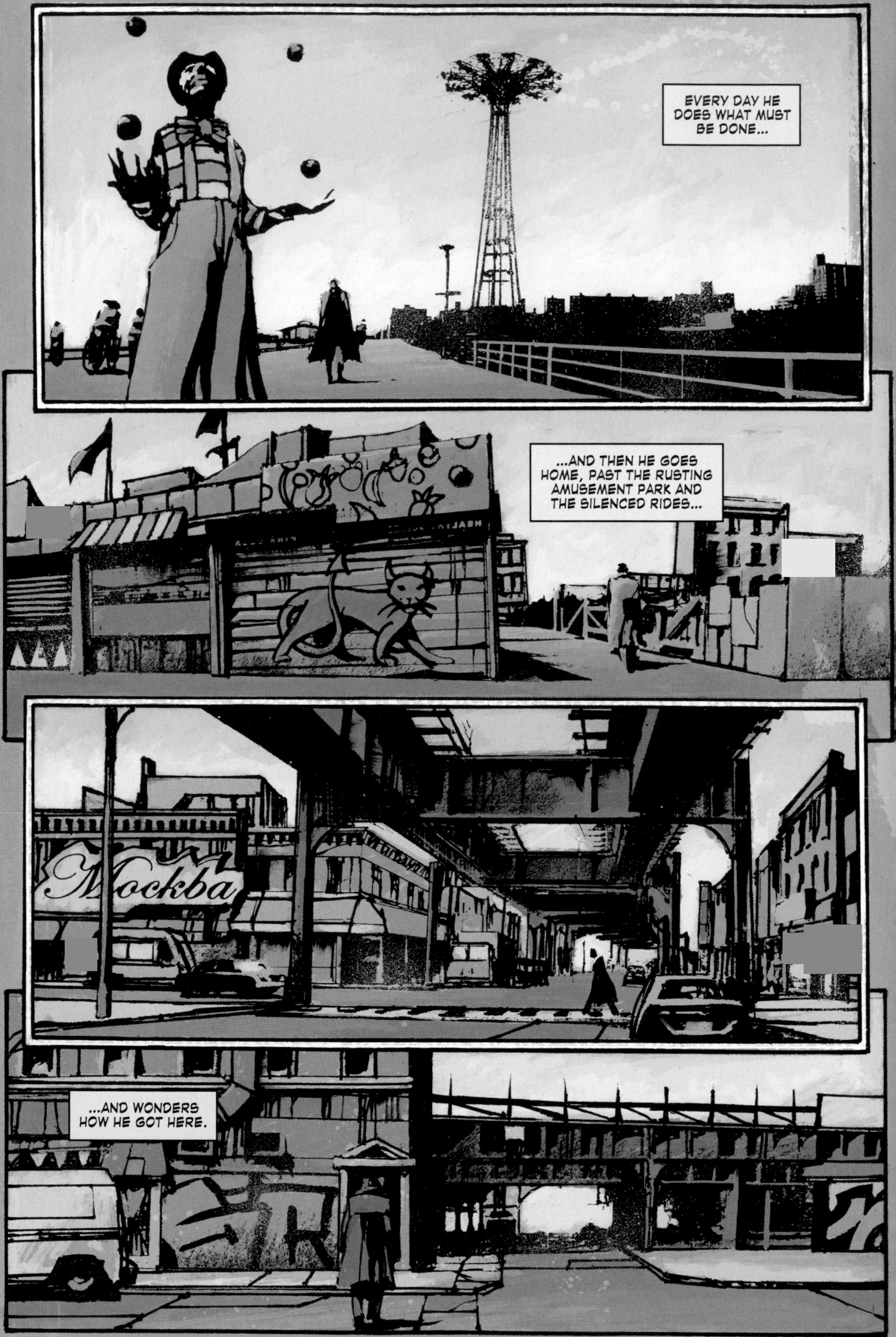
EVERY DAY HE DOES WHAT MUST BE DONE...
...AND THEN HE GOES HOME, PAST THE RUSTING AMUSEMENT PARK AND THE SILENCED RIDES...
Москва
...AND WONDERS HOW HE GOT HERE.

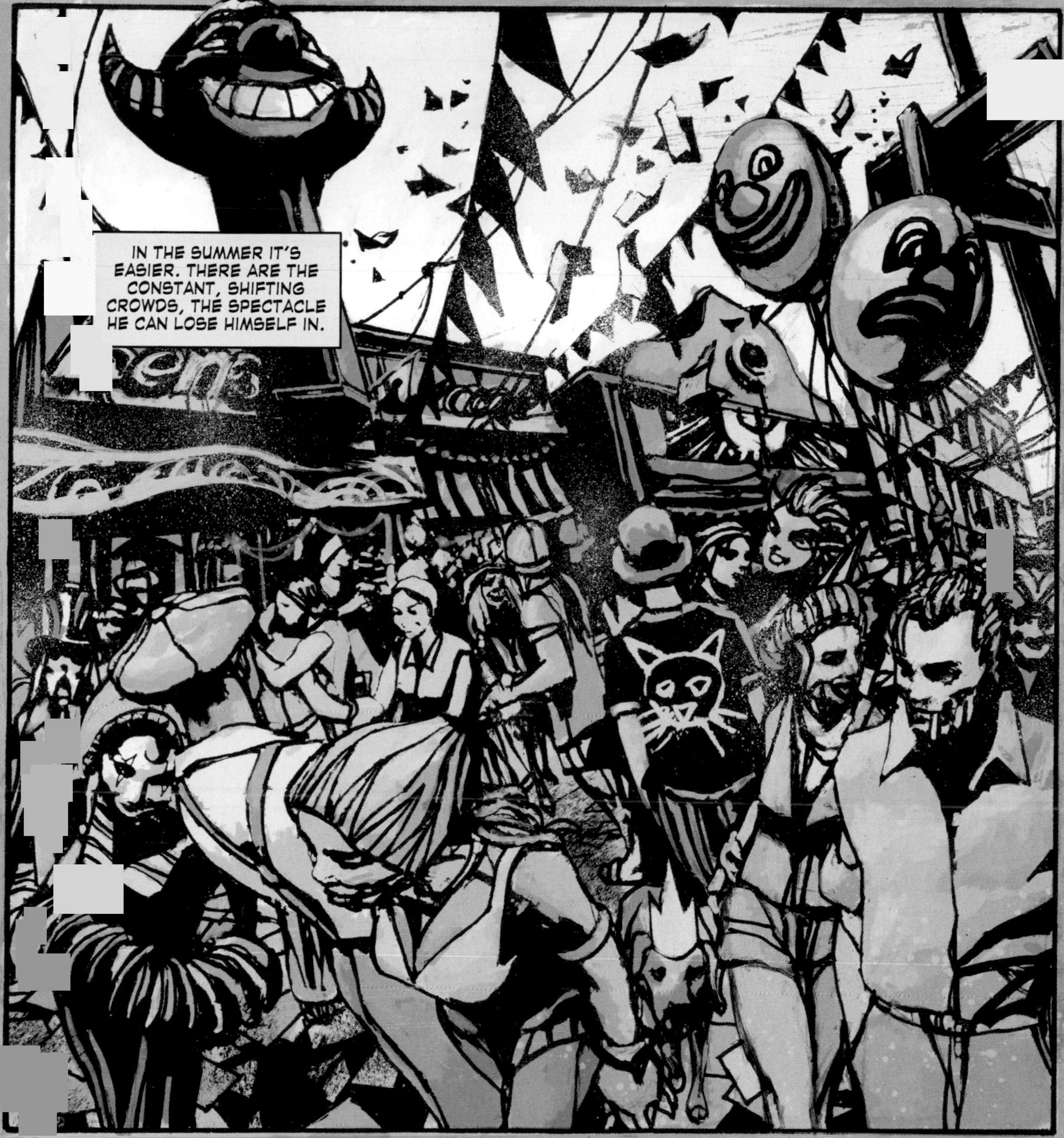
IN THE SUMMER IT'S EASIER. THERE ARE THE CONSTANT, SHIFTING CROWDS, THE SPECTACLE HE CAN LOSE HIMSELF IN.

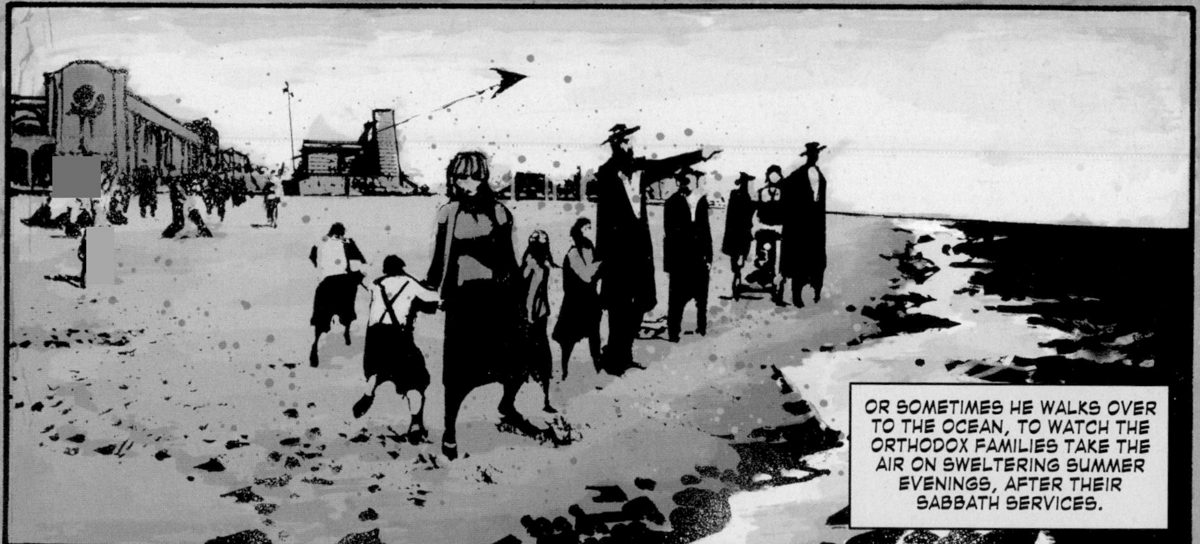
OR SOMETIMES HE WALKS OVER TO THE OCEAN, TO WATCH THE ORTHODOX FAMILIES TAKE THE AIR ON SWELTERING SUMMER EVENINGS, AFTER THEIR SABBATH SERVICES.

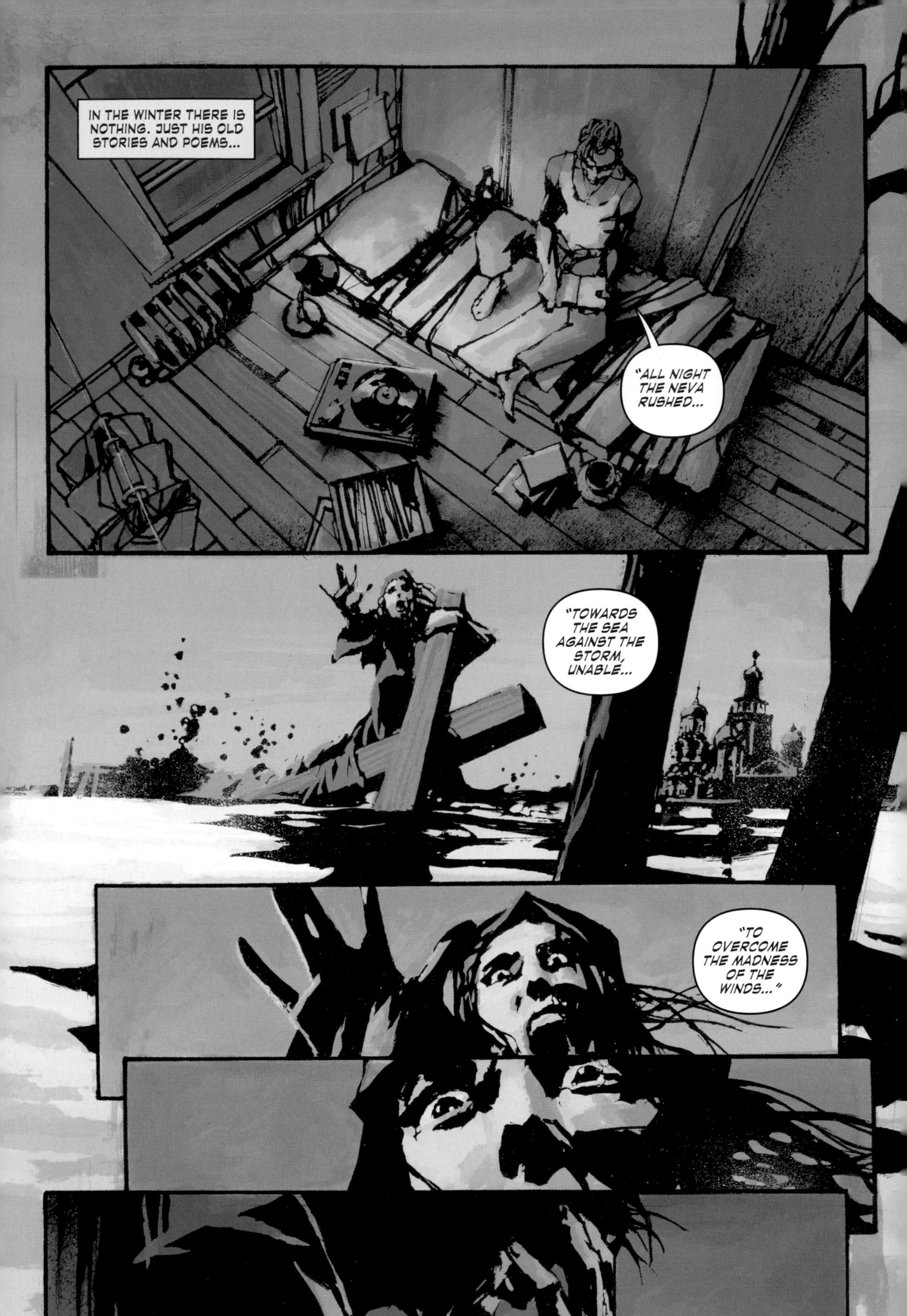
IN THE WINTER THERE IS NOTHING. JUST HIS OLD STORIES AND POEMS...
"ALL NIGHT THE NEVA RUSHED...
"TOWARDS THE SEA AGAINST THE STORM, UNABLE...
"TO OVERCOME THE MADNESS OF THE WINDS..."

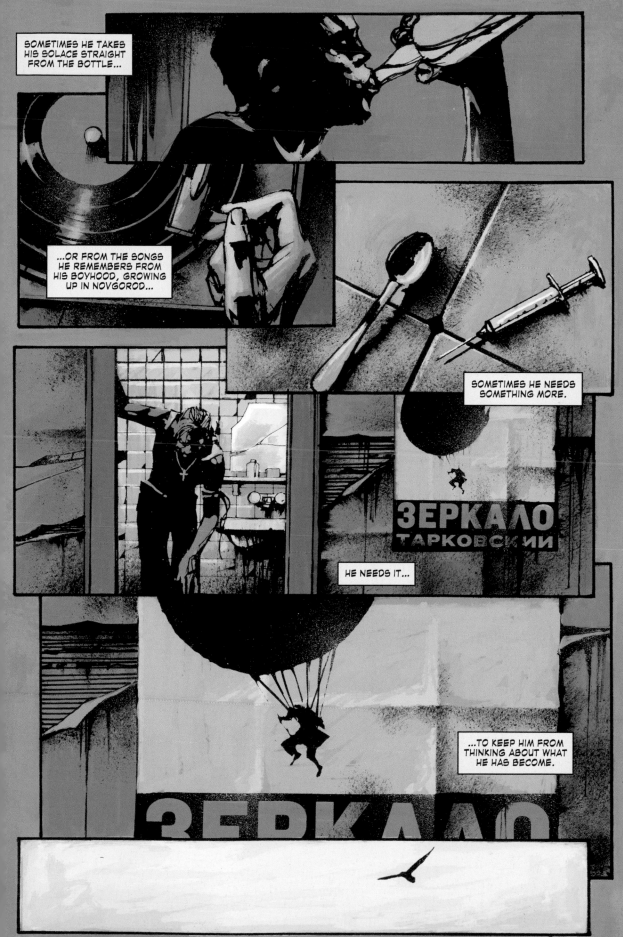

SOMETIMES HE TAKES HIS SOLACE STRAIGHT FROM THE BOTTLE...

...OR FROM THE SONGS HE REMEMBERS FROM HIS BOYHOOD, GROWING UP IN NOVGOROD...

SOMETIMES HE NEEDS SOMETHING MORE.

ЗЕРКАЛО
ТАРКОВСКИИ

HE NEEDS IT...

...TO KEEP HIM FROM THINKING ABOUT WHAT HE HAS BECOME.

ЗЕРКАЛО

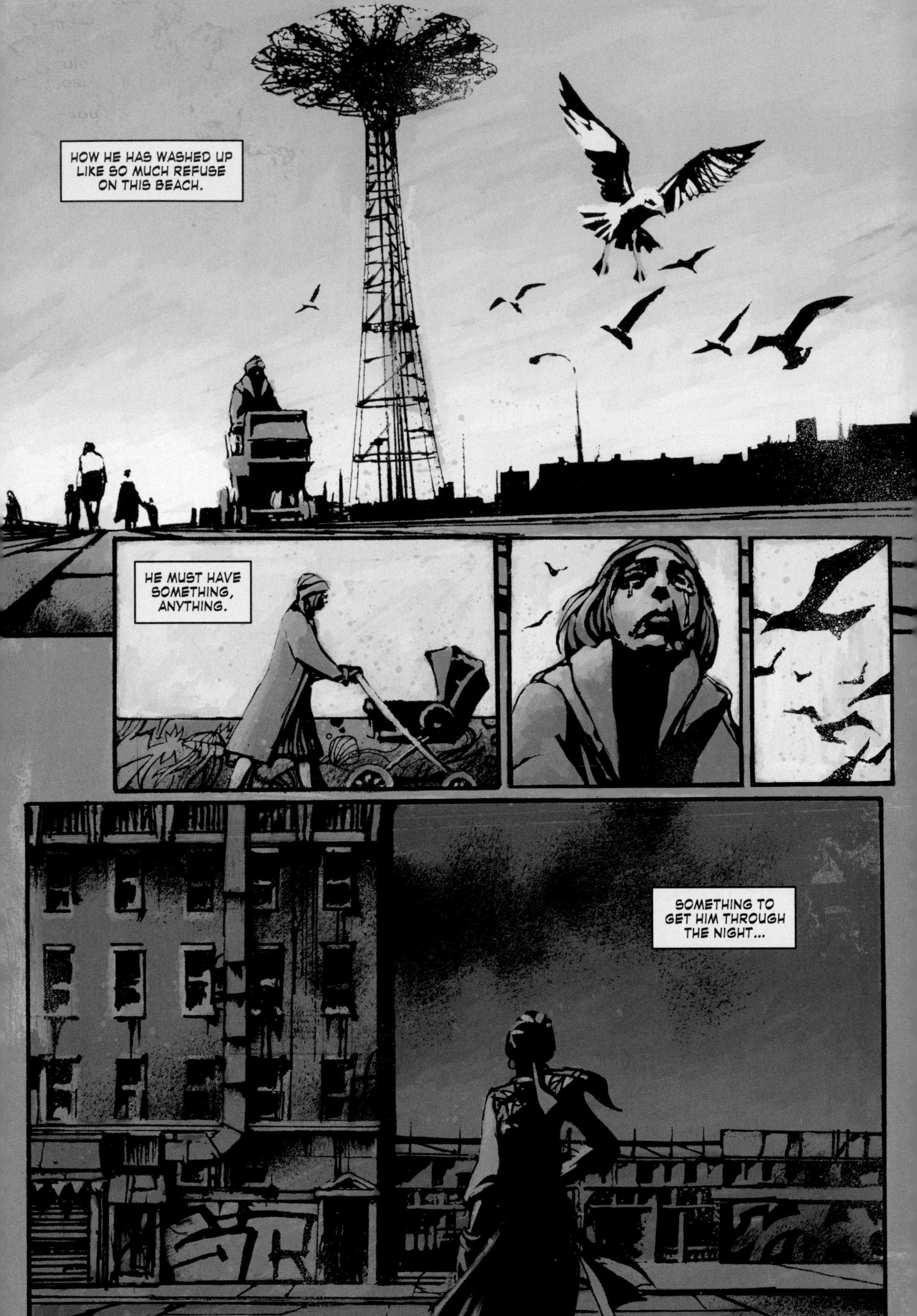
HOW HE HAS WASHED UP LIKE SO MUCH REFUSE ON THIS BEACH.
HE MUST HAVE SOMETHING, ANYTHING.
SOMETHING TO GET HIM THROUGH THE NIGHT...

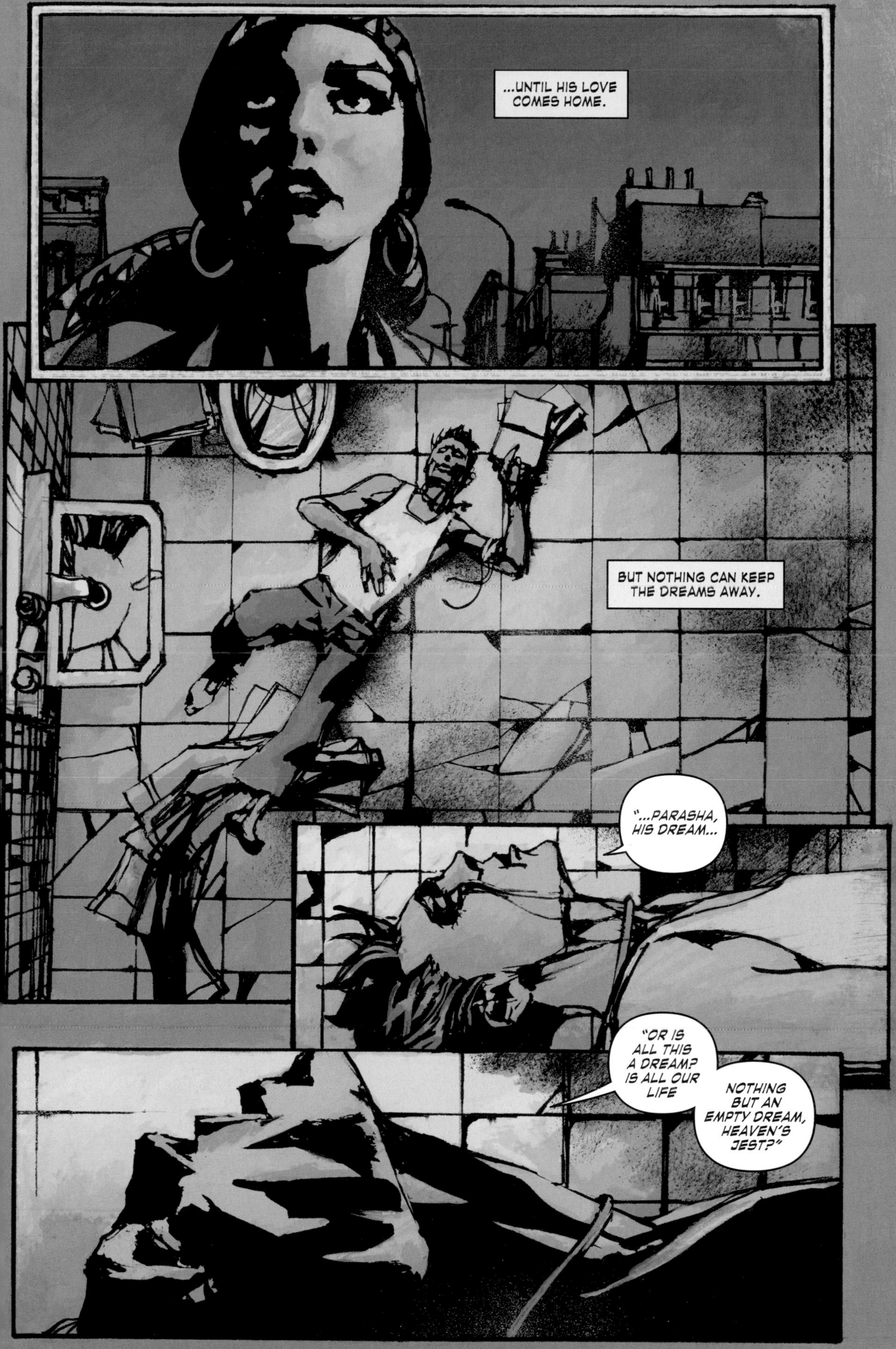
...UNTIL HIS LOVE COMES HOME.
BUT NOTHING CAN KEEP THE DREAMS AWAY.
"...PARASHA, HIS DREAM...
"OR IS ALL THIS A DREAM? IS ALL OUR LIFE
NOTHING BUT AN EMPTY DREAM, HEAVEN'S JEST?"

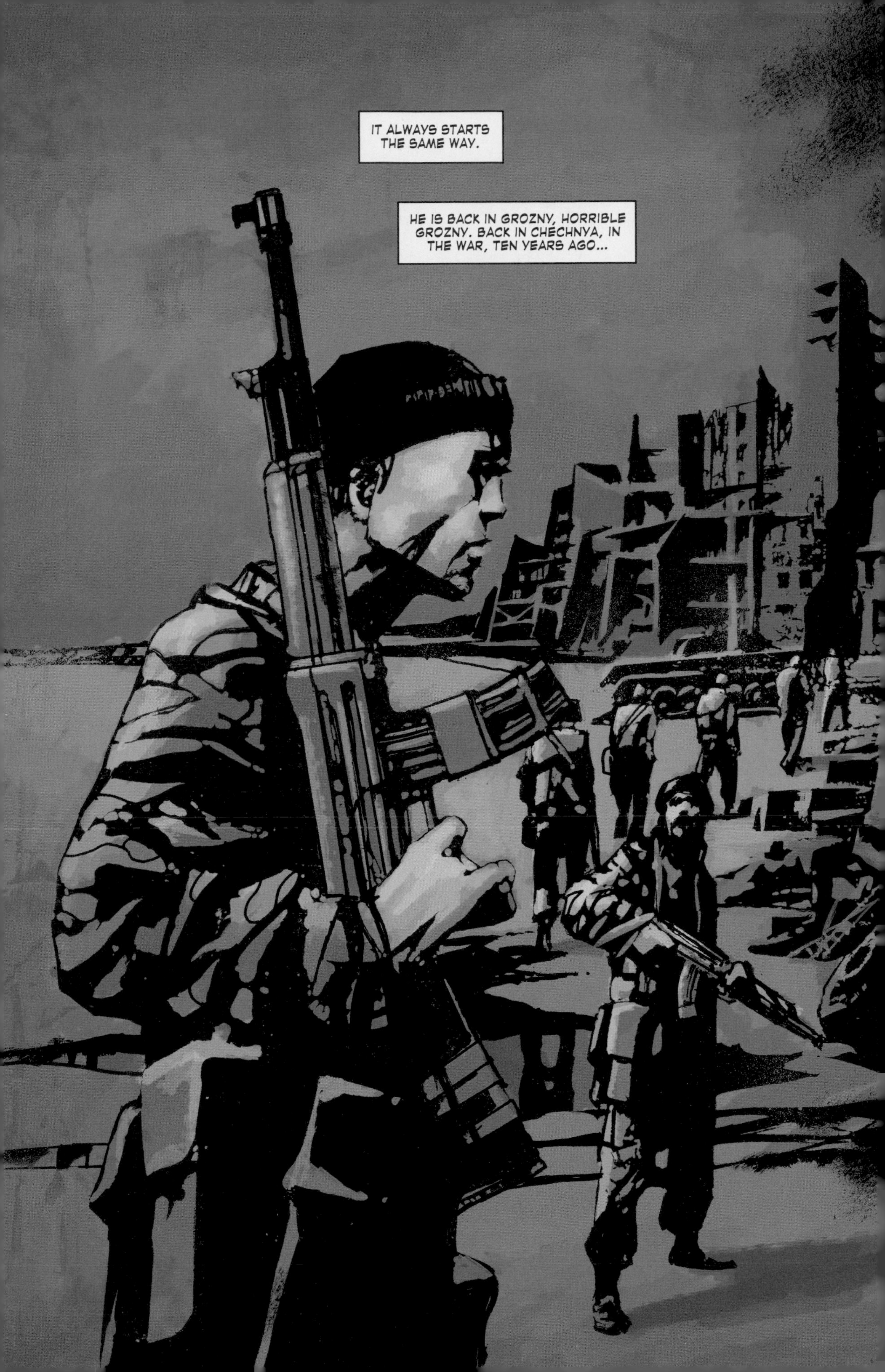
IT ALWAYS STARTS THE SAME WAY.
HE IS BACK IN GROZNY, HORRIBLE GROZNY. BACK IN CHECHNYA, IN THE WAR, TEN YEARS AGO...

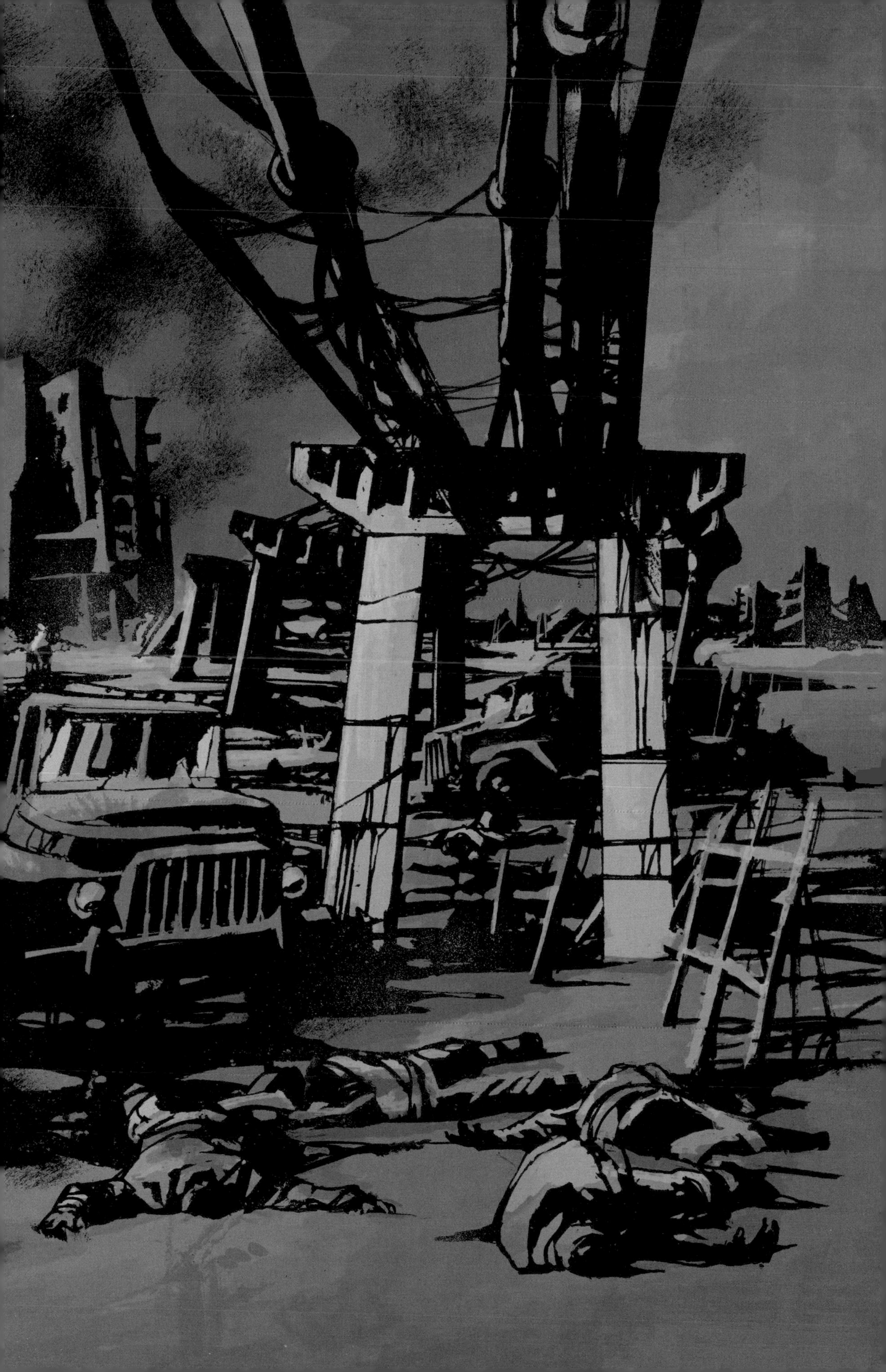

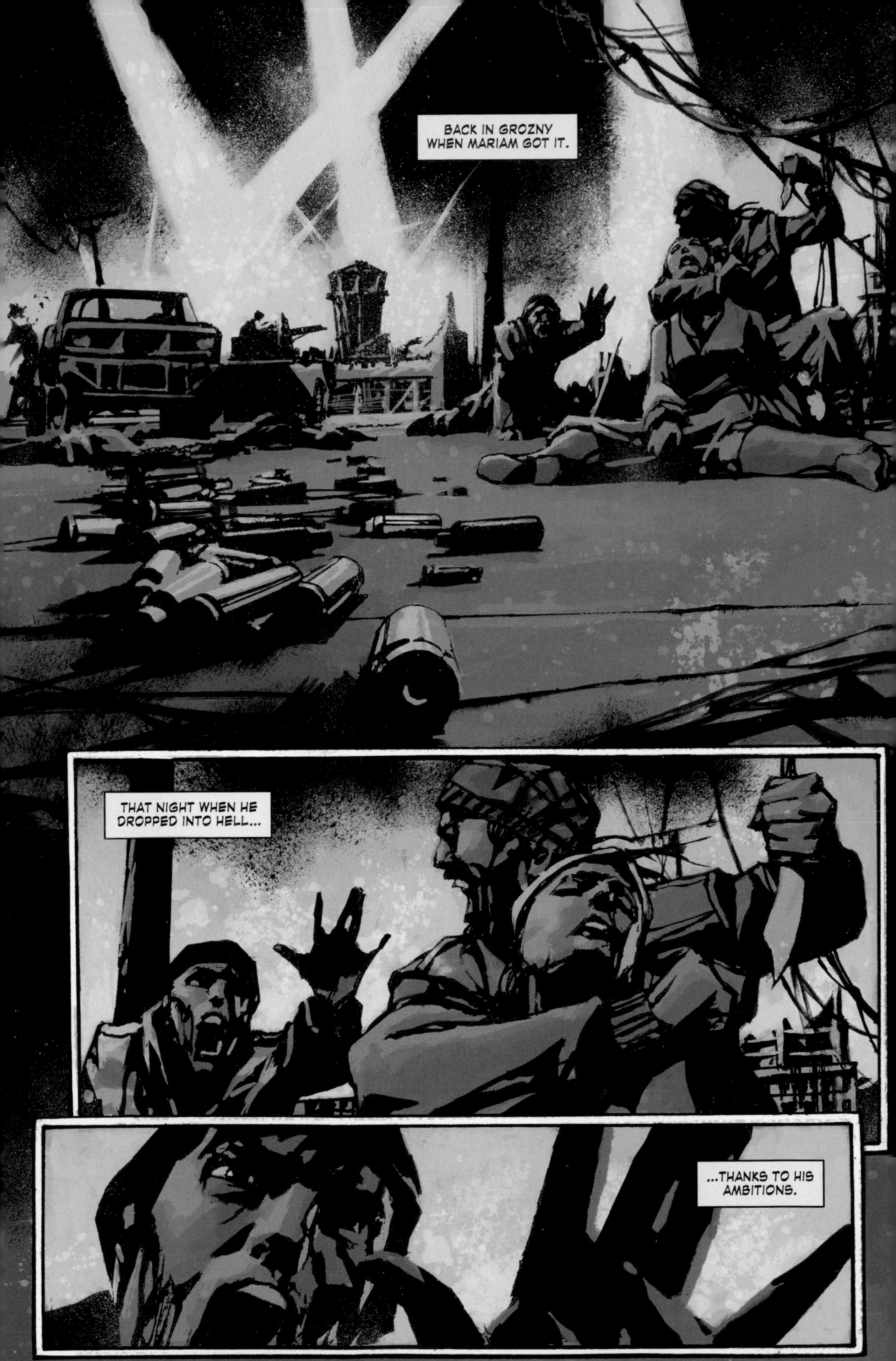
BACK IN GROZNY WHEN MARIAM GOT IT.
THAT NIGHT WHEN HE DROPPED INTO HELL...
...THANKS TO HIS AMBITIONS.

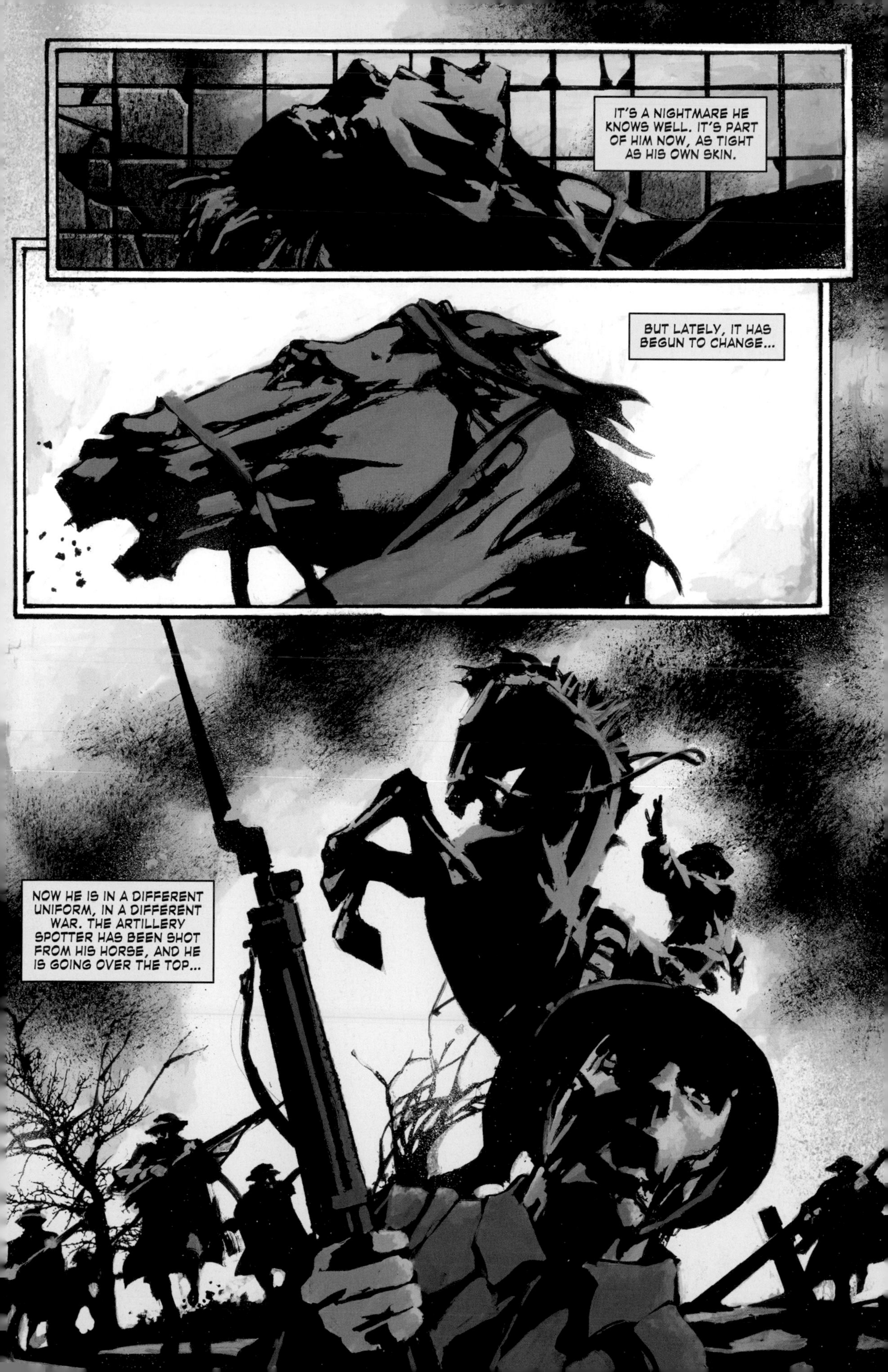
IT'S A NIGHTMARE HE KNOWS WELL. IT'S PART OF HIM NOW, AS TIGHT AS HIS OWN SKIN.
BUT LATELY, IT HAS BEGUN TO CHANGE...
NOW HE IS IN A DIFFERENT UNIFORM, IN A DIFFERENT WAR. THE ARTILLERY SPOTTER HAS BEEN SHOT FROM HIS HORSE, AND HE IS GOING OVER THE TOP...

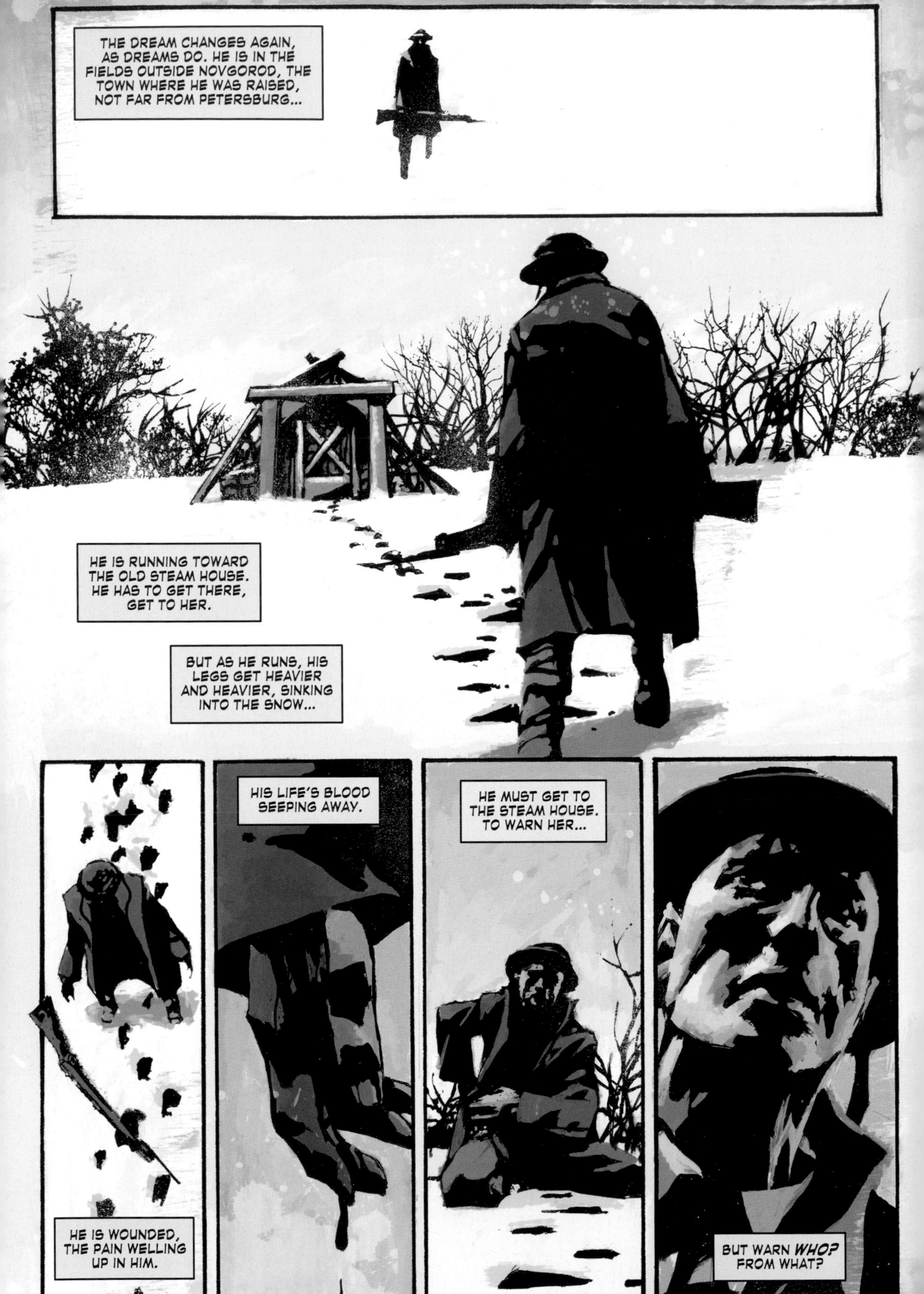
THE DREAM CHANGES AGAIN, AS DREAMS DO. HE IS IN THE FIELDS OUTSIDE NOVGOROD, THE TOWN WHERE HE WAS RAISED, NOT FAR FROM PETERSBURG...
HE IS RUNNING TOWARD THE OLD STEAM HOUSE. HE HAS TO GET THERE, GET TO HER.
BUT AS HE RUNS, HIS LEGS GET HEAVIER AND HEAVIER, SINKING INTO THE SNOW...
HE IS WOUNDED, THE PAIN WELLING UP IN HIM.
HIS LIFE'S BLOOD SEEPING AWAY.
HE MUST GET TO THE STEAM HOUSE. TO WARN HER...
BUT WARN *WHO?* FROM WHAT?

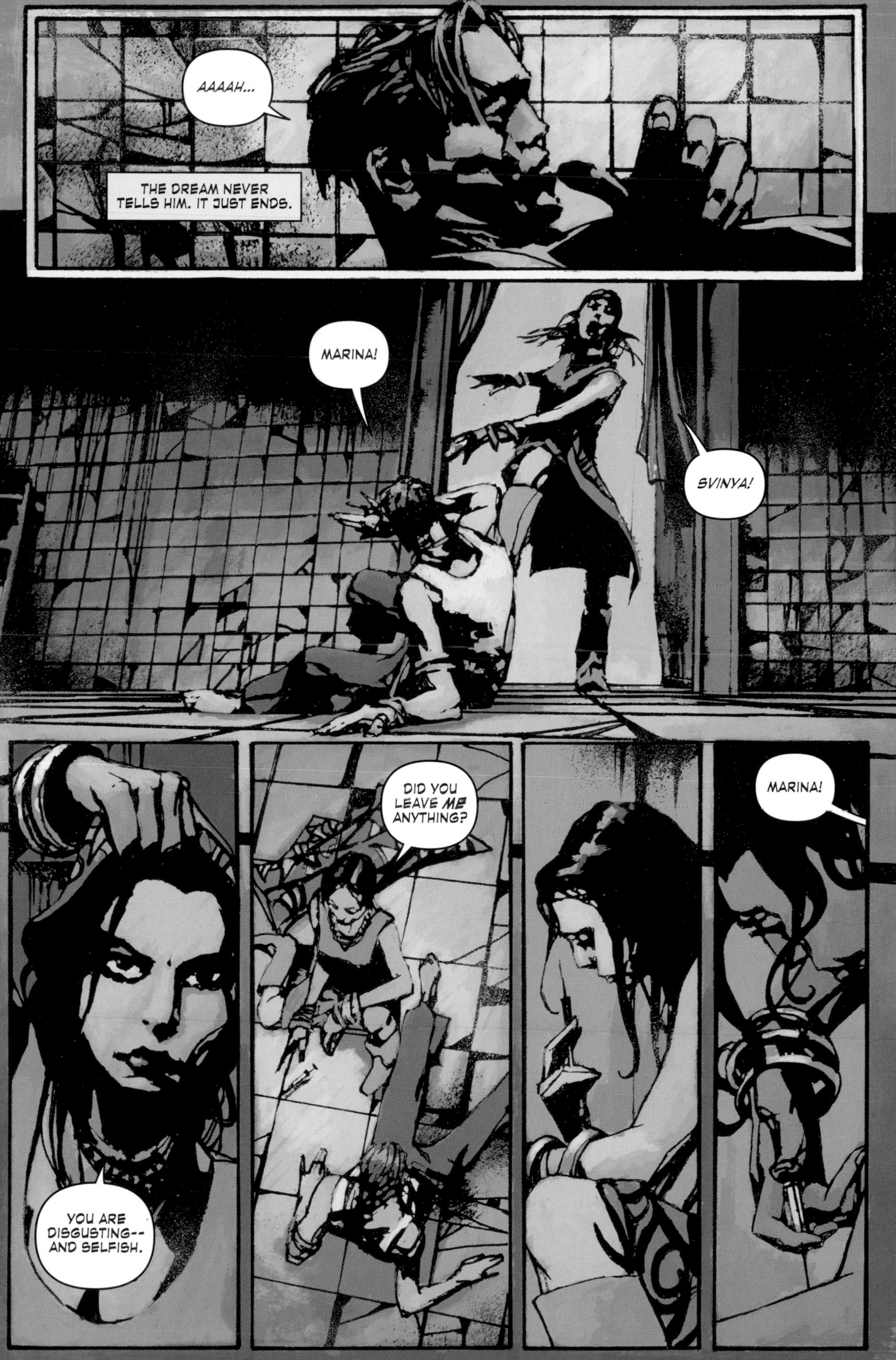
AAAAH...
THE DREAM NEVER TELLS HIM. IT JUST ENDS.
MARINA!
SVINYA!
YOU ARE DISGUSTING-- AND SELFISH.
DID YOU LEAVE *ME* ANYTHING?
MARINA!

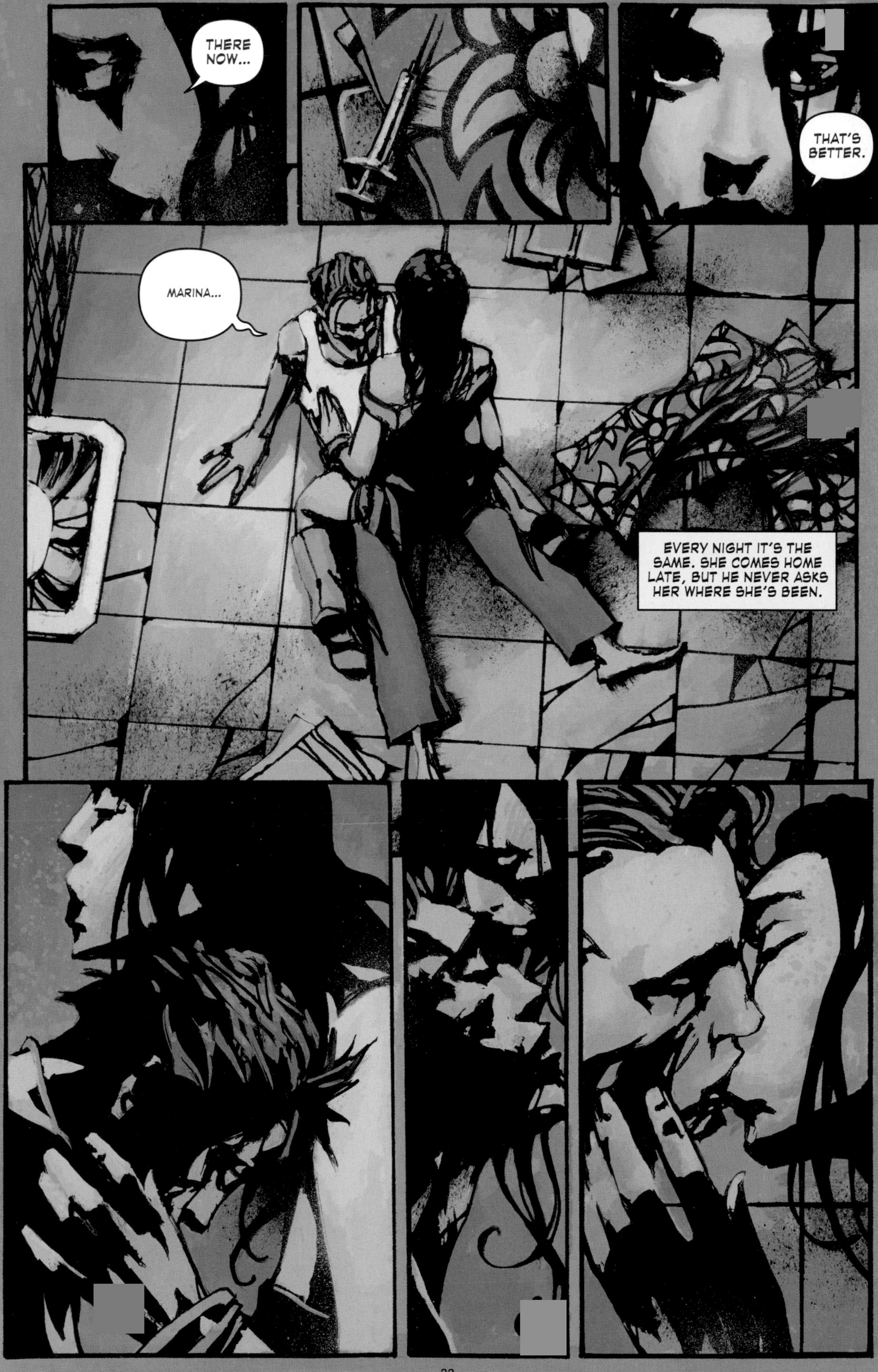
THERE NOW...
THAT'S BETTER.
MARINA...
EVERY NIGHT IT'S THE SAME. SHE COMES HOME LATE, BUT HE NEVER ASKS HER WHERE SHE'S BEEN.

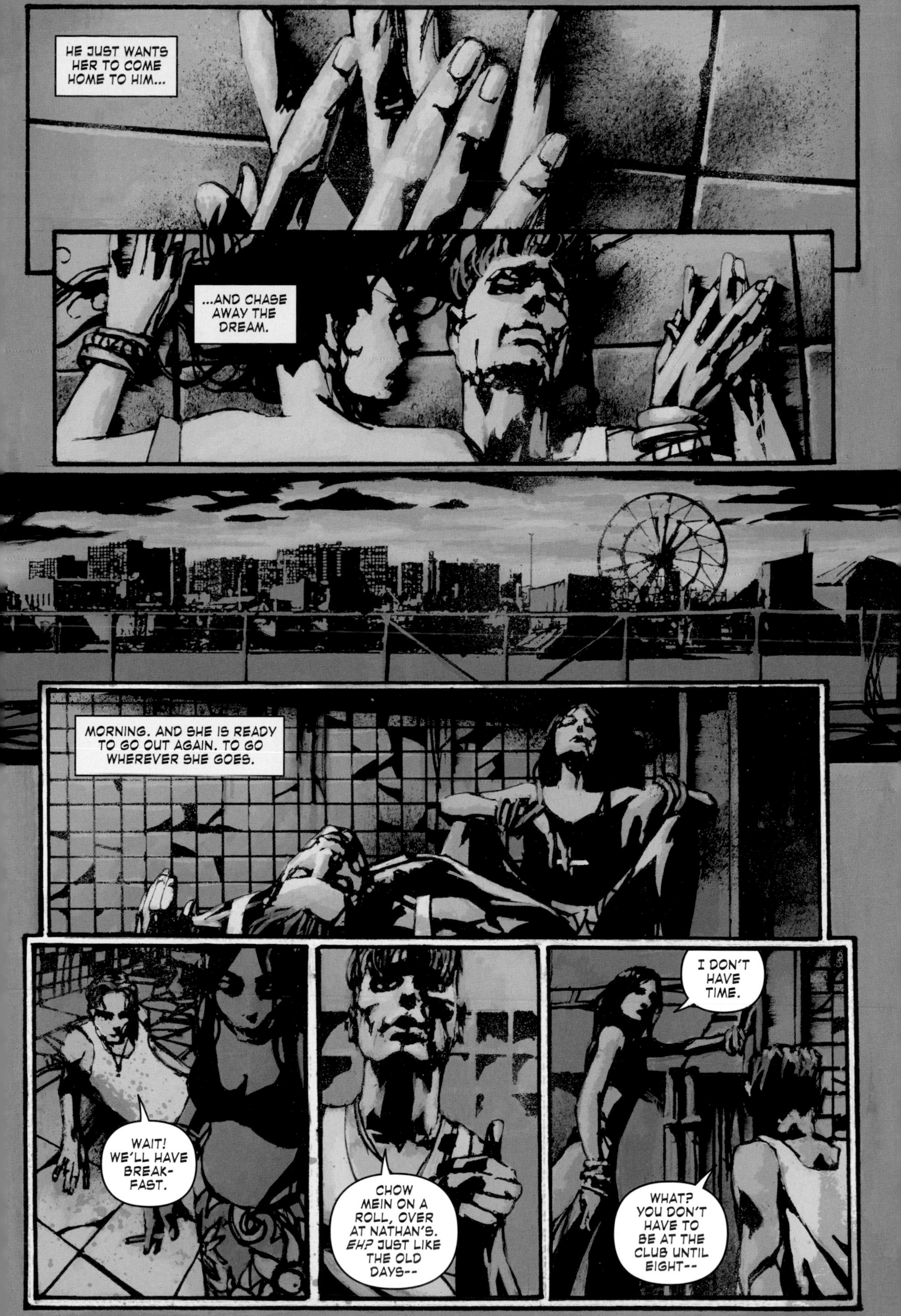
HE JUST WANTS HER TO COME HOME TO HIM...
...AND CHASE AWAY THE DREAM.
MORNING. AND SHE IS READY TO GO OUT AGAIN. TO GO WHEREVER SHE GOES.
WAIT! WE'LL HAVE BREAK-FAST.
CHOW MEIN ON A ROLL, OVER AT NATHAN'S. *EH?* JUST LIKE THE OLD DAYS--
I DON'T HAVE TIME.
WHAT? YOU DON'T HAVE TO BE AT THE CLUB UNTIL EIGHT--

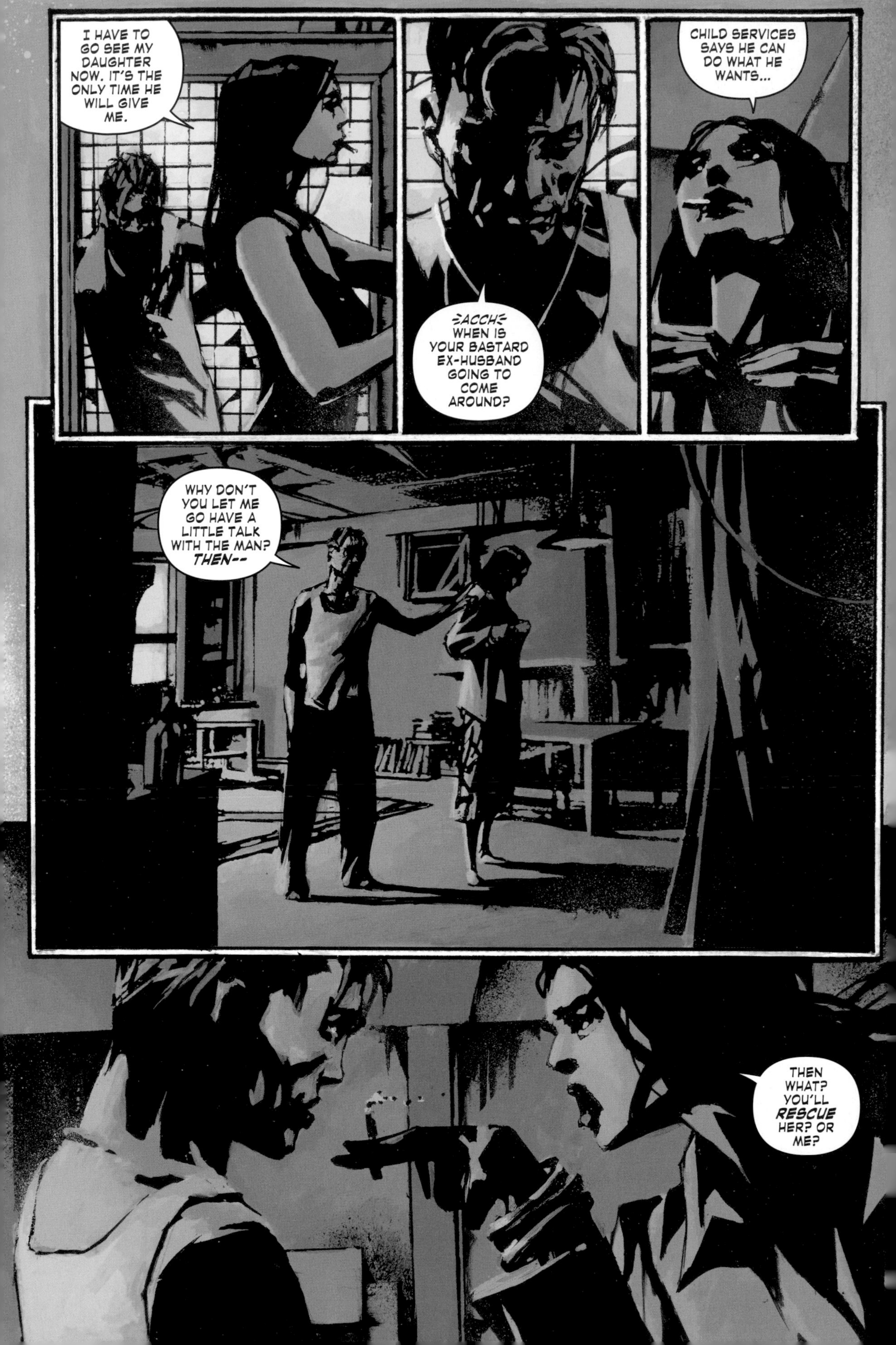
I HAVE TO GO SEE MY DAUGHTER NOW. IT'S THE ONLY TIME HE WILL GIVE ME.
=ACCH= WHEN IS YOUR BASTARD EX-HUSBAND GOING TO COME AROUND?
CHILD SERVICES SAYS HE CAN DO WHAT HE WANTS...
WHY DON'T YOU LET ME GO HAVE A LITTLE TALK WITH THE MAN? THEN--
THEN WHAT? YOU'LL RESCUE HER? OR ME?

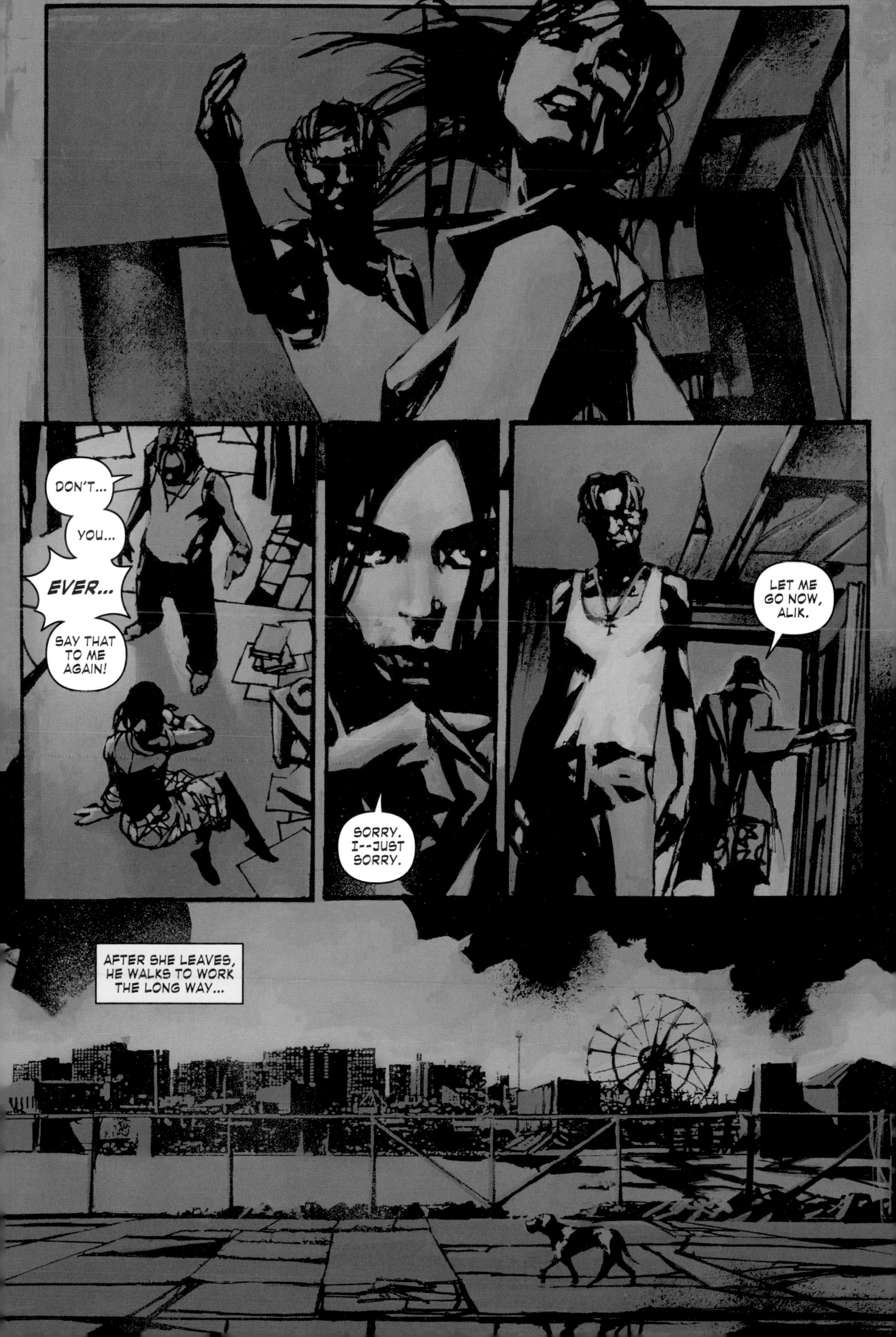
DON'T...
YOU...
EVER...
SAY THAT TO ME AGAIN!
SORRY. I--JUST SORRY.
LET ME GO NOW, ALIK.
AFTER SHE LEAVES, HE WALKS TO WORK THE LONG WAY...

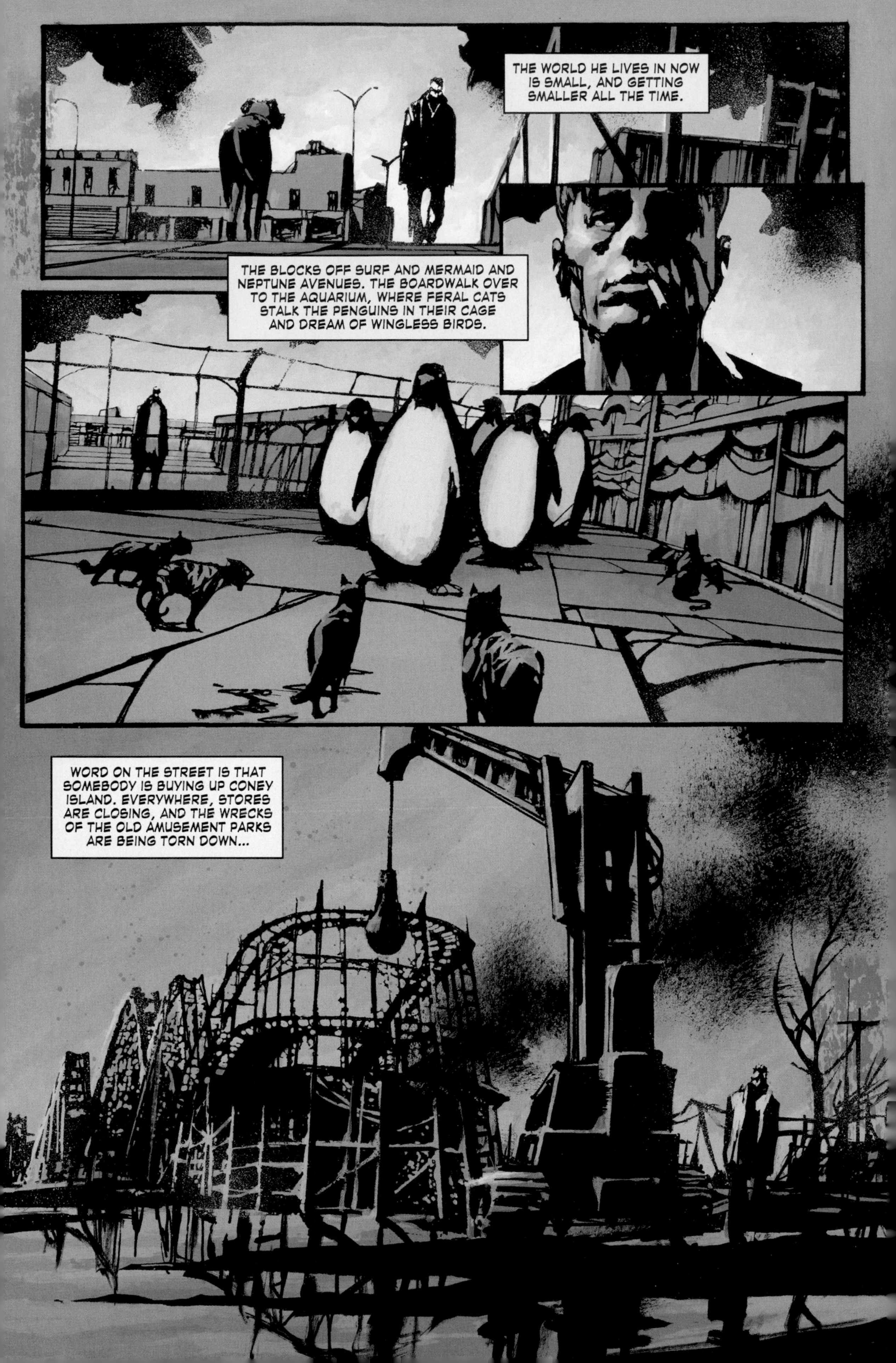
THE WORLD HE LIVES IN NOW IS SMALL, AND GETTING SMALLER ALL THE TIME.
THE BLOCKS OFF SURF AND MERMAID AND NEPTUNE AVENUES. THE BOARDWALK OVER TO THE AQUARIUM, WHERE FERAL CATS STALK THE PENGUINS IN THEIR CAGE AND DREAM OF WINGLESS BIRDS.
WORD ON THE STREET IS THAT SOMEBODY IS BUYING UP CONEY ISLAND. EVERYWHERE, STORES ARE CLOSING, AND THE WRECKS OF THE OLD AMUSEMENT PARKS ARE BEING TORN DOWN...

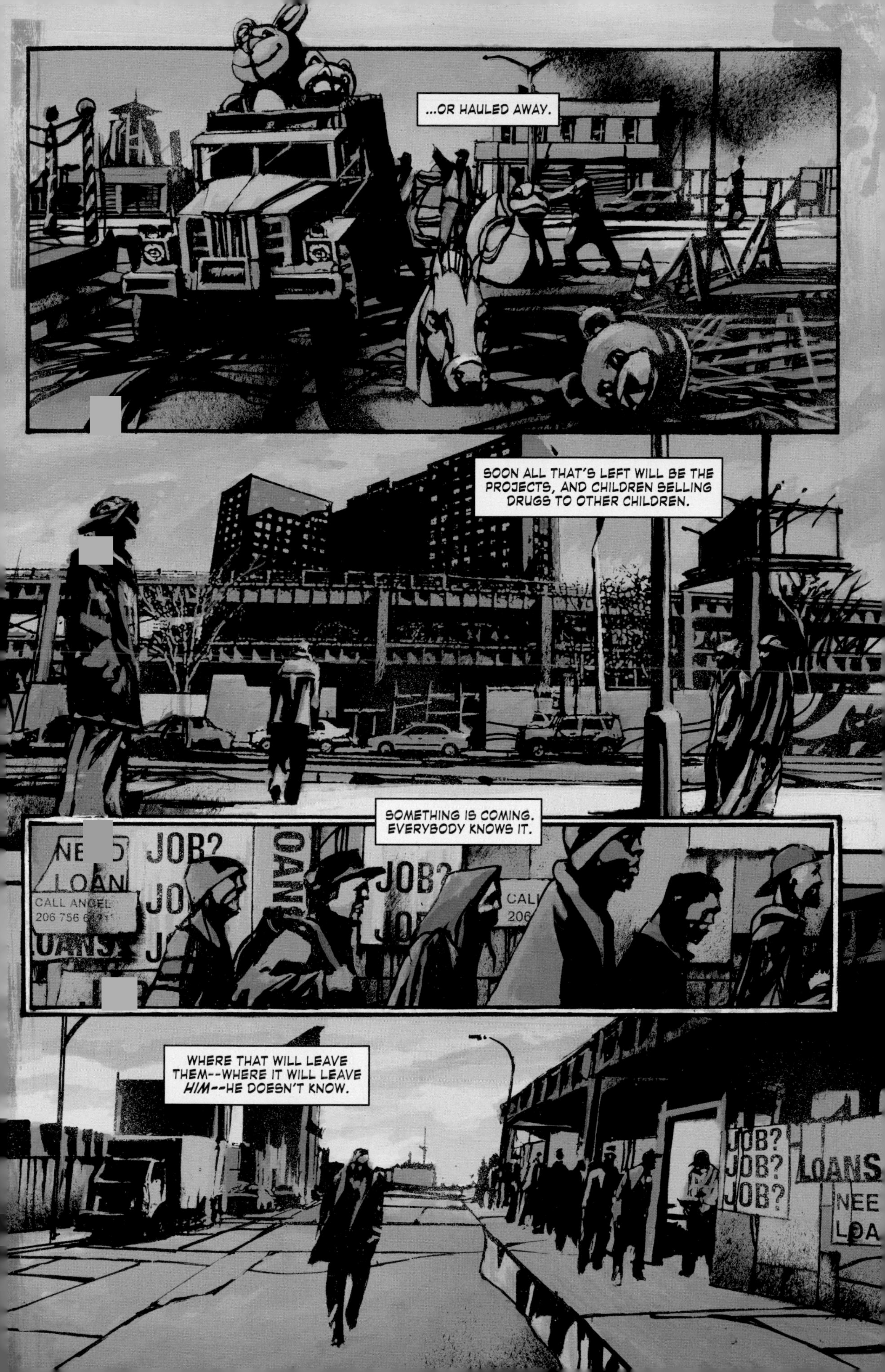
...OR HAULED AWAY.
SOON ALL THAT'S LEFT WILL BE THE PROJECTS, AND CHILDREN SELLING DRUGS TO OTHER CHILDREN.
SOMETHING IS COMING. EVERYBODY KNOWS IT.
JOB?
JOB?
WHERE THAT WILL LEAVE THEM--WHERE IT WILL LEAVE *HIM*--HE DOESN'T KNOW.
JOB?
JOB?
JOB?
LOANS

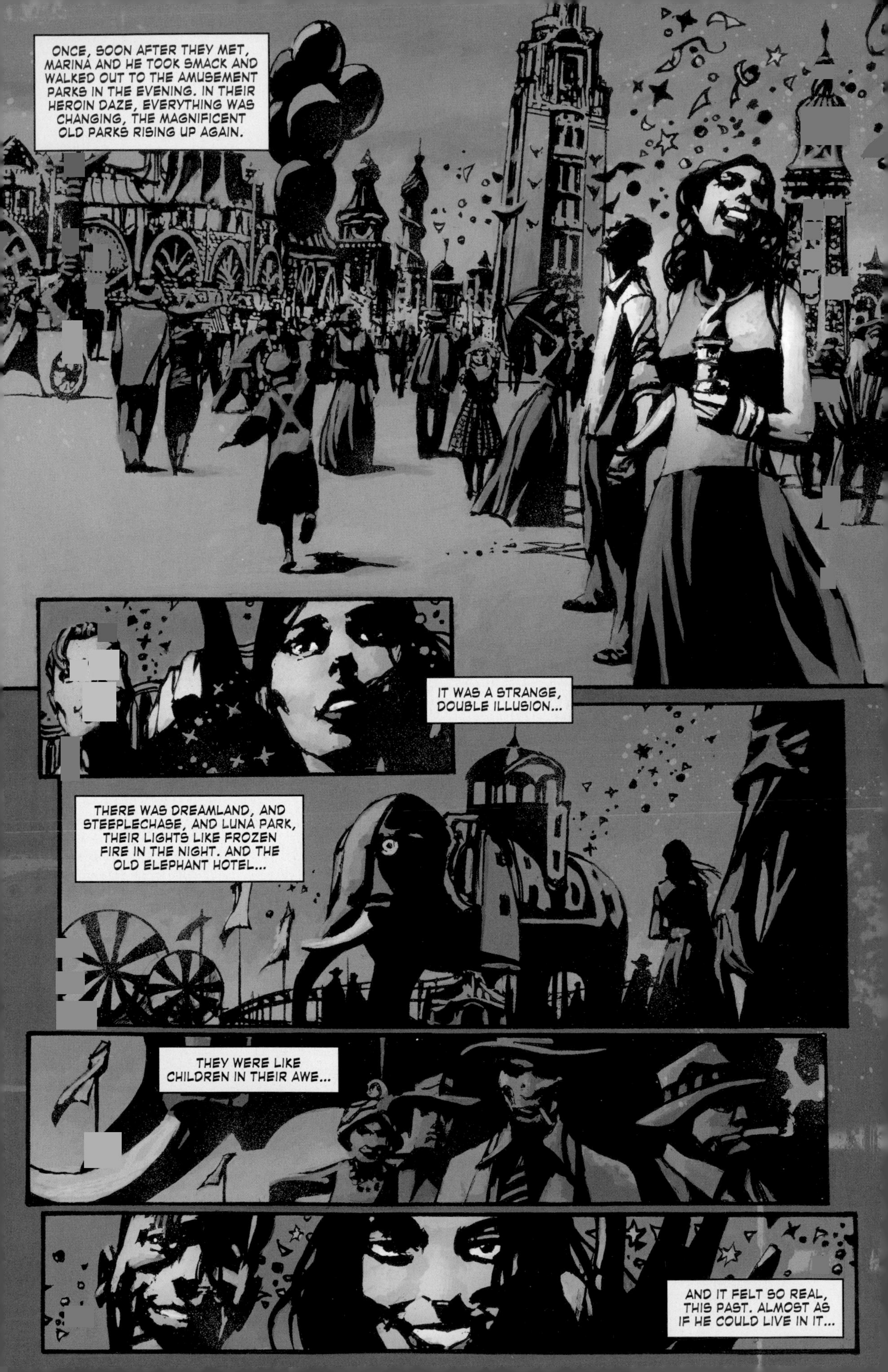
ONCE, SOON AFTER THEY MET, MARINA AND HE TOOK SMACK AND WALKED OUT TO THE AMUSEMENT PARKS IN THE EVENING. IN THEIR HEROIN DAZE, EVERYTHING WAS CHANGING, THE MAGNIFICENT OLD PARKS RISING UP AGAIN.
IT WAS A STRANGE, DOUBLE ILLUSION...
THERE WAS DREAMLAND, AND STEEPLECHASE, AND LUNA PARK, THEIR LIGHTS LIKE FROZEN FIRE IN THE NIGHT. AND THE OLD ELEPHANT HOTEL...
THEY WERE LIKE CHILDREN IN THEIR AWE...
AND IT FELT SO REAL, THIS PAST. ALMOST AS IF HE COULD LIVE IN IT...

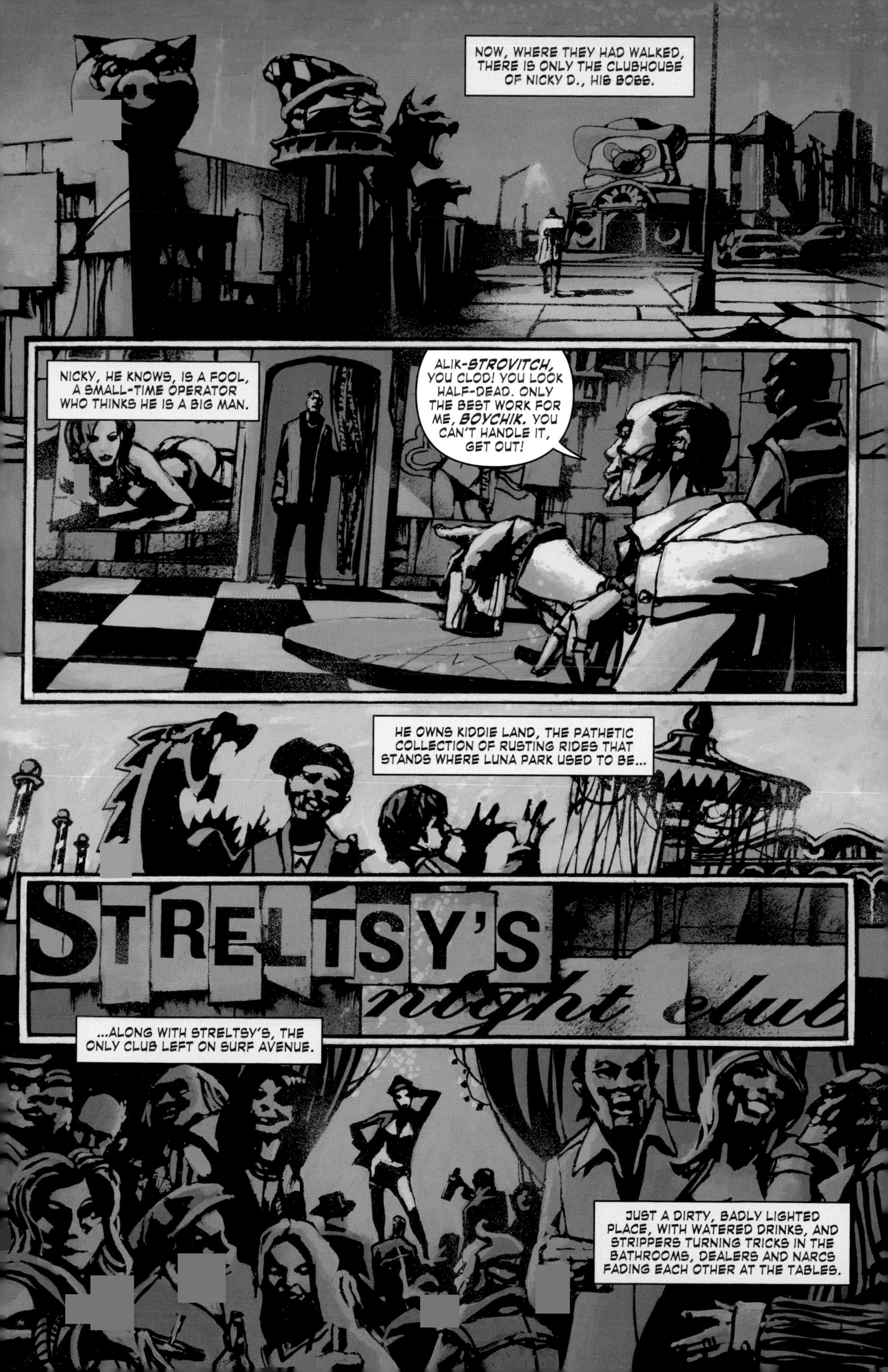
NOW, WHERE THEY HAD WALKED, THERE IS ONLY THE CLUBHOUSE OF NICKY D., HIS BOSS.
NICKY, HE KNOWS, IS A FOOL, A SMALL-TIME OPERATOR WHO THINKS HE IS A BIG MAN.
ALIK-STROVITCH, YOU CLOD! YOU LOOK HALF-DEAD. ONLY THE BEST WORK FOR ME, BOYCHIK. YOU CAN'T HANDLE IT, GET OUT!
HE OWNS KIDDIE LAND, THE PATHETIC COLLECTION OF RUSTING RIDES THAT STANDS WHERE LUNA PARK USED TO BE...
STRELTSY'S
night club
...ALONG WITH STRELTSY'S, THE ONLY CLUB LEFT ON SURF AVENUE.
JUST A DIRTY, BADLY LIGHTED PLACE, WITH WATERED DRINKS, AND STRIPPERS TURNING TRICKS IN THE BATHROOMS, DEALERS AND NARCS FADING EACH OTHER AT THE TABLES.

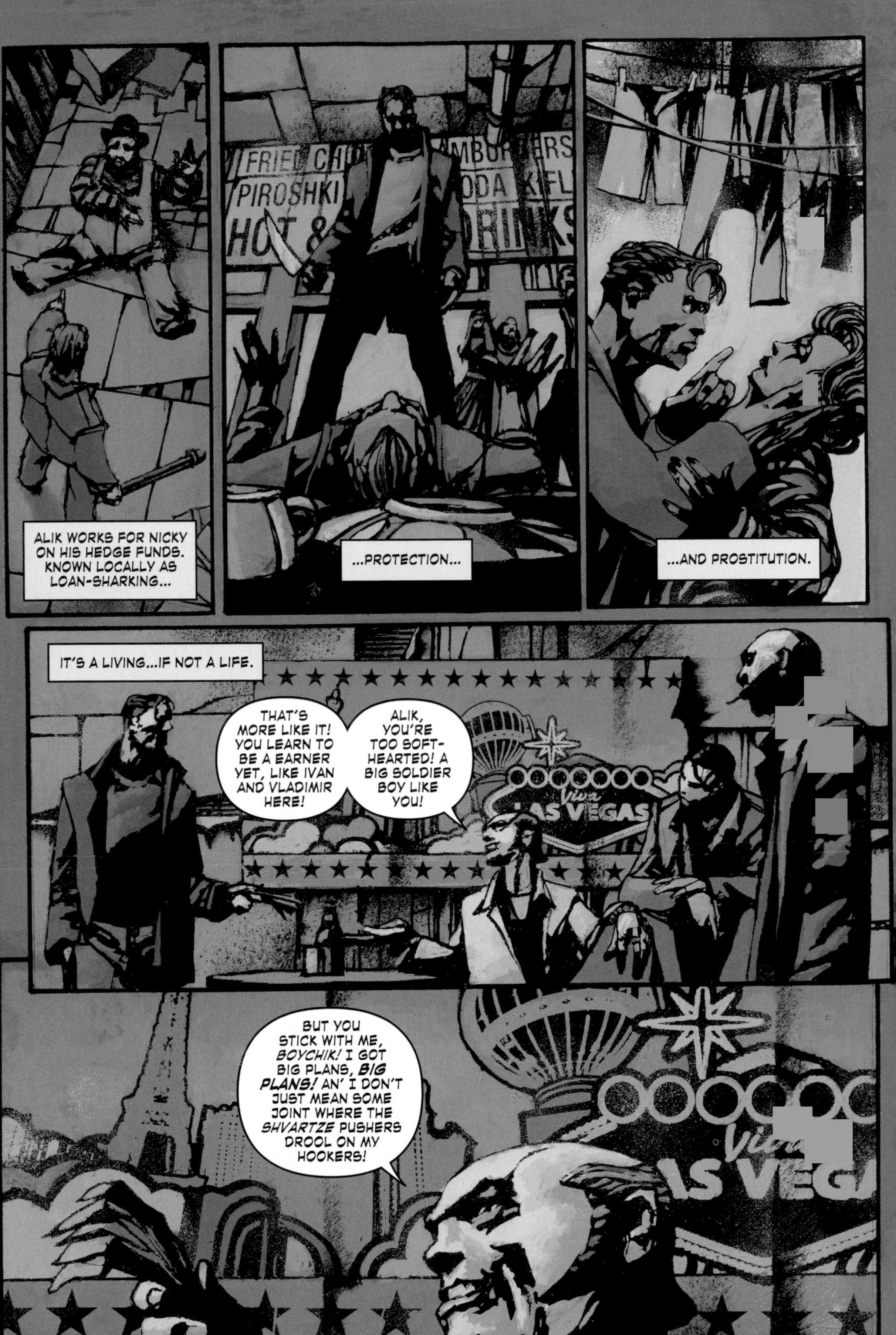
FRIED CH
PIROSHKI
HOT &
AMBURGERS
ODA KEFI
DRINKS
ALIK WORKS FOR NICKY ON HIS HEDGE FUNDS. KNOWN LOCALLY AS LOAN-SHARKING...
...PROTECTION...
...AND PROSTITUTION.
IT'S A LIVING...IF NOT A LIFE.
THAT'S MORE LIKE IT! YOU LEARN TO BE A EARNER YET, LIKE IVAN AND VLADIMIR HERE!
ALIK, YOU'RE TOO SOFT-HEARTED! A BIG SOLDIER BOY LIKE YOU!
BUT YOU STICK WITH ME, *BOYCHIK!* I GOT BIG PLANS, ***BIG PLANS!*** AN' I DON'T JUST MEAN SOME JOINT WHERE THE *SHVARTZE* PUSHERS DROOL ON MY HOOKERS!

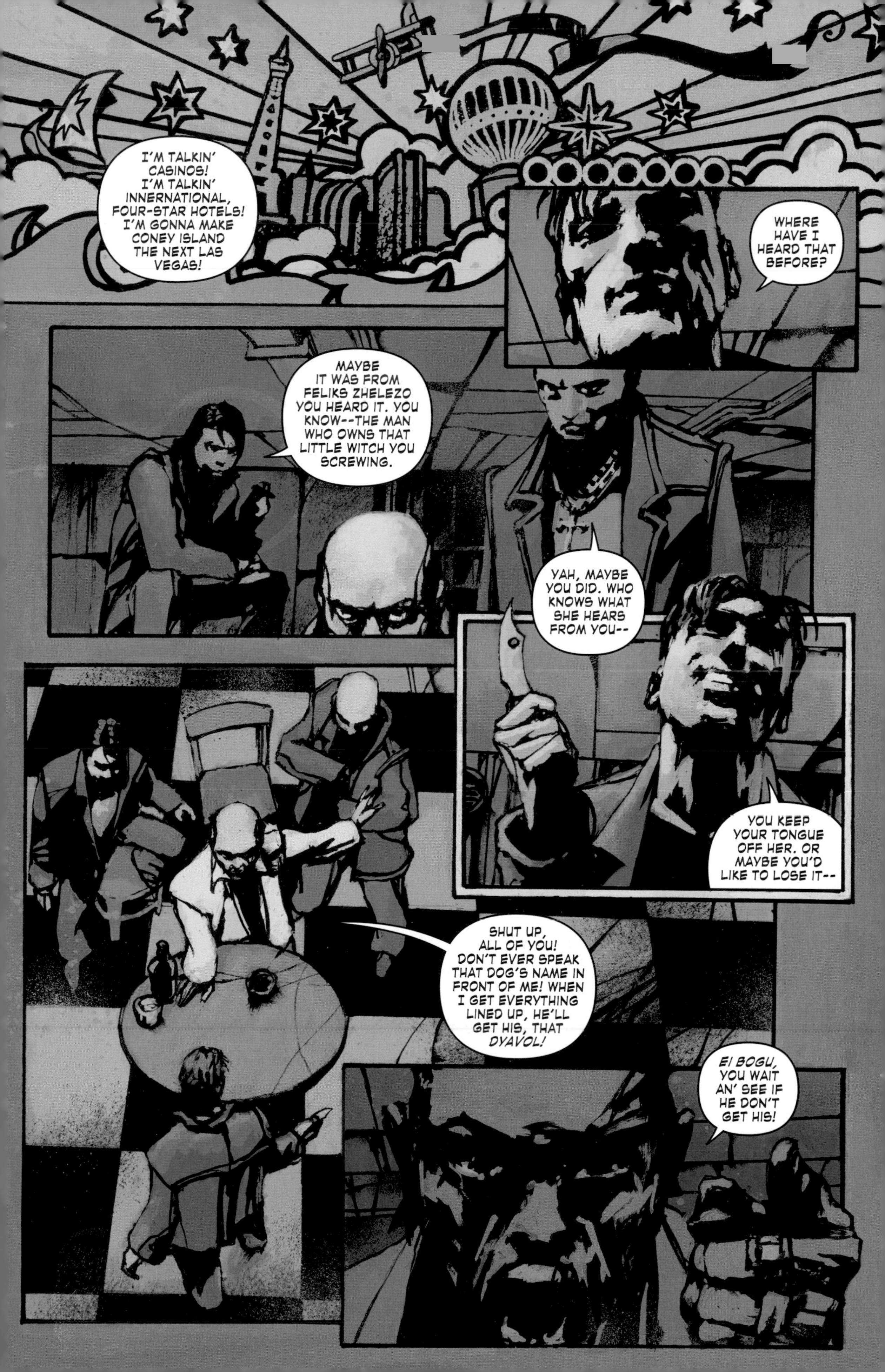
I'M TALKIN' CASINOS! I'M TALKIN' INNERNATIONAL, FOUR-STAR HOTELS! I'M GONNA MAKE CONEY ISLAND THE NEXT LAS VEGAS!
WHERE HAVE I HEARD THAT BEFORE?
MAYBE IT WAS FROM FELIKS ZHELEZO YOU HEARD IT. YOU KNOW--THE MAN WHO OWNS THAT LITTLE WITCH YOU SCREWING.
YAH, MAYBE YOU DID. WHO KNOWS WHAT SHE HEARS FROM YOU--
YOU KEEP YOUR TONGUE OFF HER. OR MAYBE YOU'D LIKE TO LOSE IT--
SHUT UP, ALL OF YOU! DON'T EVER SPEAK THAT DOG'S NAME IN FRONT OF ME! WHEN I GET EVERYTHING LINED UP, HE'LL GET HIS, THAT *DYAVOL!*
*EI BOGU,* YOU WAIT AN' SEE IF HE DON'T GET HIS!

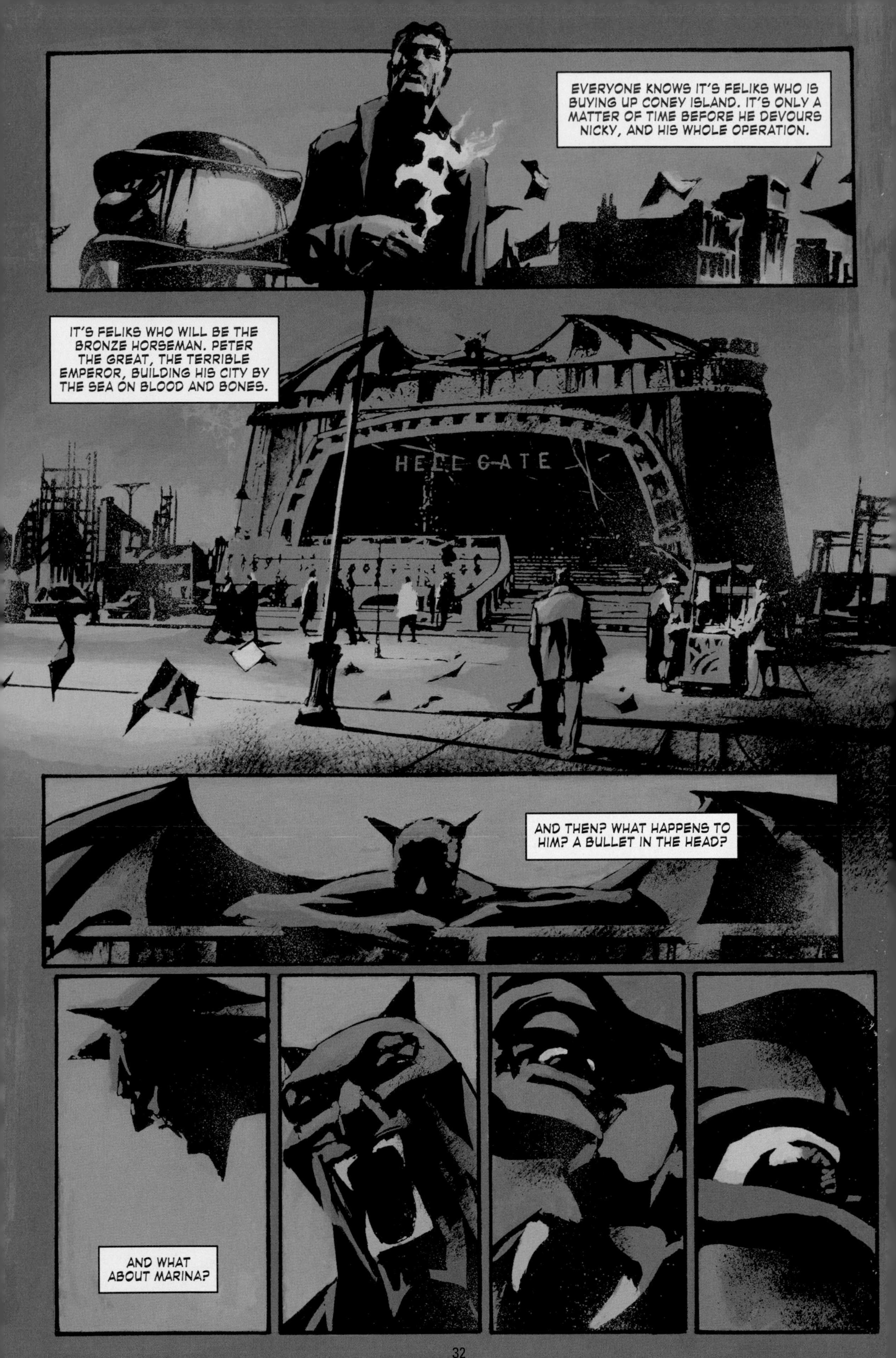
EVERYONE KNOWS IT'S FELIKS WHO IS BUYING UP CONEY ISLAND. IT'S ONLY A MATTER OF TIME BEFORE HE DEVOURS NICKY, AND HIS WHOLE OPERATION.
IT'S FELIKS WHO WILL BE THE BRONZE HORSEMAN. PETER THE GREAT, THE TERRIBLE EMPEROR, BUILDING HIS CITY BY THE SEA ON BLOOD AND BONES.
HELL GATE
AND THEN? WHAT HAPPENS TO HIM? A BULLET IN THE HEAD?
AND WHAT ABOUT MARINA?

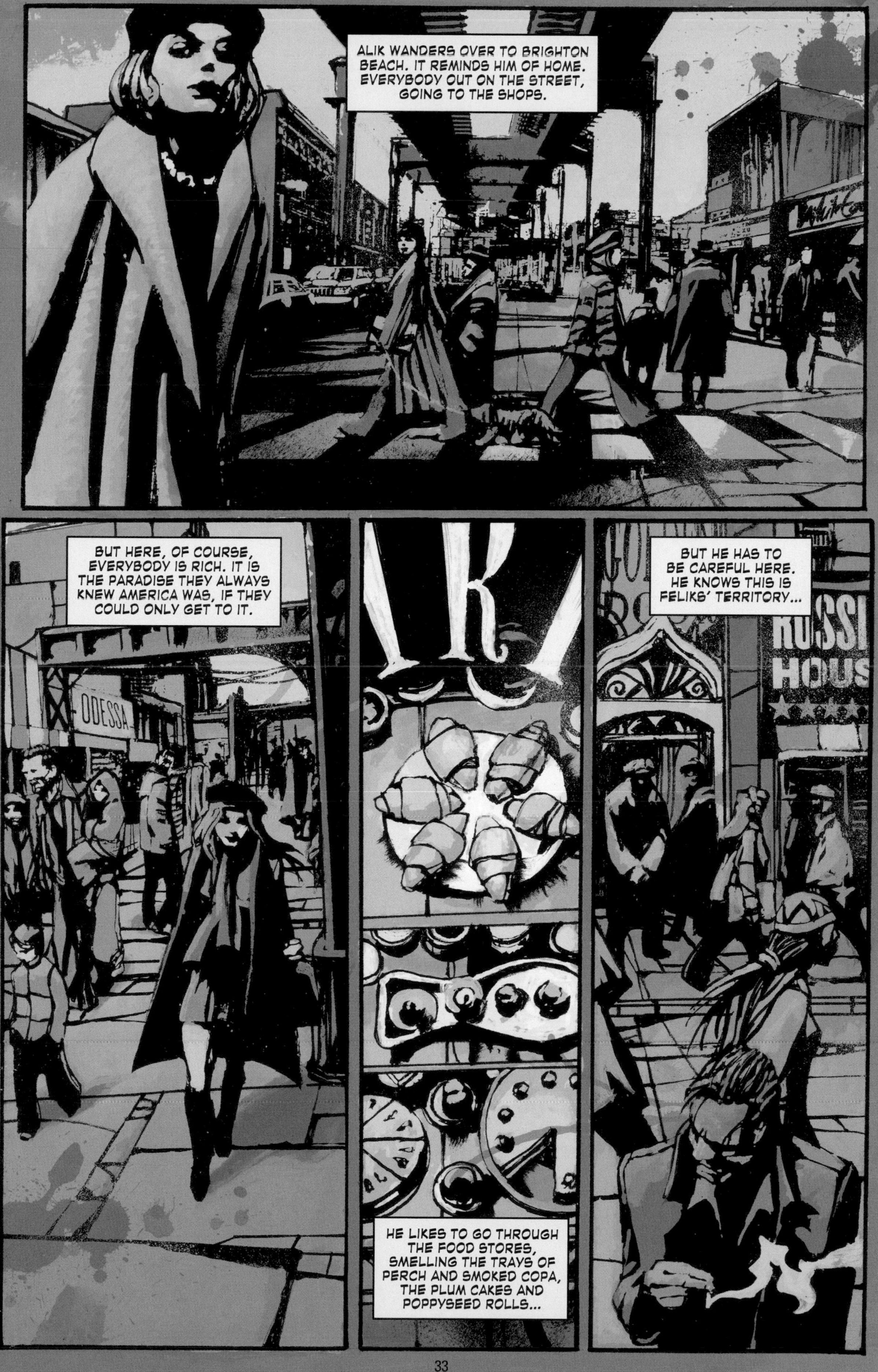
ALIK WANDERS OVER TO BRIGHTON BEACH. IT REMINDS HIM OF HOME. EVERYBODY OUT ON THE STREET, GOING TO THE SHOPS.
BUT HERE, OF COURSE, EVERYBODY IS RICH. IT IS THE PARADISE THEY ALWAYS KNEW AMERICA WAS, IF THEY COULD ONLY GET TO IT.
ODESSA
HE LIKES TO GO THROUGH THE FOOD STORES, SMELLING THE TRAYS OF PERCH AND SMOKED COPA, THE PLUM CAKES AND POPPYSEED ROLLS...
BUT HE HAS TO BE CAREFUL HERE. HE KNOWS THIS IS FELIKS' TERRITORY...
RUSSI
HOUS

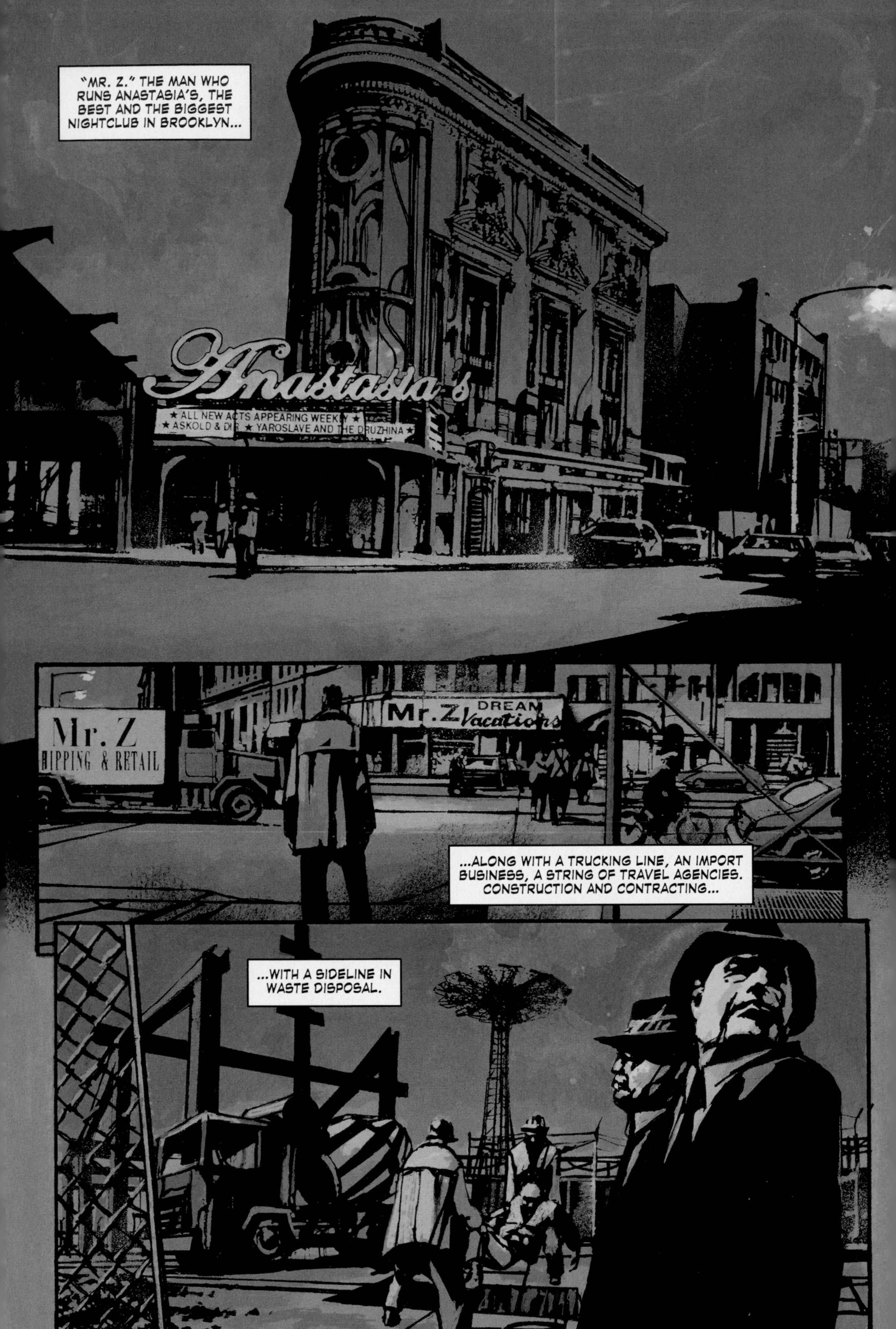
"MR. Z." THE MAN WHO RUNS ANASTASIA'S, THE BEST AND THE BIGGEST NIGHTCLUB IN BROOKLYN...
Anastasia's
★ ALL NEW ACTS APPEARING WEEKLY ★
★ ASKOLD & DIR ★ YAROSLAVE AND THE DRUZHINA ★
Mr. Z
Mr. Z DREAM
...ALONG WITH A TRUCKING LINE, AN IMPORT BUSINESS, A STRING OF TRAVEL AGENCIES. CONSTRUCTION AND CONTRACTING...
...WITH A SIDELINE IN WASTE DISPOSAL.

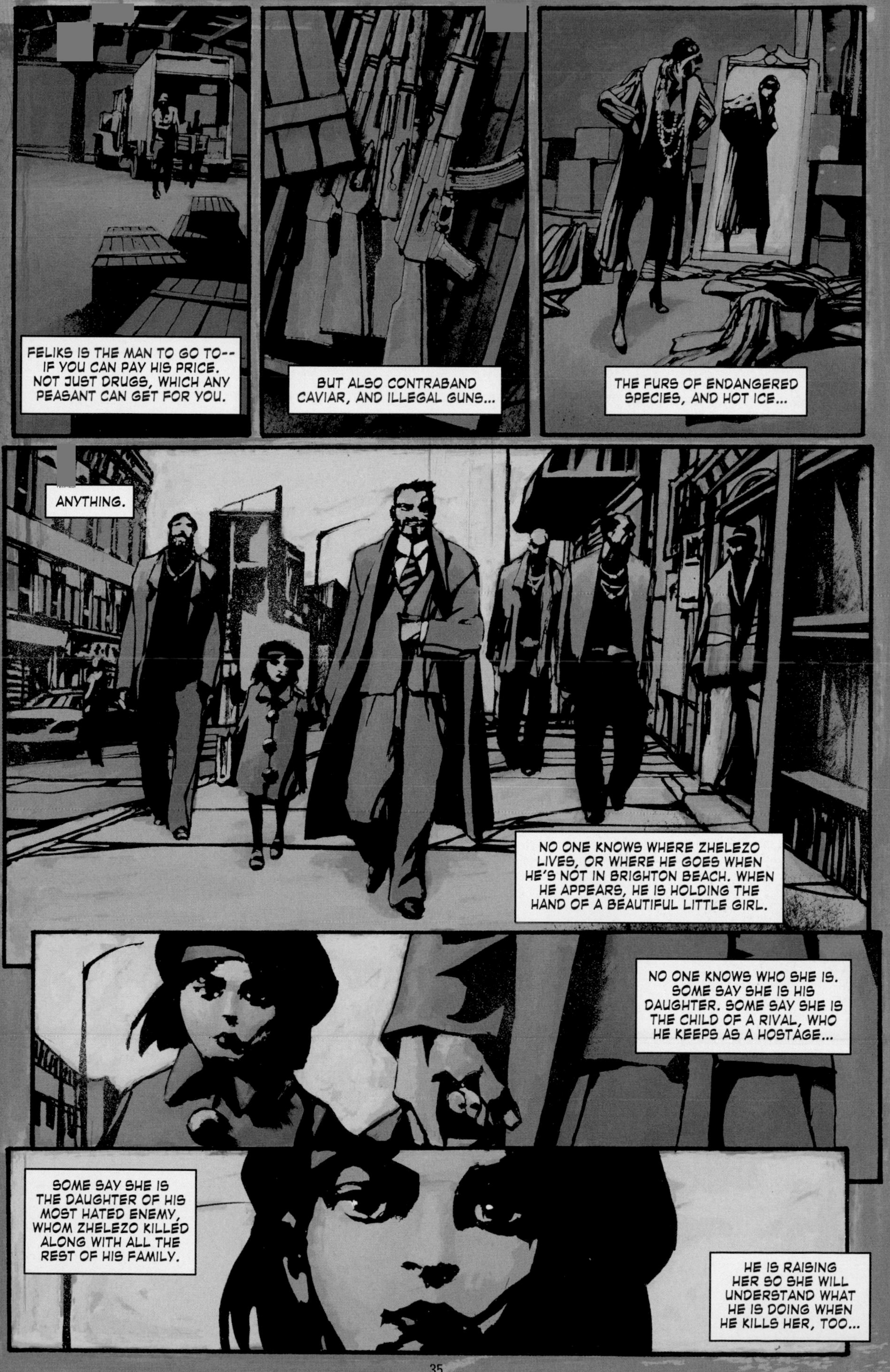
FELIKS IS THE MAN TO GO TO--
IF YOU CAN PAY HIS PRICE.
NOT JUST DRUGS, WHICH ANY
PEASANT CAN GET FOR YOU.
BUT ALSO CONTRABAND
CAVIAR, AND ILLEGAL GUNS...
THE FURS OF ENDANGERED
SPECIES, AND HOT ICE...
ANYTHING.
NO ONE KNOWS WHERE ZHELEZO
LIVES, OR WHERE HE GOES WHEN
HE'S NOT IN BRIGHTON BEACH. WHEN
HE APPEARS, HE IS HOLDING THE
HAND OF A BEAUTIFUL LITTLE GIRL.
NO ONE KNOWS WHO SHE IS.
SOME SAY SHE IS HIS
DAUGHTER. SOME SAY SHE IS
THE CHILD OF A RIVAL, WHO
HE KEEPS AS A HOSTAGE...
SOME SAY SHE IS
THE DAUGHTER OF HIS
MOST HATED ENEMY,
WHOM ZHELEZO KILLED
ALONG WITH ALL THE
REST OF HIS FAMILY.
HE IS RAISING
HER SO SHE WILL
UNDERSTAND WHAT
HE IS DOING WHEN
HE KILLS HER, TOO...

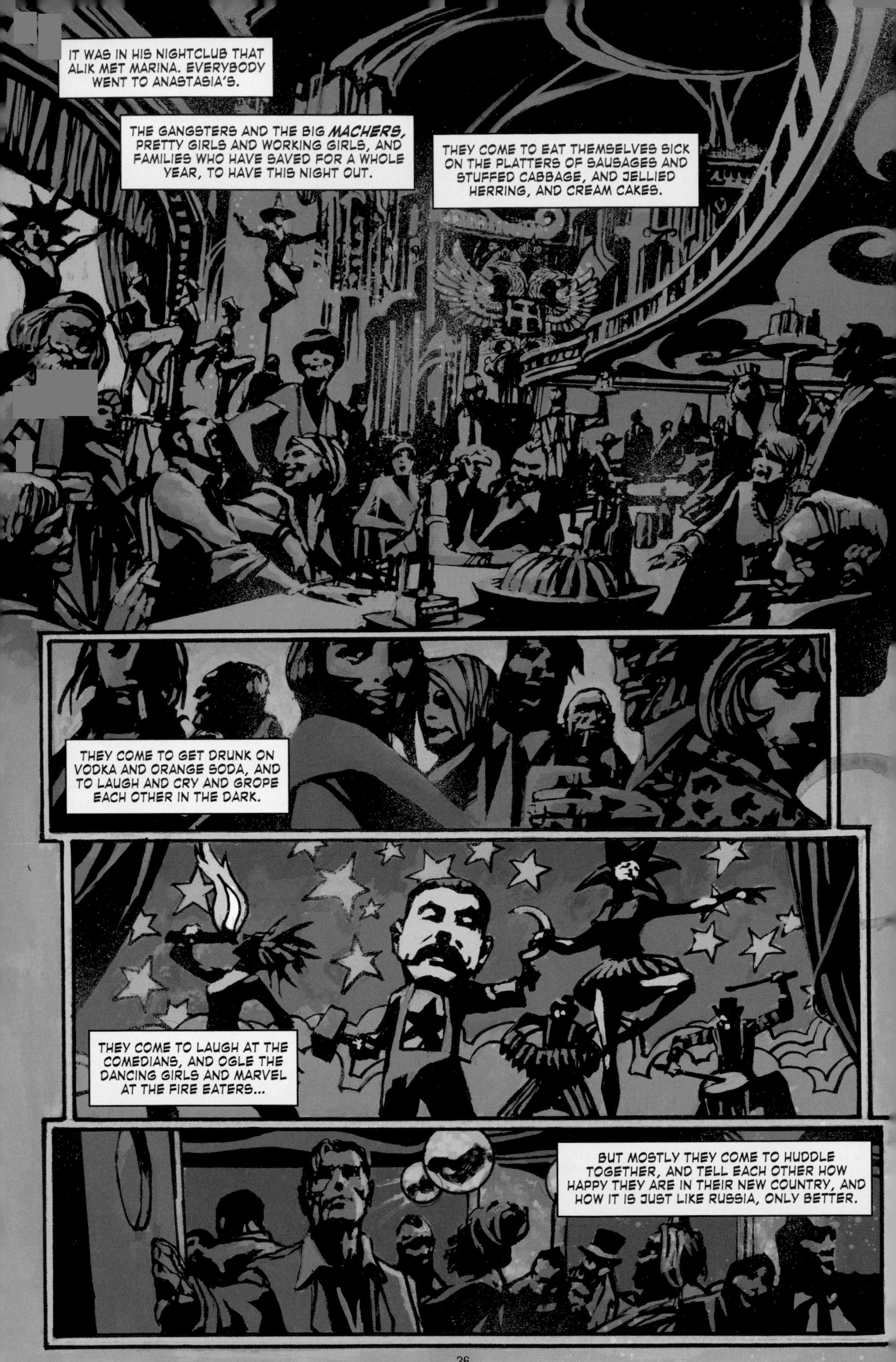
IT WAS IN HIS NIGHTCLUB THAT ALIK MET MARINA. EVERYBODY WENT TO ANASTASIA'S.
THE GANGSTERS AND THE BIG *MACHERS,* PRETTY GIRLS AND WORKING GIRLS, AND FAMILIES WHO HAVE SAVED FOR A WHOLE YEAR, TO HAVE THIS NIGHT OUT.
THEY COME TO EAT THEMSELVES SICK ON THE PLATTERS OF SAUSAGES AND STUFFED CABBAGE, AND JELLIED HERRING, AND CREAM CAKES.
THEY COME TO GET DRUNK ON VODKA AND ORANGE SODA, AND TO LAUGH AND CRY AND GROPE EACH OTHER IN THE DARK.
THEY COME TO LAUGH AT THE COMEDIANS, AND OGLE THE DANCING GIRLS AND MARVEL AT THE FIRE EATERS...
BUT MOSTLY THEY COME TO HUDDLE TOGETHER, AND TELL EACH OTHER HOW HAPPY THEY ARE IN THEIR NEW COUNTRY, AND HOW IT IS JUST LIKE RUSSIA, ONLY BETTER.

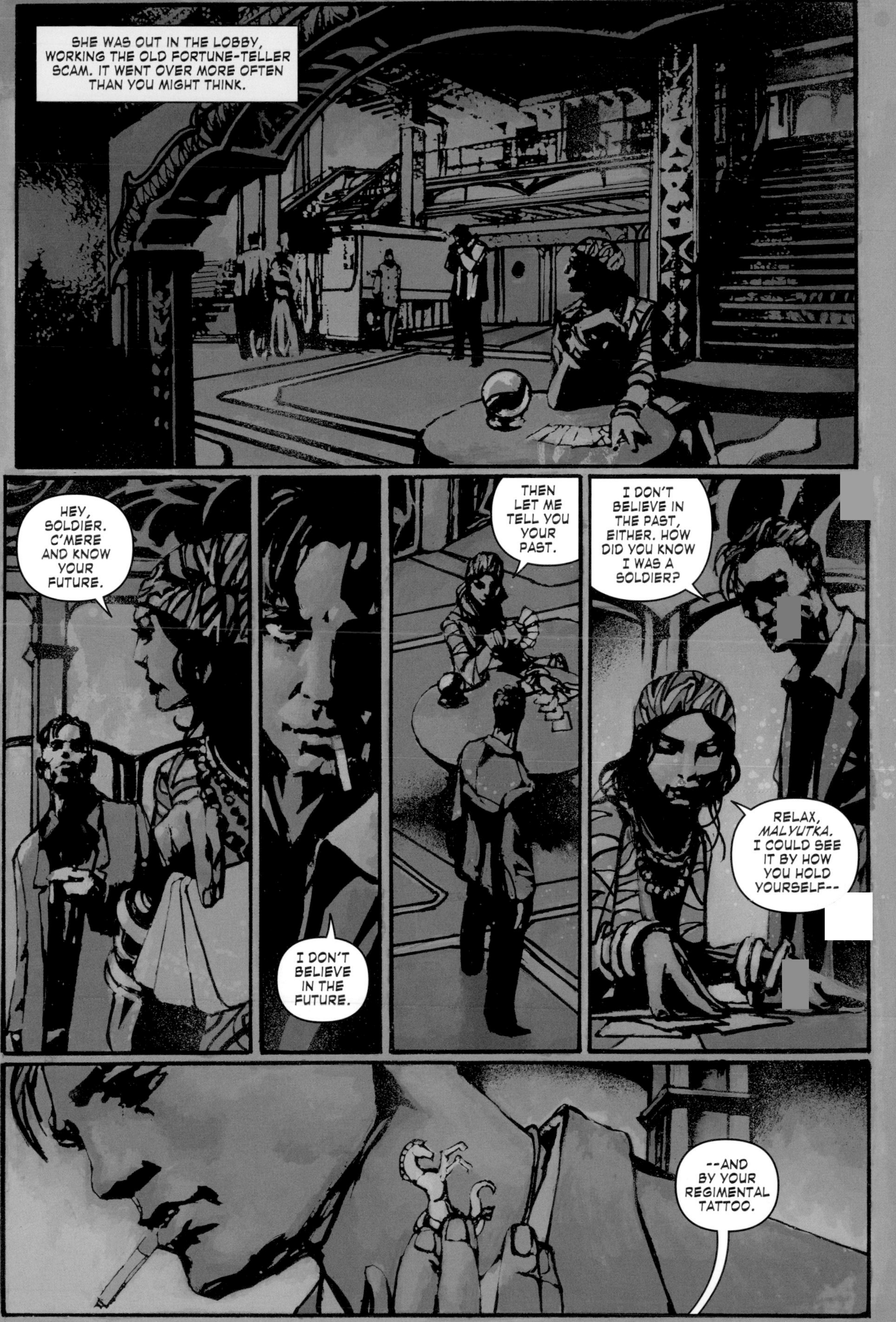
SHE WAS OUT IN THE LOBBY, WORKING THE OLD FORTUNE-TELLER SCAM. IT WENT OVER MORE OFTEN THAN YOU MIGHT THINK.
HEY, SOLDIER. C'MERE AND KNOW YOUR FUTURE.
I DON'T BELIEVE IN THE FUTURE.
THEN LET ME TELL YOU YOUR PAST.
I DON'T BELIEVE IN THE PAST, EITHER. HOW DID YOU KNOW I WAS A SOLDIER?
RELAX, *MALYUTKA.* I COULD SEE IT BY HOW YOU HOLD YOURSELF--
--AND BY YOUR REGIMENTAL TATTOO.

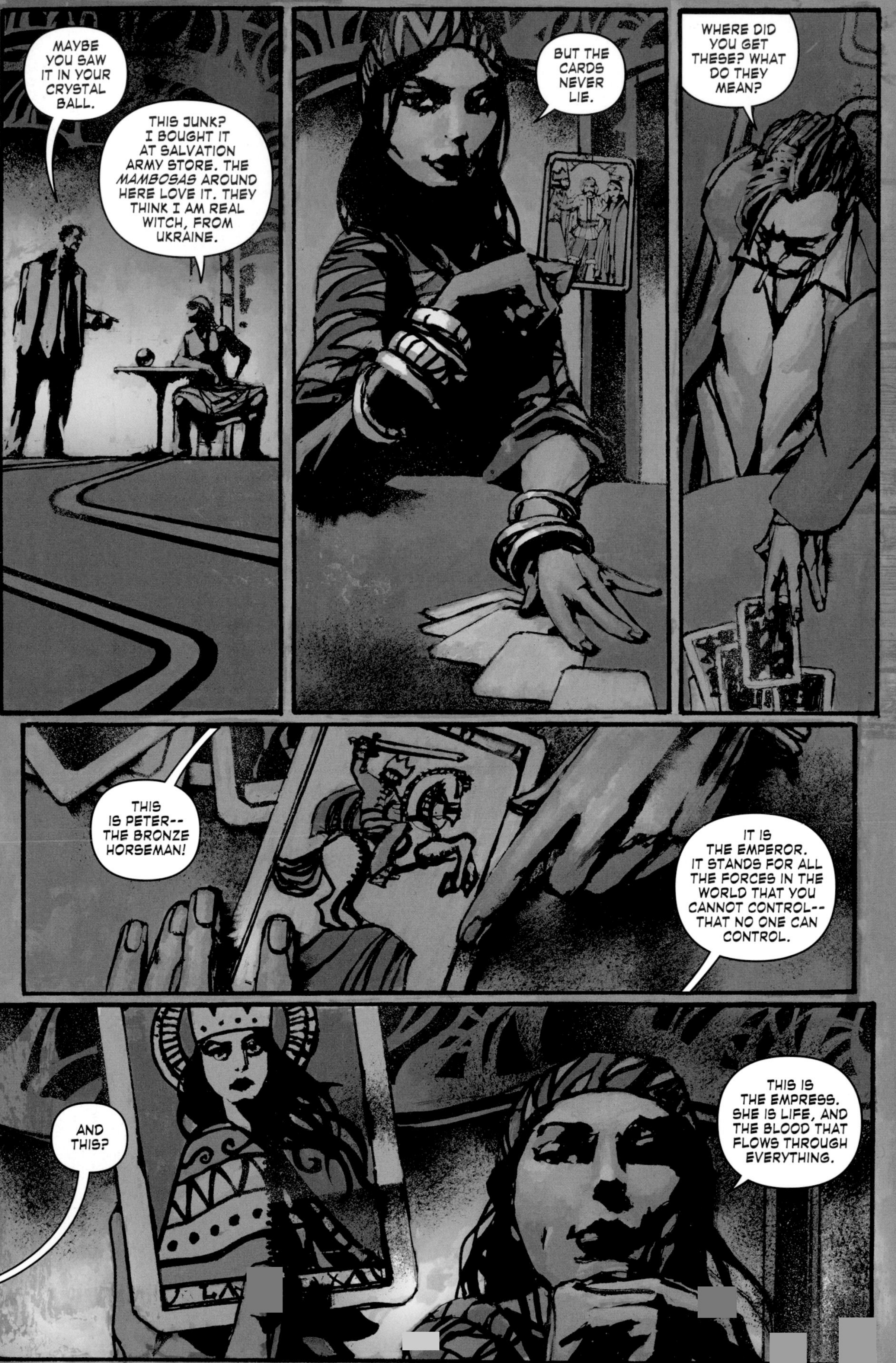
MAYBE YOU SAW IT IN YOUR CRYSTAL BALL.
THIS JUNK? I BOUGHT IT AT SALVATION ARMY STORE. THE *MAMBOSAS* AROUND HERE LOVE IT. THEY THINK I AM REAL WITCH, FROM UKRAINE.
BUT THE CARDS NEVER LIE.
WHERE DID YOU GET THESE? WHAT DO THEY MEAN?
THIS IS PETER-- THE BRONZE HORSEMAN!
IT IS THE EMPEROR. IT STANDS FOR ALL THE FORCES IN THE WORLD THAT YOU CANNOT CONTROL-- THAT NO ONE CAN CONTROL.
AND THIS?
THIS IS THE EMPRESS. SHE IS LIFE, AND THE BLOOD THAT FLOWS THROUGH EVERYTHING.

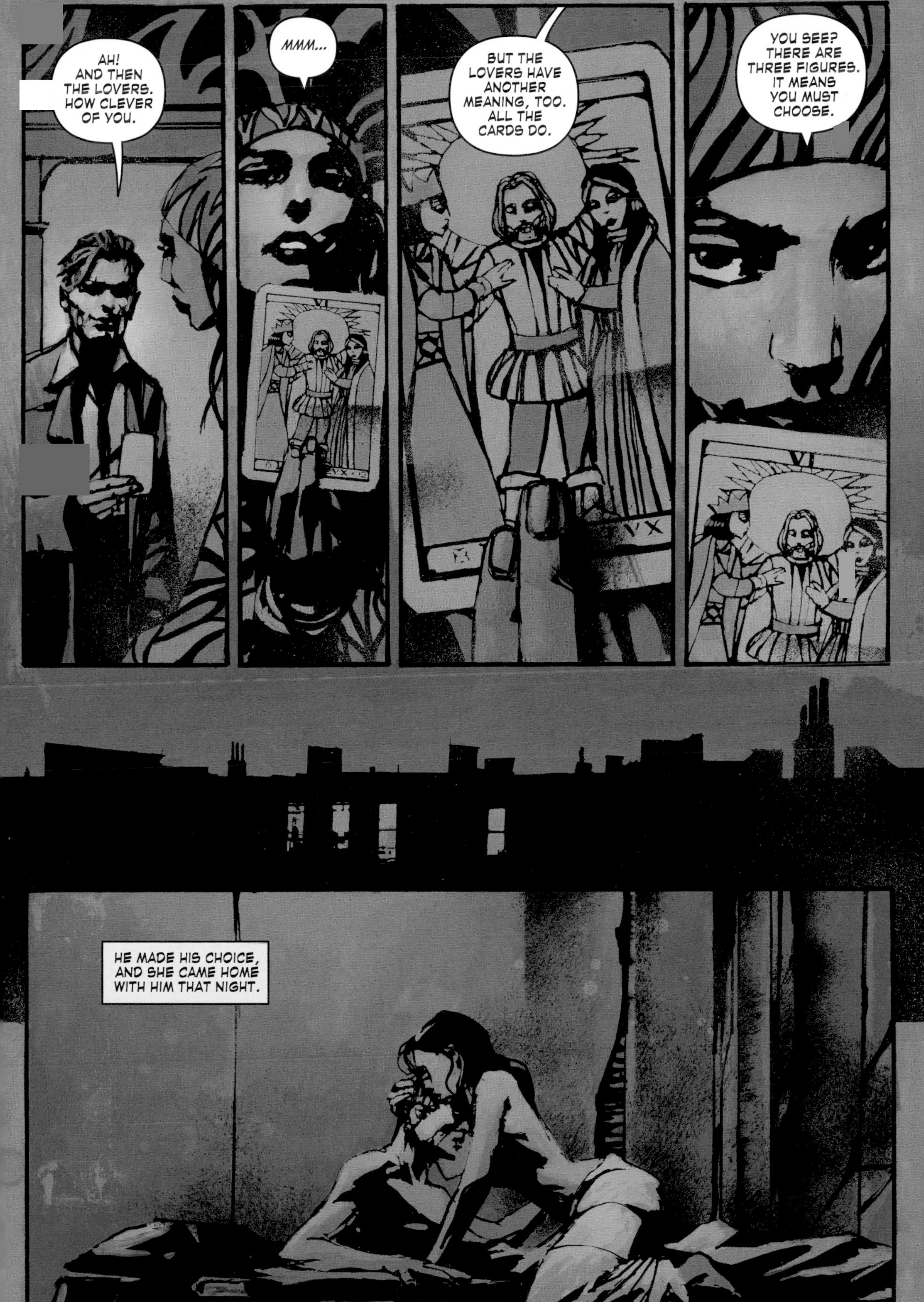
AH! AND THEN THE LOVERS. HOW CLEVER OF YOU.
MMM...
BUT THE LOVERS HAVE ANOTHER MEANING, TOO. ALL THE CARDS DO.
YOU SEE? THERE ARE THREE FIGURES. IT MEANS YOU MUST CHOOSE.
HE MADE HIS CHOICE, AND SHE CAME HOME WITH HIM THAT NIGHT.

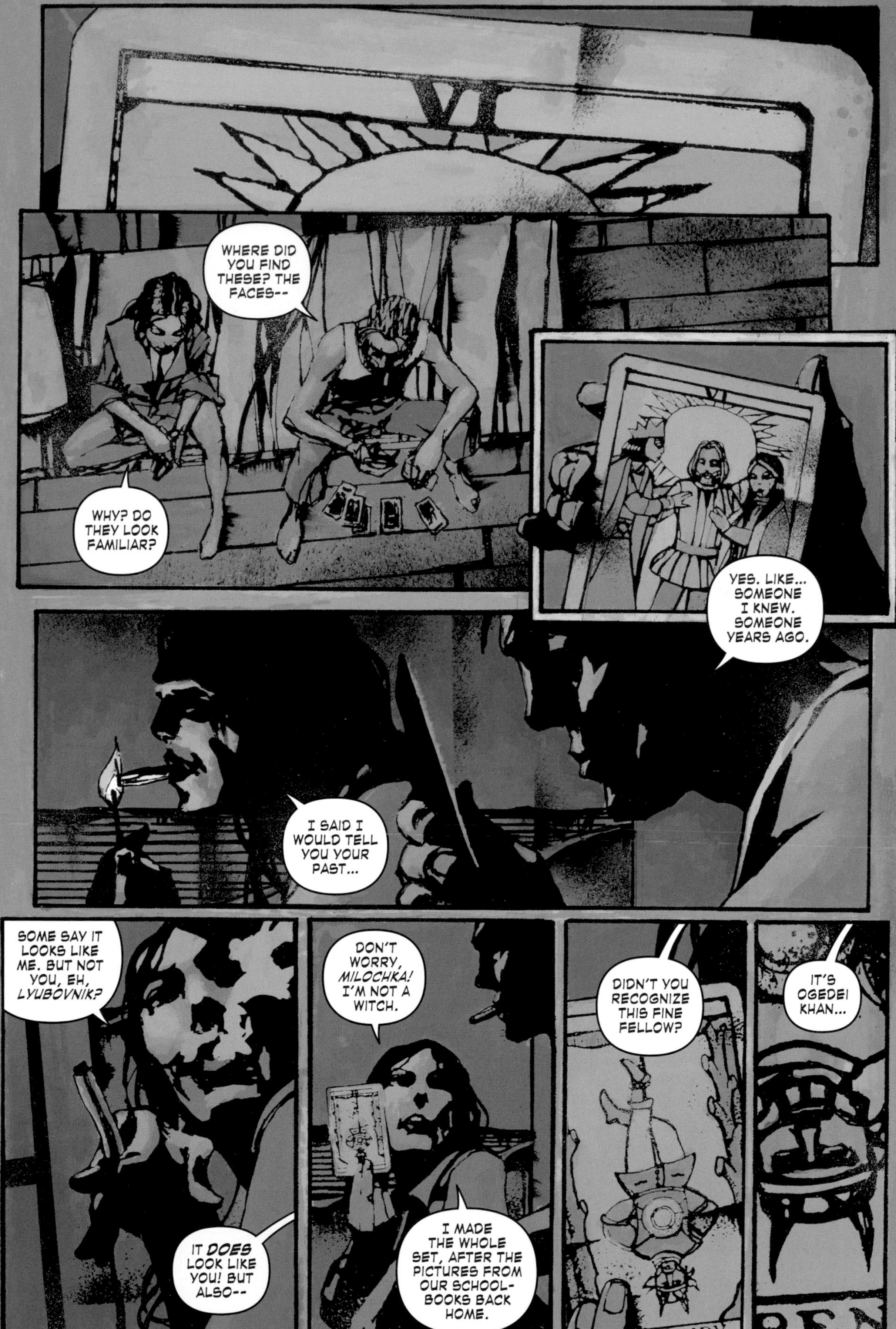
WHERE DID YOU FIND THESE? THE FACES--
WHY? DO THEY LOOK FAMILIAR?
YES. LIKE... SOMEONE I KNEW. SOMEONE YEARS AGO.
I SAID I WOULD TELL YOU YOUR PAST...
SOME SAY IT LOOKS LIKE ME. BUT NOT YOU, EH, *LYUBOVNIK?*
IT ***DOES*** LOOK LIKE YOU! BUT ALSO--
DON'T WORRY, *MILOCHKA!* I'M NOT A WITCH.
I MADE THE WHOLE SET, AFTER THE PICTURES FROM OUR SCHOOL-BOOKS BACK HOME.
DIDN'T YOU RECOGNIZE THIS FINE FELLOW?
PENDV
IT'S OGEDEI KHAN...
PEN

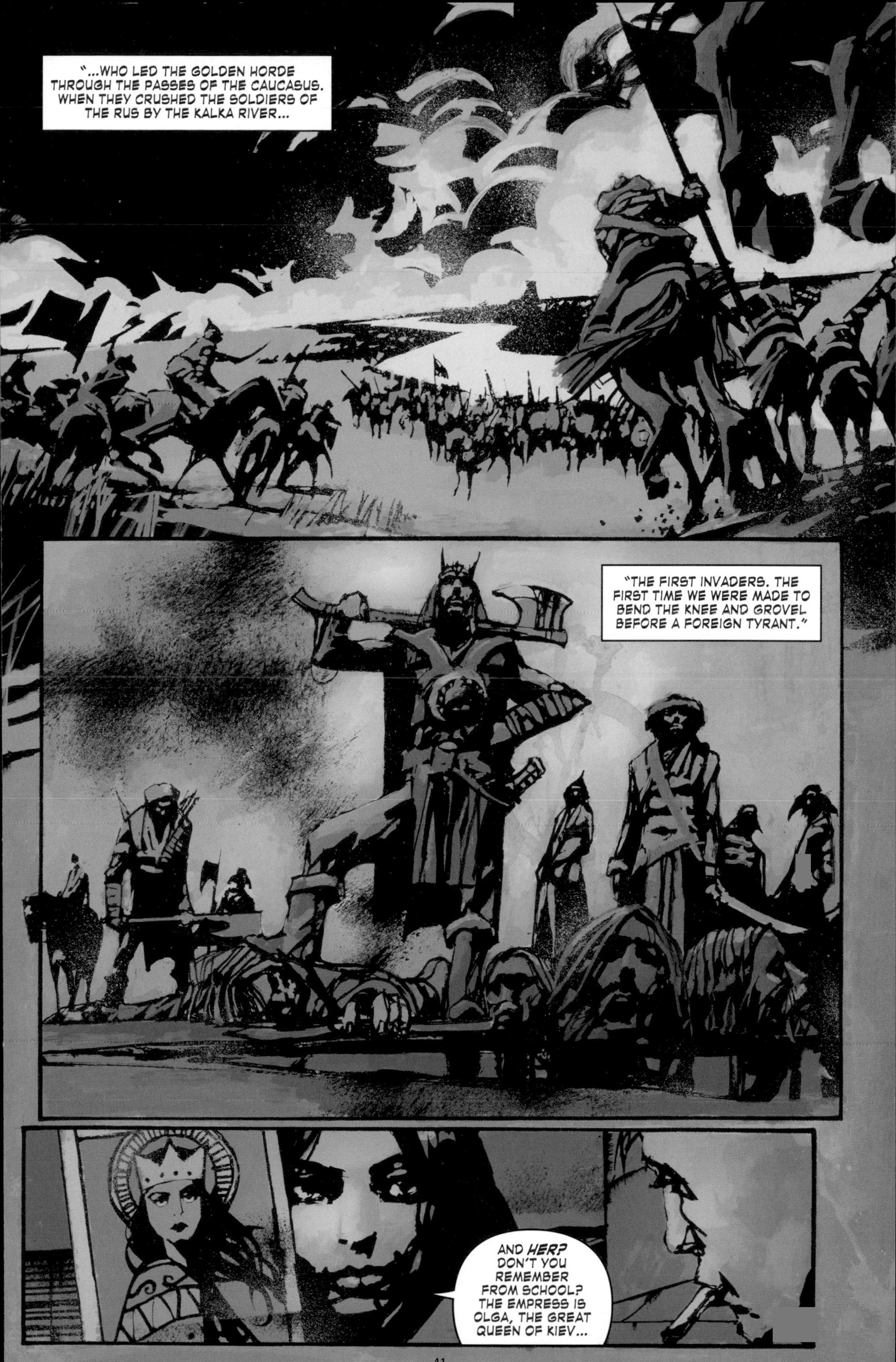
"...WHO LED THE GOLDEN HORDE THROUGH THE PASSES OF THE CAUCASUS. WHEN THEY CRUSHED THE SOLDIERS OF THE RUS BY THE KALKA RIVER...
"THE FIRST INVADERS. THE FIRST TIME WE WERE MADE TO BEND THE KNEE AND GROVEL BEFORE A FOREIGN TYRANT."
AND HER? DON'T YOU REMEMBER FROM SCHOOL? THE EMPRESS IS OLGA, THE GREAT QUEEN OF KIEV...

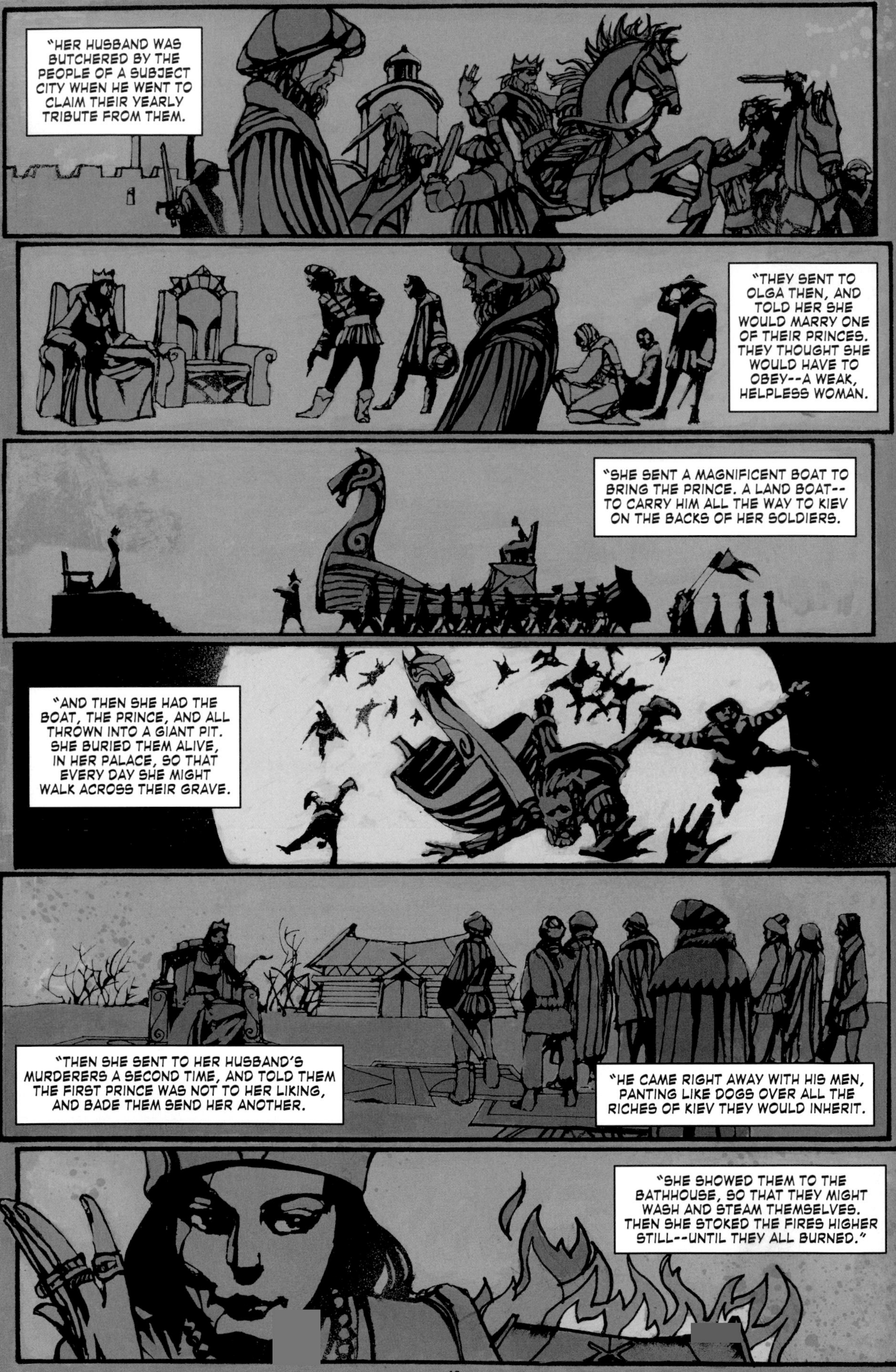
"HER HUSBAND WAS BUTCHERED BY THE PEOPLE OF A SUBJECT CITY WHEN HE WENT TO CLAIM THEIR YEARLY TRIBUTE FROM THEM.
"THEY SENT TO OLGA THEN, AND TOLD HER SHE WOULD MARRY ONE OF THEIR PRINCES. THEY THOUGHT SHE WOULD HAVE TO OBEY--A WEAK, HELPLESS WOMAN.
"SHE SENT A MAGNIFICENT BOAT TO BRING THE PRINCE. A LAND BOAT--TO CARRY HIM ALL THE WAY TO KIEV ON THE BACKS OF HER SOLDIERS.
"AND THEN SHE HAD THE BOAT, THE PRINCE, AND ALL THROWN INTO A GIANT PIT. SHE BURIED THEM ALIVE, IN HER PALACE, SO THAT EVERY DAY SHE MIGHT WALK ACROSS THEIR GRAVE.
"THEN SHE SENT TO HER HUSBAND'S MURDERERS A SECOND TIME, AND TOLD THEM THE FIRST PRINCE WAS NOT TO HER LIKING, AND BADE THEM SEND HER ANOTHER.
"HE CAME RIGHT AWAY WITH HIS MEN, PANTING LIKE DOGS OVER ALL THE RICHES OF KIEV THEY WOULD INHERIT.
"SHE SHOWED THEM TO THE BATHHOUSE, SO THAT THEY MIGHT WASH AND STEAM THEMSELVES. THEN SHE STOKED THE FIRES HIGHER STILL--UNTIL THEY ALL BURNED."

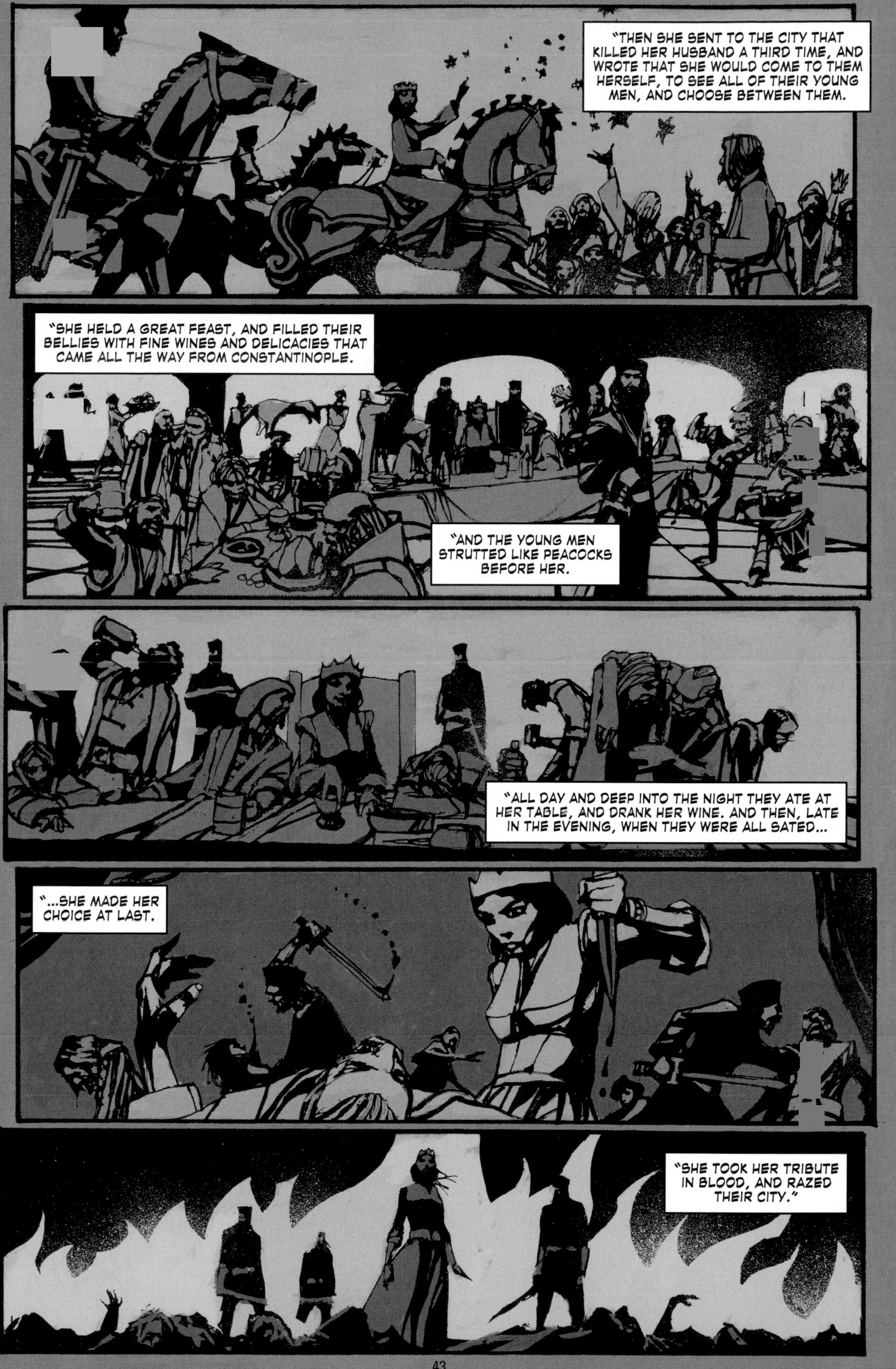
"THEN SHE SENT TO THE CITY THAT KILLED HER HUSBAND A THIRD TIME, AND WROTE THAT SHE WOULD COME TO THEM HERSELF, TO SEE ALL OF THEIR YOUNG MEN, AND CHOOSE BETWEEN THEM.
"SHE HELD A GREAT FEAST, AND FILLED THEIR BELLIES WITH FINE WINES AND DELICACIES THAT CAME ALL THE WAY FROM CONSTANTINOPLE.
"AND THE YOUNG MEN STRUTTED LIKE PEACOCKS BEFORE HER.
"ALL DAY AND DEEP INTO THE NIGHT THEY ATE AT HER TABLE, AND DRANK HER WINE. AND THEN, LATE IN THE EVENING, WHEN THEY WERE ALL SATED...
"...SHE MADE HER CHOICE AT LAST.
"SHE TOOK HER TRIBUTE IN BLOOD, AND RAZED THEIR CITY."

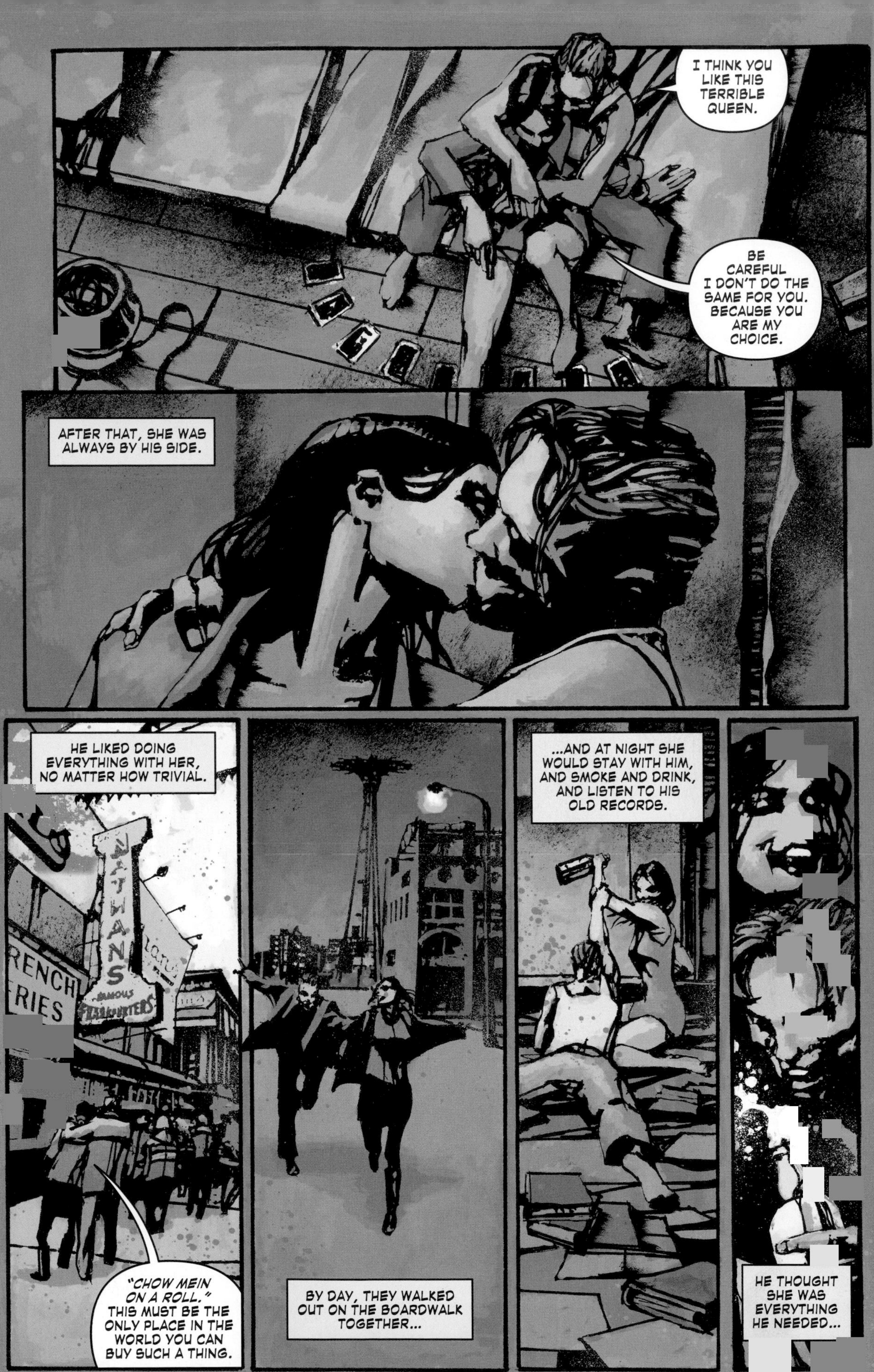

I THINK YOU LIKE THIS TERRIBLE QUEEN.
BE CAREFUL I DON'T DO THE SAME FOR YOU. BECAUSE YOU ARE MY CHOICE.
AFTER THAT, SHE WAS ALWAYS BY HIS SIDE.
HE LIKED DOING EVERYTHING WITH HER, NO MATTER HOW TRIVIAL.
"CHOW MEIN ON A ROLL." THIS MUST BE THE ONLY PLACE IN THE WORLD YOU CAN BUY SUCH A THING.
BY DAY, THEY WALKED OUT ON THE BOARDWALK TOGETHER...
...AND AT NIGHT SHE WOULD STAY WITH HIM, AND SMOKE AND DRINK, AND LISTEN TO HIS OLD RECORDS.
HE THOUGHT SHE WAS EVERYTHING HE NEEDED...

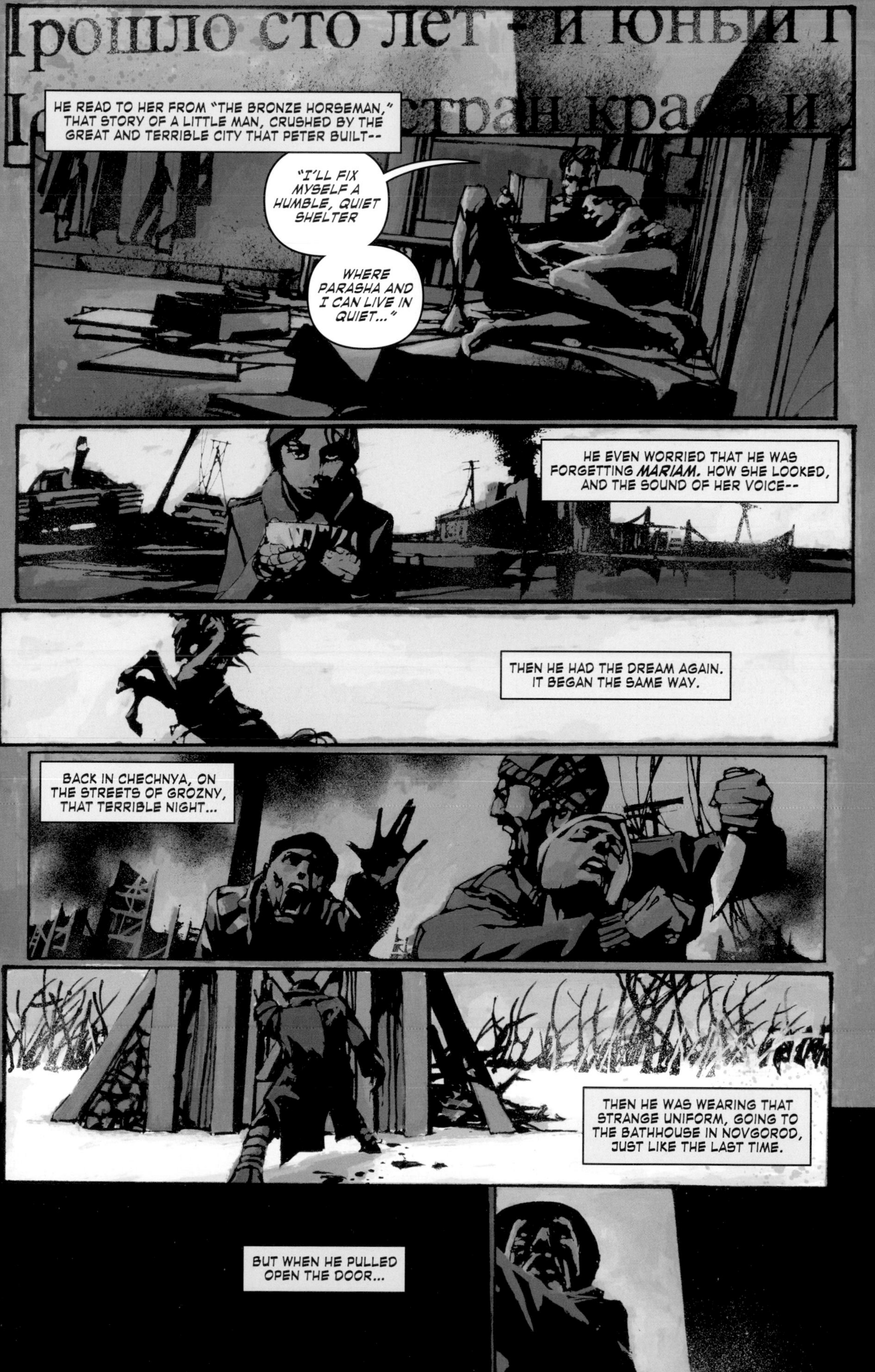
рошло сто лет - и юный
HE READ TO HER FROM "THE BRONZE HORSEMAN," THAT STORY OF A LITTLE MAN, CRUSHED BY THE GREAT AND TERRIBLE CITY THAT PETER BUILT--
"I'LL FIX MYSELF A HUMBLE, QUIET SHELTER
WHERE PARASHA AND I CAN LIVE IN QUIET..."
HE EVEN WORRIED THAT HE WAS FORGETTING *MARIAM.* HOW SHE LOOKED, AND THE SOUND OF HER VOICE--
THEN HE HAD THE DREAM AGAIN. IT BEGAN THE SAME WAY.
BACK IN CHECHNYA, ON THE STREETS OF GROZNY, THAT TERRIBLE NIGHT...
THEN HE WAS WEARING THAT STRANGE UNIFORM, GOING TO THE BATHHOUSE IN NOVGOROD, JUST LIKE THE LAST TIME.
BUT WHEN HE PULLED OPEN THE DOOR...

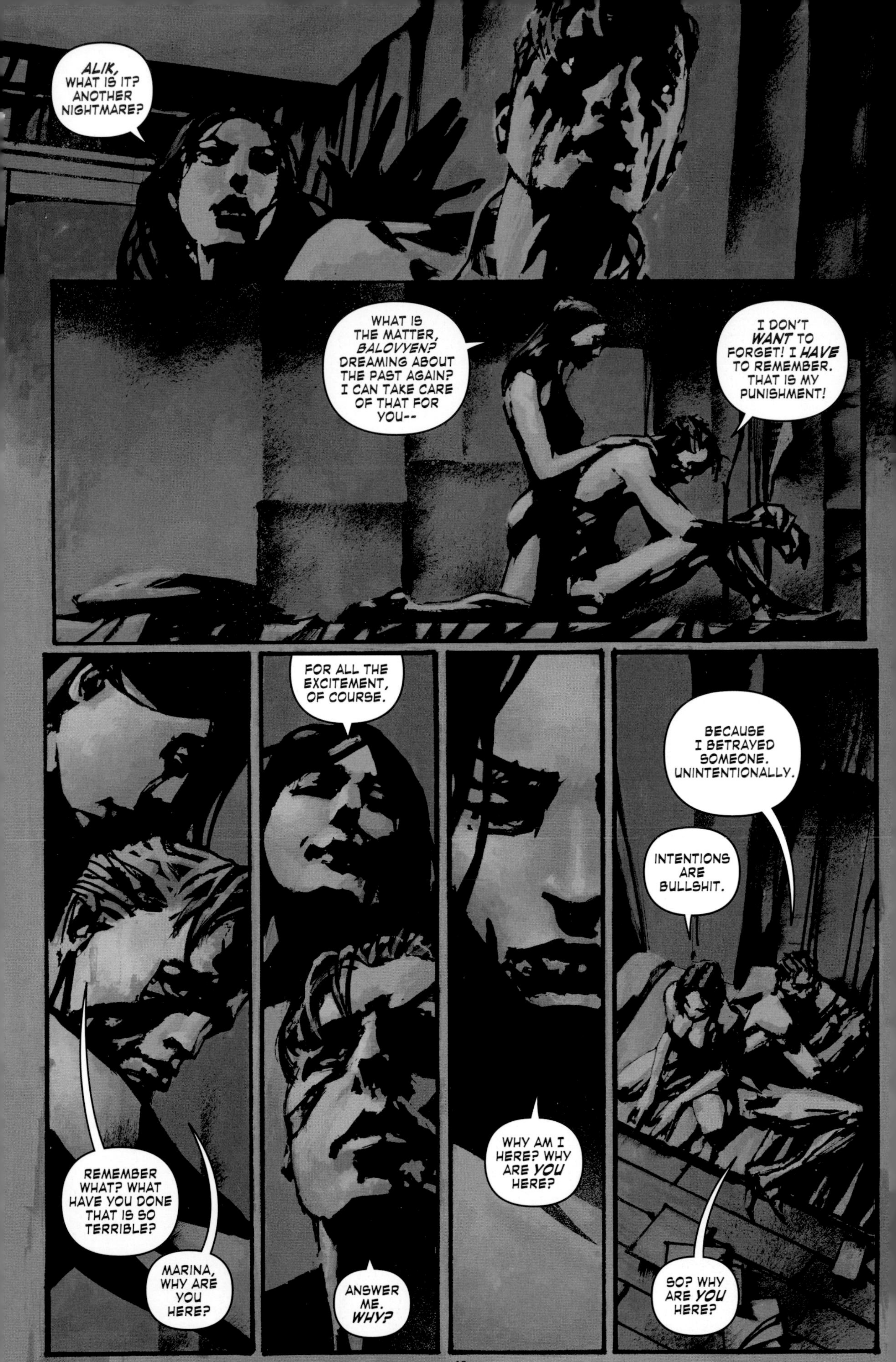
ALIK, WHAT IS IT? ANOTHER NIGHTMARE?
WHAT IS THE MATTER, BALOVYEN? DREAMING ABOUT THE PAST AGAIN? I CAN TAKE CARE OF THAT FOR YOU--
I DON'T WANT TO FORGET! I HAVE TO REMEMBER. THAT IS MY PUNISHMENT!
REMEMBER WHAT? WHAT HAVE YOU DONE THAT IS SO TERRIBLE?
MARINA, WHY ARE YOU HERE?
FOR ALL THE EXCITEMENT, OF COURSE.
ANSWER ME. WHY?
WHY AM I HERE? WHY ARE YOU HERE?
BECAUSE I BETRAYED SOMEONE. UNINTENTIONALLY.
INTENTIONS ARE BULLSHIT.
SO? WHY ARE YOU HERE?

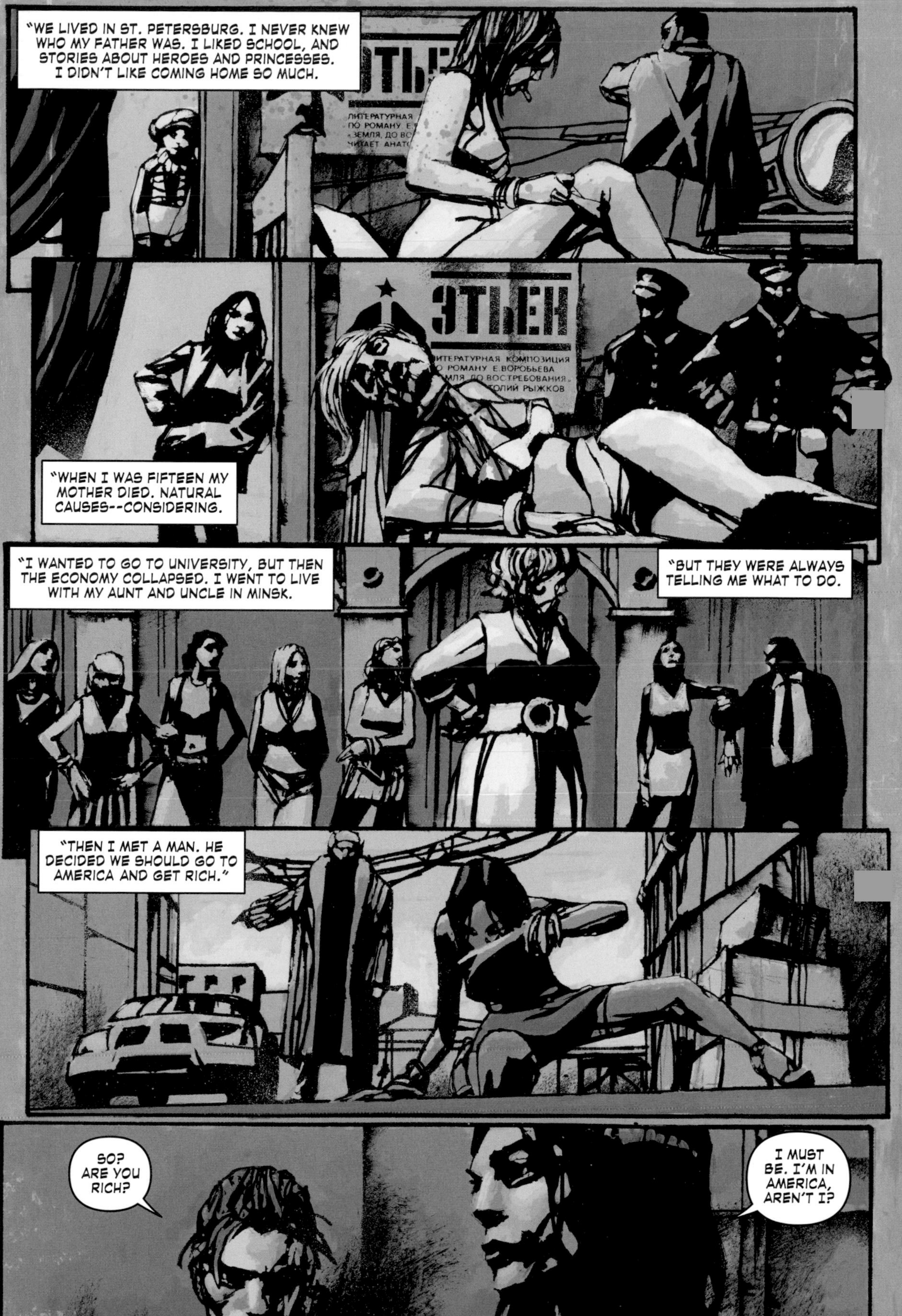
"WE LIVED IN ST. PETERSBURG. I NEVER KNEW WHO MY FATHER WAS. I LIKED SCHOOL, AND STORIES ABOUT HEROES AND PRINCESSES. I DIDN'T LIKE COMING HOME SO MUCH.
"WHEN I WAS FIFTEEN MY MOTHER DIED. NATURAL CAUSES--CONSIDERING.
"I WANTED TO GO TO UNIVERSITY, BUT THEN THE ECONOMY COLLAPSED. I WENT TO LIVE WITH MY AUNT AND UNCLE IN MINSK.
"BUT THEY WERE ALWAYS TELLING ME WHAT TO DO.
"THEN I MET A MAN. HE DECIDED WE SHOULD GO TO AMERICA AND GET RICH."
SO? ARE YOU RICH?
I MUST BE. I'M IN AMERICA, AREN'T I?

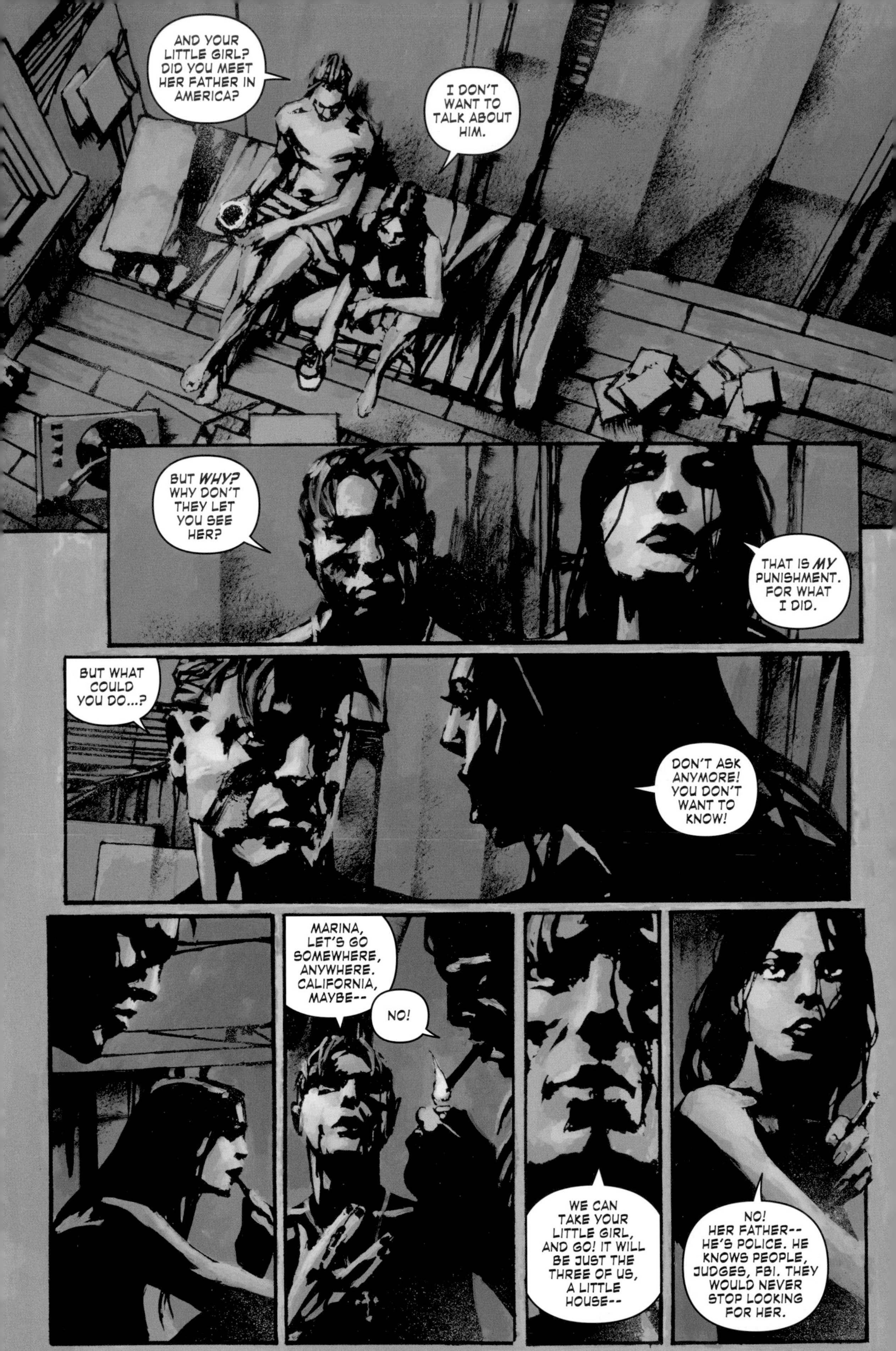
AND YOUR LITTLE GIRL? DID YOU MEET HER FATHER IN AMERICA?
I DON'T WANT TO TALK ABOUT HIM.
BUT WHY? WHY DON'T THEY LET YOU SEE HER?
THAT IS MY PUNISHMENT. FOR WHAT I DID.
BUT WHAT COULD YOU DO...?
DON'T ASK ANYMORE! YOU DON'T WANT TO KNOW!
MARINA, LET'S GO SOMEWHERE, ANYWHERE. CALIFORNIA, MAYBE--
NO!
WE CAN TAKE YOUR LITTLE GIRL, AND GO! IT WILL BE JUST THE THREE OF US, A LITTLE HOUSE--
NO! HER FATHER-- HE'S POLICE. HE KNOWS PEOPLE, JUDGES, FBI. THEY WOULD NEVER STOP LOOKING FOR HER.

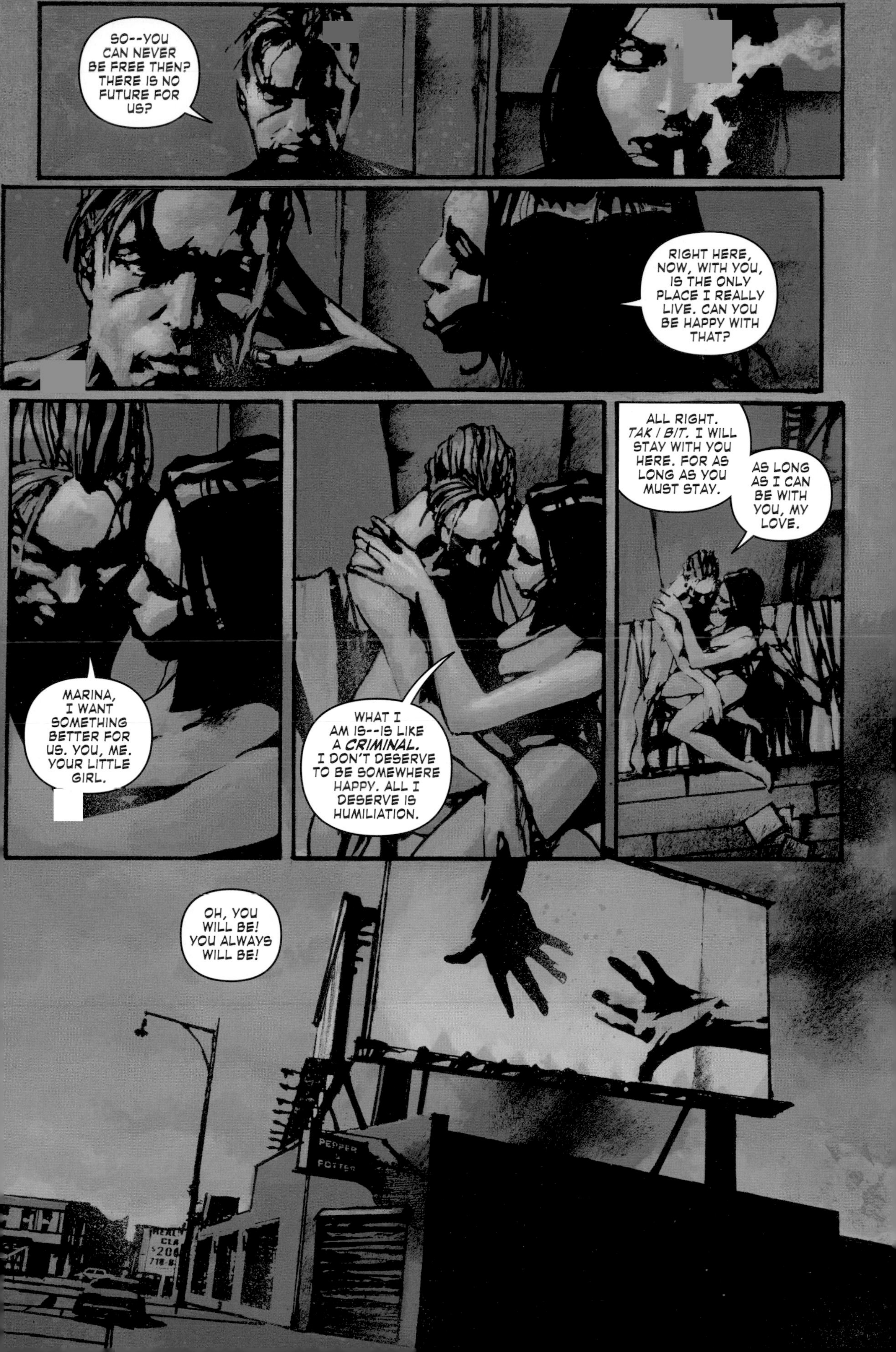
SO--YOU CAN NEVER BE FREE THEN? THERE IS NO FUTURE FOR US?
RIGHT HERE, NOW, WITH YOU, IS THE ONLY PLACE I REALLY LIVE. CAN YOU BE HAPPY WITH THAT?
MARINA, I WANT SOMETHING BETTER FOR US. YOU, ME. YOUR LITTLE GIRL.
WHAT I AM IS--IS LIKE A *CRIMINAL.* I DON'T DESERVE TO BE SOMEWHERE HAPPY. ALL I DESERVE IS HUMILIATION.
ALL RIGHT. *TAK I BIT.* I WILL STAY WITH YOU HERE. FOR AS LONG AS YOU MUST STAY.
AS LONG AS I CAN BE WITH YOU, MY LOVE.
OH, YOU WILL BE! YOU ALWAYS WILL BE!

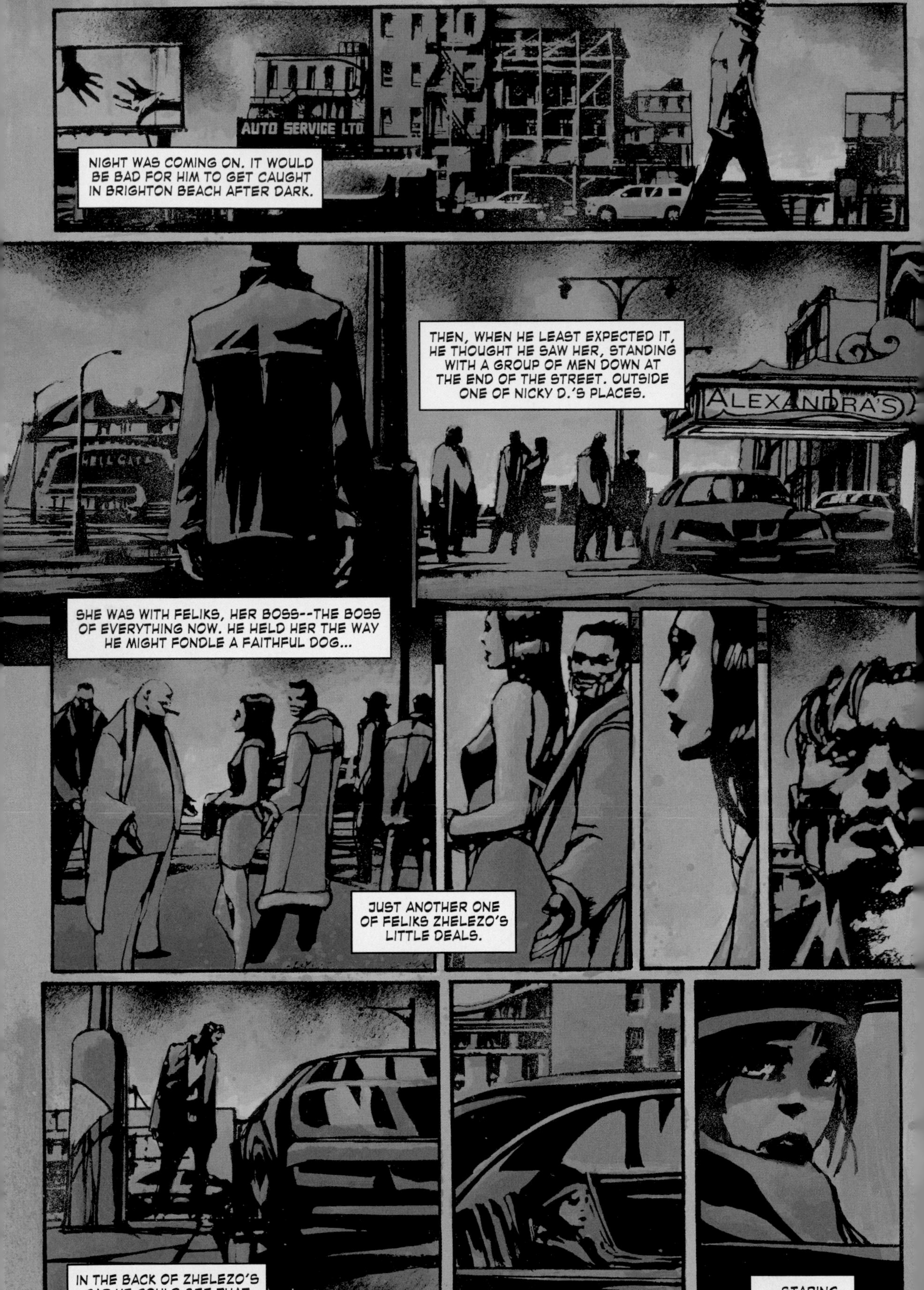
AUTO SERVICE LTD
NIGHT WAS COMING ON. IT WOULD BE BAD FOR HIM TO GET CAUGHT IN BRIGHTON BEACH AFTER DARK.
THEN, WHEN HE LEAST EXPECTED IT, HE THOUGHT HE SAW HER, STANDING WITH A GROUP OF MEN DOWN AT THE END OF THE STREET. OUTSIDE ONE OF NICKY D.'S PLACES.
ALEXANDRA'S
SHE WAS WITH FELIKS, HER BOSS--THE BOSS OF EVERYTHING NOW. HE HELD HER THE WAY HE MIGHT FONDLE A FAITHFUL DOG...
JUST ANOTHER ONE OF FELIKS ZHELEZO'S LITTLE DEALS.
IN THE BACK OF ZHELEZO'S CAR HE COULD SEE THAT LITTLE GIRL AGAIN...
...STARING BACK AT HIM.

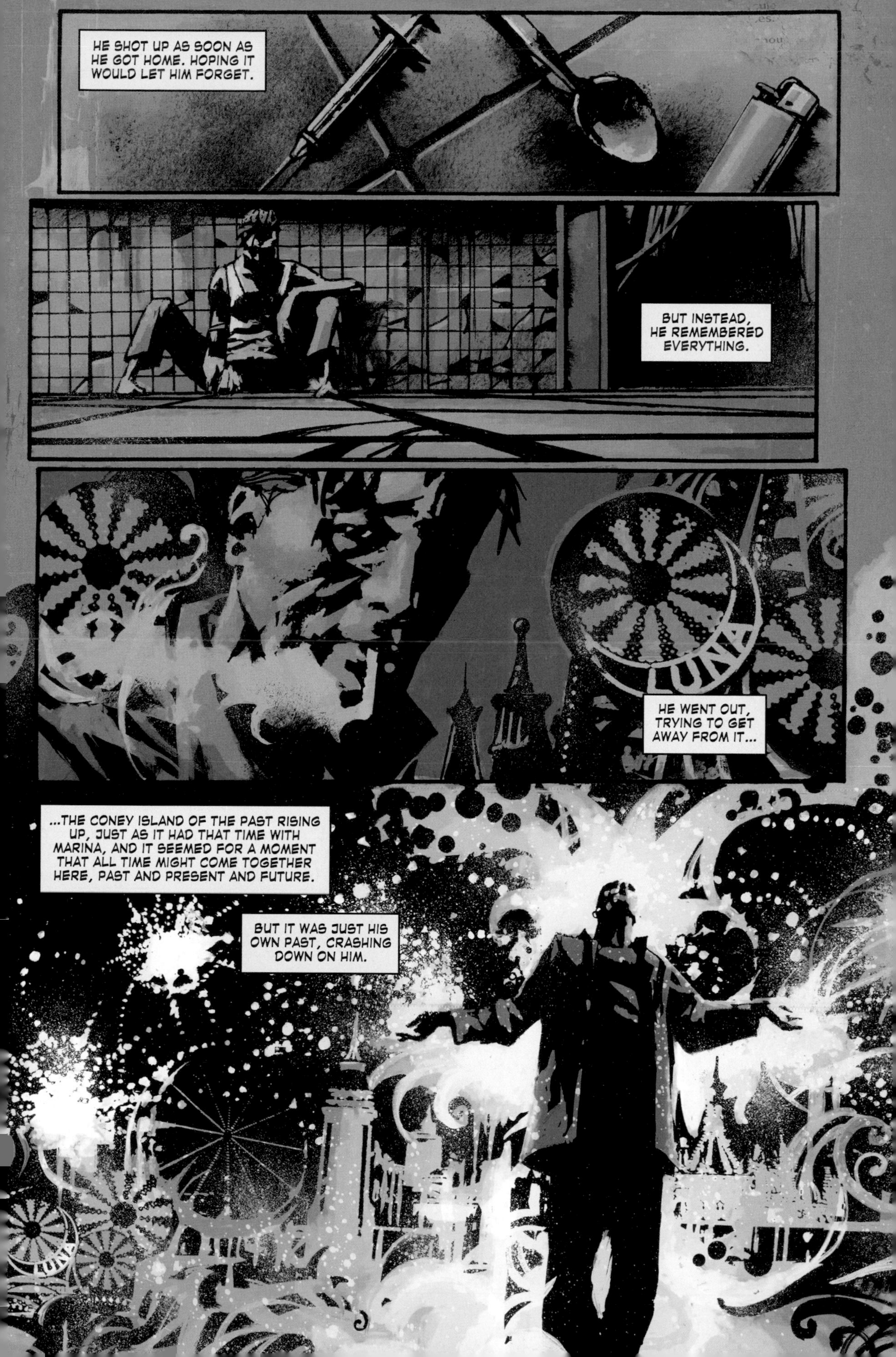
HE SHOT UP AS SOON AS HE GOT HOME. HOPING IT WOULD LET HIM FORGET.
BUT INSTEAD, HE REMEMBERED EVERYTHING.
LUNA
HE WENT OUT, TRYING TO GET AWAY FROM IT...
...THE CONEY ISLAND OF THE PAST RISING UP, JUST AS IT HAD THAT TIME WITH MARINA, AND IT SEEMED FOR A MOMENT THAT ALL TIME MIGHT COME TOGETHER HERE, PAST AND PRESENT AND FUTURE.
BUT IT WAS JUST HIS OWN PAST, CRASHING DOWN ON HIM.
LUNA

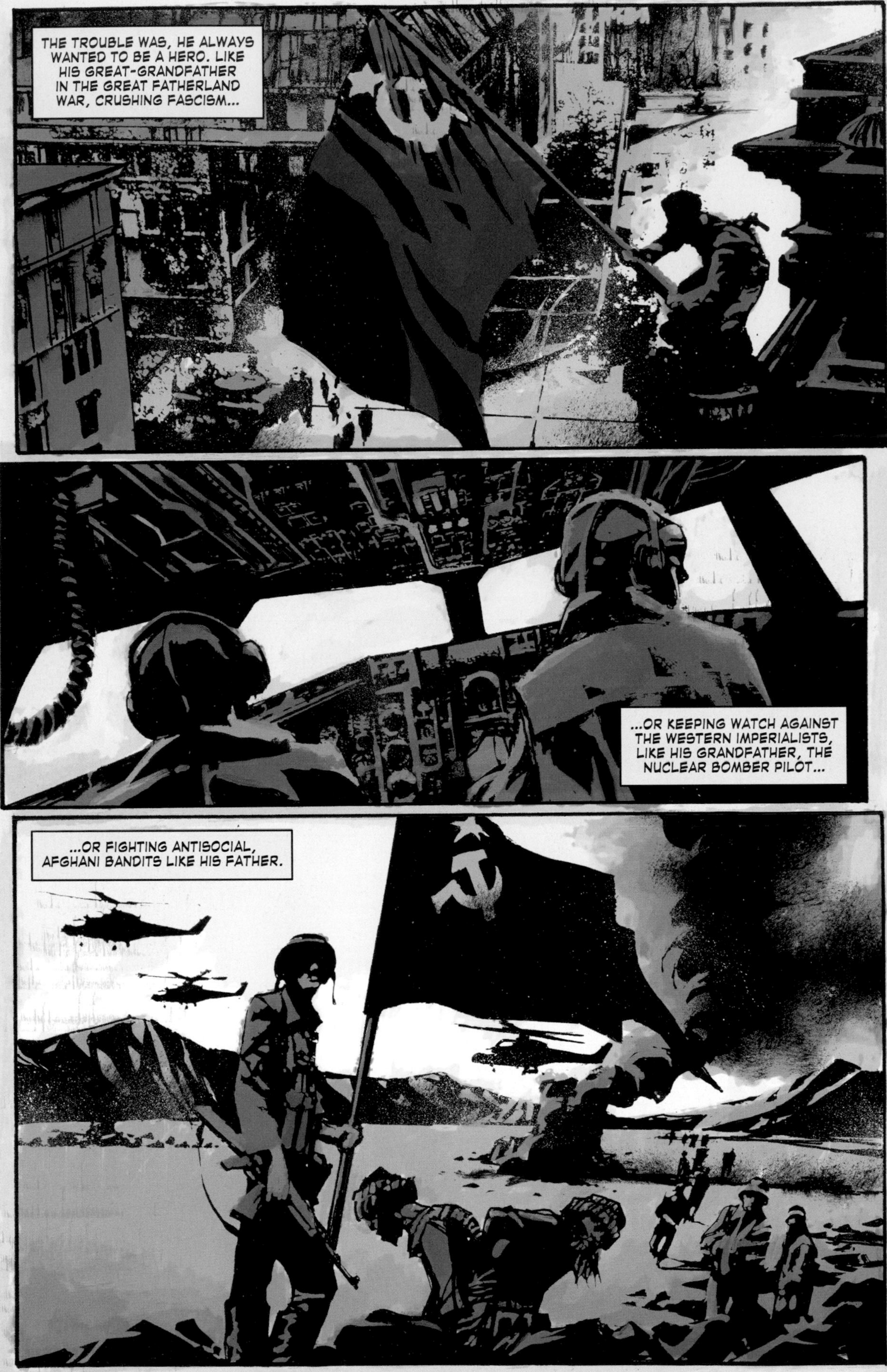
THE TROUBLE WAS, HE ALWAYS WANTED TO BE A HERO. LIKE HIS GREAT-GRANDFATHER IN THE GREAT FATHERLAND WAR, CRUSHING FASCISM...
...OR KEEPING WATCH AGAINST THE WESTERN IMPERIALISTS, LIKE HIS GRANDFATHER, THE NUCLEAR BOMBER PILOT...
...OR FIGHTING ANTISOCIAL, AFGHANI BANDITS LIKE HIS FATHER.

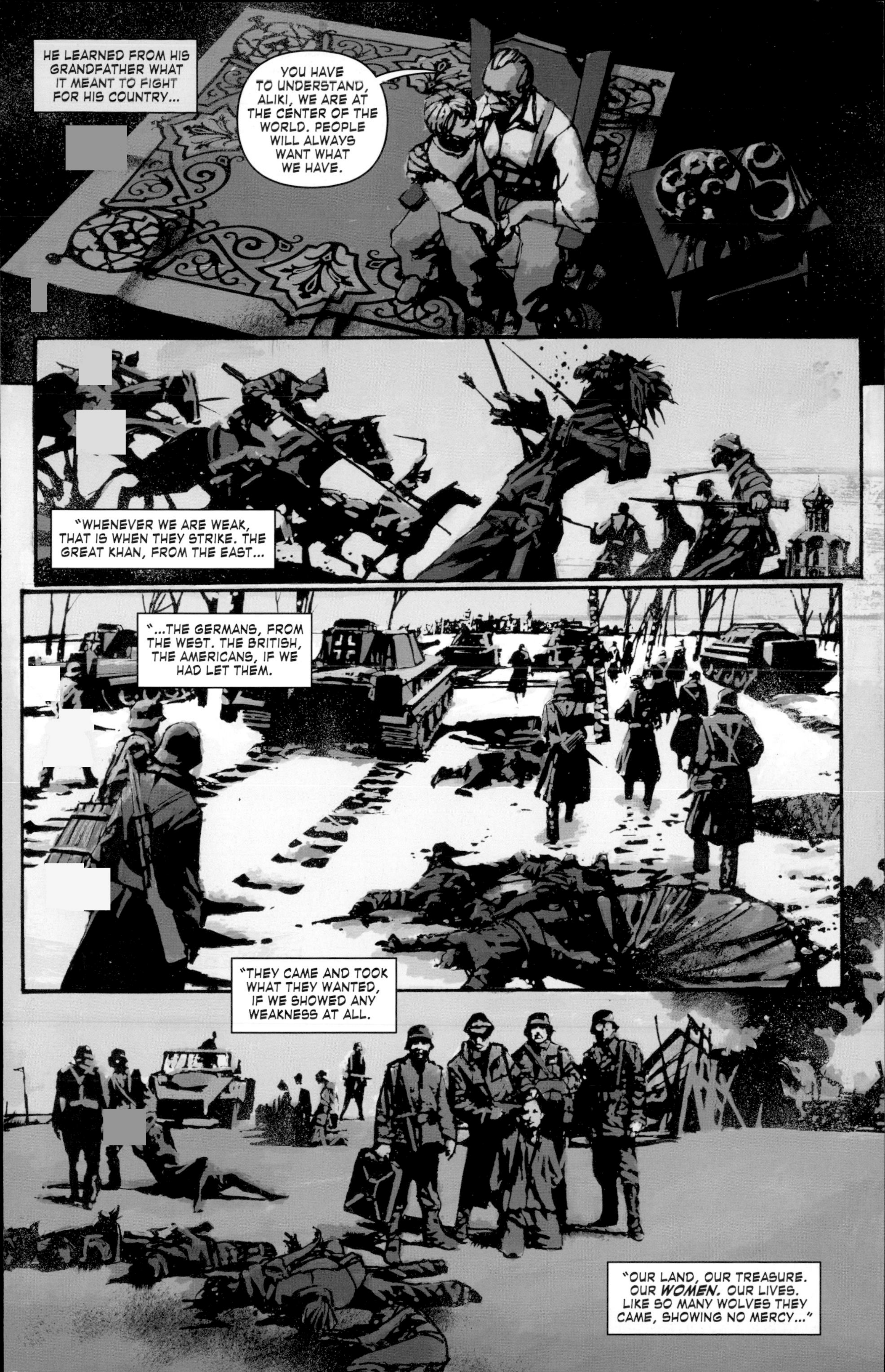
HE LEARNED FROM HIS GRANDFATHER WHAT IT MEANT TO FIGHT FOR HIS COUNTRY...
YOU HAVE TO UNDERSTAND, ALIKI, WE ARE AT THE CENTER OF THE WORLD. PEOPLE WILL ALWAYS WANT WHAT WE HAVE.
"WHENEVER WE ARE WEAK, THAT IS WHEN THEY STRIKE. THE GREAT KHAN, FROM THE EAST...
"...THE GERMANS, FROM THE WEST. THE BRITISH, THE AMERICANS, IF WE HAD LET THEM.
"THEY CAME AND TOOK WHAT THEY WANTED, IF WE SHOWED ANY WEAKNESS AT ALL.
"OUR LAND, OUR TREASURE. OUR *WOMEN.* OUR LIVES. LIKE SO MANY WOLVES THEY CAME, SHOWING NO MERCY..."

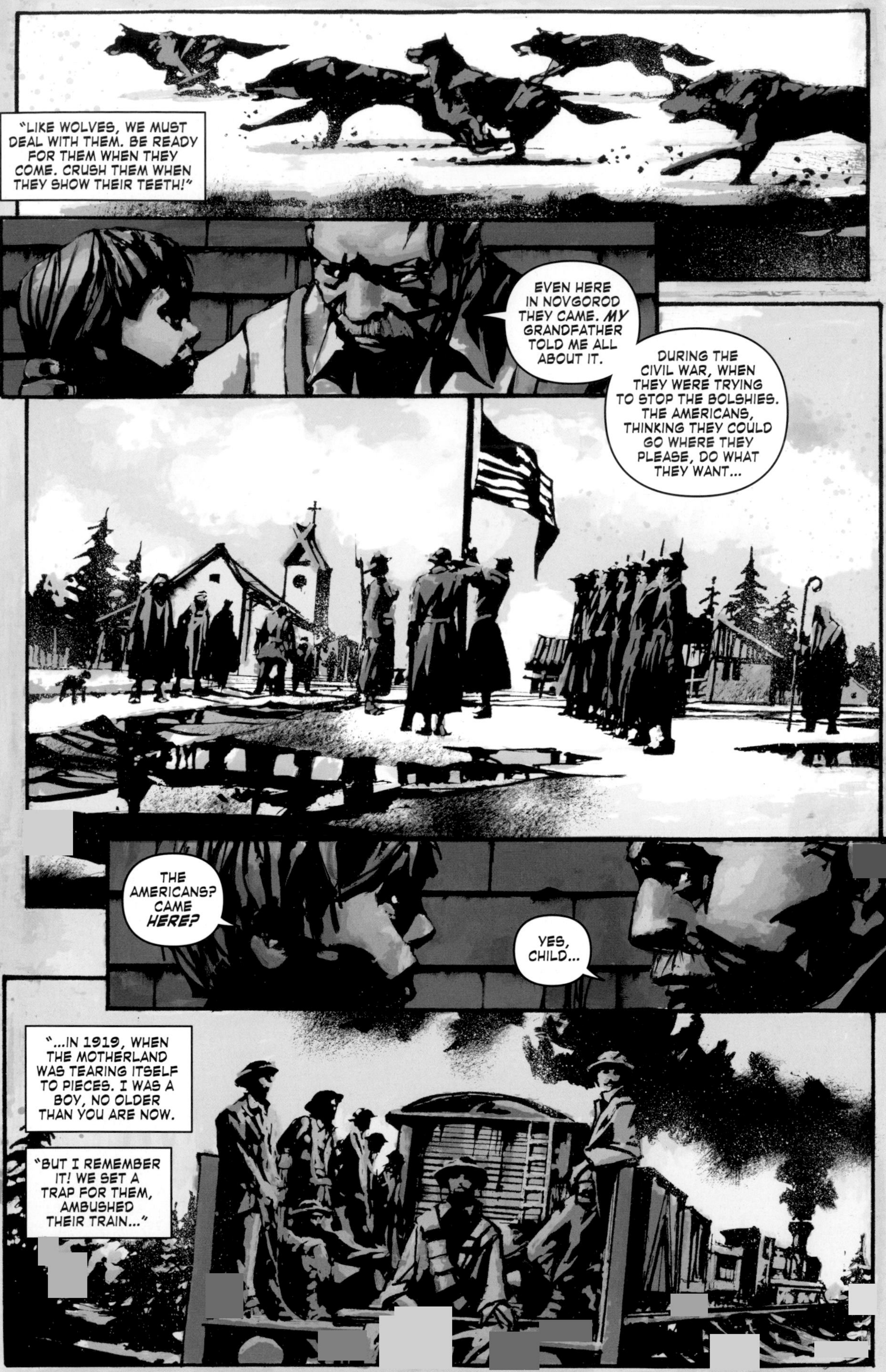
"LIKE WOLVES, WE MUST DEAL WITH THEM. BE READY FOR THEM WHEN THEY COME. CRUSH THEM WHEN THEY SHOW THEIR TEETH!"
EVEN HERE IN NOVGOROD THEY CAME. MY GRANDFATHER TOLD ME ALL ABOUT IT.
DURING THE CIVIL WAR, WHEN THEY WERE TRYING TO STOP THE BOLSHIES. THE AMERICANS, THINKING THEY COULD GO WHERE THEY PLEASE, DO WHAT THEY WANT...
THE AMERICANS? CAME HERE?
YES, CHILD...
"...IN 1919, WHEN THE MOTHERLAND WAS TEARING ITSELF TO PIECES. I WAS A BOY, NO OLDER THAN YOU ARE NOW.
"BUT I REMEMBER IT! WE SET A TRAP FOR THEM, AMBUSHED THEIR TRAIN..."

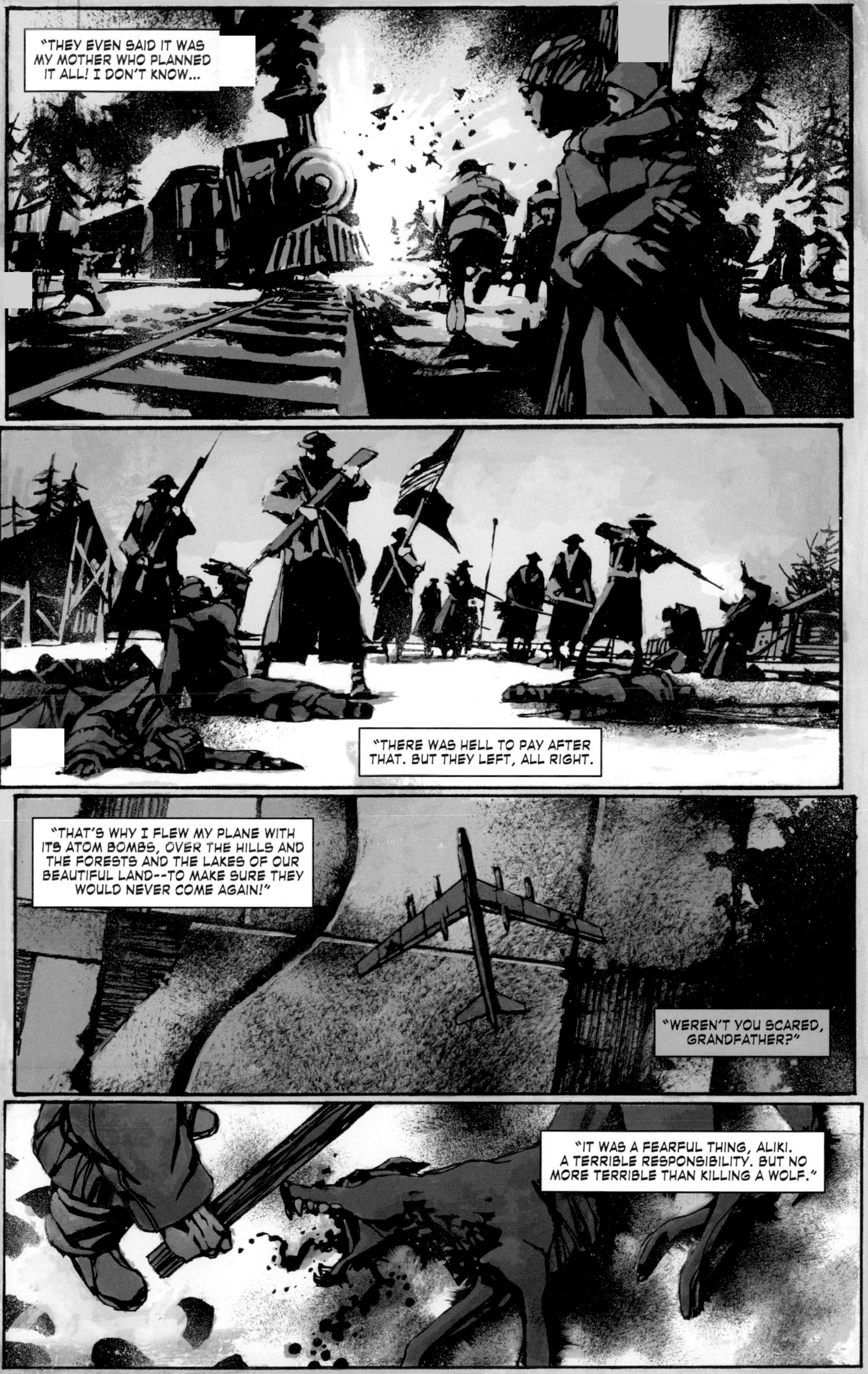
"THEY EVEN SAID IT WAS MY MOTHER WHO PLANNED IT ALL! I DON'T KNOW...
"THERE WAS HELL TO PAY AFTER THAT. BUT THEY LEFT, ALL RIGHT.
"THAT'S WHY I FLEW MY PLANE WITH ITS ATOM BOMBS, OVER THE HILLS AND THE FORESTS AND THE LAKES OF OUR BEAUTIFUL LAND--TO MAKE SURE THEY WOULD NEVER COME AGAIN!"
"WEREN'T YOU SCARED, GRANDFATHER?"
"IT WAS A FEARFUL THING, ALIKI. A TERRIBLE RESPONSIBILITY. BUT NO MORE TERRIBLE THAN KILLING A WOLF."

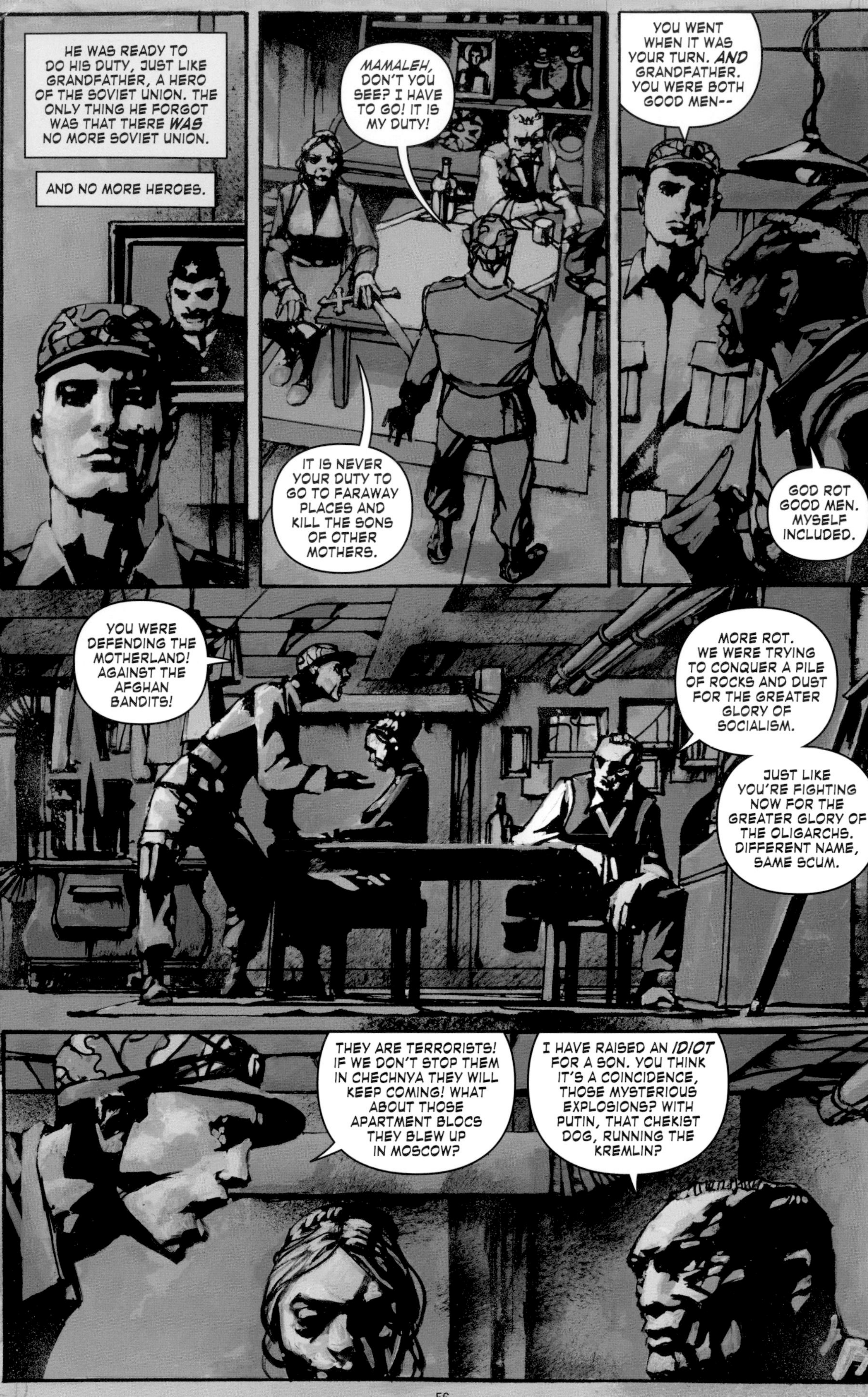
HE WAS READY TO DO HIS DUTY, JUST LIKE GRANDFATHER, A HERO OF THE SOVIET UNION. THE ONLY THING HE FORGOT WAS THAT THERE *WAS* NO MORE SOVIET UNION.
AND NO MORE HEROES.
*MAMALEH*, DON'T YOU SEE? I HAVE TO GO! IT IS MY DUTY!
IT IS NEVER YOUR DUTY TO GO TO FARAWAY PLACES AND KILL THE SONS OF OTHER MOTHERS.
YOU WENT WHEN IT WAS YOUR TURN. *AND* GRANDFATHER. YOU WERE BOTH GOOD MEN--
GOD ROT GOOD MEN. MYSELF INCLUDED.
YOU WERE DEFENDING THE MOTHERLAND! AGAINST THE AFGHAN BANDITS!
MORE ROT. WE WERE TRYING TO CONQUER A PILE OF ROCKS AND DUST FOR THE GREATER GLORY OF SOCIALISM.
JUST LIKE YOU'RE FIGHTING NOW FOR THE GREATER GLORY OF THE OLIGARCHS. DIFFERENT NAME, SAME SCUM.
THEY ARE TERRORISTS! IF WE DON'T STOP THEM IN CHECHNYA THEY WILL KEEP COMING! WHAT ABOUT THOSE APARTMENT BLOCS THEY BLEW UP IN MOSCOW?
I HAVE RAISED AN *IDIOT* FOR A SON. YOU THINK IT'S A COINCIDENCE, THOSE MYSTERIOUS EXPLOSIONS? WITH PUTIN, THAT CHEKIST DOG, RUNNING THE KREMLIN?

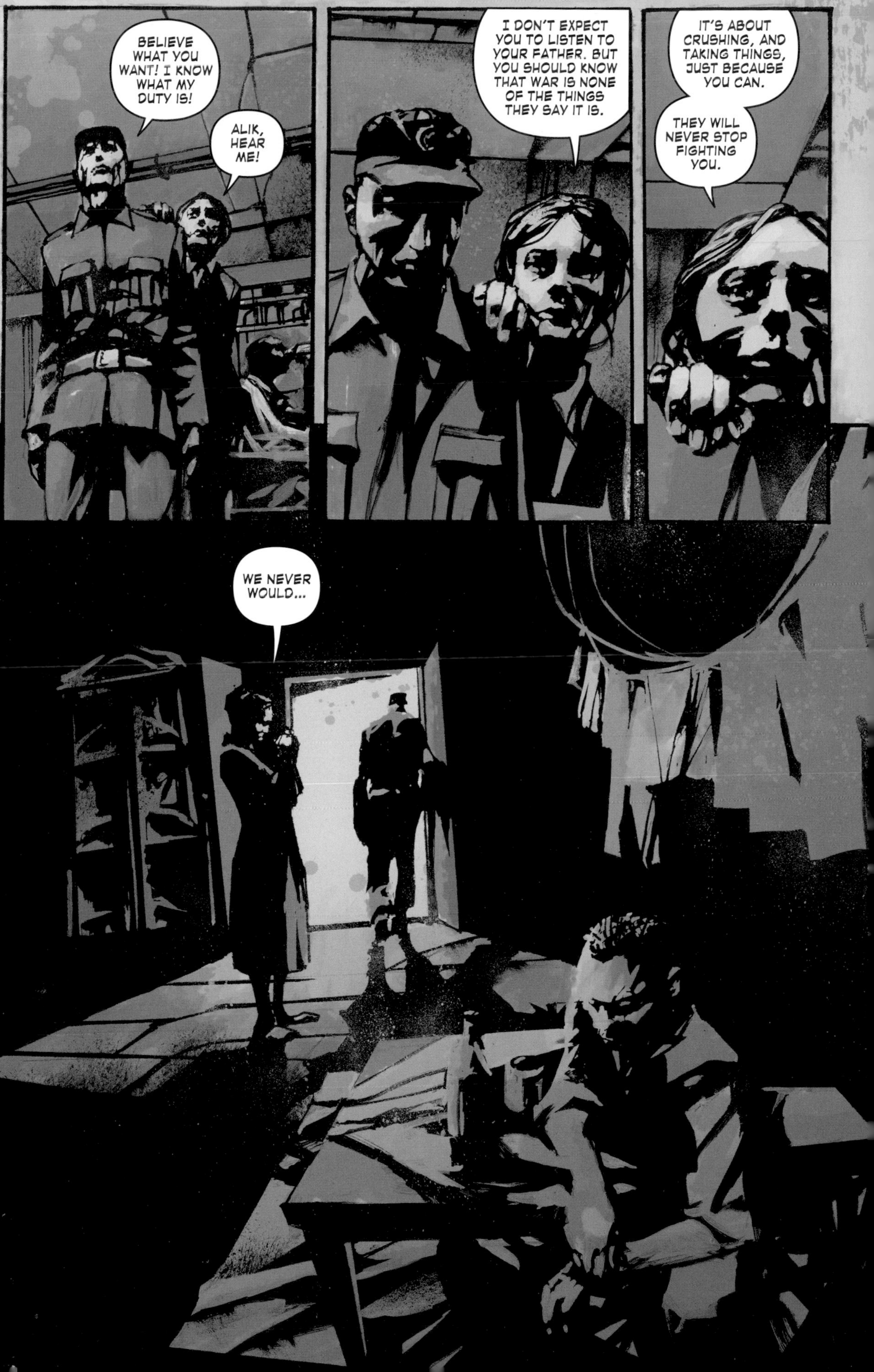
BELIEVE WHAT YOU WANT! I KNOW WHAT MY DUTY IS!
ALIK, HEAR ME!
I DON'T EXPECT YOU TO LISTEN TO YOUR FATHER. BUT YOU SHOULD KNOW THAT WAR IS NONE OF THE THINGS THEY SAY IT IS.
IT'S ABOUT CRUSHING, AND TAKING THINGS, JUST BECAUSE YOU CAN.
THEY WILL NEVER STOP FIGHTING YOU.
WE NEVER WOULD...

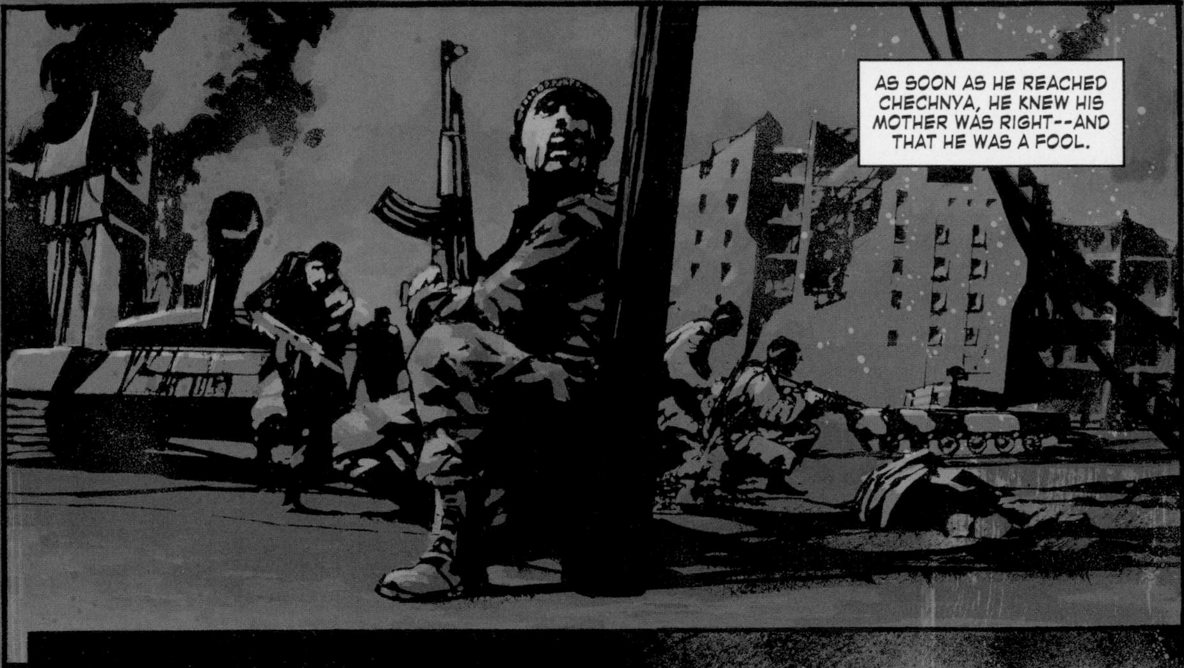
AS SOON AS HE REACHED CHECHNYA, HE KNEW HIS MOTHER WAS RIGHT--AND THAT HE WAS A FOOL.

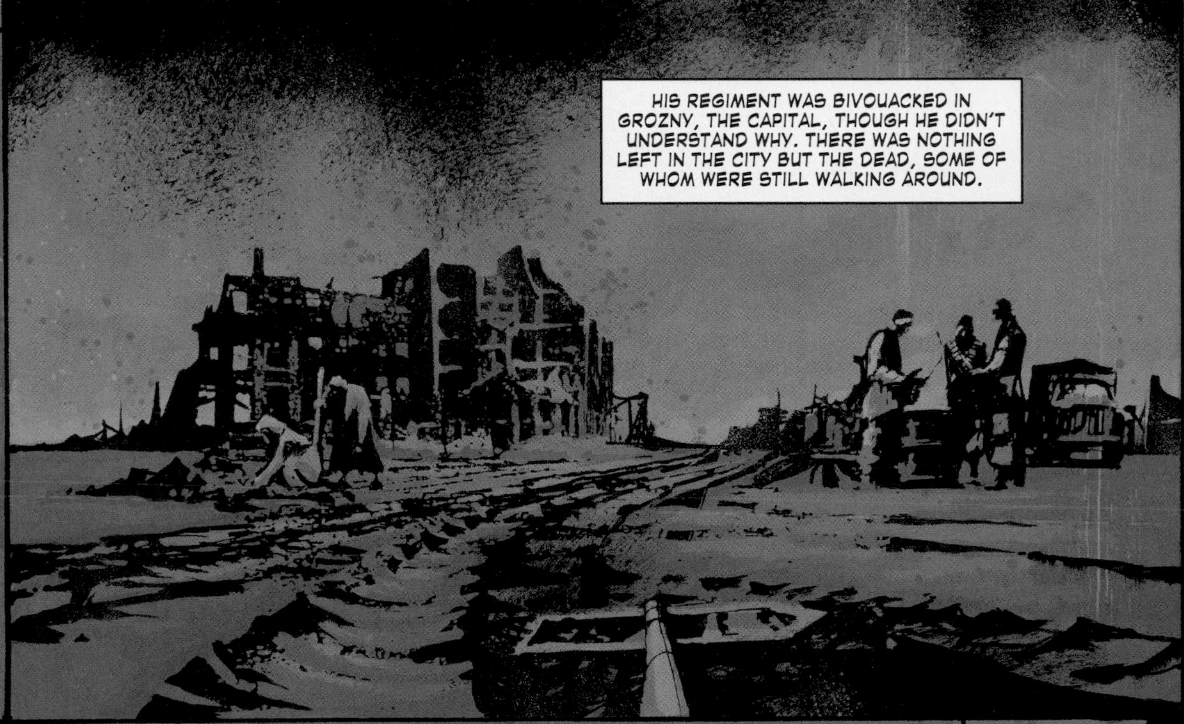
HIS REGIMENT WAS BIVOUACKED IN GROZNY, THE CAPITAL, THOUGH HE DIDN'T UNDERSTAND WHY. THERE WAS NOTHING LEFT IN THE CITY BUT THE DEAD, SOME OF WHOM WERE STILL WALKING AROUND.

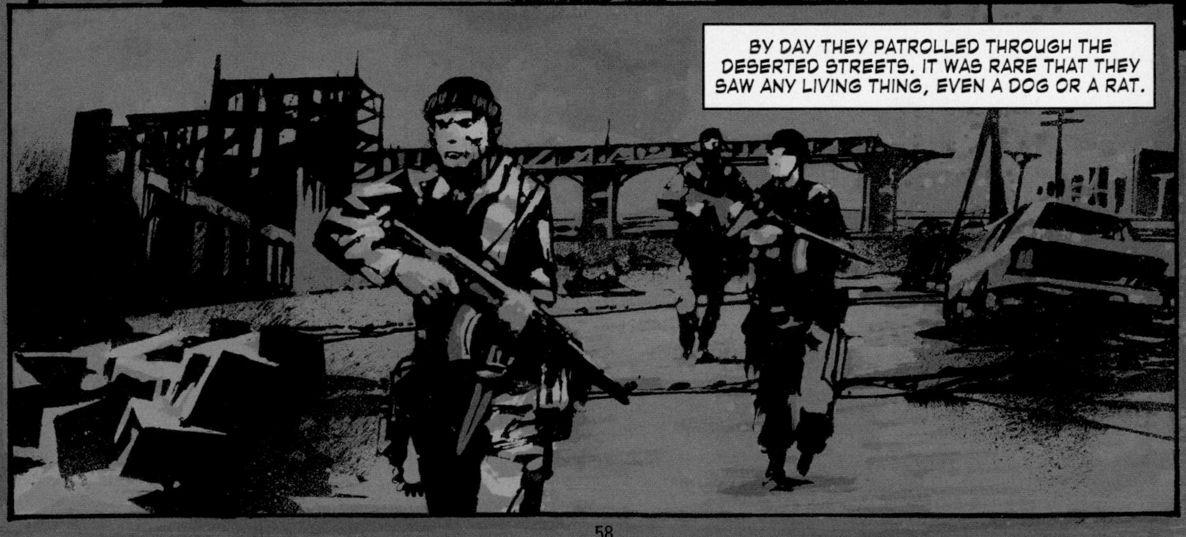
BY DAY THEY PATROLLED THROUGH THE DESERTED STREETS. IT WAS RARE THAT THEY SAW ANY LIVING THING, EVEN A DOG OR A RAT.

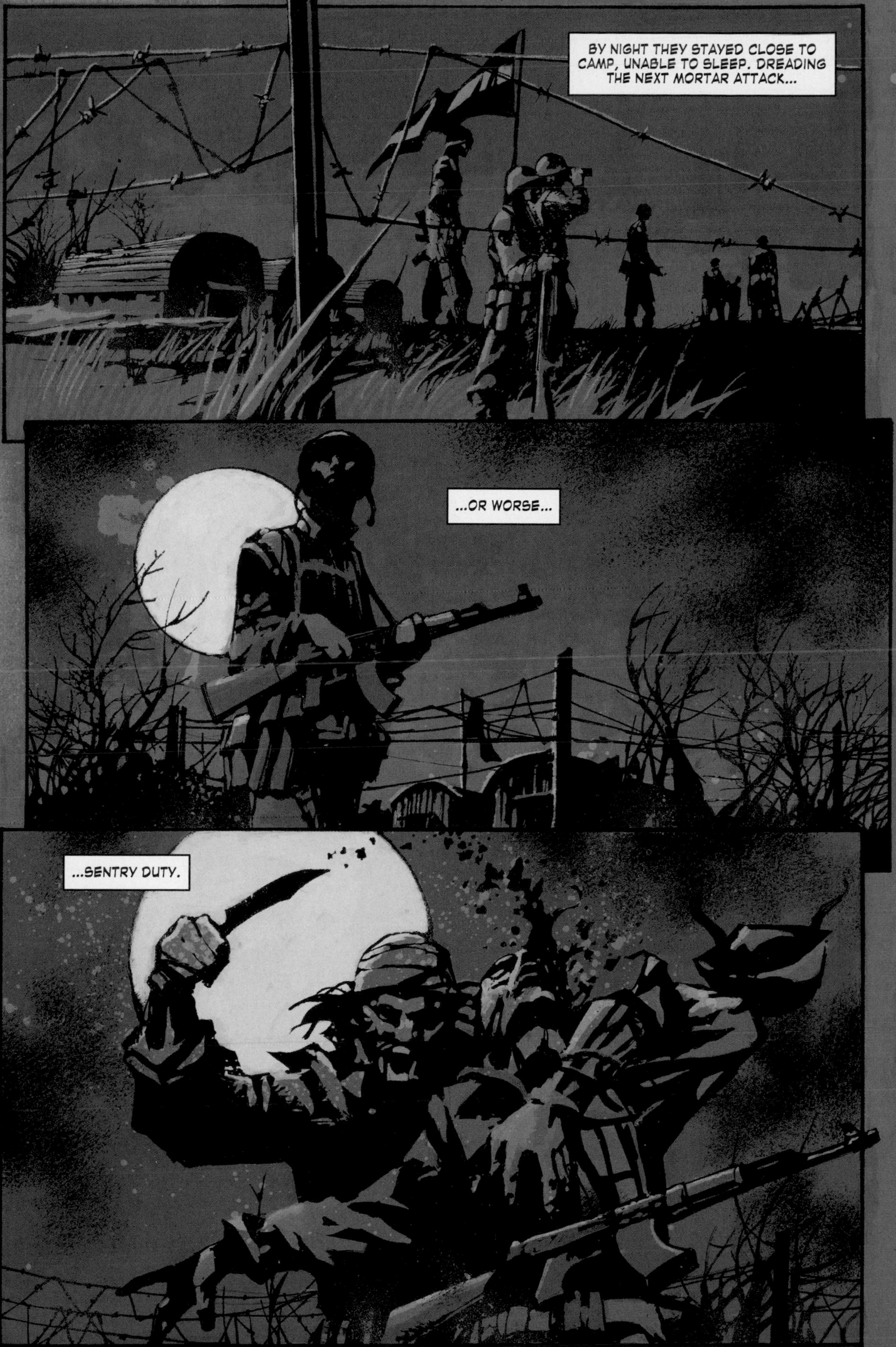
BY NIGHT THEY STAYED CLOSE TO CAMP, UNABLE TO SLEEP. DREADING THE NEXT MORTAR ATTACK...
...OR WORSE...
...SENTRY DUTY.

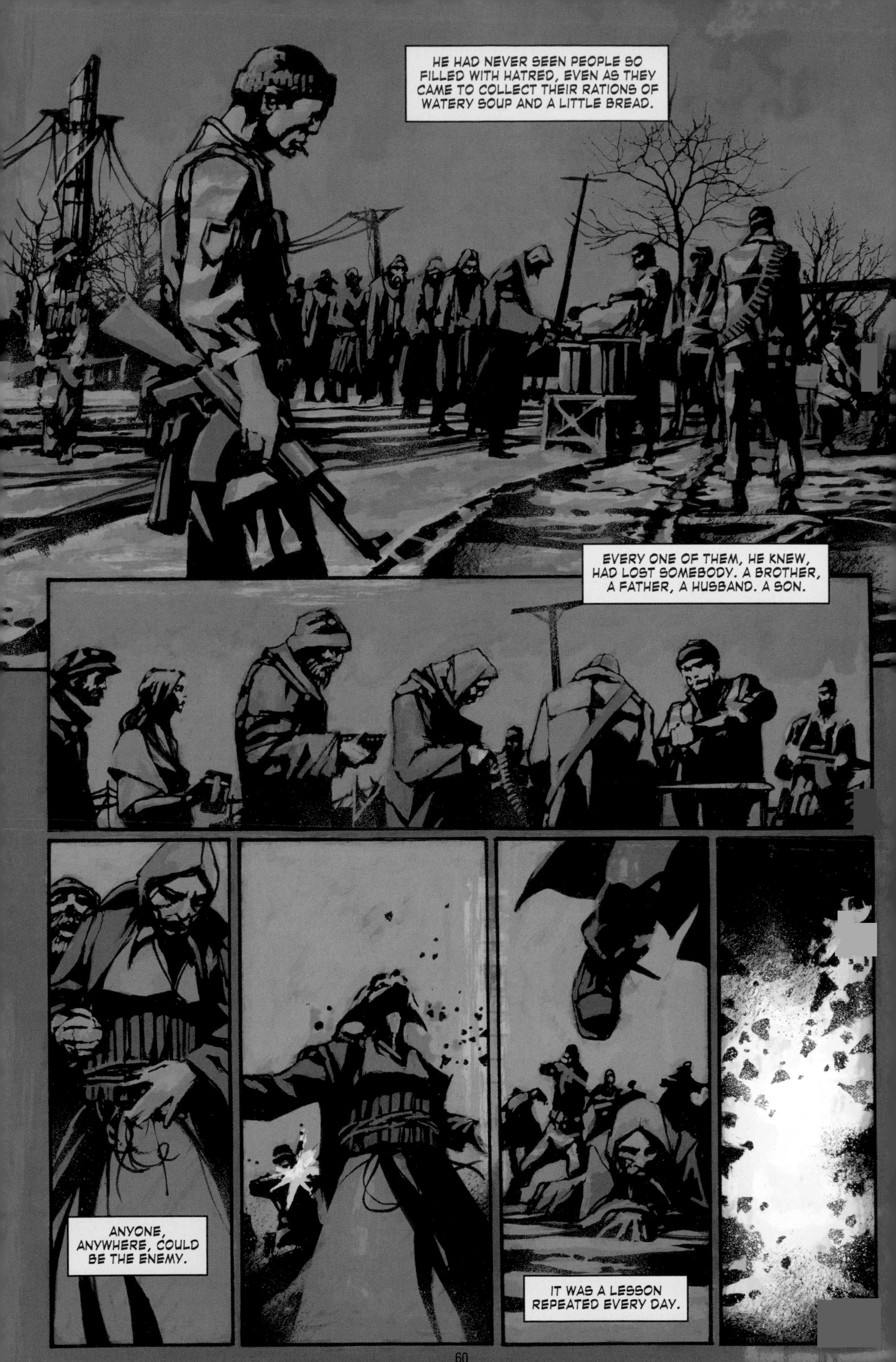
HE HAD NEVER SEEN PEOPLE SO FILLED WITH HATRED, EVEN AS THEY CAME TO COLLECT THEIR RATIONS OF WATERY SOUP AND A LITTLE BREAD.
EVERY ONE OF THEM, HE KNEW, HAD LOST SOMEBODY. A BROTHER, A FATHER, A HUSBAND. A SON.
ANYONE, ANYWHERE, COULD BE THE ENEMY.
IT WAS A LESSON REPEATED EVERY DAY.

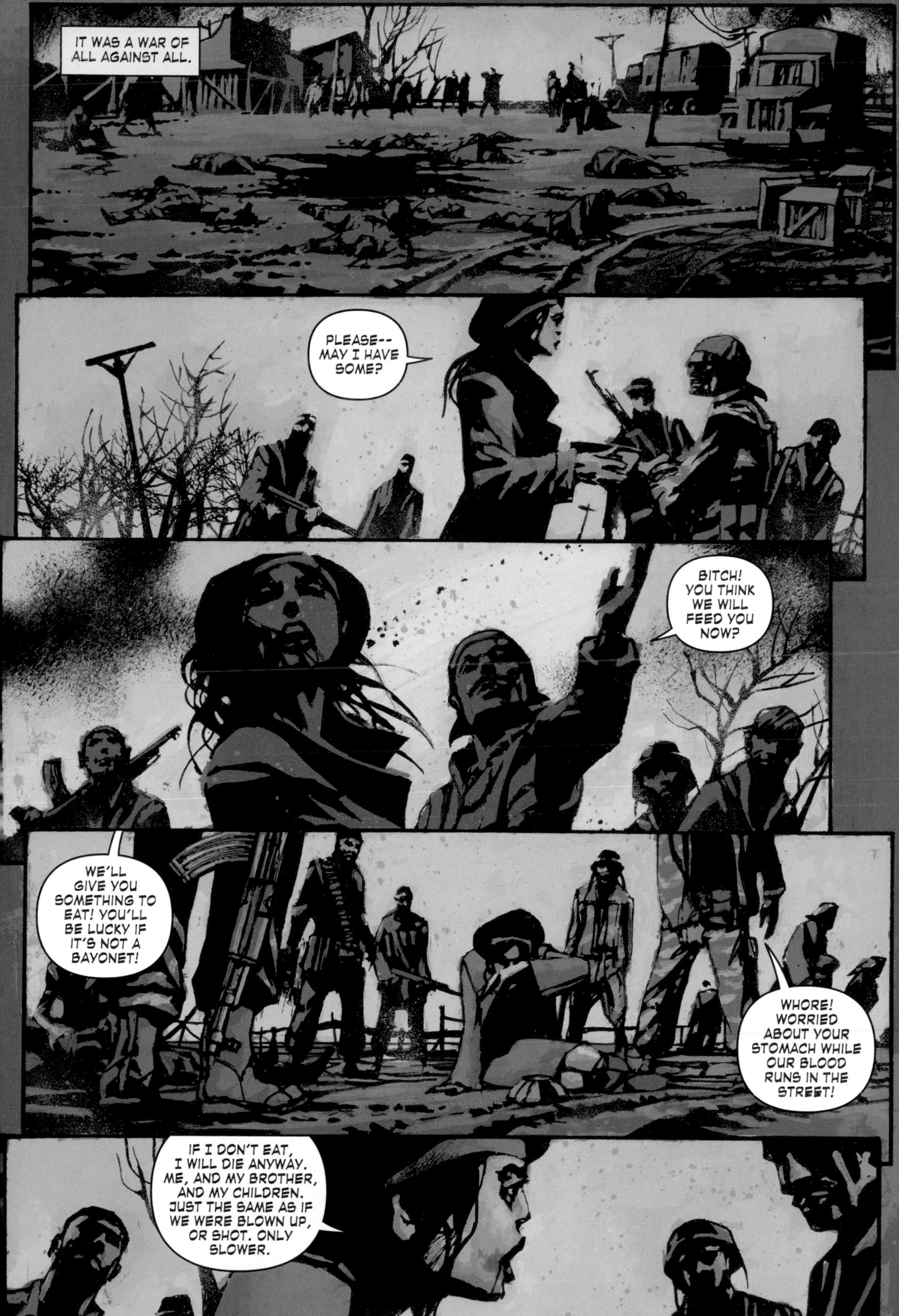
IT WAS A WAR OF ALL AGAINST ALL.
PLEASE-- MAY I HAVE SOME?
BITCH! YOU THINK WE WILL FEED YOU NOW?
WE'LL GIVE YOU SOMETHING TO EAT! YOU'LL BE LUCKY IF IT'S NOT A BAYONET!
WHORE! WORRIED ABOUT YOUR STOMACH WHILE OUR BLOOD RUNS IN THE STREET!
IF I DON'T EAT, I WILL DIE ANYWAY. ME, AND MY BROTHER, AND MY CHILDREN. JUST THE SAME AS IF WE WERE BLOWN UP, OR SHOT. ONLY SLOWER.

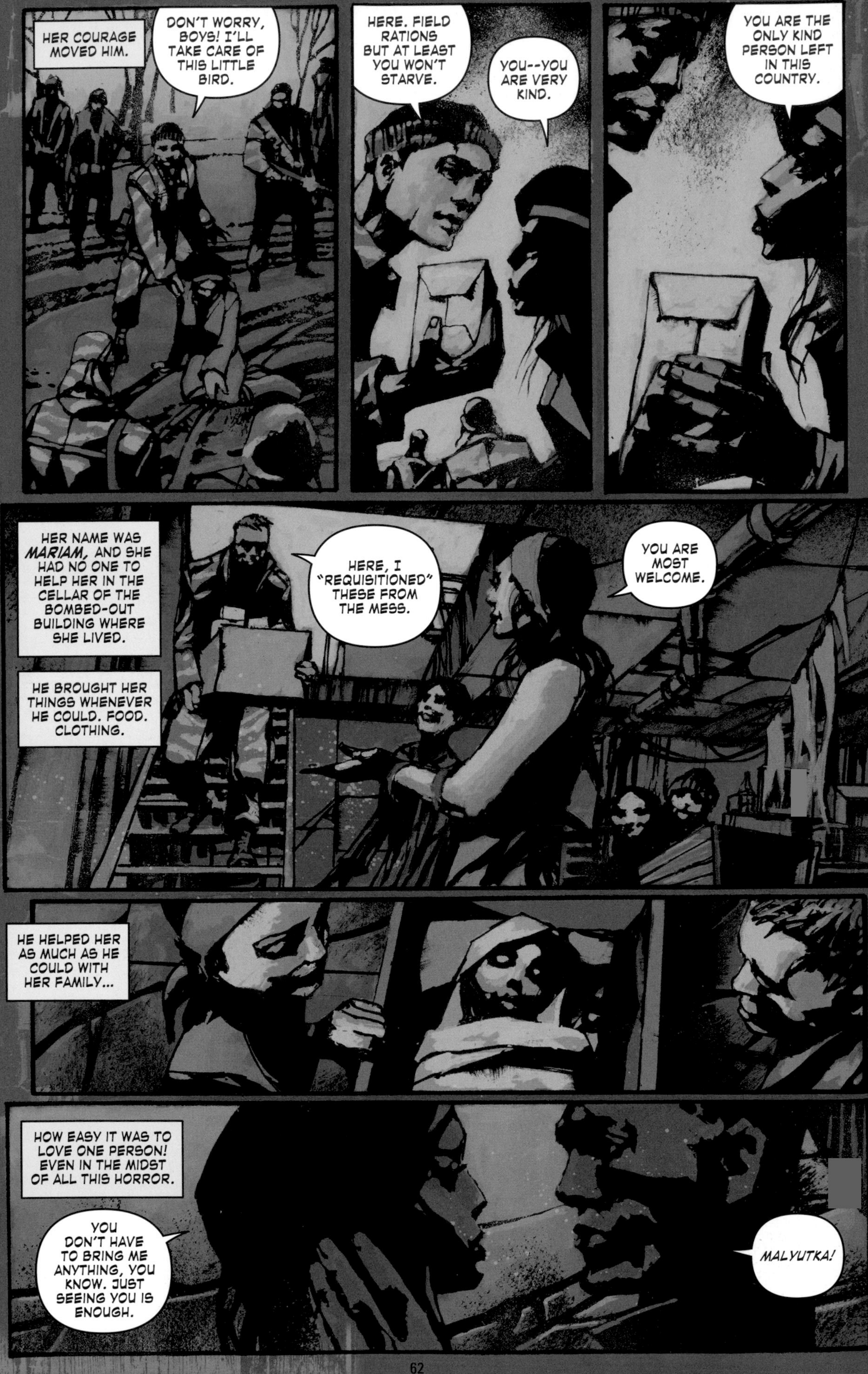

HER COURAGE MOVED HIM.
DON'T WORRY, BOYS! I'LL TAKE CARE OF THIS LITTLE BIRD.
HERE. FIELD RATIONS BUT AT LEAST YOU WON'T STARVE.
YOU--YOU ARE VERY KIND.
YOU ARE THE ONLY KIND PERSON LEFT IN THIS COUNTRY.
HER NAME WAS *MARIAM,* AND SHE HAD NO ONE TO HELP HER IN THE CELLAR OF THE BOMBED-OUT BUILDING WHERE SHE LIVED.
HE BROUGHT HER THINGS WHENEVER HE COULD. FOOD. CLOTHING.
HERE, I "REQUISITIONED" THESE FROM THE MESS.
YOU ARE MOST WELCOME.
HE HELPED HER AS MUCH AS HE COULD WITH HER FAMILY...
HOW EASY IT WAS TO LOVE ONE PERSON! EVEN IN THE MIDST OF ALL THIS HORROR.
YOU DON'T HAVE TO BRING ME ANYTHING, YOU KNOW. JUST SEEING YOU IS ENOUGH.
*MALYUTKA!*

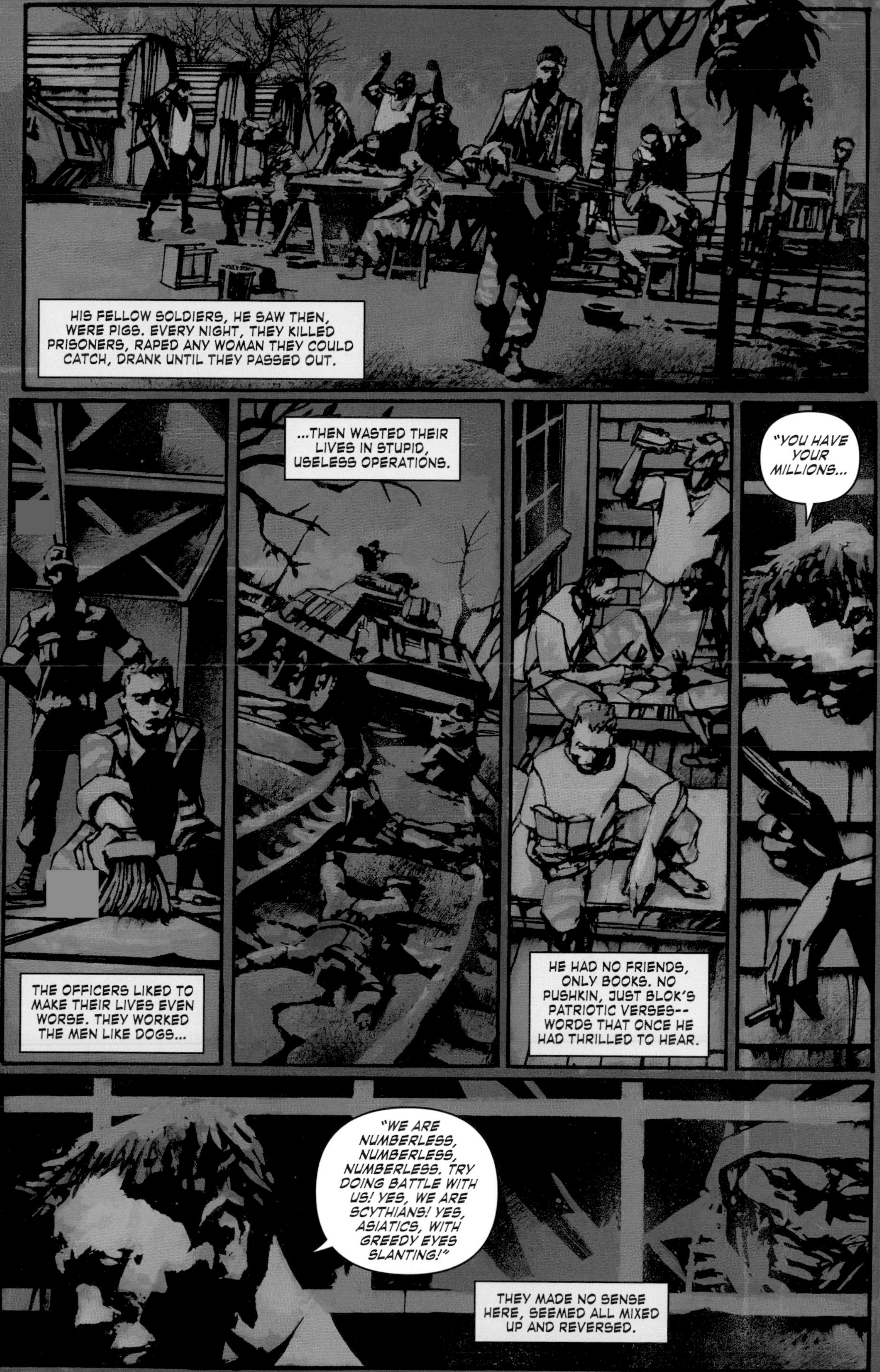
HIS FELLOW SOLDIERS, HE SAW THEN, WERE PIGS. EVERY NIGHT, THEY KILLED PRISONERS, RAPED ANY WOMAN THEY COULD CATCH, DRANK UNTIL THEY PASSED OUT.
THE OFFICERS LIKED TO MAKE THEIR LIVES EVEN WORSE. THEY WORKED THE MEN LIKE DOGS...
...THEN WASTED THEIR LIVES IN STUPID, USELESS OPERATIONS.
HE HAD NO FRIENDS, ONLY BOOKS. NO PUSHKIN, JUST BLOK'S PATRIOTIC VERSES--WORDS THAT ONCE HE HAD THRILLED TO HEAR.
"YOU HAVE YOUR MILLIONS...
"WE ARE NUMBERLESS, NUMBERLESS, NUMBERLESS. TRY DOING BATTLE WITH US! YES, WE ARE SCYTHIANS! YES, ASIATICS, WITH GREEDY EYES SLANTING!"
THEY MADE NO SENSE HERE, SEEMED ALL MIXED UP AND REVERSED.

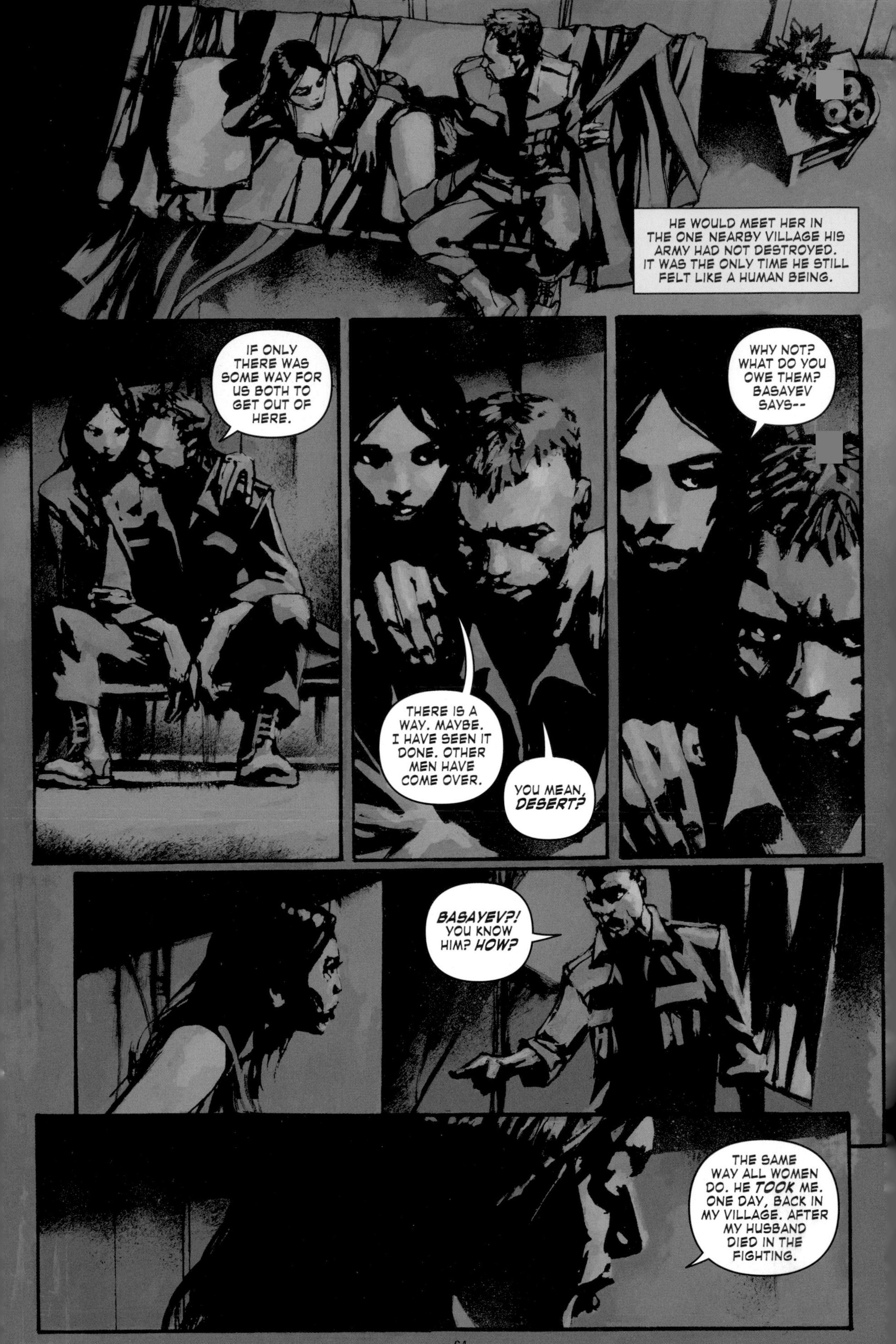
HE WOULD MEET HER IN THE ONE NEARBY VILLAGE HIS ARMY HAD NOT DESTROYED. IT WAS THE ONLY TIME HE STILL FELT LIKE A HUMAN BEING.
IF ONLY THERE WAS SOME WAY FOR US BOTH TO GET OUT OF HERE.
THERE IS A WAY. MAYBE. I HAVE SEEN IT DONE. OTHER MEN HAVE COME OVER.
YOU MEAN, DESERT?
WHY NOT? WHAT DO YOU OWE THEM? BASAYEV SAYS--
BASAYEV?! YOU KNOW HIM? HOW?
THE SAME WAY ALL WOMEN DO. HE TOOK ME. ONE DAY, BACK IN MY VILLAGE. AFTER MY HUSBAND DIED IN THE FIGHTING.

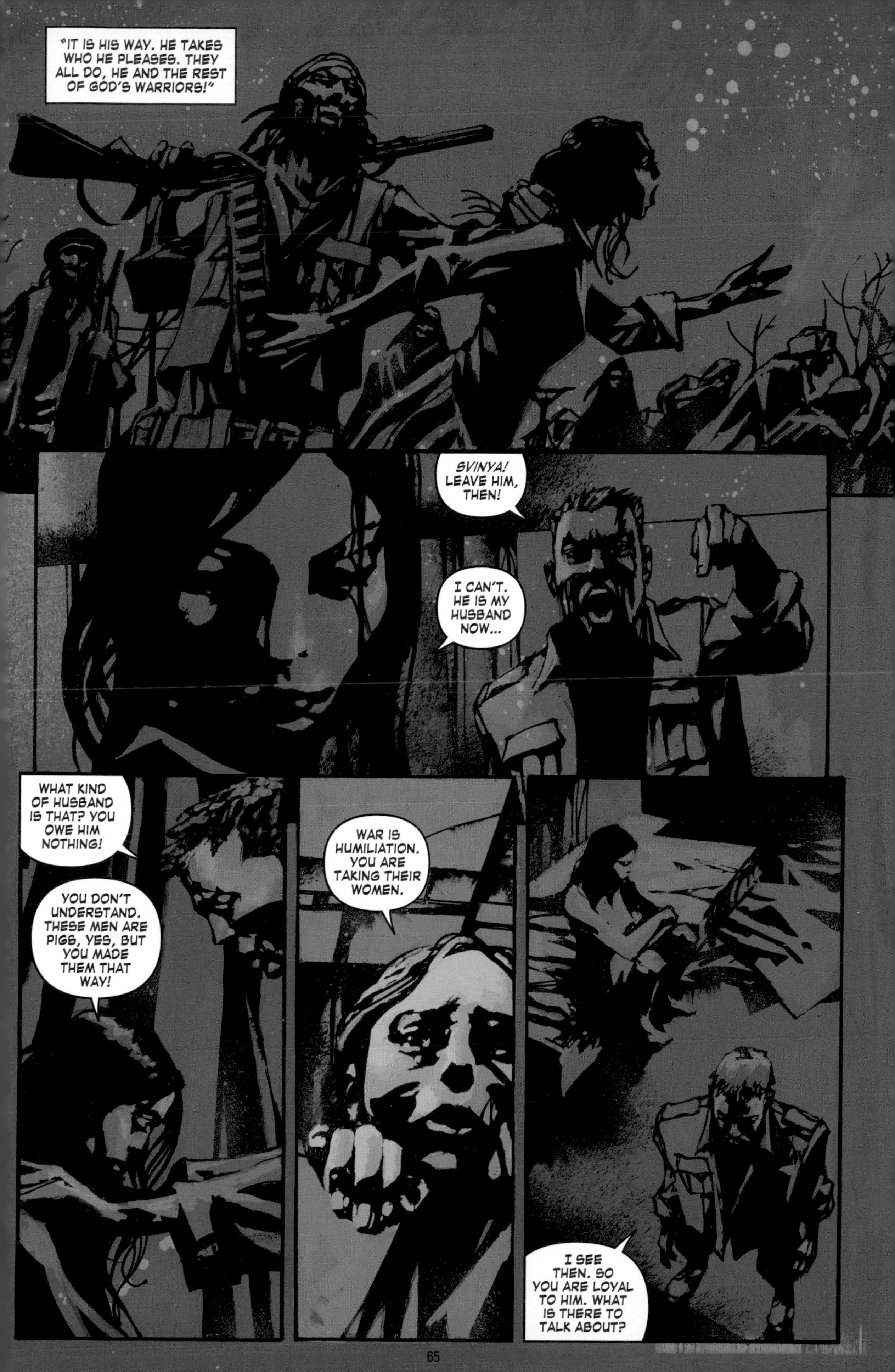
"IT IS HIS WAY. HE TAKES WHO HE PLEASES. THEY ALL DO, HE AND THE REST OF GOD'S WARRIORS!"
*SVINYA!* LEAVE HIM, THEN!
I CAN'T. HE IS MY HUSBAND NOW...
WHAT KIND OF HUSBAND IS THAT? YOU OWE HIM NOTHING!
YOU DON'T UNDERSTAND. THESE MEN ARE PIGS, YES, BUT YOU MADE THEM THAT WAY!
WAR IS HUMILIATION. YOU ARE TAKING THEIR WOMEN.
I SEE THEN. SO YOU ARE LOYAL TO HIM. WHAT IS THERE TO TALK ABOUT?

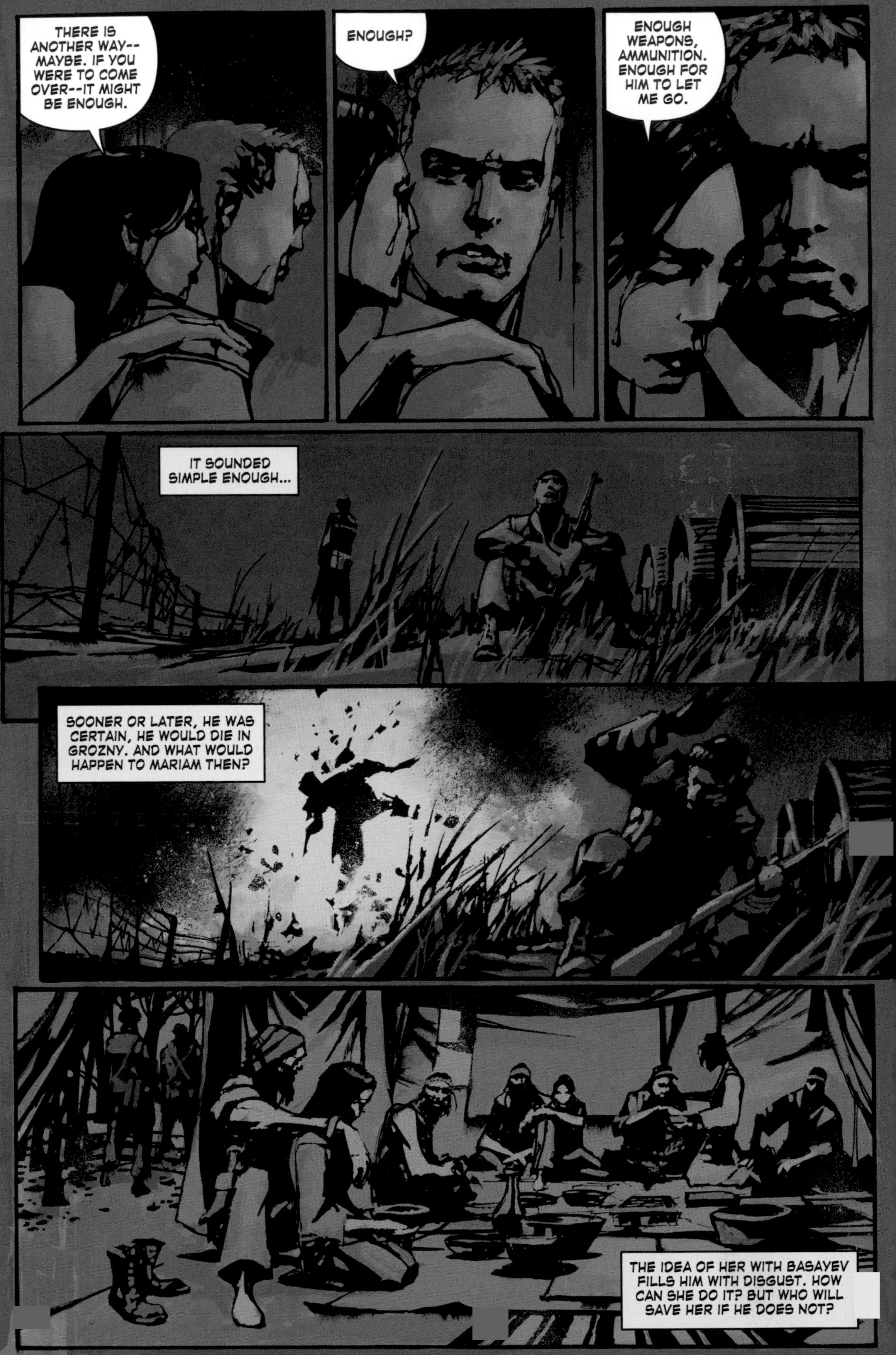
THERE IS ANOTHER WAY-- MAYBE. IF YOU WERE TO COME OVER--IT MIGHT BE ENOUGH.
ENOUGH?
ENOUGH WEAPONS, AMMUNITION. ENOUGH FOR HIM TO LET ME GO.
IT SOUNDED SIMPLE ENOUGH...
SOONER OR LATER, HE WAS CERTAIN, HE WOULD DIE IN GROZNY. AND WHAT WOULD HAPPEN TO MARIAM THEN?
THE IDEA OF HER WITH BASAYEV FILLS HIM WITH DISGUST. HOW CAN SHE DO IT? BUT WHO WILL SAVE HER IF HE DOES NOT?

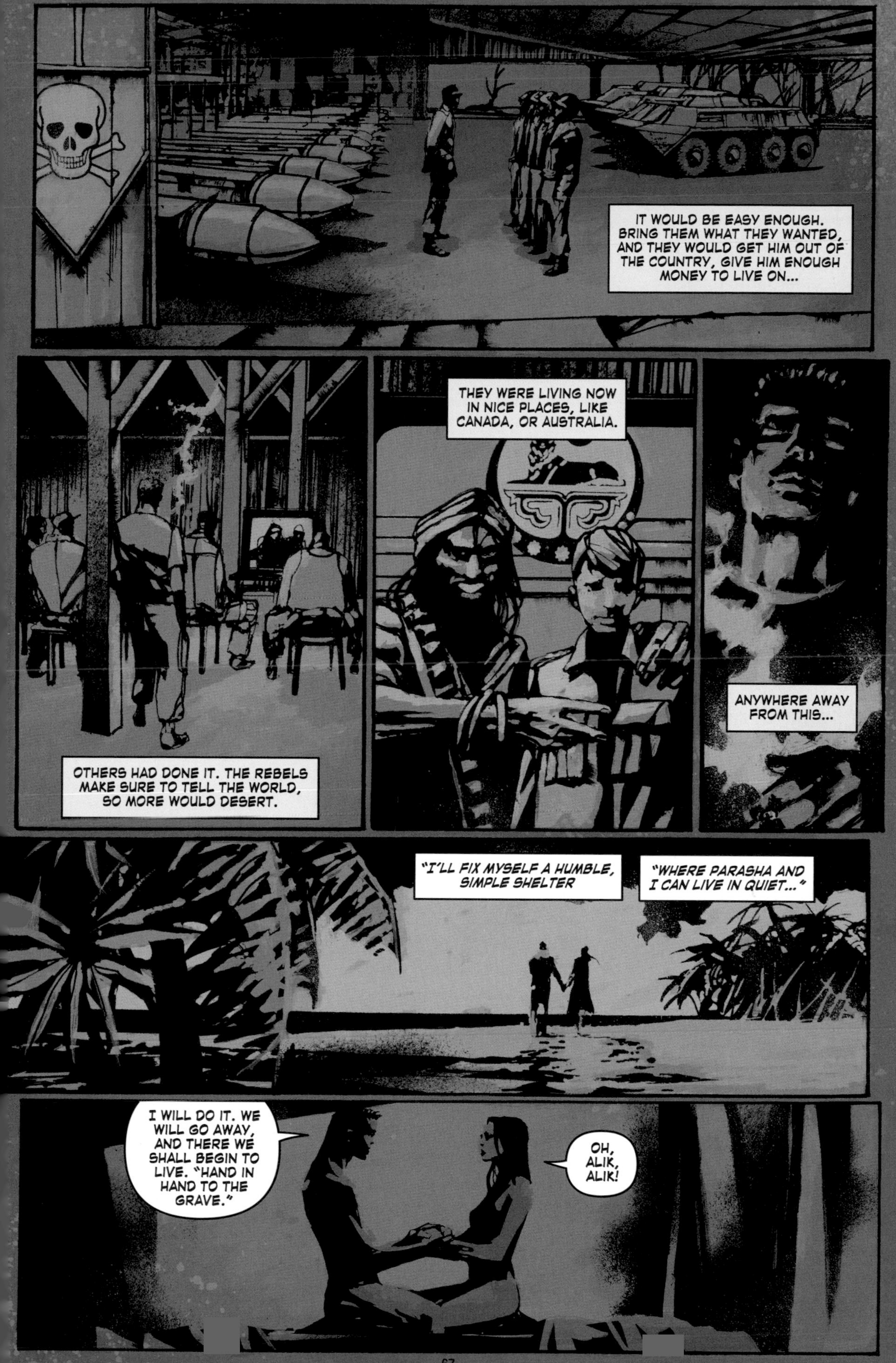
IT WOULD BE EASY ENOUGH. BRING THEM WHAT THEY WANTED, AND THEY WOULD GET HIM OUT OF THE COUNTRY, GIVE HIM ENOUGH MONEY TO LIVE ON...
OTHERS HAD DONE IT. THE REBELS MAKE SURE TO TELL THE WORLD, SO MORE WOULD DESERT.
THEY WERE LIVING NOW IN NICE PLACES, LIKE CANADA, OR AUSTRALIA.
ANYWHERE AWAY FROM THIS...
"I'LL FIX MYSELF A HUMBLE, SIMPLE SHELTER
"WHERE PARASHA AND I CAN LIVE IN QUIET..."
I WILL DO IT. WE WILL GO AWAY, AND THERE WE SHALL BEGIN TO LIVE. "HAND IN HAND TO THE GRAVE."
OH, ALIK, ALIK!

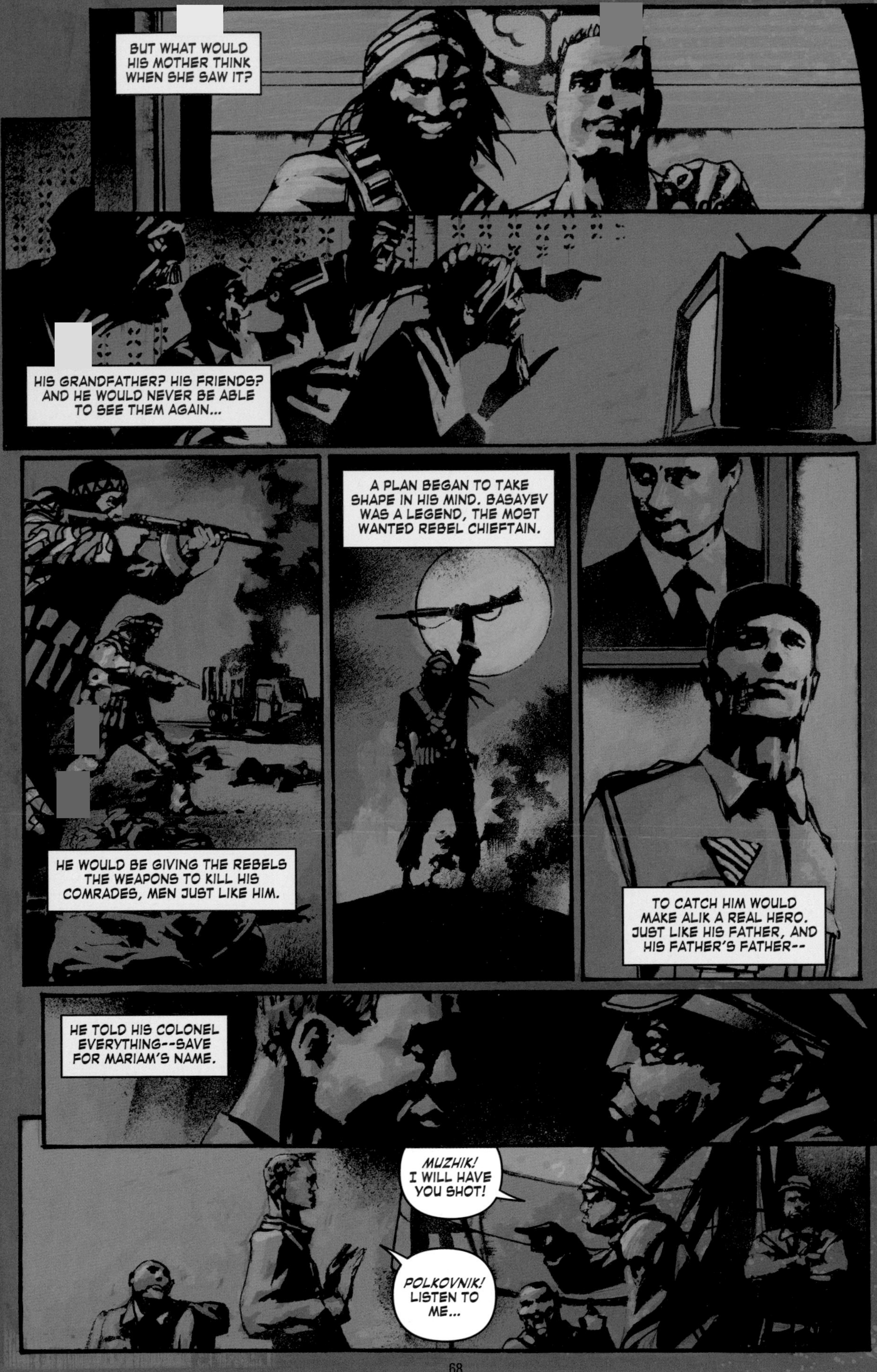
BUT WHAT WOULD HIS MOTHER THINK WHEN SHE SAW IT?
HIS GRANDFATHER? HIS FRIENDS? AND HE WOULD NEVER BE ABLE TO SEE THEM AGAIN...
HE WOULD BE GIVING THE REBELS THE WEAPONS TO KILL HIS COMRADES, MEN JUST LIKE HIM.
A PLAN BEGAN TO TAKE SHAPE IN HIS MIND. BASAYEV WAS A LEGEND, THE MOST WANTED REBEL CHIEFTAIN.
TO CATCH HIM WOULD MAKE ALIK A REAL HERO. JUST LIKE HIS FATHER, AND HIS FATHER'S FATHER--
HE TOLD HIS COLONEL EVERYTHING--SAVE FOR MARIAM'S NAME.
*MUZHIK!* I WILL HAVE YOU SHOT!
*POLKOVNIK!* LISTEN TO ME...

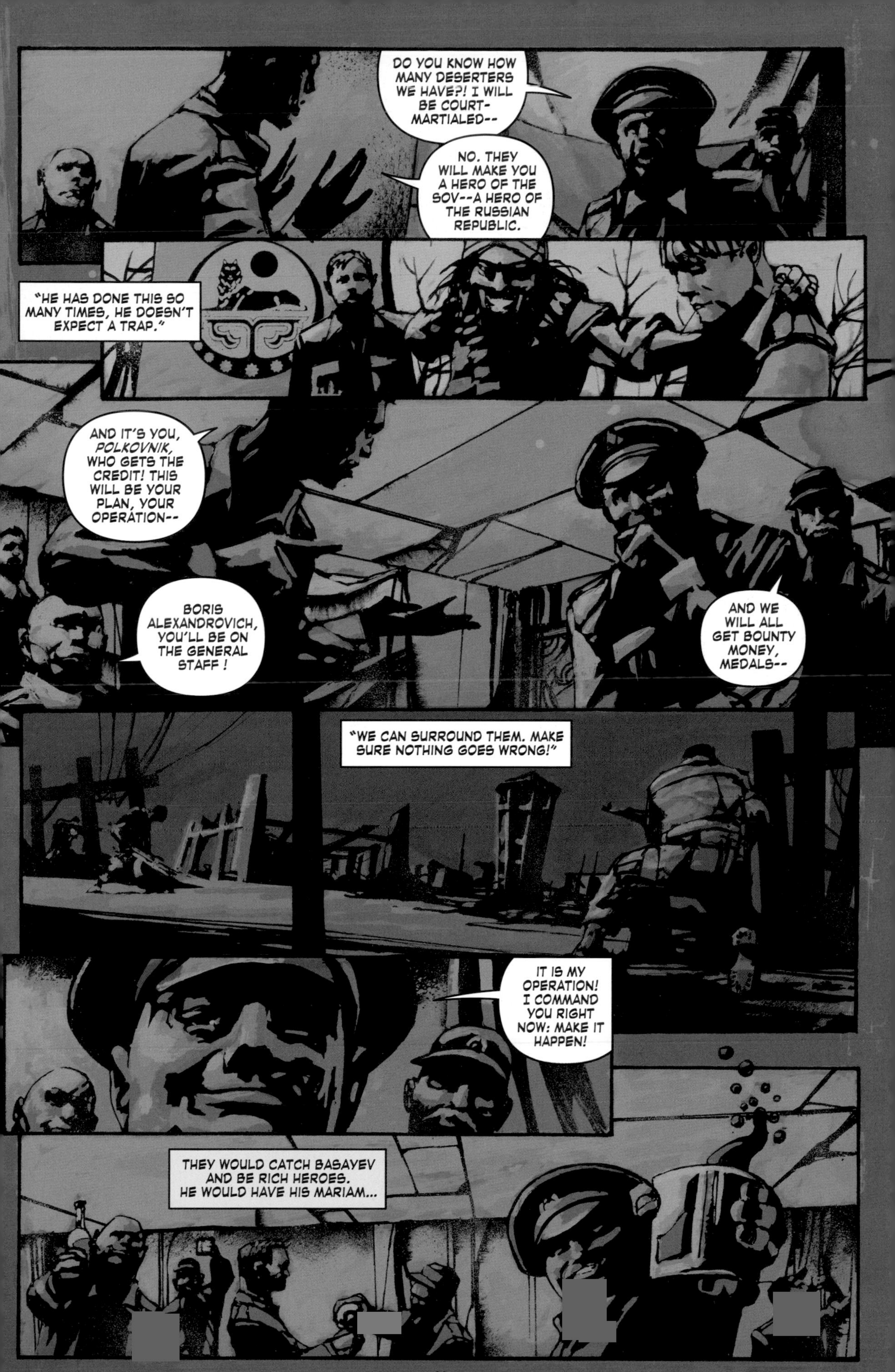
DO YOU KNOW HOW MANY DESERTERS WE HAVE?! I WILL BE COURT-MARTIALED--
NO. THEY WILL MAKE YOU A HERO OF THE SOV--A HERO OF THE RUSSIAN REPUBLIC.
"HE HAS DONE THIS SO MANY TIMES, HE DOESN'T EXPECT A TRAP."
AND IT'S YOU, *POLKOVNIK*, WHO GETS THE CREDIT! THIS WILL BE YOUR PLAN, YOUR OPERATION--
BORIS ALEXANDROVICH, YOU'LL BE ON THE GENERAL STAFF !
AND WE WILL ALL GET BOUNTY MONEY, MEDALS--
"WE CAN SURROUND THEM. MAKE SURE NOTHING GOES WRONG!"
IT IS MY OPERATION! I COMMAND YOU RIGHT NOW: MAKE IT HAPPEN!
THEY WOULD CATCH BASAYEV AND BE RICH HEROES. HE WOULD HAVE HIS MARIAM...

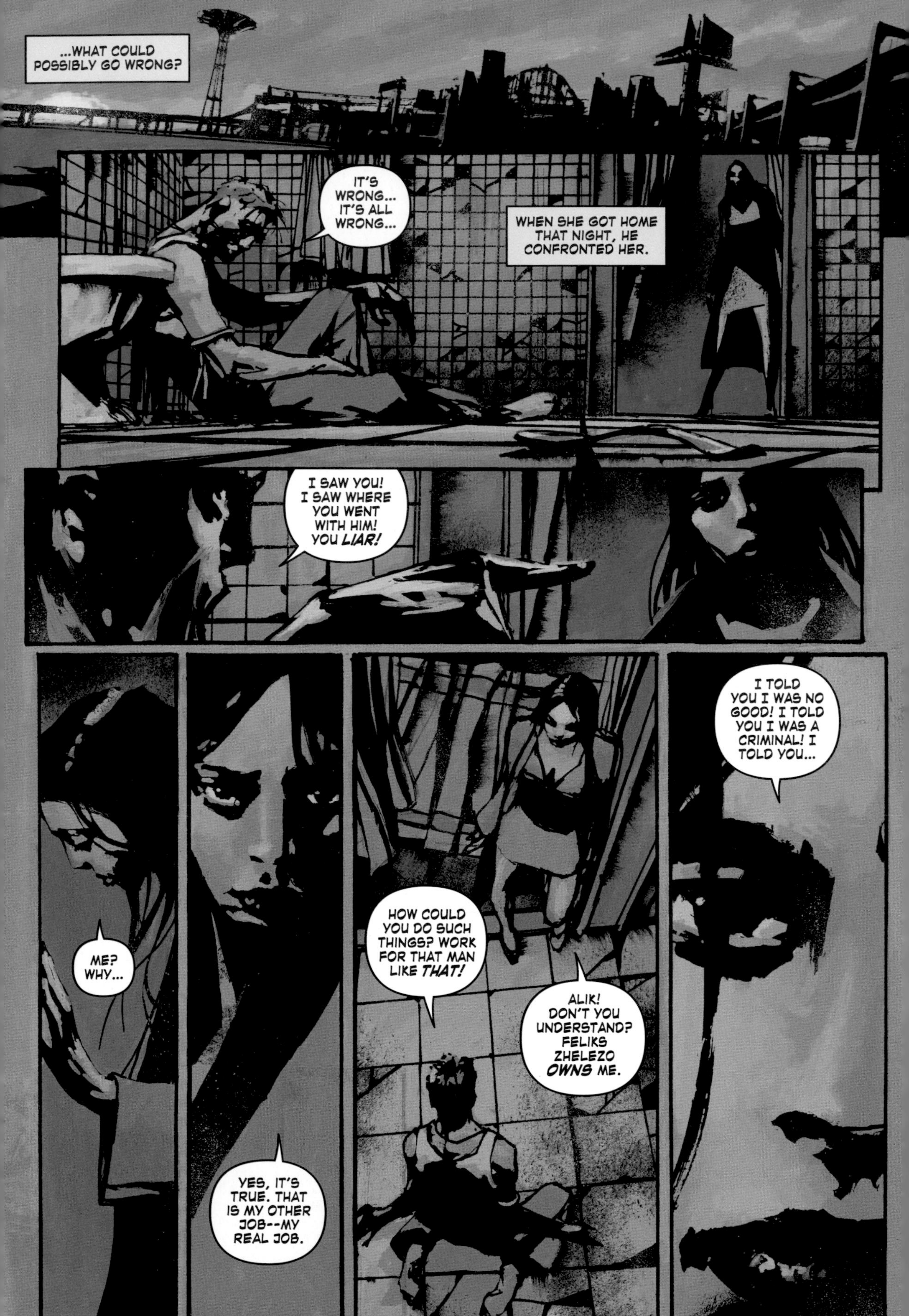
...WHAT COULD POSSIBLY GO WRONG?
IT'S WRONG... IT'S ALL WRONG...
WHEN SHE GOT HOME THAT NIGHT, HE CONFRONTED HER.
I SAW YOU! I SAW WHERE YOU WENT WITH HIM! YOU *LIAR!*
ME? WHY...
YES, IT'S TRUE. THAT IS MY OTHER JOB--MY REAL JOB.
HOW COULD YOU DO SUCH THINGS? WORK FOR THAT MAN LIKE *THAT!*
ALIK! DON'T YOU UNDERSTAND? FELIKS ZHELEZO *OWNS* ME.
I TOLD YOU I WAS NO GOOD! I TOLD YOU I WAS A CRIMINAL! I TOLD YOU...

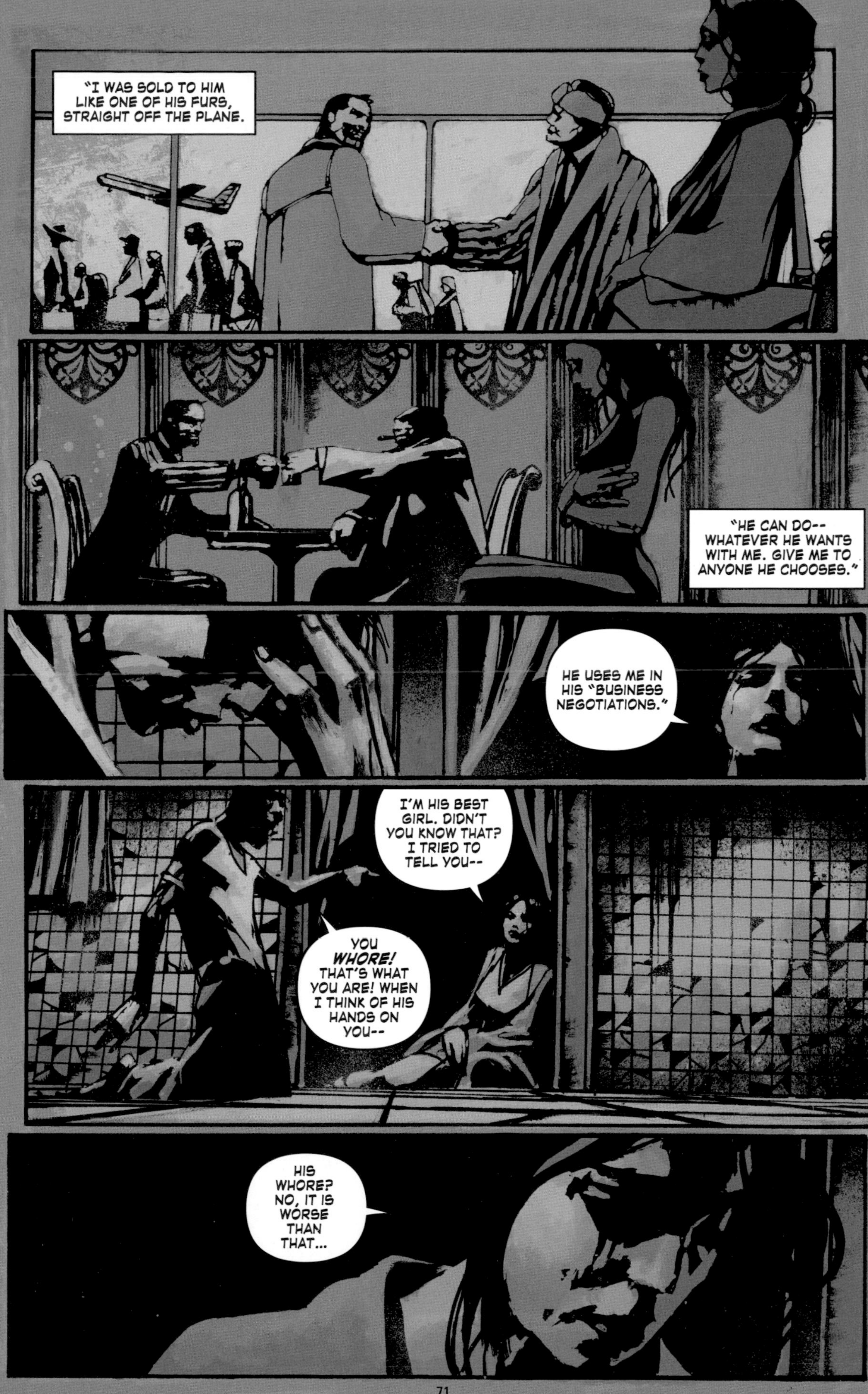

"I WAS SOLD TO HIM LIKE ONE OF HIS FURS, STRAIGHT OFF THE PLANE.
"HE CAN DO--WHATEVER HE WANTS WITH ME. GIVE ME TO ANYONE HE CHOOSES."
HE USES ME IN HIS "BUSINESS NEGOTIATIONS."
I'M HIS BEST GIRL. DIDN'T YOU KNOW THAT? I TRIED TO TELL YOU--
YOU *WHORE!* THAT'S WHAT YOU ARE! WHEN I THINK OF HIS HANDS ON YOU--
HIS WHORE? NO, IT IS WORSE THAN THAT...

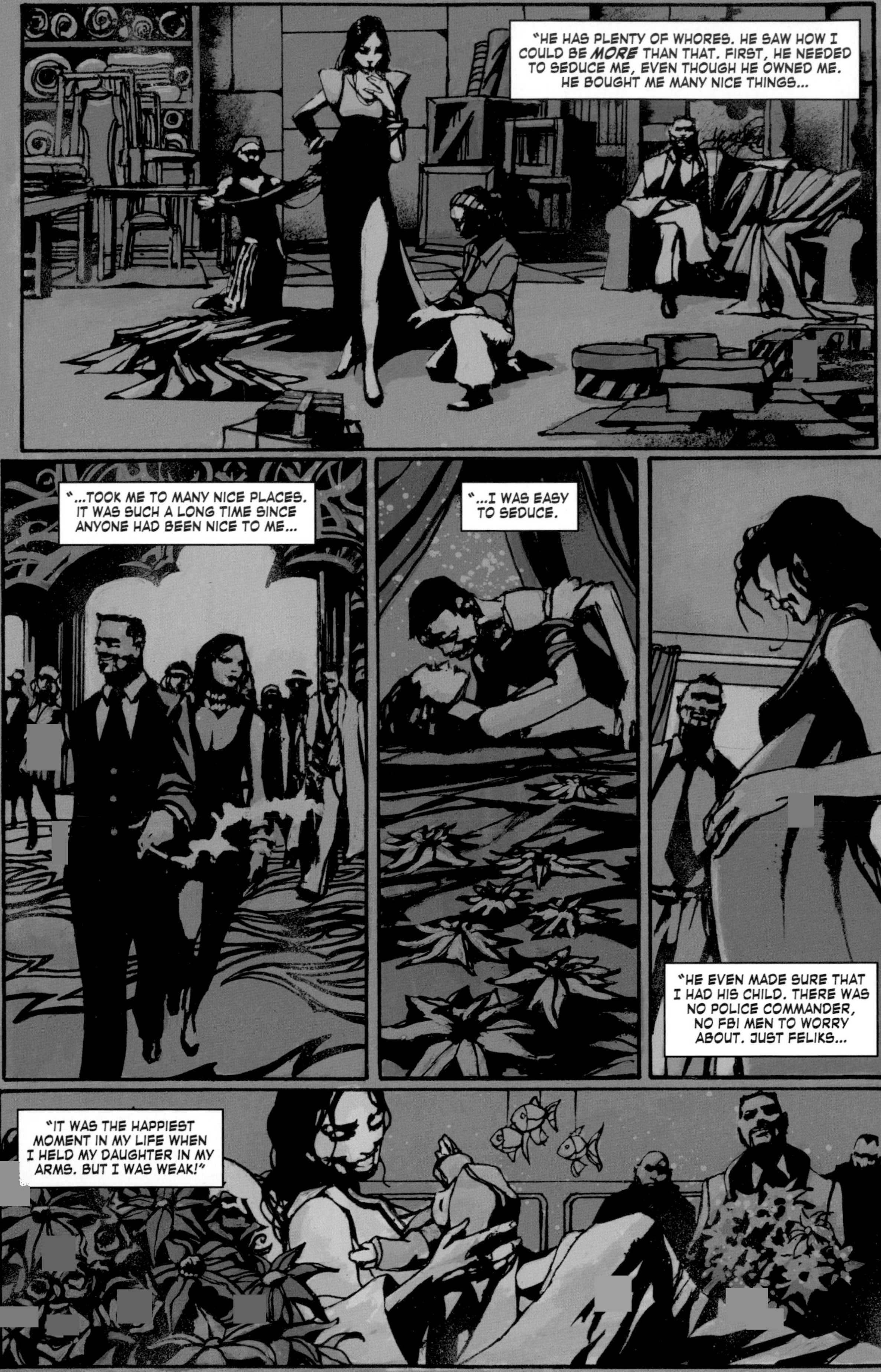
"HE HAS PLENTY OF WHORES. HE SAW HOW I COULD BE MORE THAN THAT. FIRST, HE NEEDED TO SEDUCE ME, EVEN THOUGH HE OWNED ME. HE BOUGHT ME MANY NICE THINGS...
"...TOOK ME TO MANY NICE PLACES. IT WAS SUCH A LONG TIME SINCE ANYONE HAD BEEN NICE TO ME...
"...I WAS EASY TO SEDUCE.
"HE EVEN MADE SURE THAT I HAD HIS CHILD. THERE WAS NO POLICE COMMANDER, NO FBI MEN TO WORRY ABOUT. JUST FELIKS...
"IT WAS THE HAPPIEST MOMENT IN MY LIFE WHEN I HELD MY DAUGHTER IN MY ARMS. BUT I WAS WEAK!"

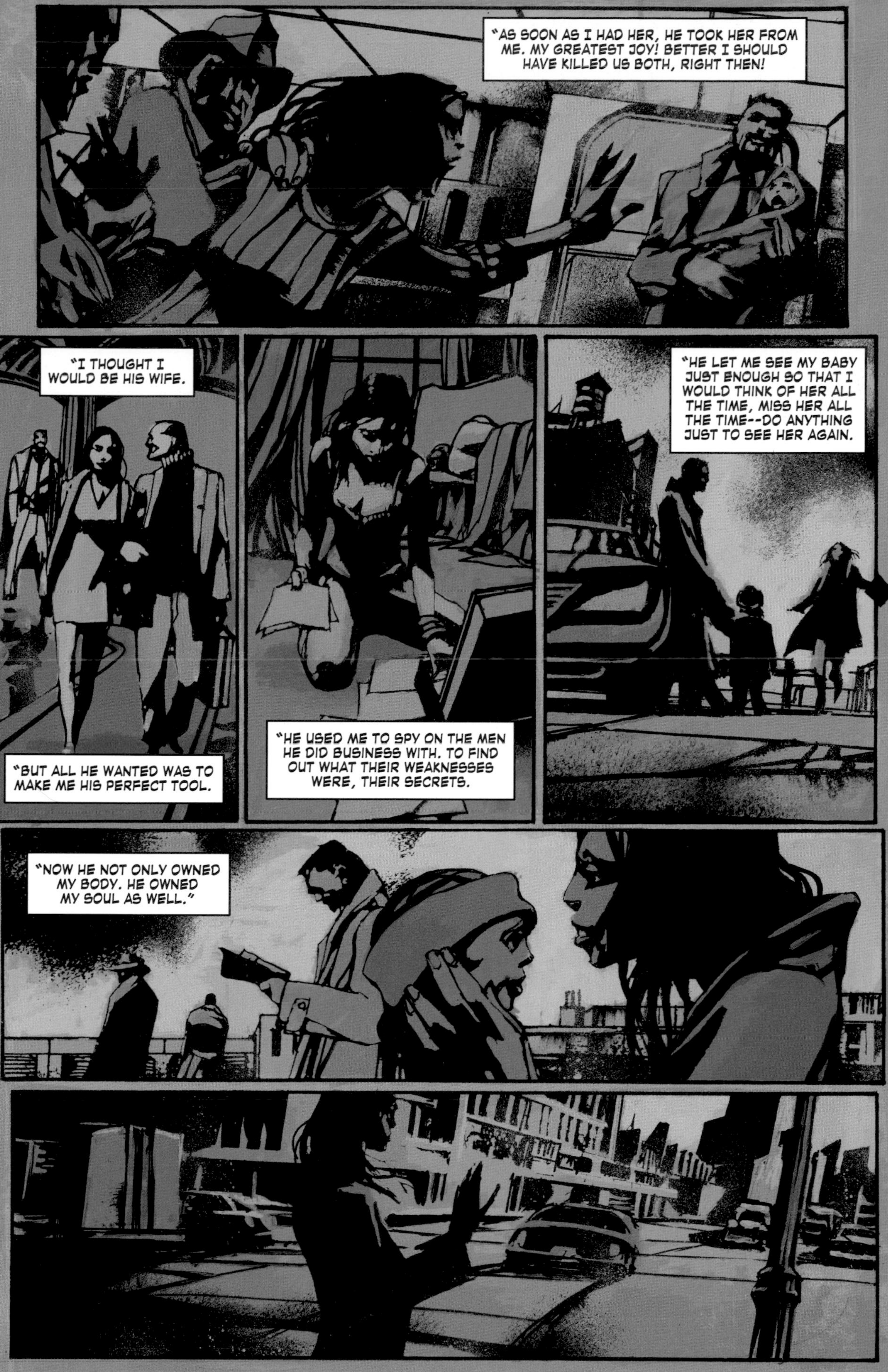
"AS SOON AS I HAD HER, HE TOOK HER FROM ME. MY GREATEST JOY! BETTER I SHOULD HAVE KILLED US BOTH, RIGHT THEN!
"I THOUGHT I WOULD BE HIS WIFE.
"BUT ALL HE WANTED WAS TO MAKE ME HIS PERFECT TOOL.
"HE USED ME TO SPY ON THE MEN HE DID BUSINESS WITH. TO FIND OUT WHAT THEIR WEAKNESSES WERE, THEIR SECRETS.
"HE LET ME SEE MY BABY JUST ENOUGH SO THAT I WOULD THINK OF HER ALL THE TIME, MISS HER ALL THE TIME--DO ANYTHING JUST TO SEE HER AGAIN.
"NOW HE NOT ONLY OWNED MY BODY. HE OWNED MY SOUL AS WELL."

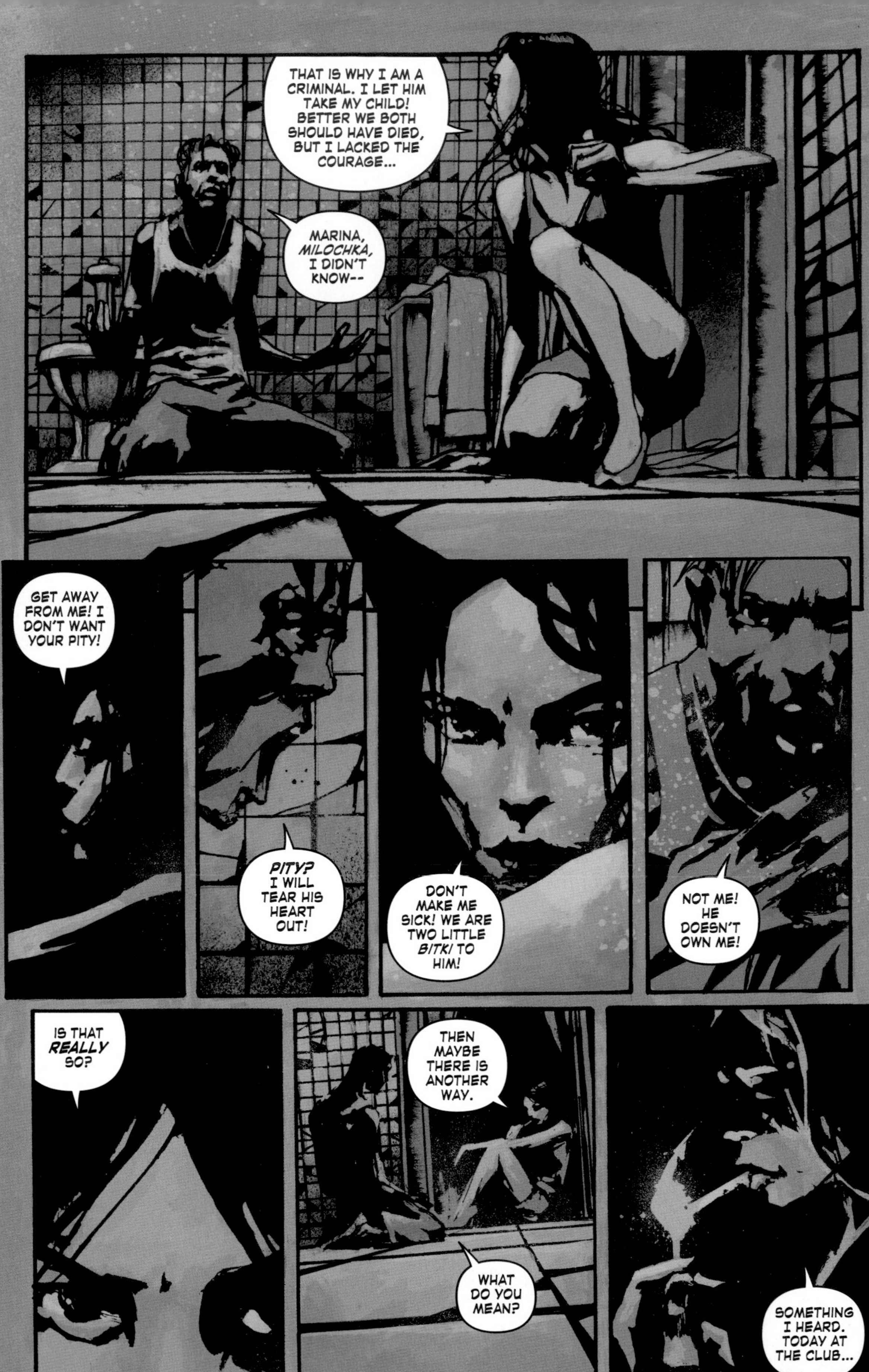
THAT IS WHY I AM A CRIMINAL. I LET HIM TAKE MY CHILD! BETTER WE BOTH SHOULD HAVE DIED, BUT I LACKED THE COURAGE...
MARINA, MILOCHKA, I DIDN'T KNOW--
GET AWAY FROM ME! I DON'T WANT YOUR PITY!
PITY? I WILL TEAR HIS HEART OUT!
DON'T MAKE ME SICK! WE ARE TWO LITTLE BITKI TO HIM!
NOT ME! HE DOESN'T OWN ME!
IS THAT REALLY SO?
THEN MAYBE THERE IS ANOTHER WAY.
WHAT DO YOU MEAN?
SOMETHING I HEARD. TODAY AT THE CLUB...

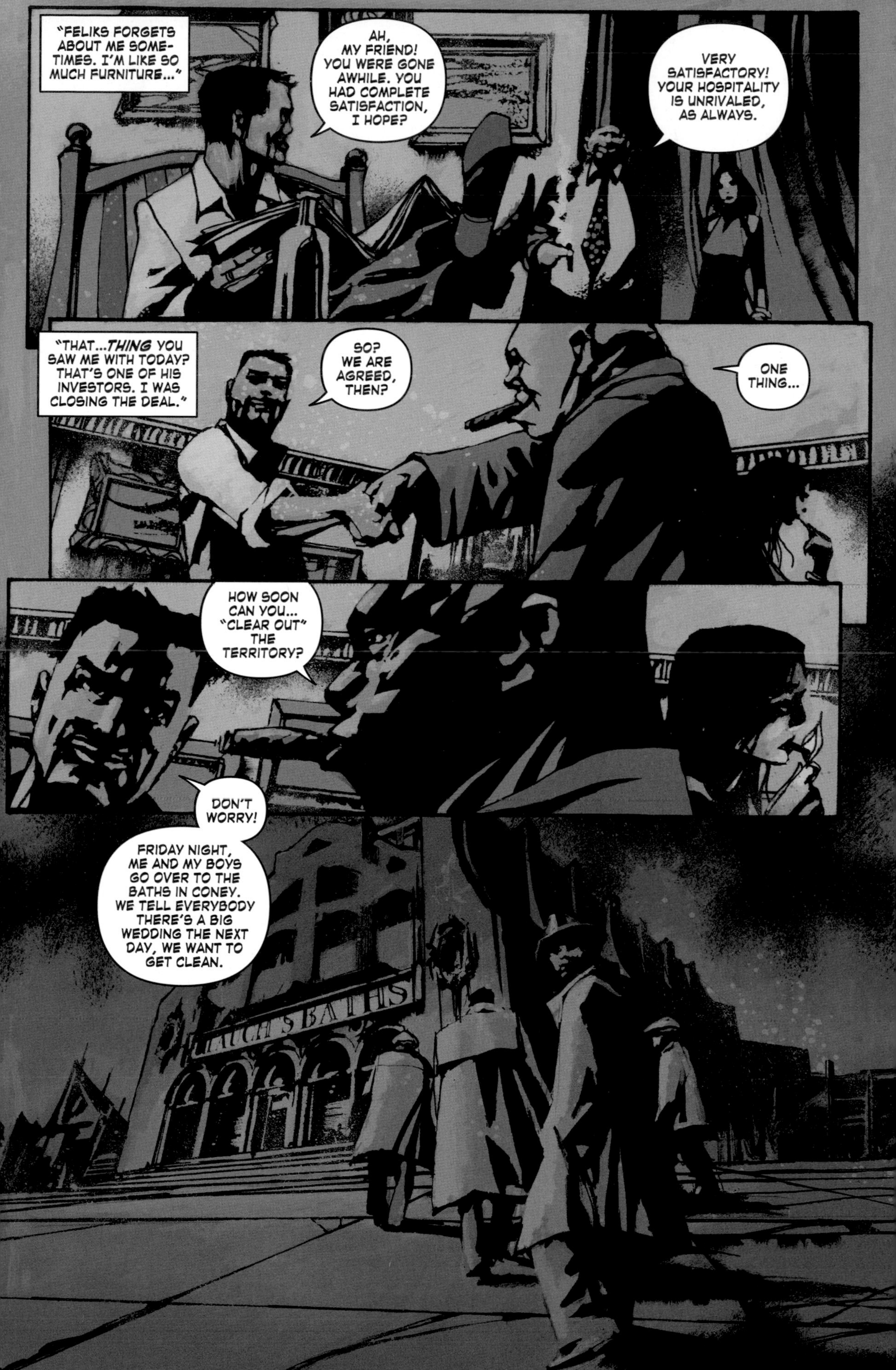
"FELIKS FORGETS ABOUT ME SOMETIMES. I'M LIKE SO MUCH FURNITURE..."
AH, MY FRIEND! YOU WERE GONE AWHILE. YOU HAD COMPLETE SATISFACTION, I HOPE?
VERY SATISFACTORY! YOUR HOSPITALITY IS UNRIVALED, AS ALWAYS.
"THAT...*THING* YOU SAW ME WITH TODAY? THAT'S ONE OF HIS INVESTORS. I WAS CLOSING THE DEAL."
SO? WE ARE AGREED, THEN?
ONE THING...
HOW SOON CAN YOU... "CLEAR OUT" THE TERRITORY?
DON'T WORRY!
FRIDAY NIGHT, ME AND MY BOYS GO OVER TO THE BATHS IN CONEY. WE TELL EVERYBODY THERE'S A BIG WEDDING THE NEXT DAY, WE WANT TO GET CLEAN.
BATHS

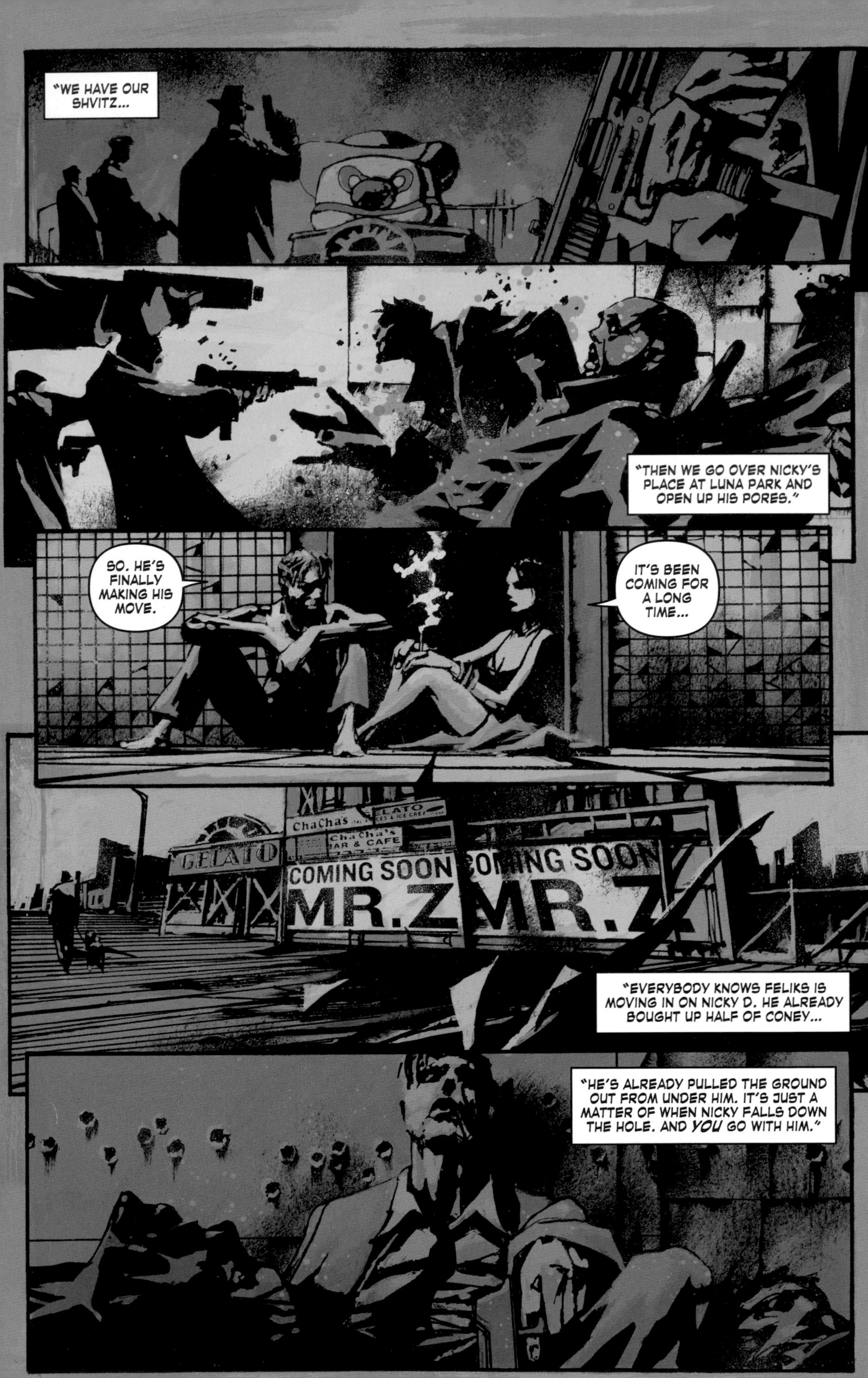
"WE HAVE OUR SHVITZ...
"THEN WE GO OVER NICKY'S PLACE AT LUNA PARK AND OPEN UP HIS PORES."
SO. HE'S FINALLY MAKING HIS MOVE.
IT'S BEEN COMING FOR A LONG TIME...
GELATO
ChaCha's
ChaCha's BAR & CAFE
COMING SOON
MR.Z
MR.Z
"EVERYBODY KNOWS FELIKS IS MOVING IN ON NICKY D. HE ALREADY BOUGHT UP HALF OF CONEY...
"HE'S ALREADY PULLED THE GROUND OUT FROM UNDER HIM. IT'S JUST A MATTER OF WHEN NICKY FALLS DOWN THE HOLE. AND *YOU* GO WITH HIM."

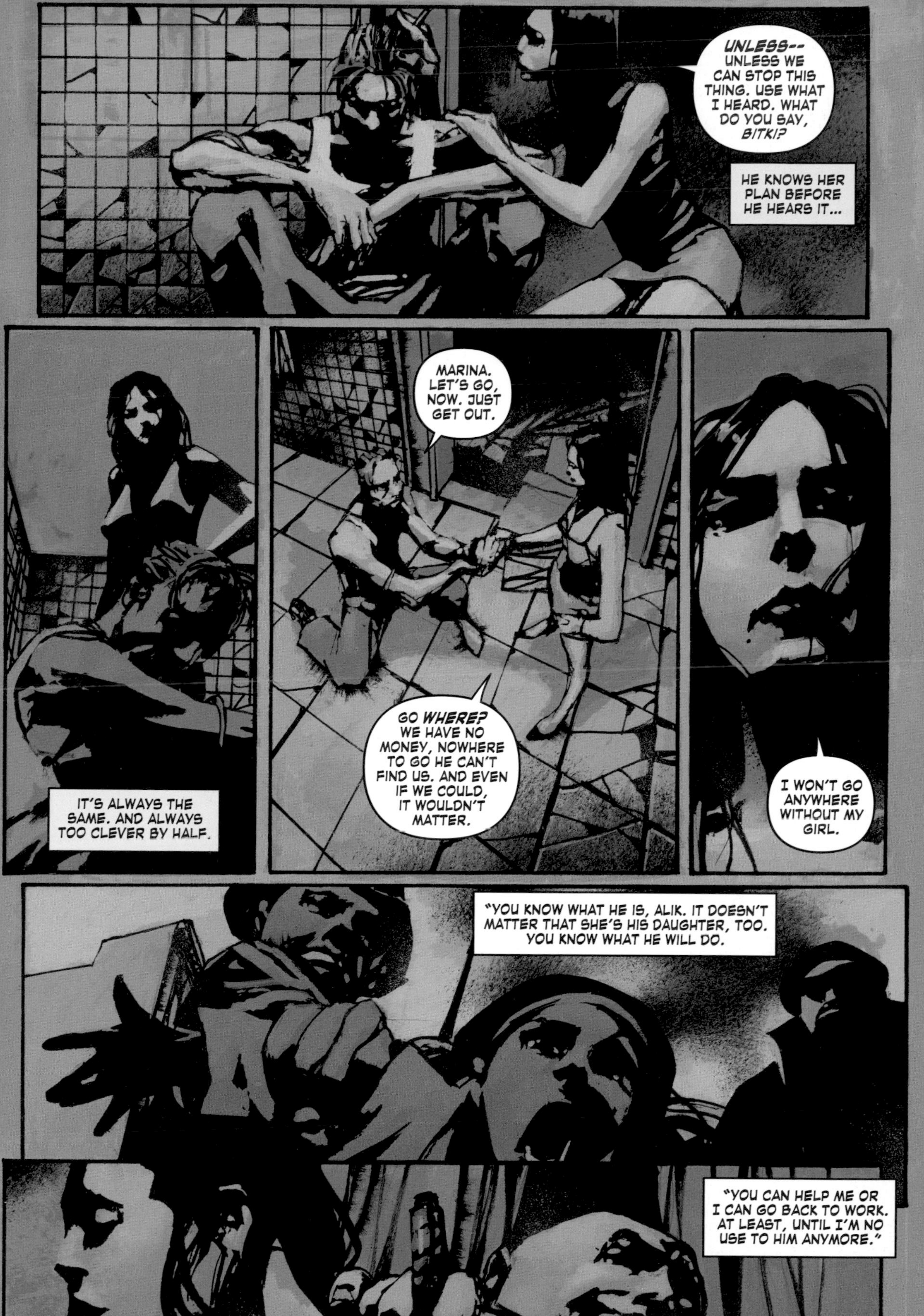
UNLESS-- UNLESS WE CAN STOP THIS THING. USE WHAT I HEARD. WHAT DO YOU SAY, BITKI?
HE KNOWS HER PLAN BEFORE HE HEARS IT...
IT'S ALWAYS THE SAME. AND ALWAYS TOO CLEVER BY HALF.
MARINA. LET'S GO, NOW. JUST GET OUT.
GO WHERE? WE HAVE NO MONEY, NOWHERE TO GO HE CAN'T FIND US. AND EVEN IF WE COULD, IT WOULDN'T MATTER.
I WON'T GO ANYWHERE WITHOUT MY GIRL.
"YOU KNOW WHAT HE IS, ALIK. IT DOESN'T MATTER THAT SHE'S HIS DAUGHTER, TOO. YOU KNOW WHAT HE WILL DO.
"YOU CAN HELP ME OR I CAN GO BACK TO WORK. AT LEAST, UNTIL I'M NO USE TO HIM ANYMORE."

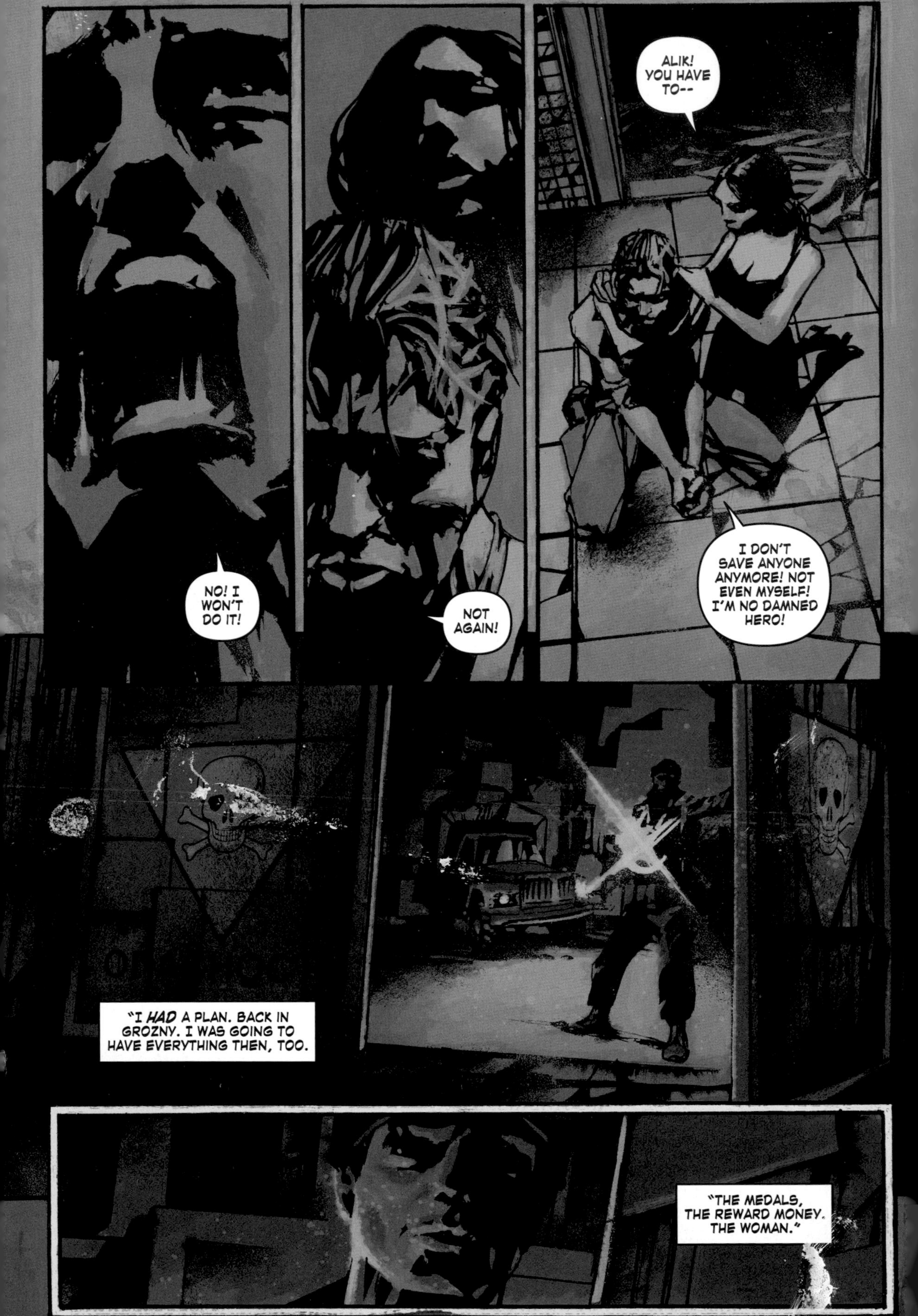
NO! I WON'T DO IT!
NOT AGAIN!
ALIK! YOU HAVE TO--
I DON'T SAVE ANYONE ANYMORE! NOT EVEN MYSELF! I'M NO DAMNED HERO!
"I HAD A PLAN. BACK IN GROZNY. I WAS GOING TO HAVE EVERYTHING THEN, TOO.
"THE MEDALS, THE REWARD MONEY. THE WOMAN."

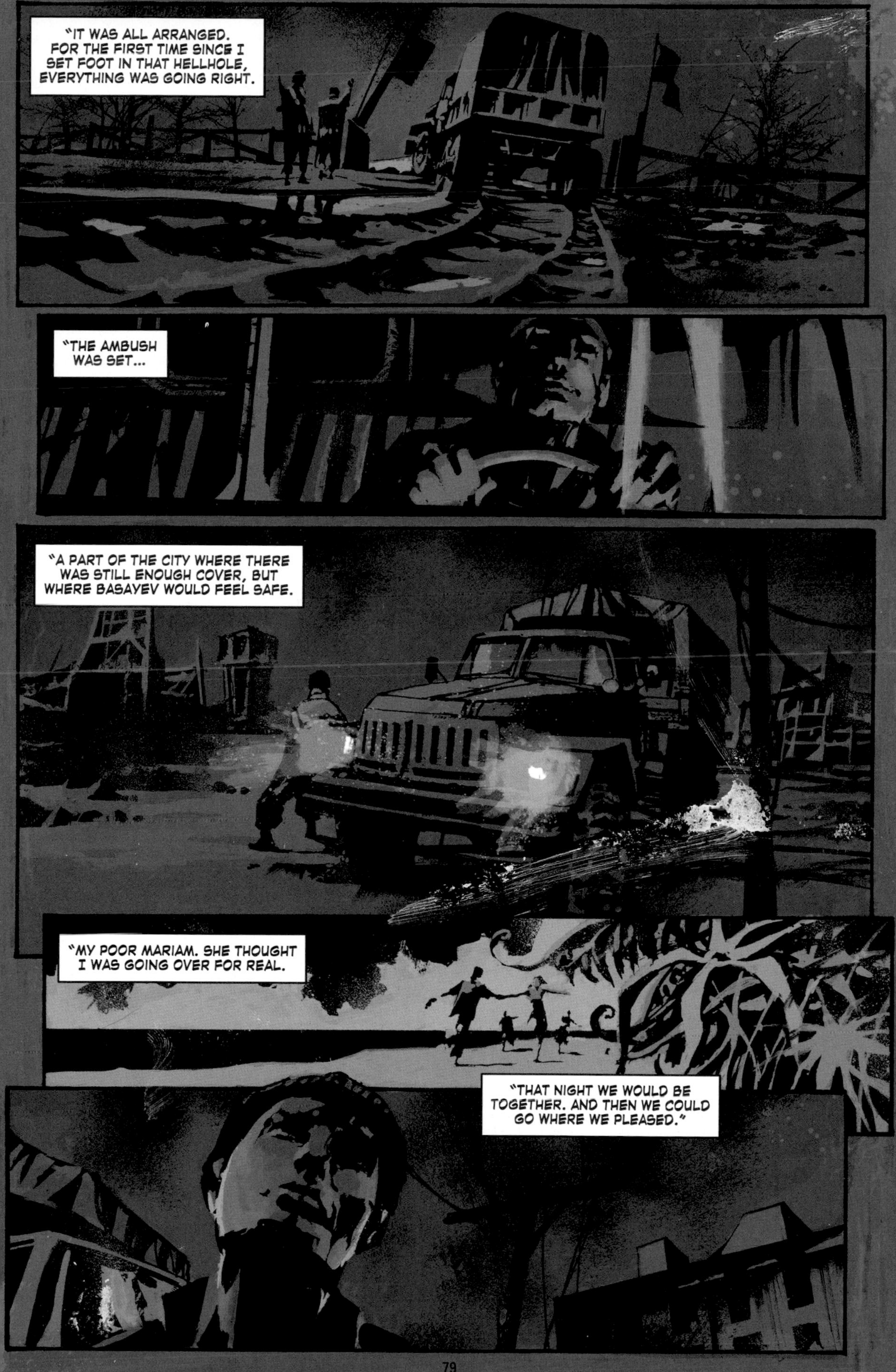
"IT WAS ALL ARRANGED. FOR THE FIRST TIME SINCE I SET FOOT IN THAT HELLHOLE, EVERYTHING WAS GOING RIGHT.
"THE AMBUSH WAS SET...
"A PART OF THE CITY WHERE THERE WAS STILL ENOUGH COVER, BUT WHERE BASAYEV WOULD FEEL SAFE.
"MY POOR MARIAM. SHE THOUGHT I WAS GOING OVER FOR REAL.
"THAT NIGHT WE WOULD BE TOGETHER. AND THEN WE COULD GO WHERE WE PLEASED."

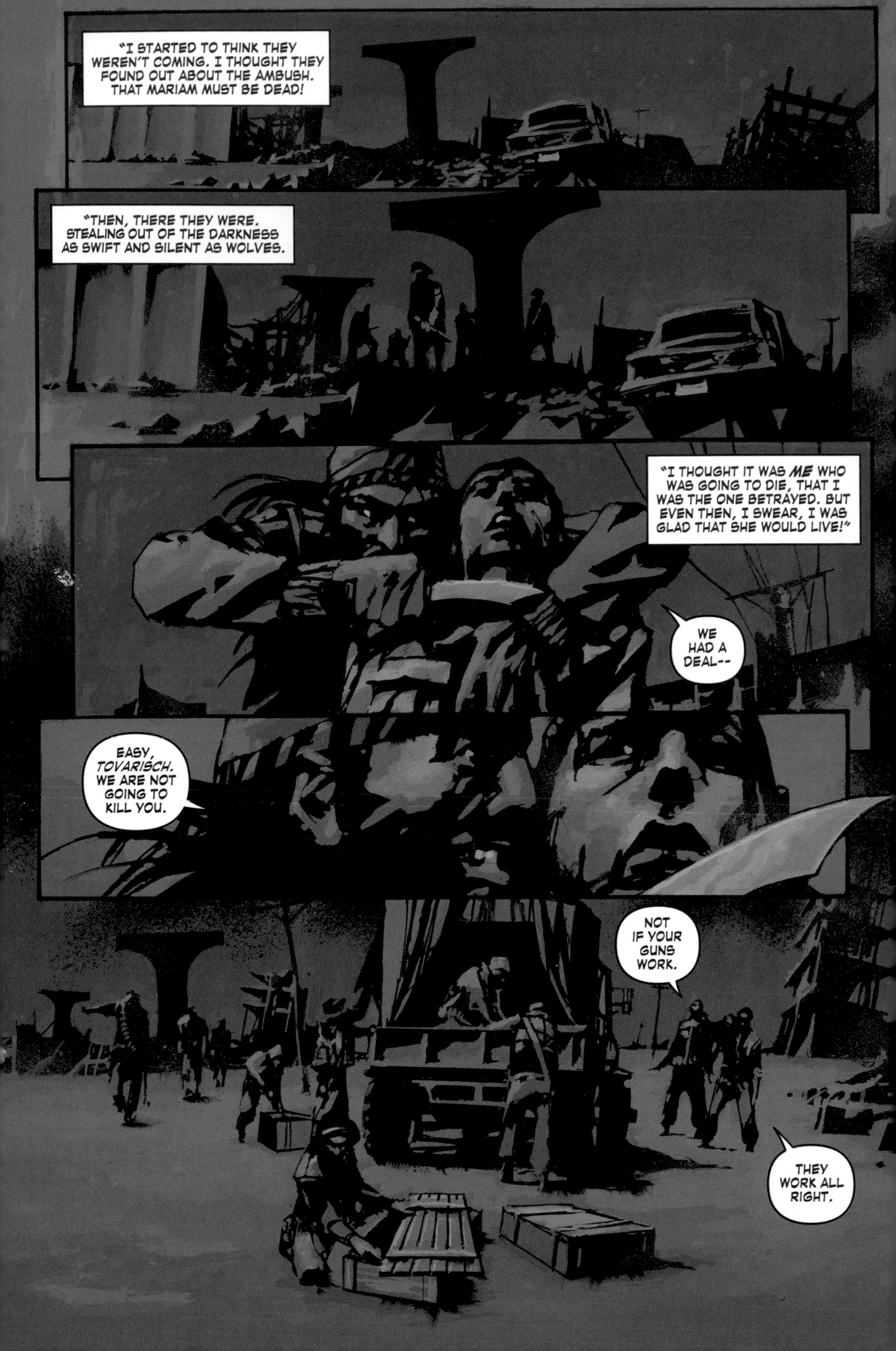
"I STARTED TO THINK THEY WEREN'T COMING. I THOUGHT THEY FOUND OUT ABOUT THE AMBUSH. THAT MARIAM MUST BE DEAD!
"THEN, THERE THEY WERE. STEALING OUT OF THE DARKNESS AS SWIFT AND SILENT AS WOLVES.
"I THOUGHT IT WAS *ME* WHO WAS GOING TO DIE, THAT I WAS THE ONE BETRAYED. BUT EVEN THEN, I SWEAR, I WAS GLAD THAT SHE WOULD LIVE!"
WE HAD A DEAL--
EASY, *TOVARISCH*. WE ARE NOT GOING TO KILL YOU.
NOT IF YOUR GUNS WORK.
THEY WORK ALL RIGHT.

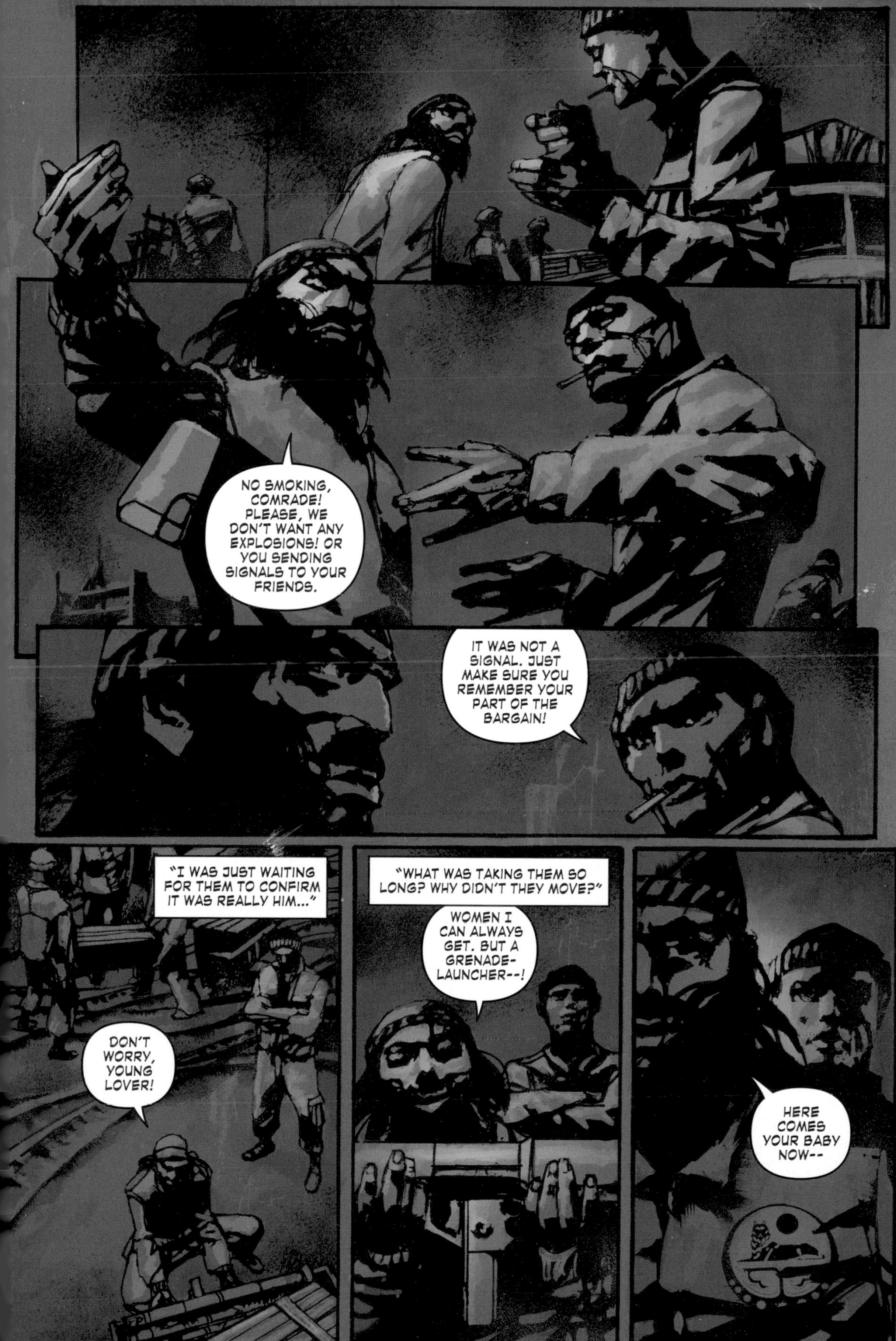
NO SMOKING, COMRADE! PLEASE, WE DON'T WANT ANY EXPLOSIONS! OR YOU SENDING SIGNALS TO YOUR FRIENDS.
IT WAS NOT A SIGNAL. JUST MAKE SURE YOU REMEMBER YOUR PART OF THE BARGAIN!
"I WAS JUST WAITING FOR THEM TO CONFIRM IT WAS REALLY HIM..."
DON'T WORRY, YOUNG LOVER!
"WHAT WAS TAKING THEM SO LONG? WHY DIDN'T THEY MOVE?"
WOMEN I CAN ALWAYS GET. BUT A GRENADE-LAUNCHER--!
HERE COMES YOUR BABY NOW--

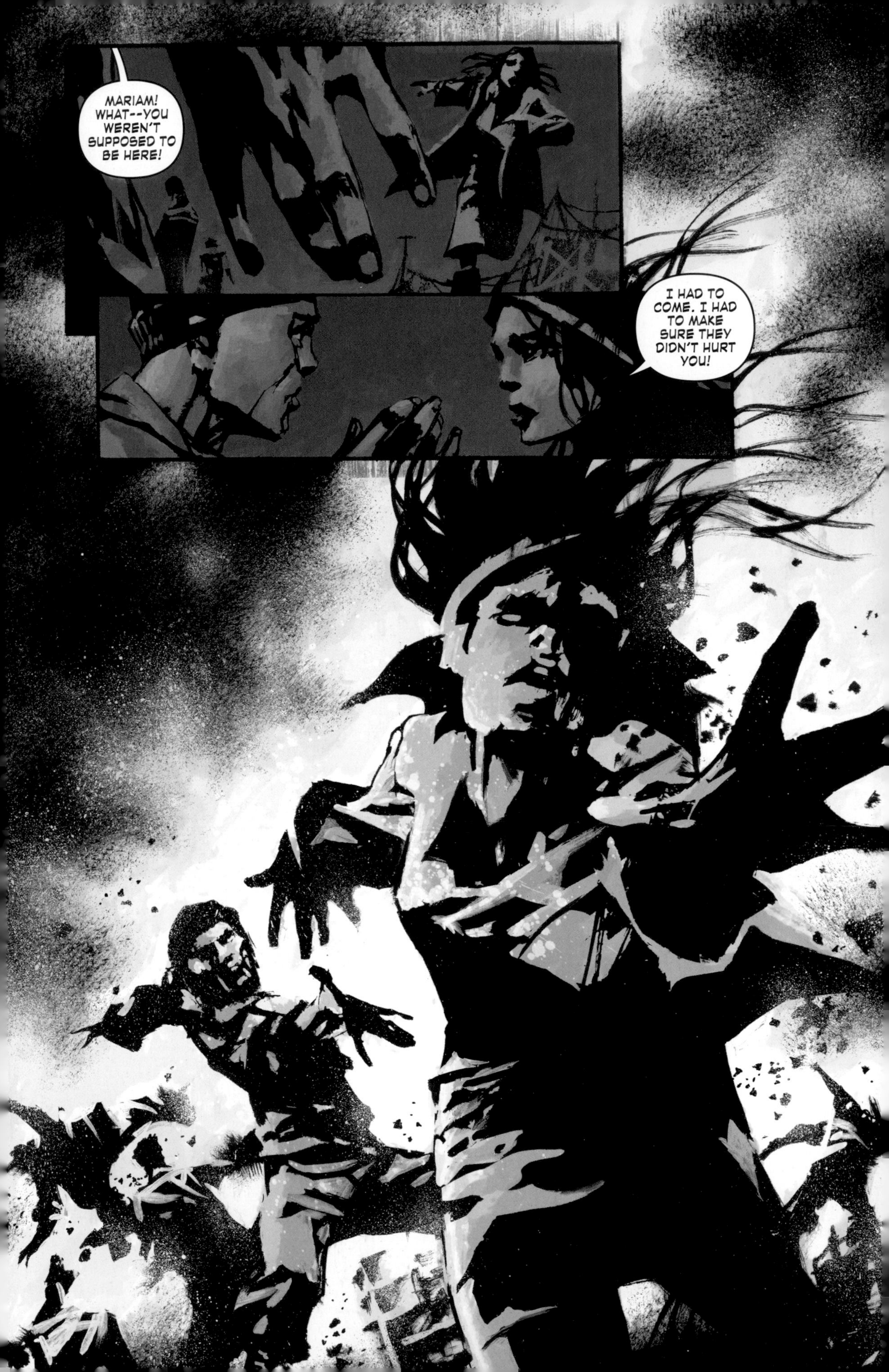
MARIAM! WHAT--YOU WEREN'T SUPPOSED TO BE HERE!
I HAD TO COME. I HAD TO MAKE SURE THEY DIDN'T HURT YOU!

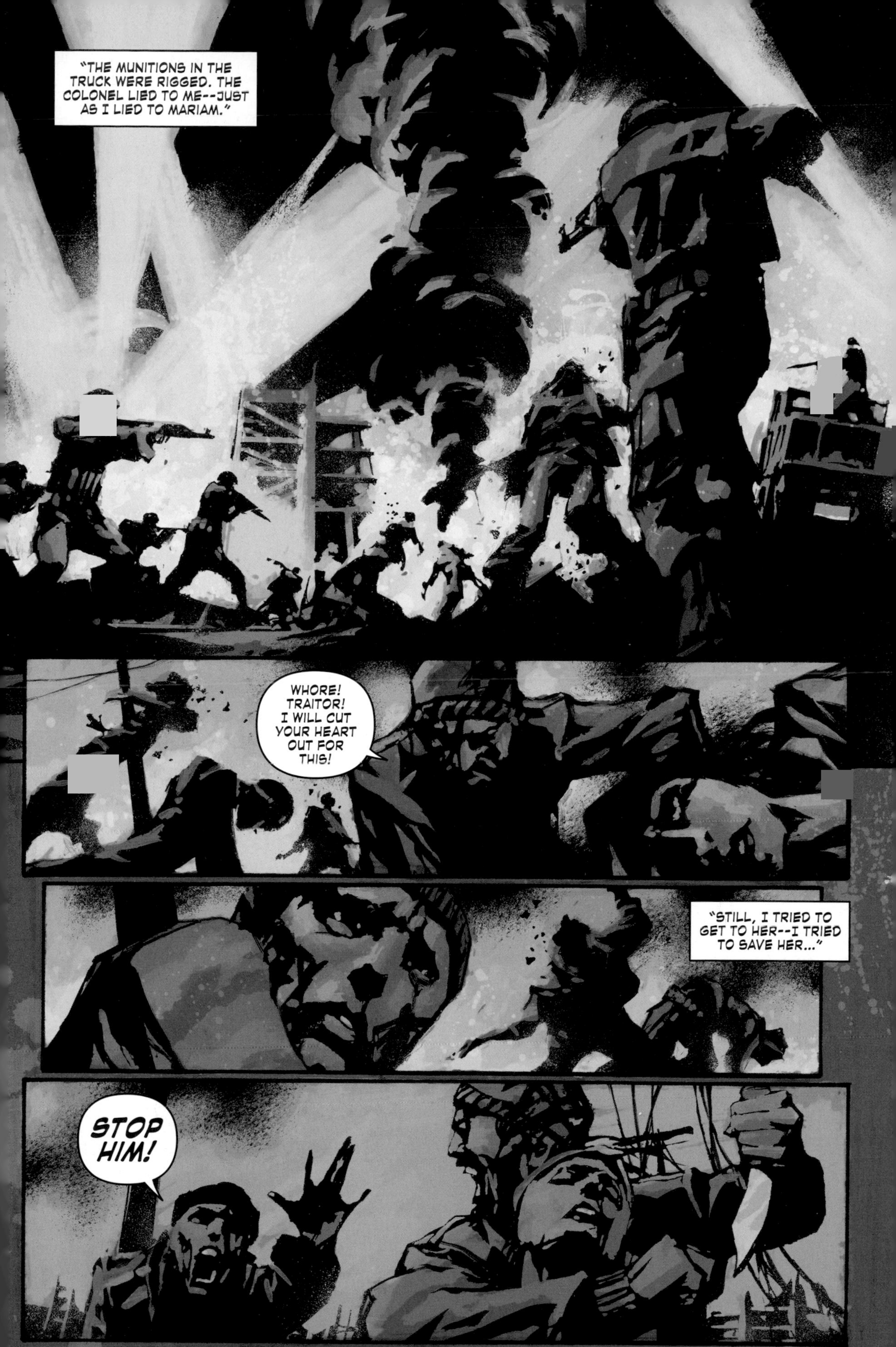
"THE MUNITIONS IN THE TRUCK WERE RIGGED. THE COLONEL LIED TO ME--JUST AS I LIED TO MARIAM."
WHORE! TRAITOR! I WILL CUT YOUR HEART OUT FOR THIS!
"STILL, I TRIED TO GET TO HER--I TRIED TO SAVE HER..."
STOP HIM!

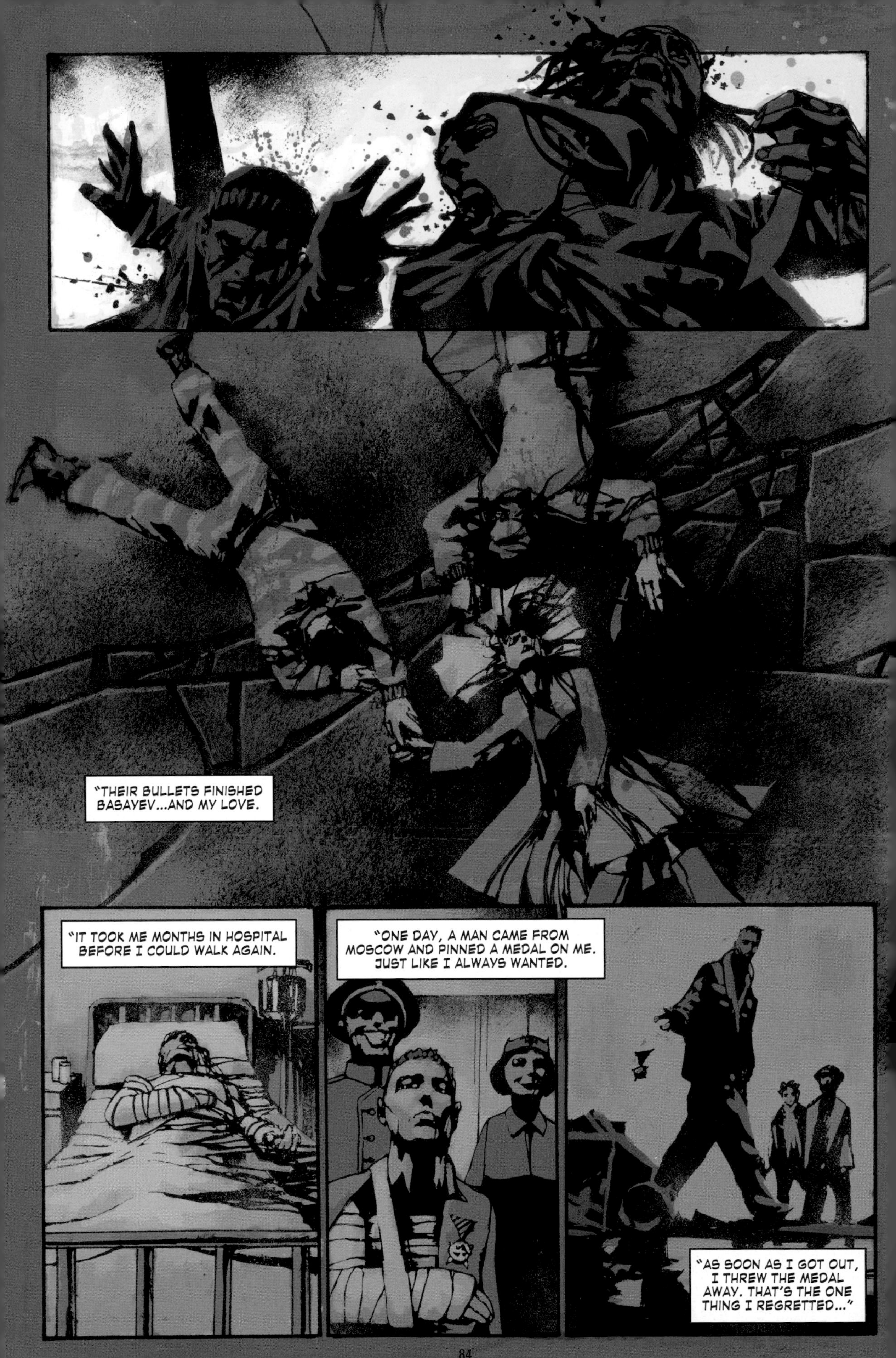
"THEIR BULLETS FINISHED
BASAYEV...AND MY LOVE.
"IT TOOK ME MONTHS IN HOSPITAL
BEFORE I COULD WALK AGAIN.
"ONE DAY, A MAN CAME FROM
MOSCOW AND PINNED A MEDAL ON ME.
JUST LIKE I ALWAYS WANTED.
"AS SOON AS I GOT OUT,
I THREW THE MEDAL
AWAY. THAT'S THE ONE
THING I REGRETTED..."

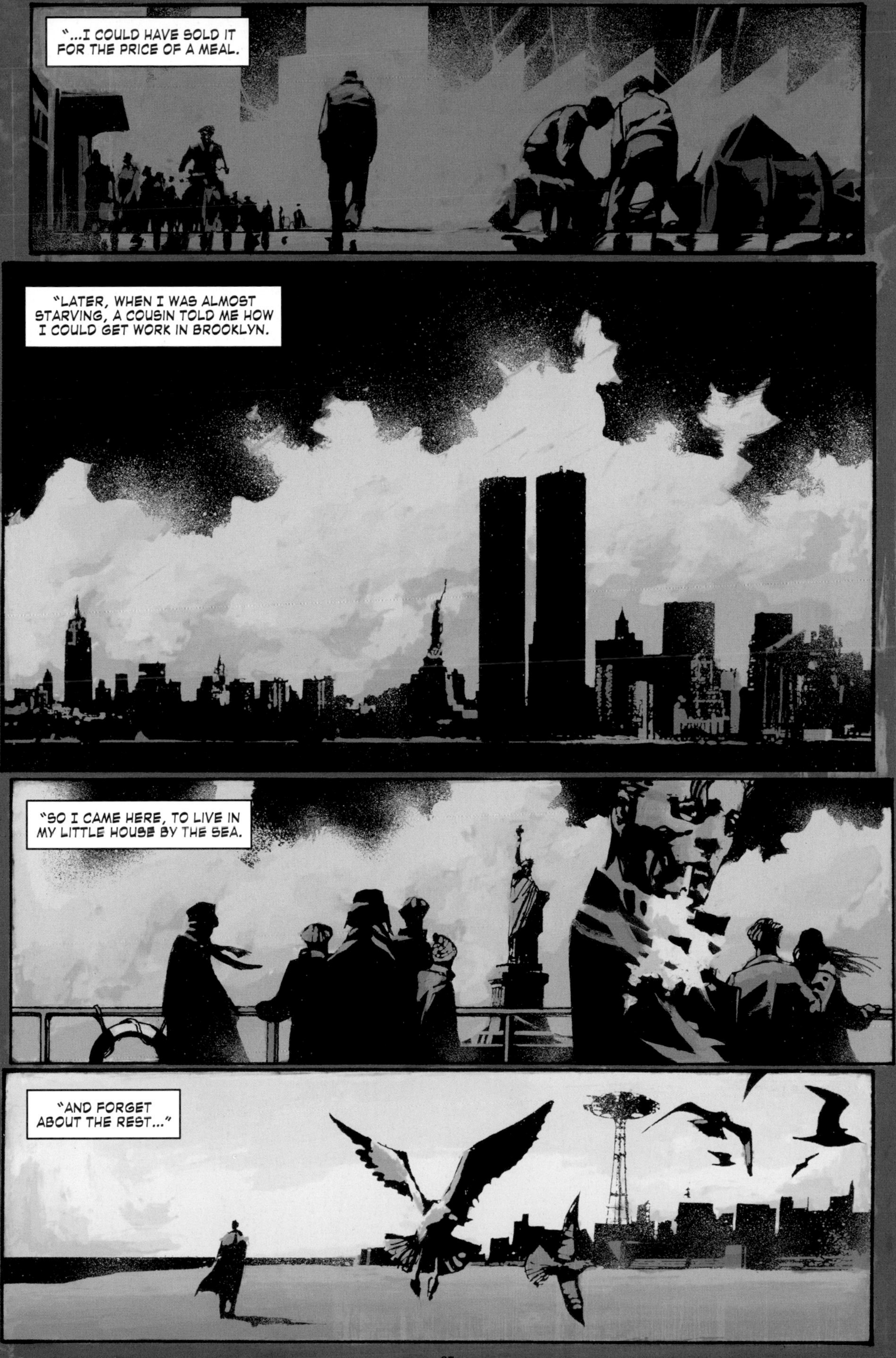
"...I COULD HAVE SOLD IT FOR THE PRICE OF A MEAL.
"LATER, WHEN I WAS ALMOST STARVING, A COUSIN TOLD ME HOW I COULD GET WORK IN BROOKLYN.
"SO I CAME HERE, TO LIVE IN MY LITTLE HOUSE BY THE SEA.
"AND FORGET ABOUT THE REST..."

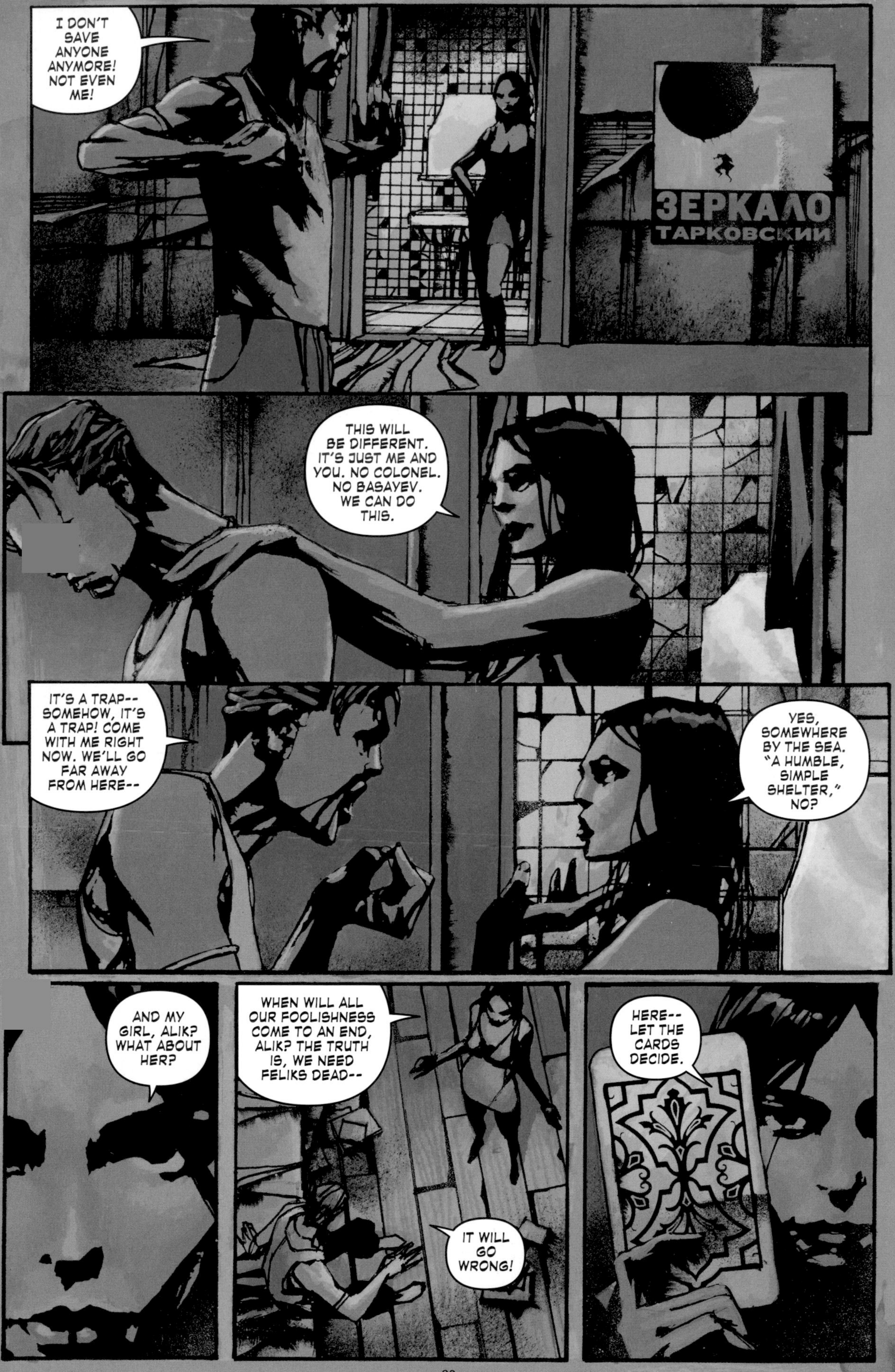
I DON'T SAVE ANYONE ANYMORE! NOT EVEN ME!
ЗЕРКАЛО
ТАРКОВСКИИ
THIS WILL BE DIFFERENT. IT'S JUST ME AND YOU. NO COLONEL. NO BASAYEV. WE CAN DO THIS.
IT'S A TRAP-- SOMEHOW, IT'S A TRAP! COME WITH ME RIGHT NOW. WE'LL GO FAR AWAY FROM HERE--
YES, SOMEWHERE BY THE SEA. "A HUMBLE, SIMPLE SHELTER," NO?
AND MY GIRL, ALIK? WHAT ABOUT HER?
WHEN WILL ALL OUR FOOLISHNESS COME TO AN END, ALIK? THE TRUTH IS, WE NEED FELIKS DEAD--
IT WILL GO WRONG!
HERE-- LET THE CARDS DECIDE.

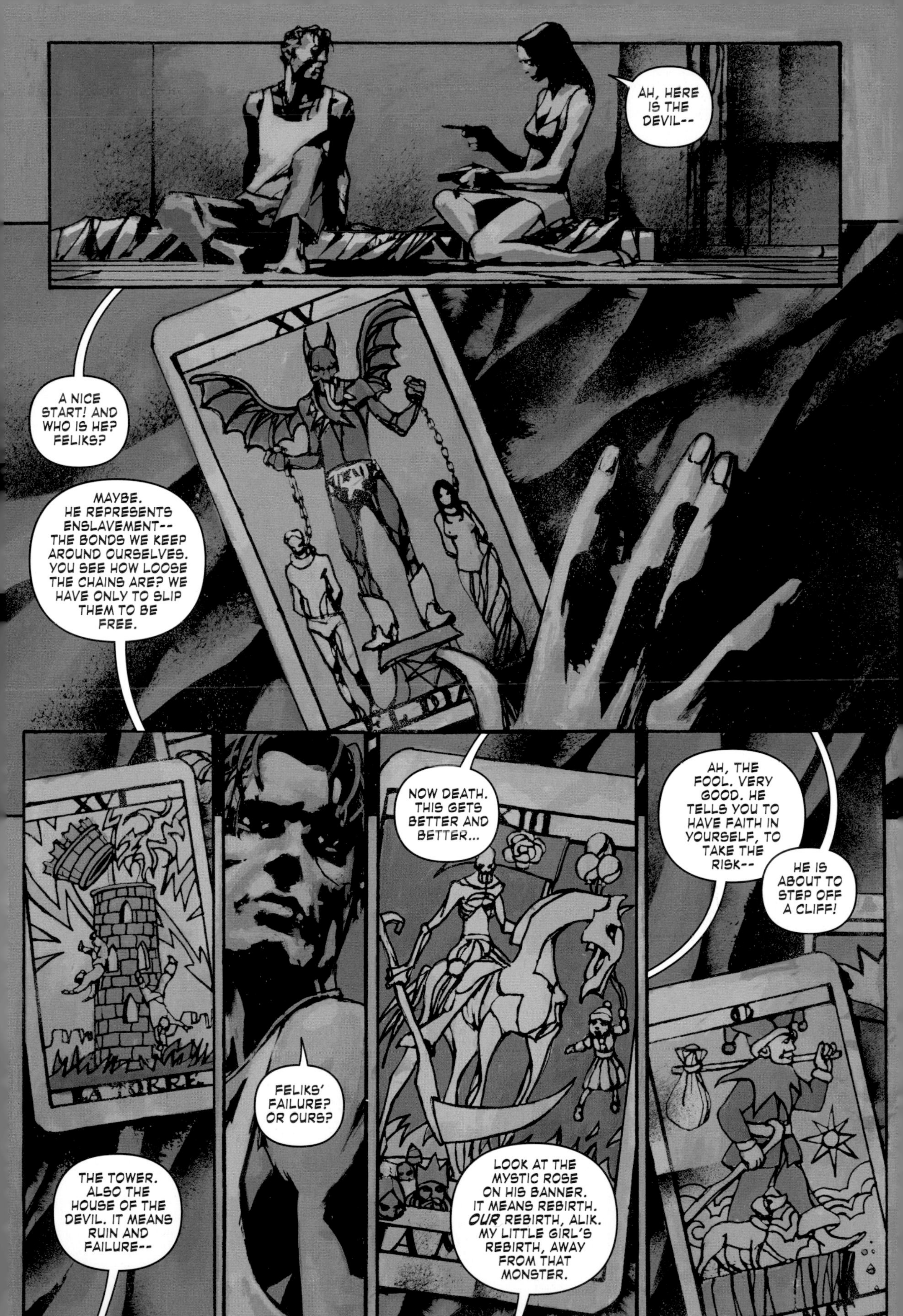
AH, HERE IS THE DEVIL--
A NICE START! AND WHO IS HE? FELIKS?
MAYBE. HE REPRESENTS ENSLAVEMENT-- THE BONDS WE KEEP AROUND OURSELVES. YOU SEE HOW LOOSE THE CHAINS ARE? WE HAVE ONLY TO SLIP THEM TO BE FREE.
XVI
THE TOWER. ALSO THE HOUSE OF THE DEVIL. IT MEANS RUIN AND FAILURE--
FELIKS' FAILURE? OR OURS?
NOW DEATH. THIS GETS BETTER AND BETTER...
LOOK AT THE MYSTIC ROSE ON HIS BANNER. IT MEANS REBIRTH. *OUR* REBIRTH, ALIK. MY LITTLE GIRL'S REBIRTH, AWAY FROM THAT MONSTER.
AH, THE FOOL. VERY GOOD. HE TELLS YOU TO HAVE FAITH IN YOURSELF, TO TAKE THE RISK--
HE IS ABOUT TO STEP OFF A CLIFF!
LE MAT

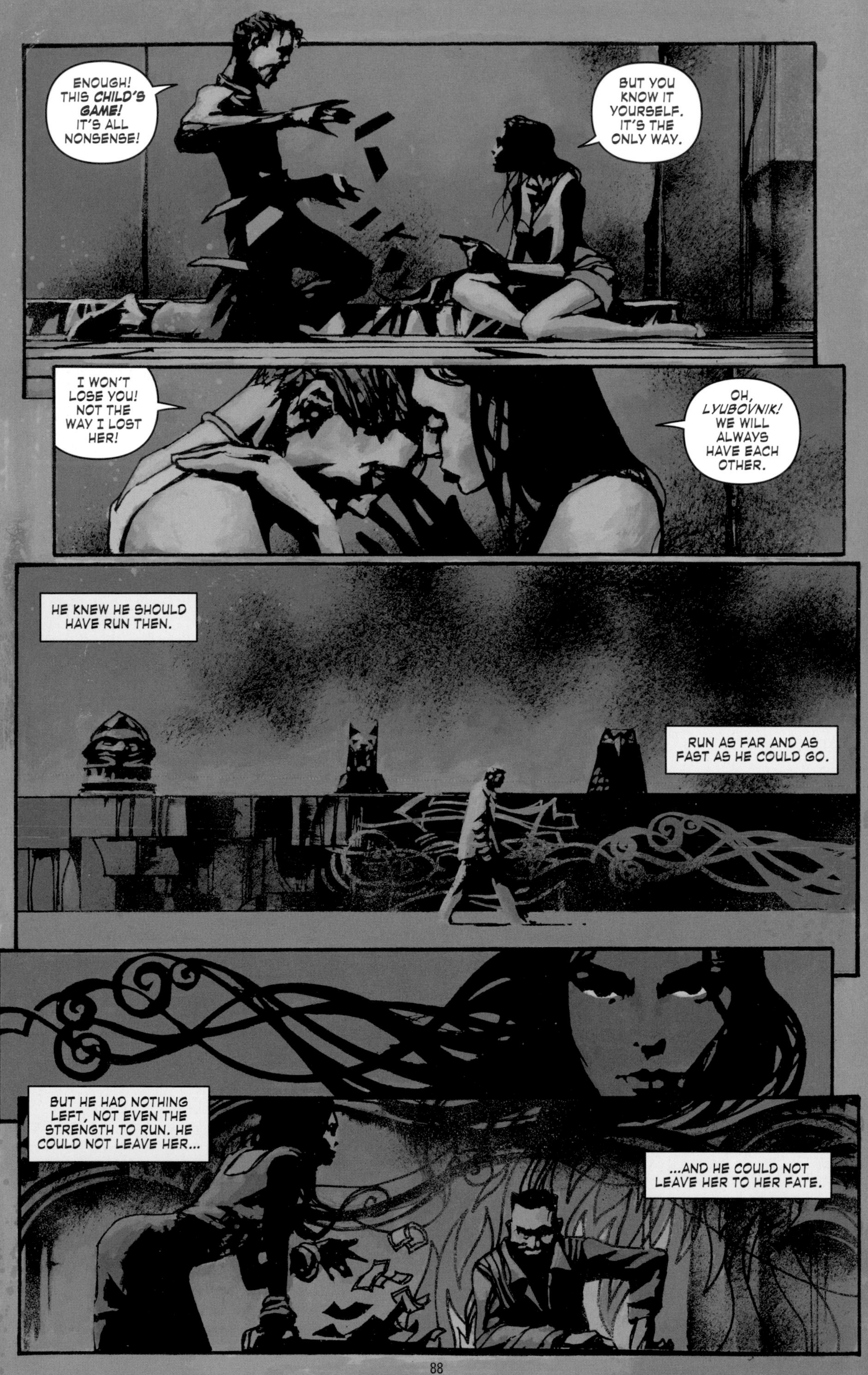
ENOUGH! THIS CHILD'S GAME! IT'S ALL NONSENSE!
BUT YOU KNOW IT YOURSELF. IT'S THE ONLY WAY.
I WON'T LOSE YOU! NOT THE WAY I LOST HER!
OH, LYUBOVNIK! WE WILL ALWAYS HAVE EACH OTHER.
HE KNEW HE SHOULD HAVE RUN THEN.
RUN AS FAR AND AS FAST AS HE COULD GO.
BUT HE HAD NOTHING LEFT, NOT EVEN THE STRENGTH TO RUN. HE COULD NOT LEAVE HER...
...AND HE COULD NOT LEAVE HER TO HER FATE.

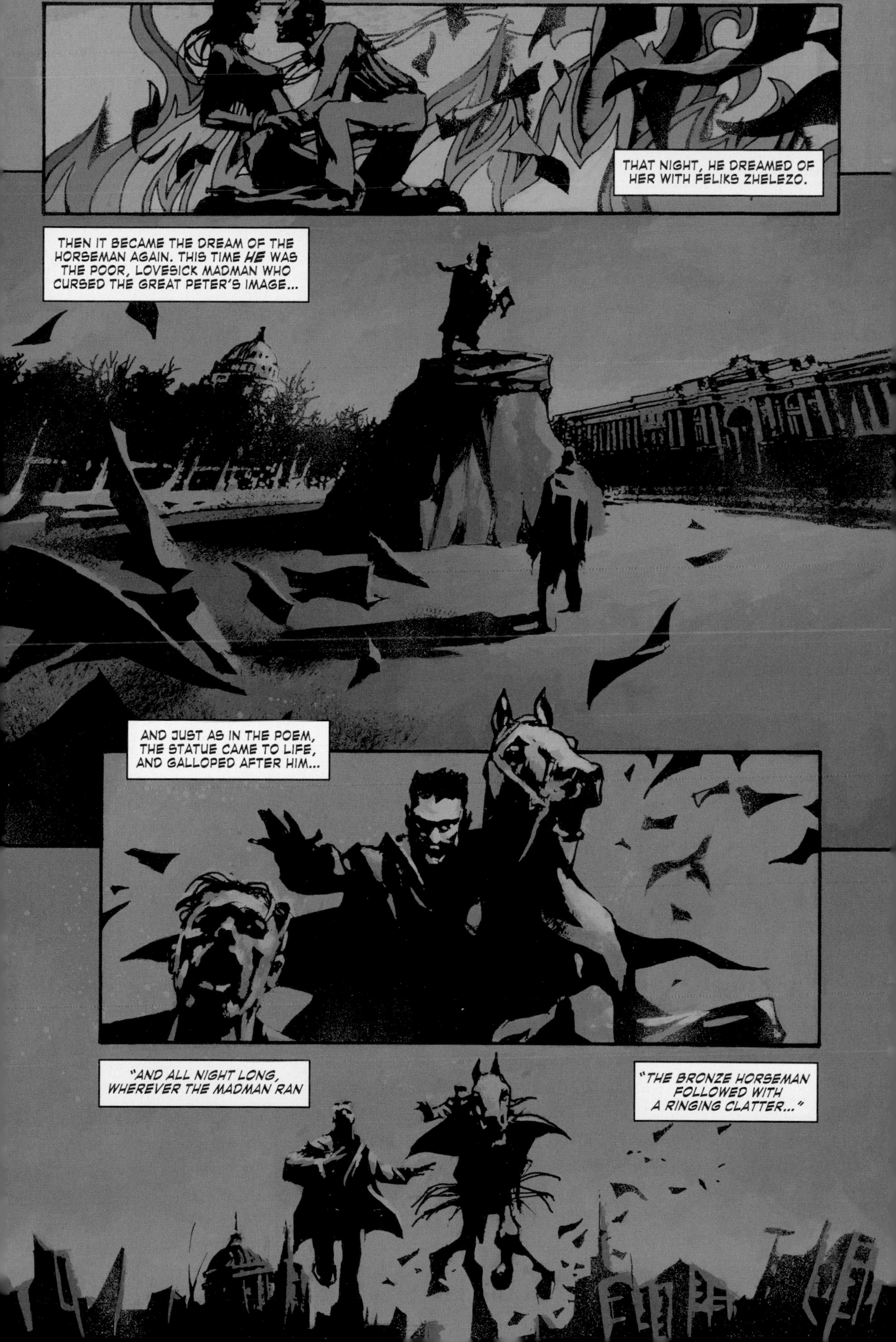
THAT NIGHT, HE DREAMED OF HER WITH FELIKS ZHELEZO.
THEN IT BECAME THE DREAM OF THE HORSEMAN AGAIN. THIS TIME *HE* WAS THE POOR, LOVESICK MADMAN WHO CURSED THE GREAT PETER'S IMAGE...
AND JUST AS IN THE POEM, THE STATUE CAME TO LIFE, AND GALLOPED AFTER HIM...
"AND ALL NIGHT LONG, WHEREVER THE MADMAN RAN
"THE BRONZE HORSEMAN FOLLOWED WITH A RINGING CLATTER..."

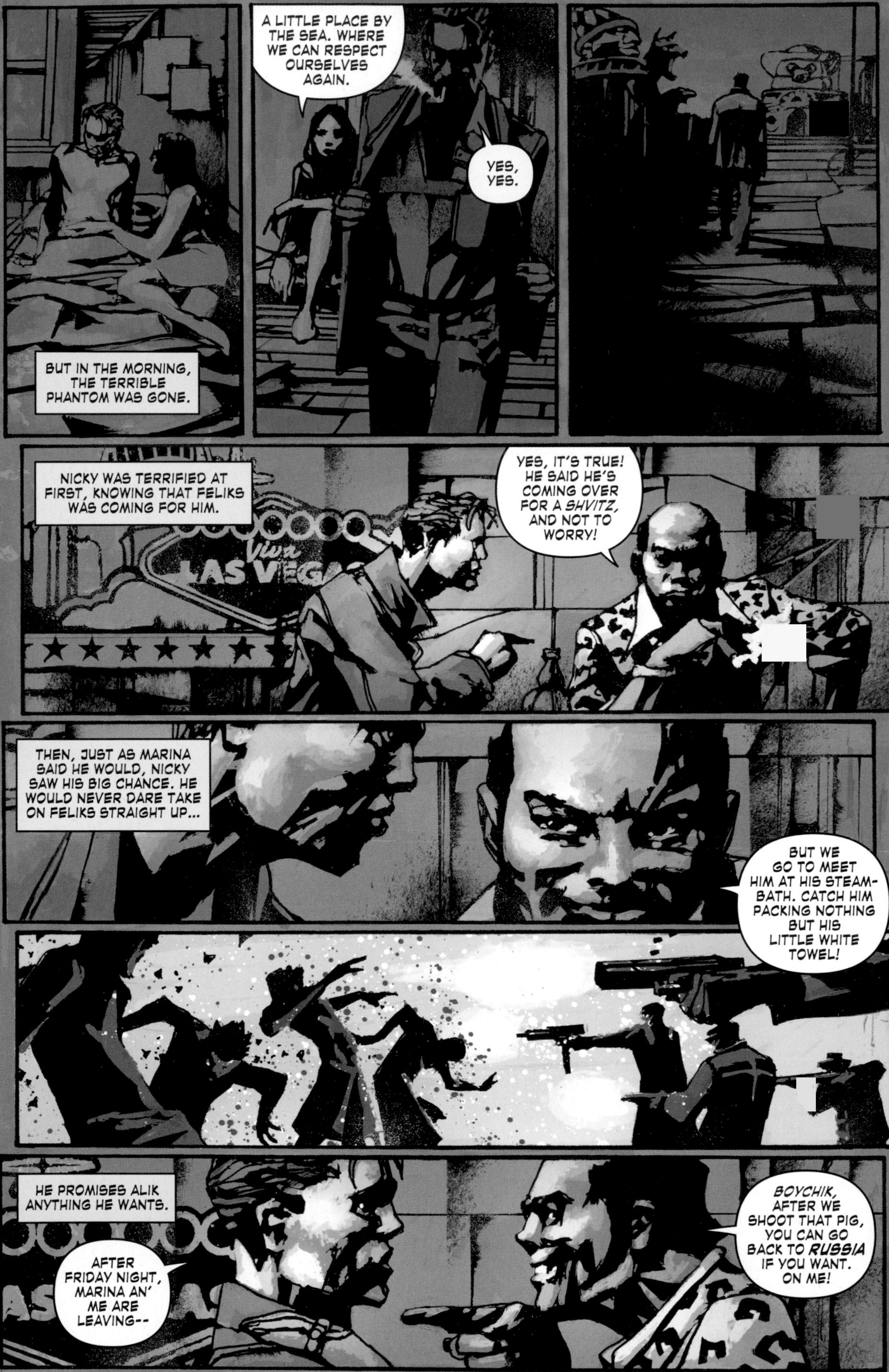
A LITTLE PLACE BY THE SEA. WHERE WE CAN RESPECT OURSELVES AGAIN.
YES, YES.
BUT IN THE MORNING, THE TERRIBLE PHANTOM WAS GONE.
NICKY WAS TERRIFIED AT FIRST, KNOWING THAT FELIKS WAS COMING FOR HIM.
YES, IT'S TRUE! HE SAID HE'S COMING OVER FOR A *SHVITZ*, AND NOT TO WORRY!
THEN, JUST AS MARINA SAID HE WOULD, NICKY SAW HIS BIG CHANCE. HE WOULD NEVER DARE TAKE ON FELIKS STRAIGHT UP...
BUT WE GO TO MEET HIM AT HIS STEAM-BATH. CATCH HIM PACKING NOTHING BUT HIS LITTLE WHITE TOWEL!
HE PROMISES ALIK ANYTHING HE WANTS.
AFTER FRIDAY NIGHT, MARINA AN' ME ARE LEAVING--
*BOYCHIK*, AFTER WE SHOOT THAT PIG, YOU CAN GO BACK TO *RUSSIA* IF YOU WANT. ON ME!

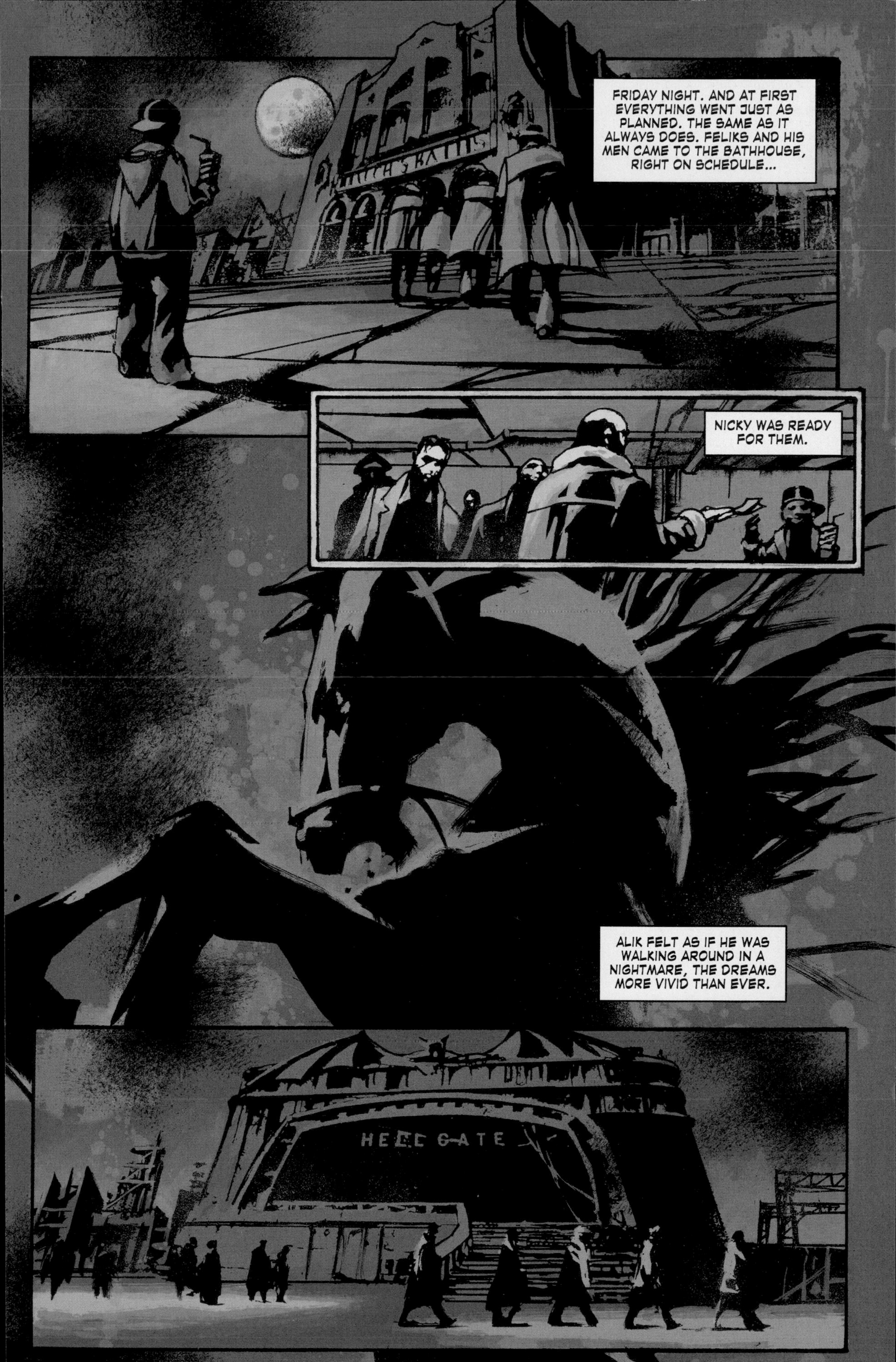
FRIDAY NIGHT. AND AT FIRST EVERYTHING WENT JUST AS PLANNED. THE SAME AS IT ALWAYS DOES. FELIKS AND HIS MEN CAME TO THE BATHHOUSE, RIGHT ON SCHEDULE...
NICKY WAS READY FOR THEM.
ALIK FELT AS IF HE WAS WALKING AROUND IN A NIGHTMARE, THE DREAMS MORE VIVID THAN EVER.
HELL GATE

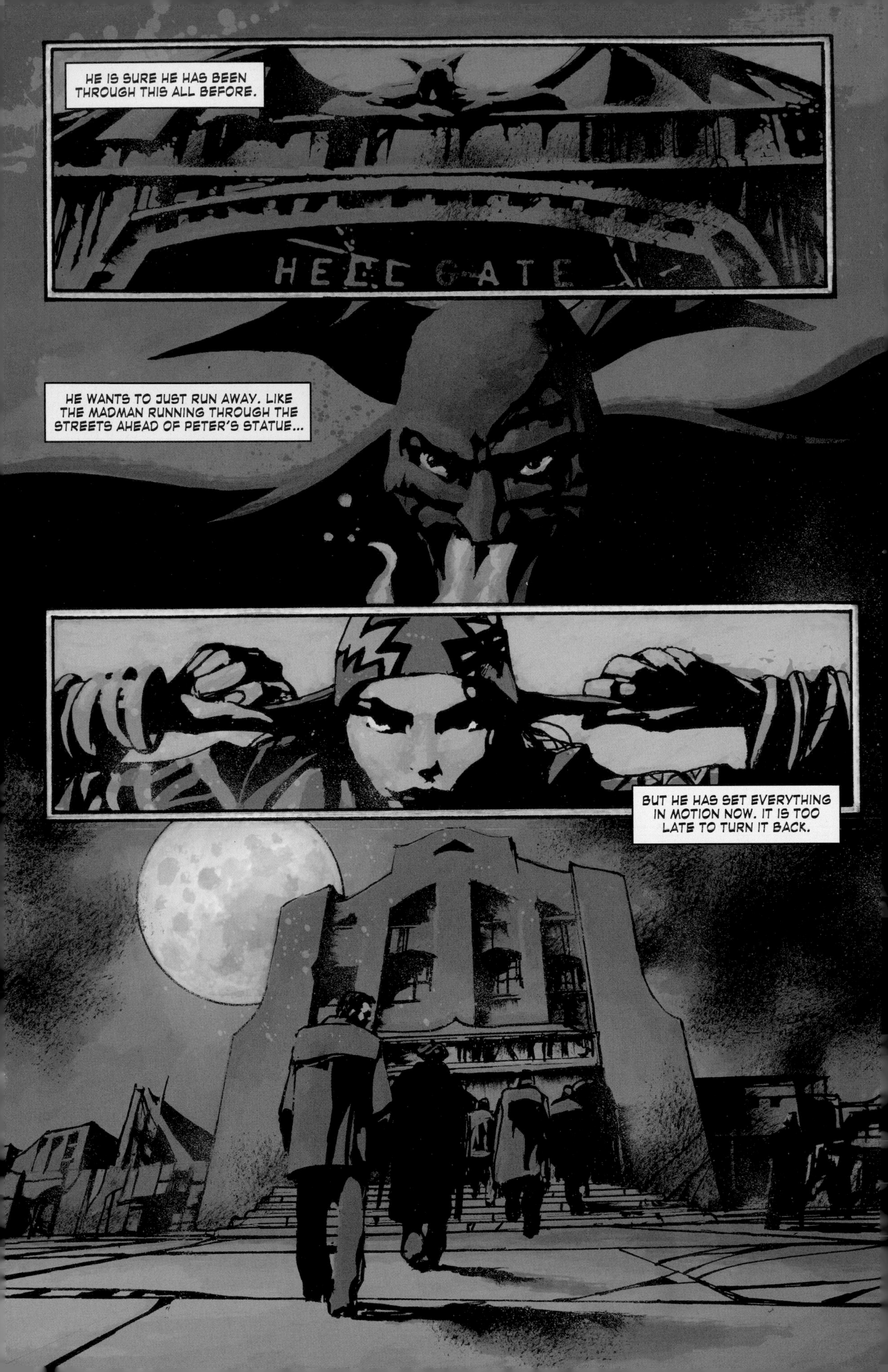
HE IS SURE HE HAS BEEN THROUGH THIS ALL BEFORE.
HELL GATE
HE WANTS TO JUST RUN AWAY. LIKE THE MADMAN RUNNING THROUGH THE STREETS AHEAD OF PETER'S STATUE...
BUT HE HAS SET EVERYTHING IN MOTION NOW. IT IS TOO LATE TO TURN IT BACK.

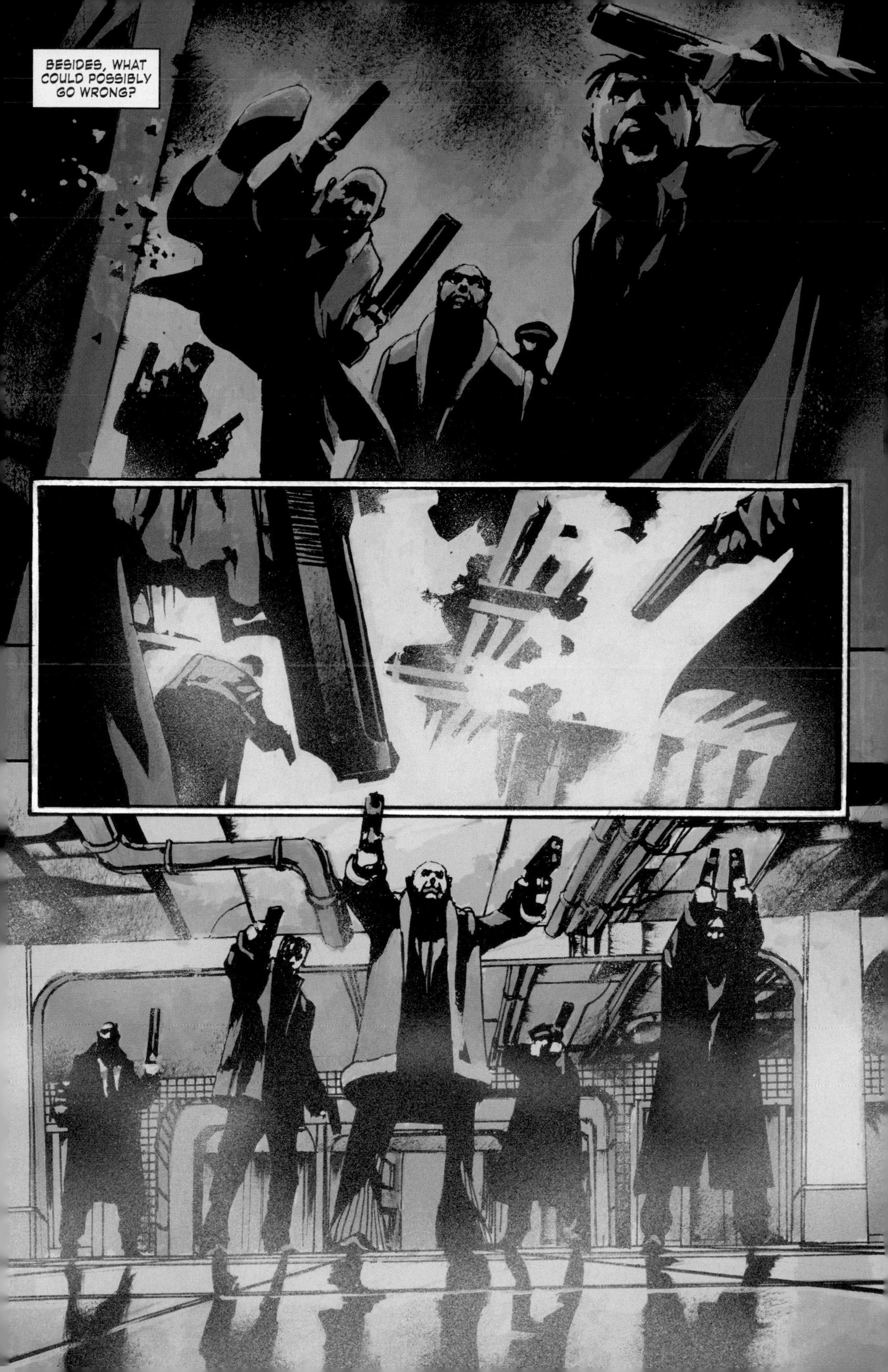
BESIDES, WHAT COULD POSSIBLY GO WRONG?

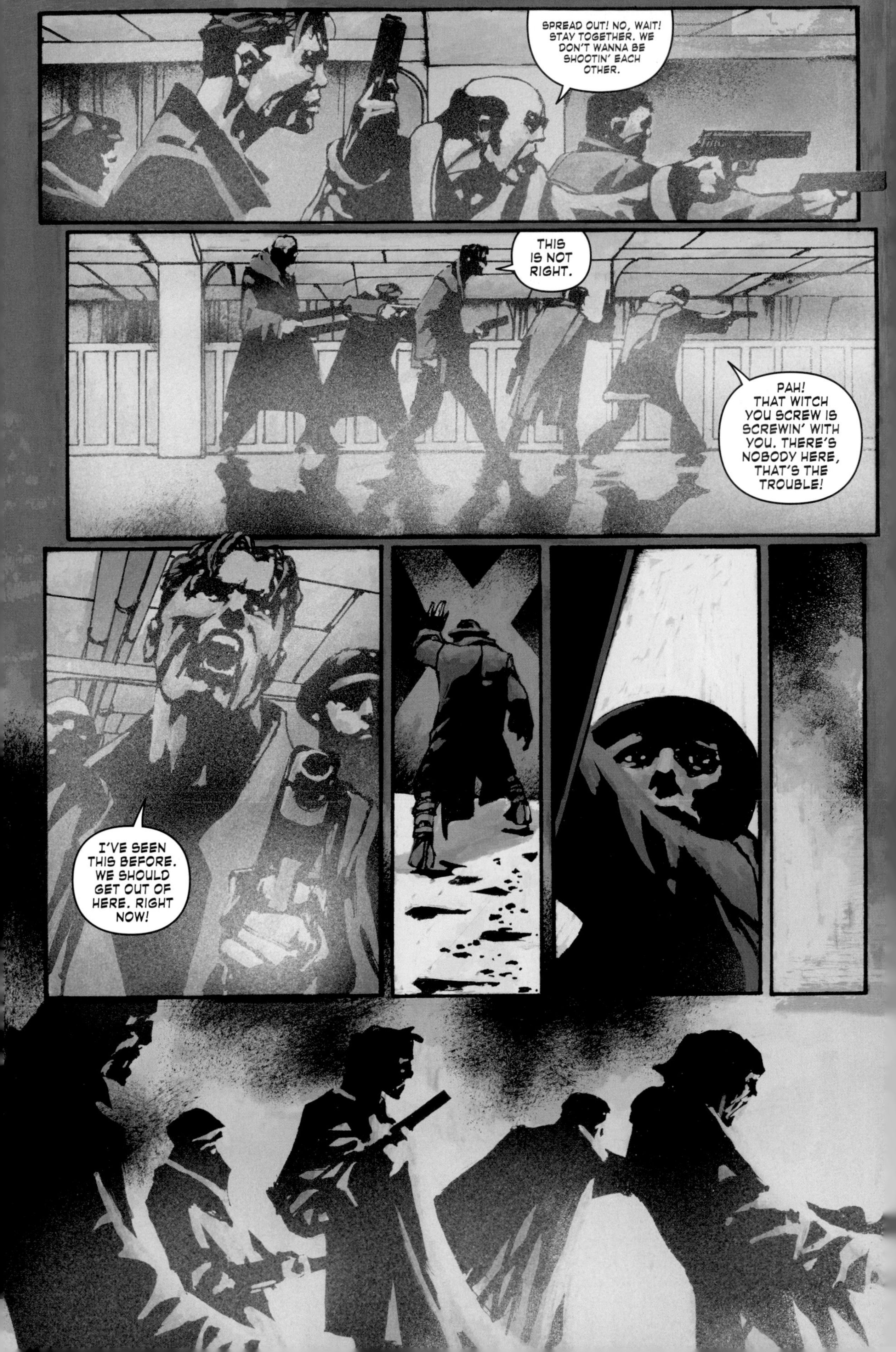
SPREAD OUT! NO, WAIT! STAY TOGETHER. WE DON'T WANNA BE SHOOTIN' EACH OTHER.
THIS IS NOT RIGHT.
PAH! THAT WITCH YOU SCREW IS SCREWIN' WITH YOU. THERE'S NOBODY HERE, THAT'S THE TROUBLE!
I'VE SEEN THIS BEFORE. WE SHOULD GET OUT OF HERE. RIGHT NOW!

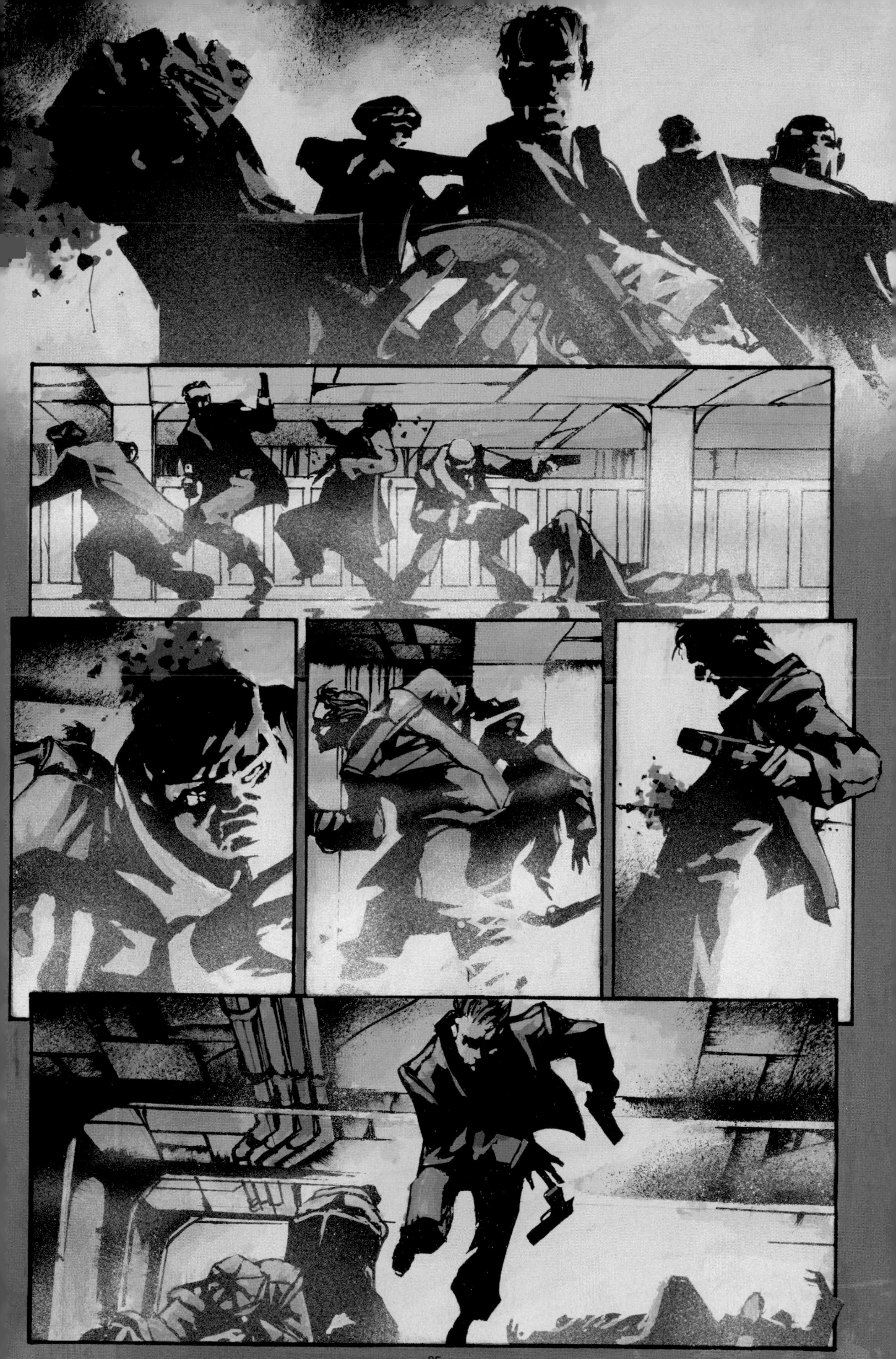

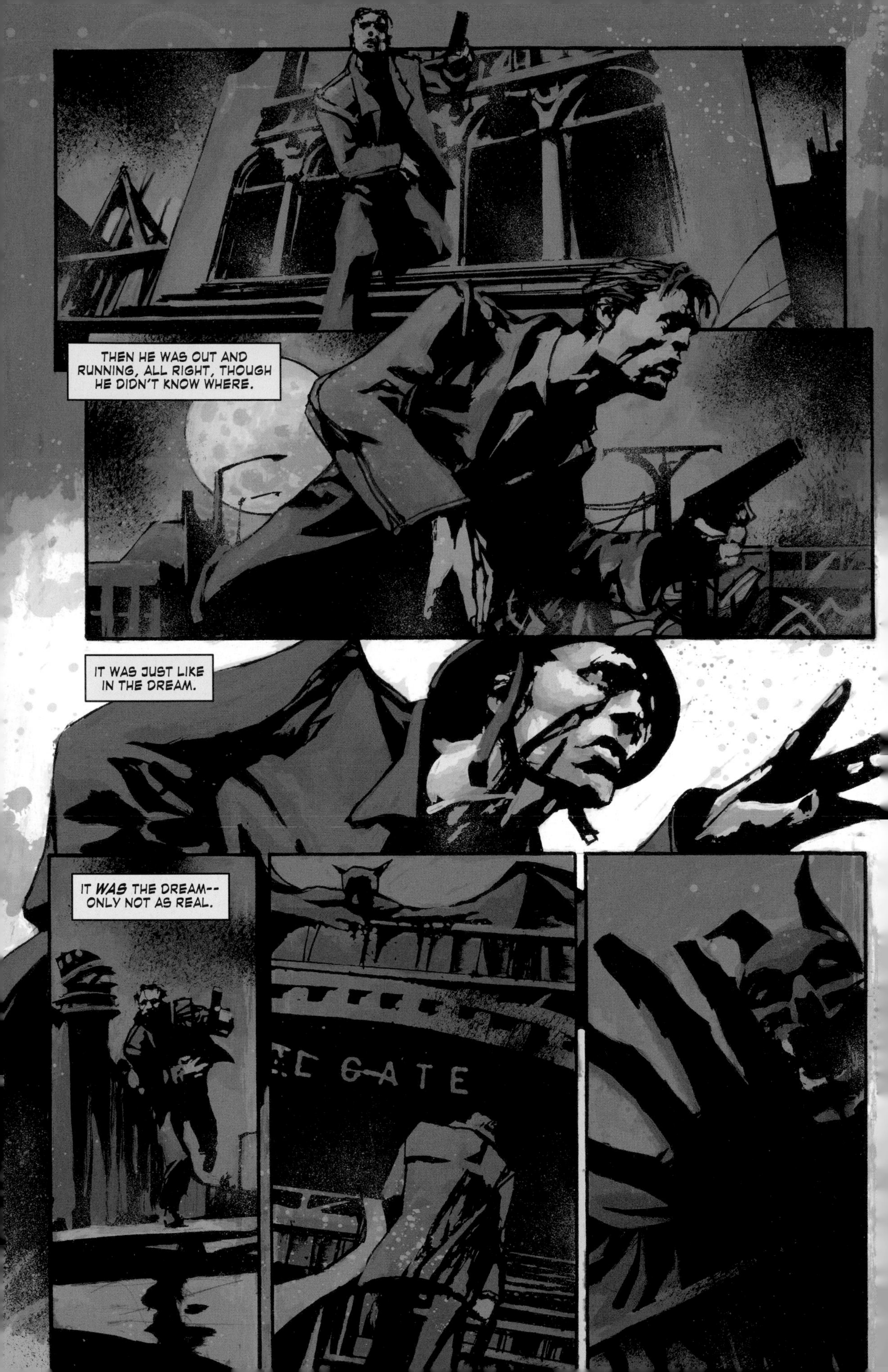
THEN HE WAS OUT AND RUNNING, ALL RIGHT, THOUGH HE DIDN'T KNOW WHERE.
IT WAS JUST LIKE IN THE DREAM.
IT *WAS* THE DREAM-- ONLY NOT AS REAL.
C GATE

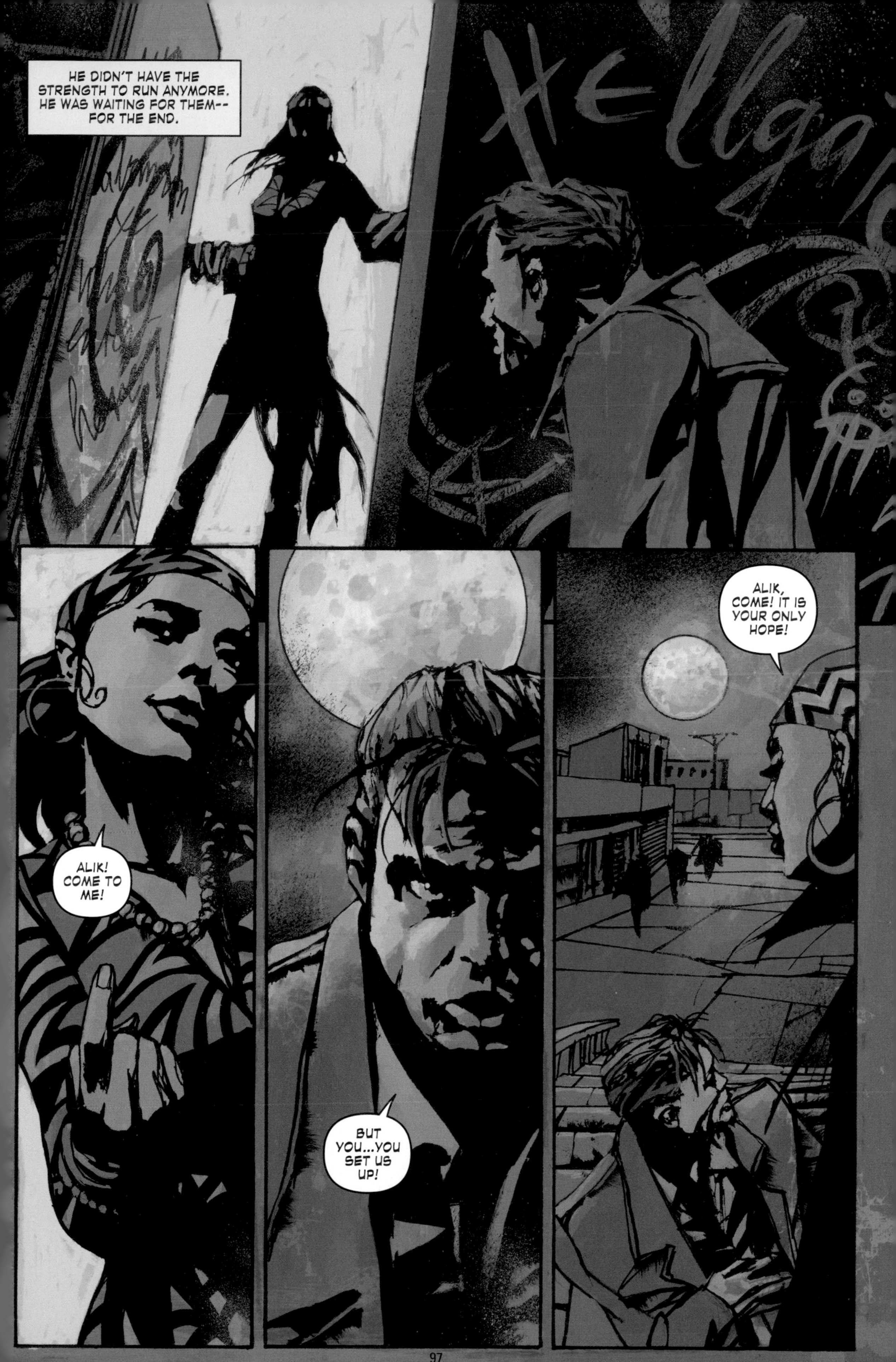
HE DIDN'T HAVE THE STRENGTH TO RUN ANYMORE. HE WAS WAITING FOR THEM-- FOR THE END.
ALIK! COME TO ME!
BUT YOU...YOU SET US UP!
ALIK, COME! IT IS YOUR ONLY HOPE!

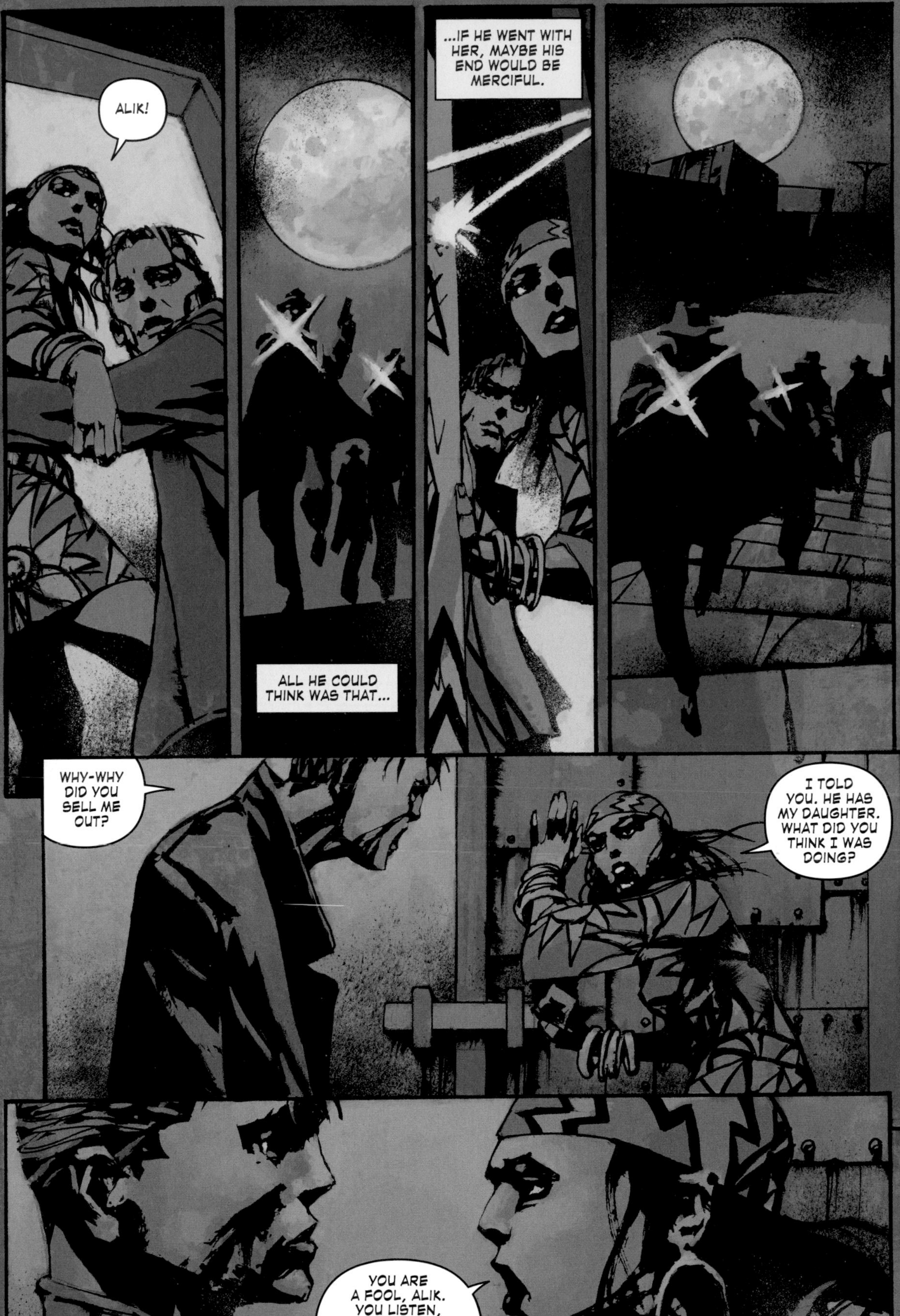

ALIK!
ALL HE COULD THINK WAS THAT...
...IF HE WENT WITH HER, MAYBE HIS END WOULD BE MERCIFUL.
WHY-WHY DID YOU SELL ME OUT?
I TOLD YOU. HE HAS MY DAUGHTER. WHAT DID YOU THINK I WAS DOING?
YOU ARE A FOOL, ALIK. YOU LISTEN, BUT YOU DO NOT UNDERSTAND. BUT I WILL HELP YOU NOW.

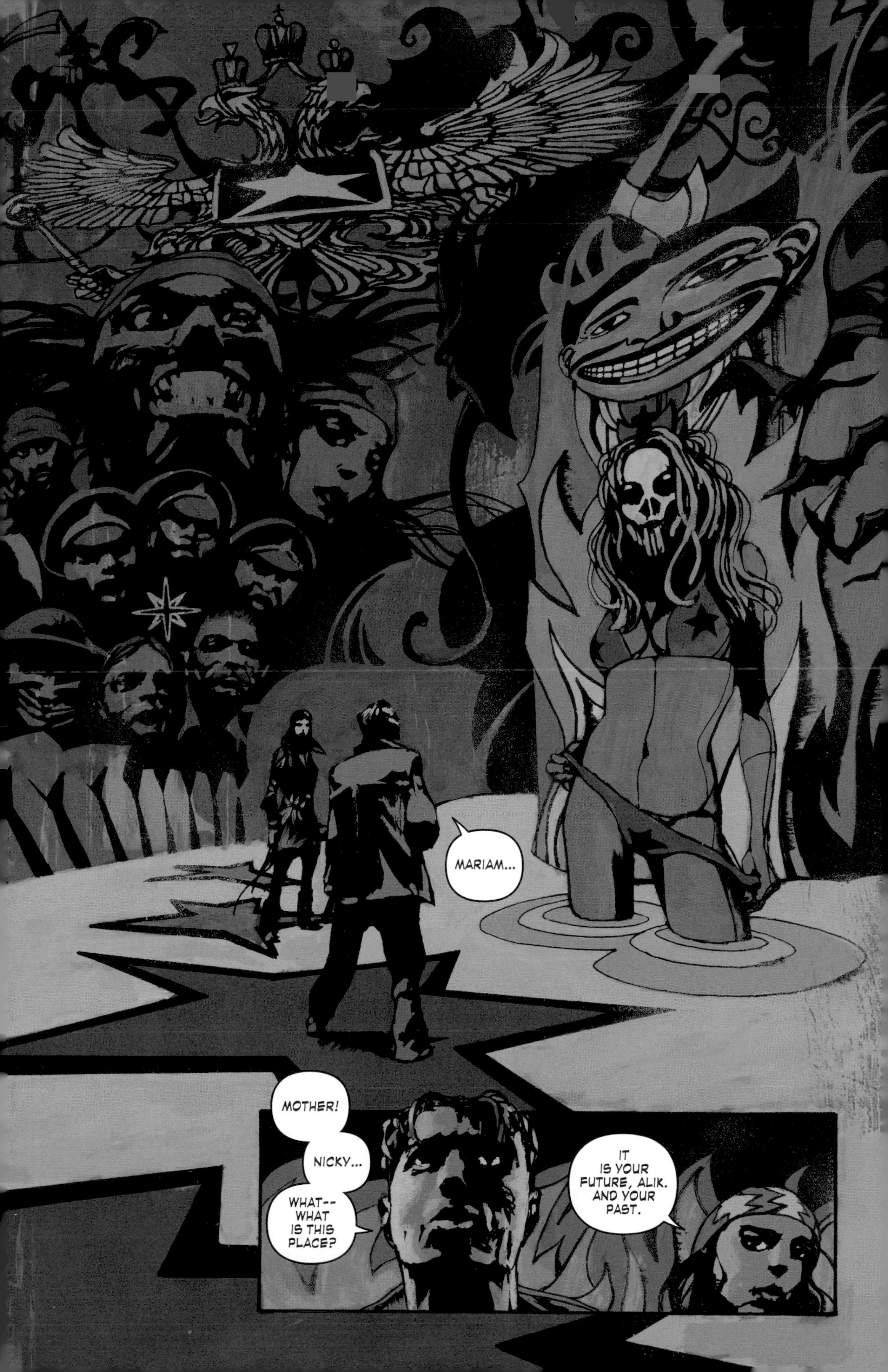
MARIAM...
MOTHER!
NICKY...
WHAT--
WHAT
IS THIS
PLACE?
IT
IS YOUR
FUTURE, ALIK.
AND YOUR
PAST.

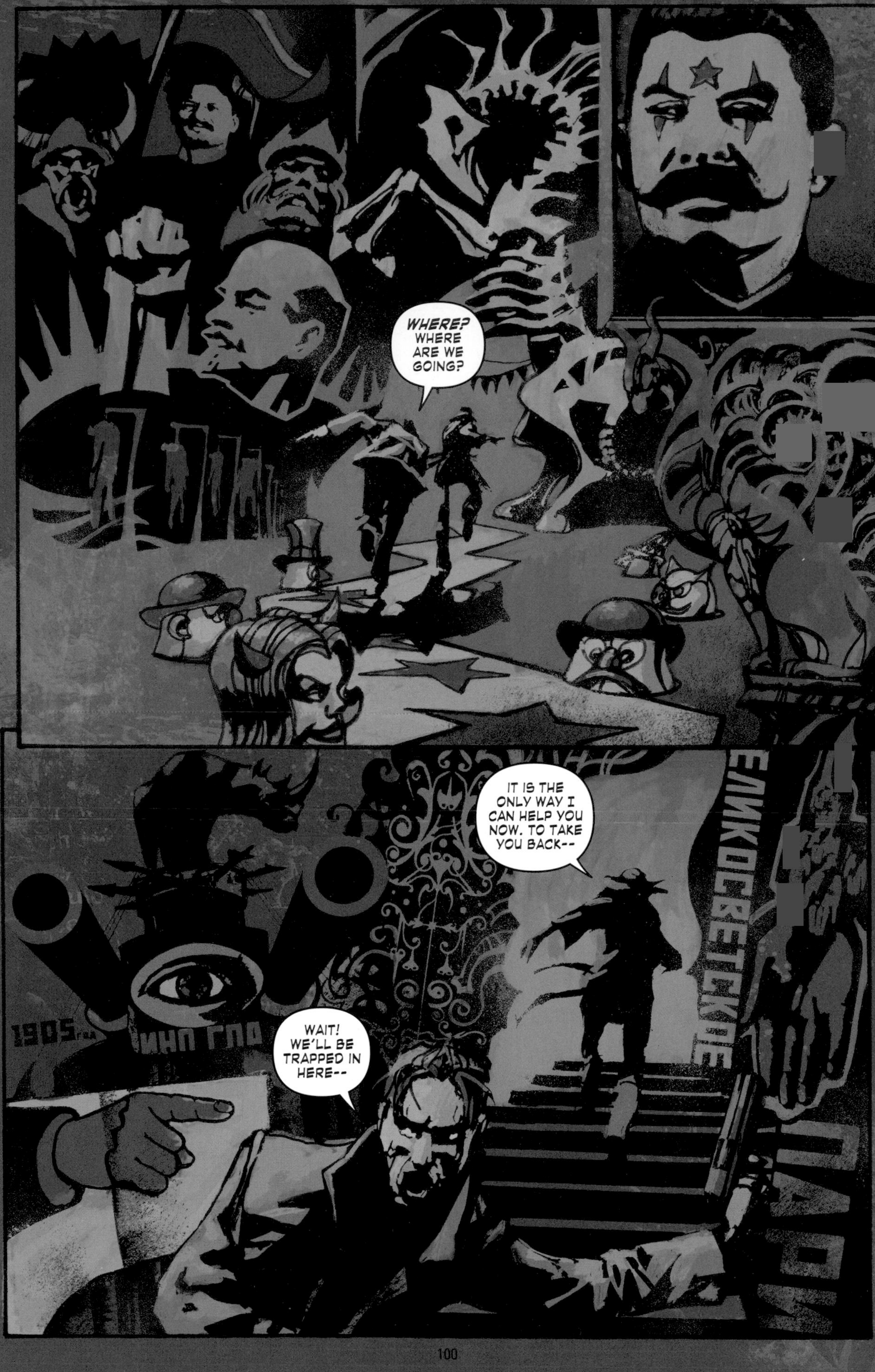
WHERE? WHERE ARE WE GOING?
IT IS THE ONLY WAY I CAN HELP YOU NOW. TO TAKE YOU BACK--
WAIT! WE'LL BE TRAPPED IN HERE--

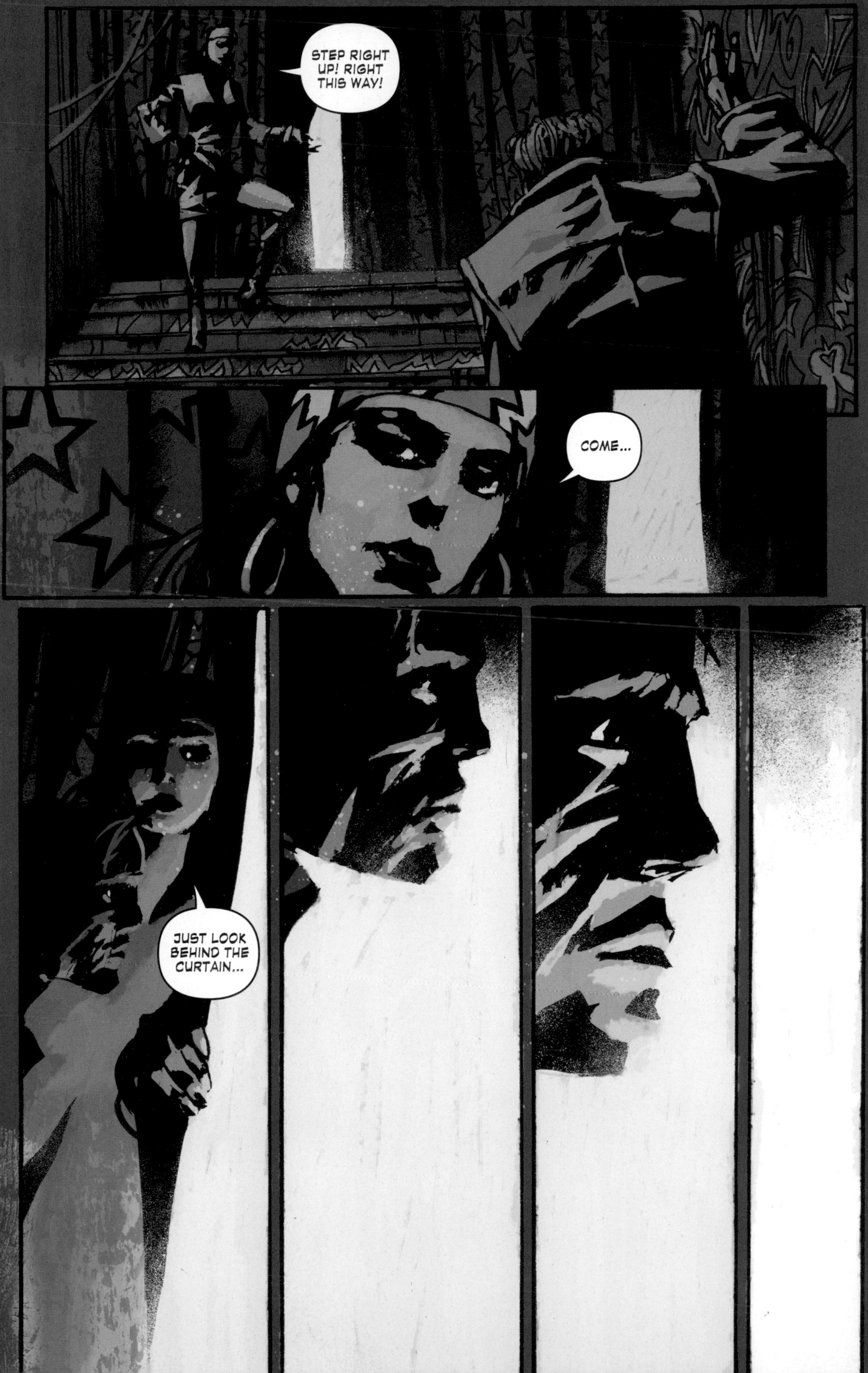
STEP RIGHT UP! RIGHT THIS WAY!
COME...
JUST LOOK BEHIND THE CURTAIN...

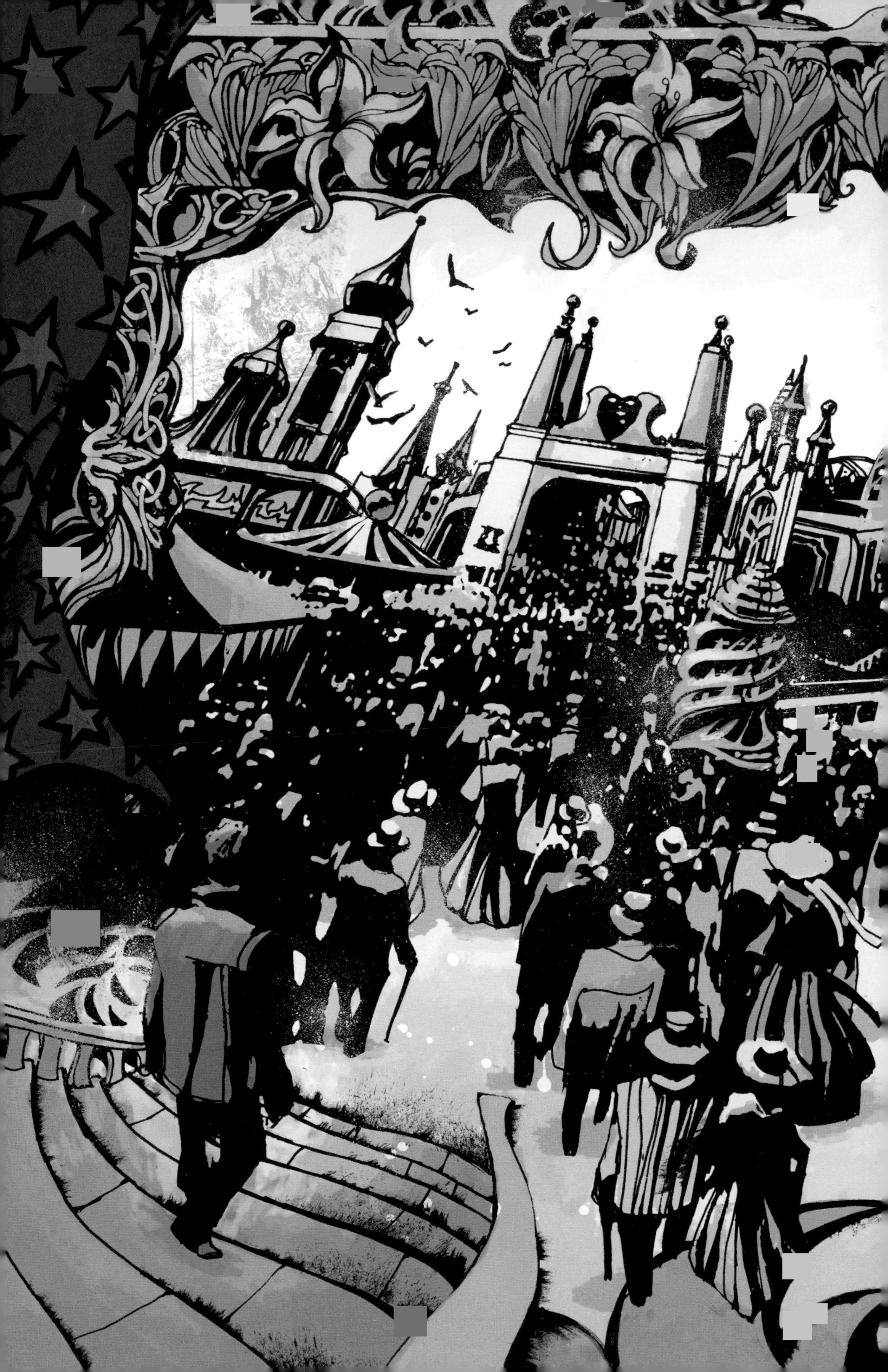

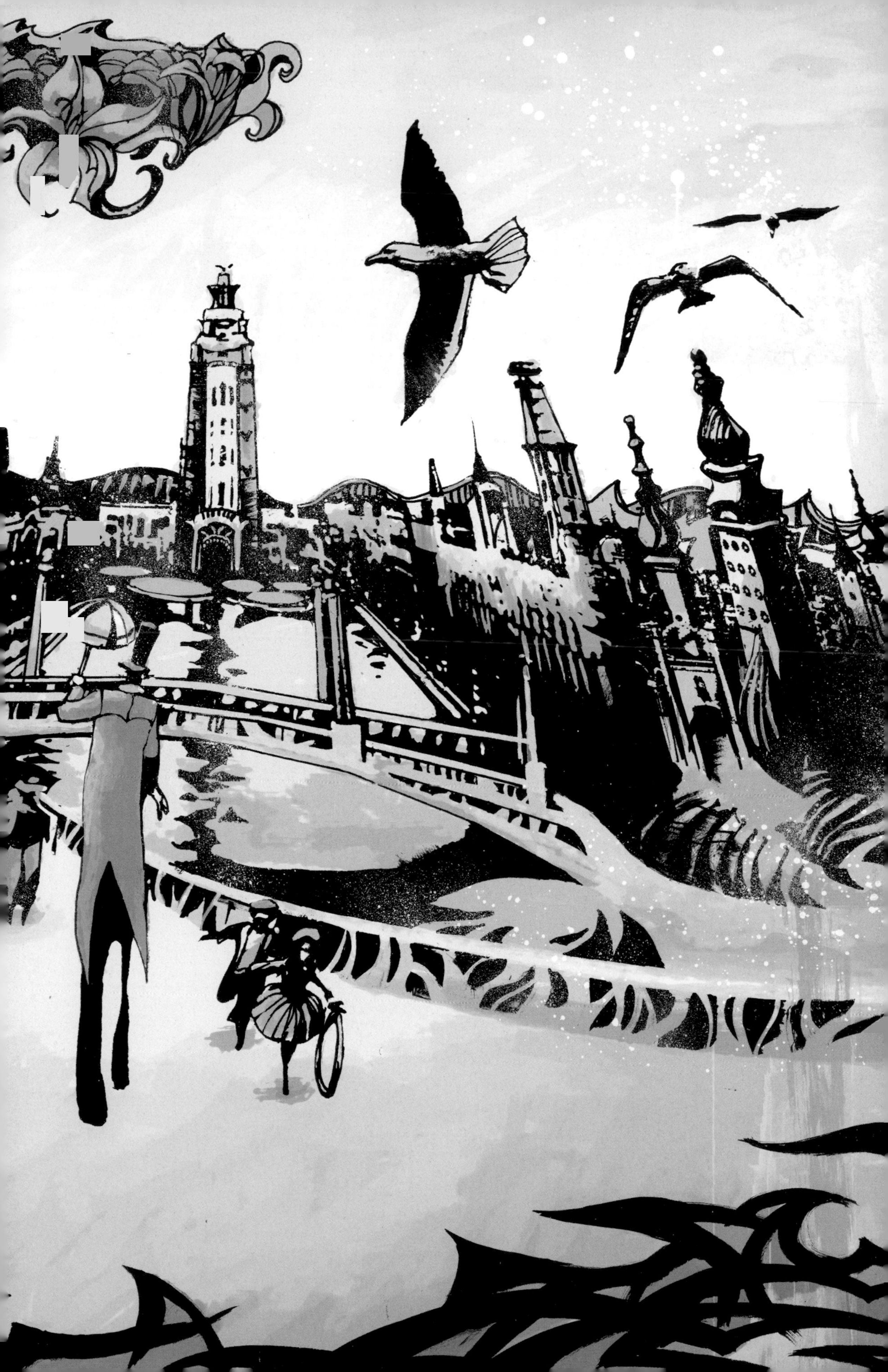

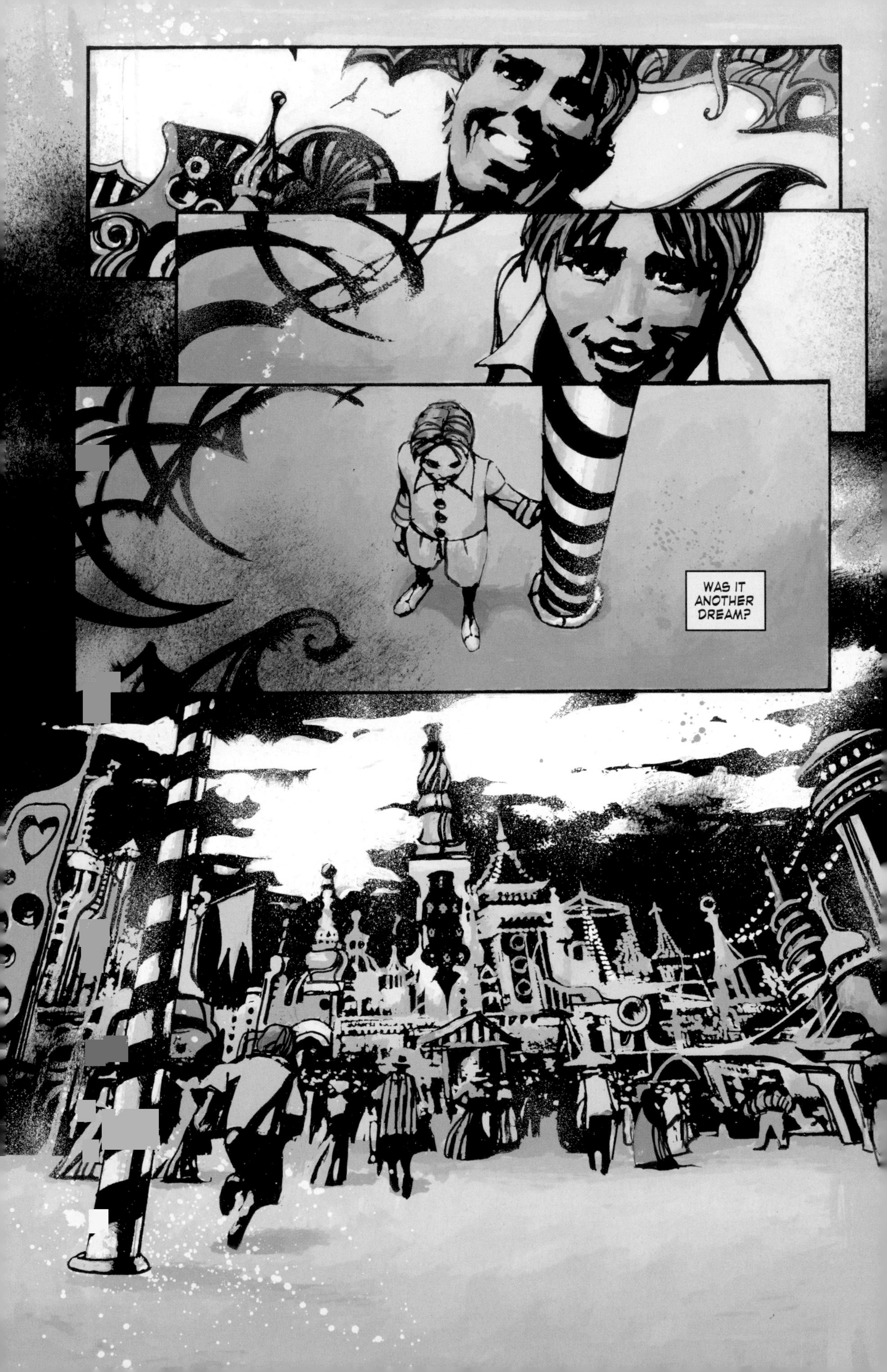
WAS IT ANOTHER DREAM?

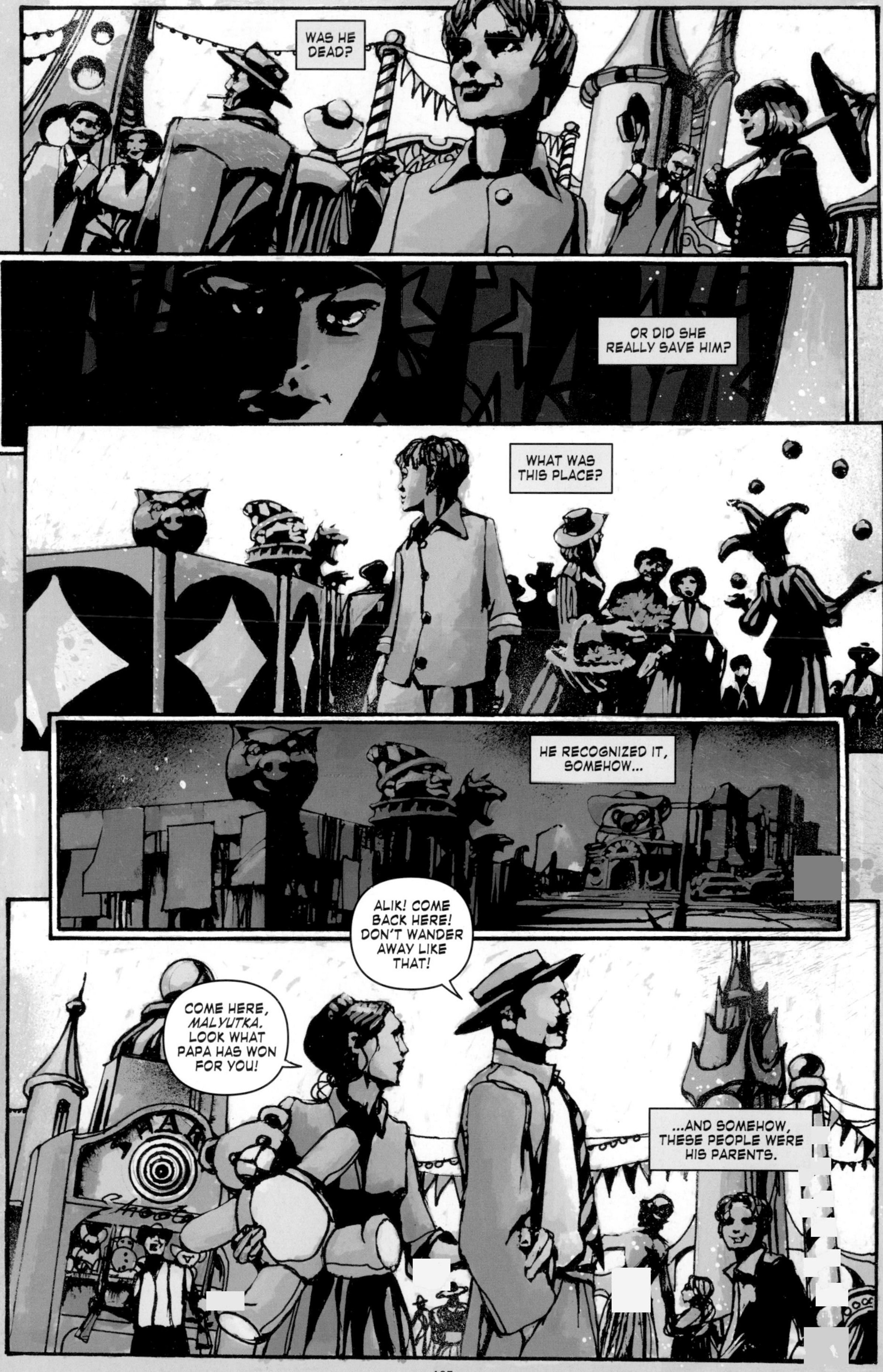
WAS HE DEAD?
OR DID SHE REALLY SAVE HIM?
WHAT WAS THIS PLACE?
HE RECOGNIZED IT, SOMEHOW...
ALIK! COME BACK HERE! DON'T WANDER AWAY LIKE THAT!
COME HERE, *MALYUTKA.* LOOK WHAT PAPA HAS WON FOR YOU!
...AND SOMEHOW, THESE PEOPLE WERE HIS PARENTS.

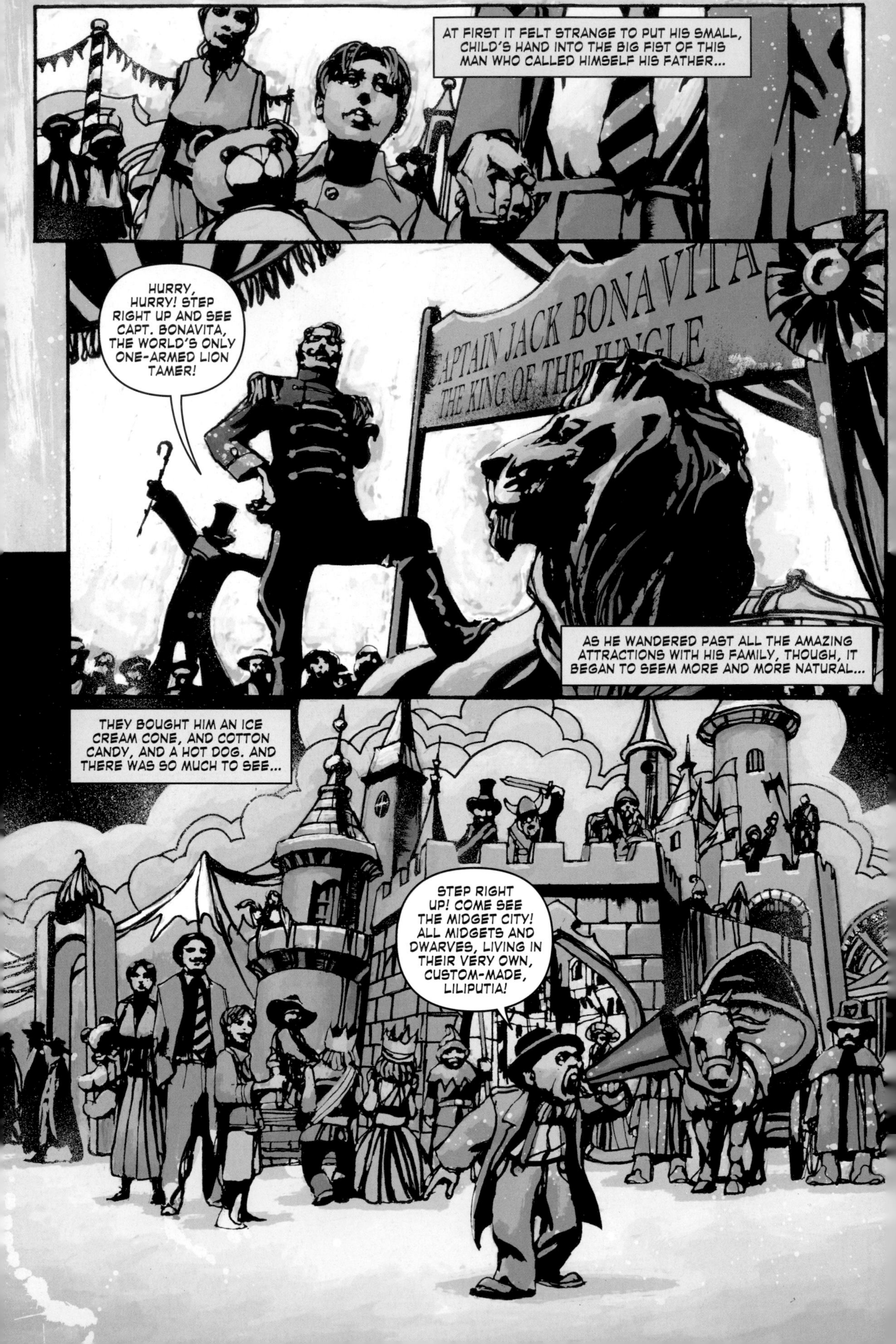
AT FIRST IT FELT STRANGE TO PUT HIS SMALL, CHILD'S HAND INTO THE BIG FIST OF THIS MAN WHO CALLED HIMSELF HIS FATHER...
HURRY, HURRY! STEP RIGHT UP AND SEE CAPT. BONAVITA, THE WORLD'S ONLY ONE-ARMED LION TAMER!
CAPTAIN JACK BONAVITA
THE KING OF THE
AS HE WANDERED PAST ALL THE AMAZING ATTRACTIONS WITH HIS FAMILY, THOUGH, IT BEGAN TO SEEM MORE AND MORE NATURAL...
THEY BOUGHT HIM AN ICE CREAM CONE, AND COTTON CANDY, AND A HOT DOG. AND THERE WAS SO MUCH TO SEE...
STEP RIGHT UP! COME SEE THE MIDGET CITY! ALL MIDGETS AND DWARVES, LIVING IN THEIR VERY OWN, CUSTOM-MADE, LILIPUTIA!

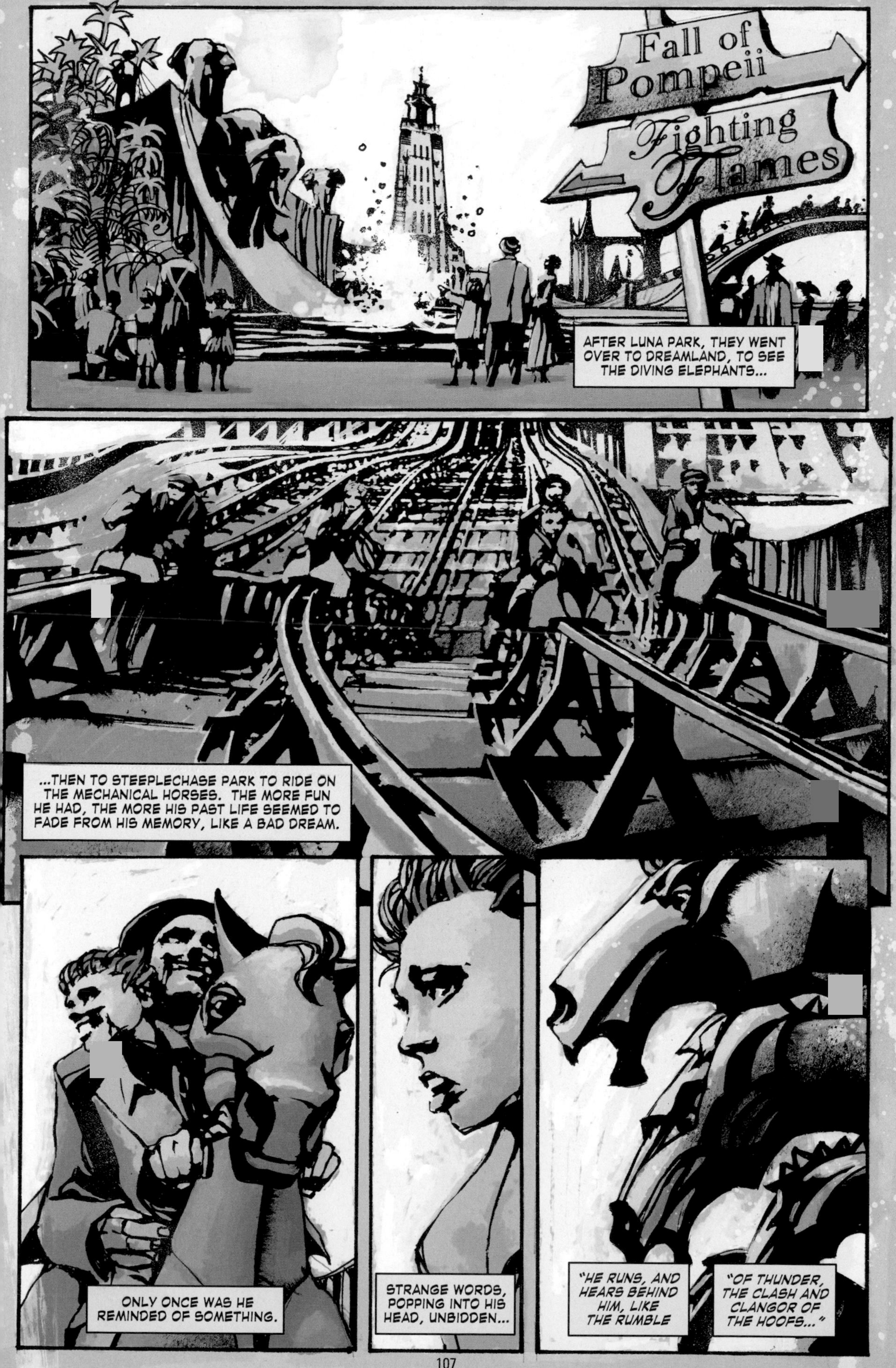
Fall of Pompeii
Fighting Flames
AFTER LUNA PARK, THEY WENT OVER TO DREAMLAND, TO SEE THE DIVING ELEPHANTS...
...THEN TO STEEPLECHASE PARK TO RIDE ON THE MECHANICAL HORSES. THE MORE FUN HE HAD, THE MORE HIS PAST LIFE SEEMED TO FADE FROM HIS MEMORY, LIKE A BAD DREAM.
ONLY ONCE WAS HE REMINDED OF SOMETHING.
STRANGE WORDS, POPPING INTO HIS HEAD, UNBIDDEN...
"HE RUNS, AND HEARS BEHIND HIM, LIKE THE RUMBLE
"OF THUNDER, THE CLASH AND CLANGOR OF THE HOOFS..."

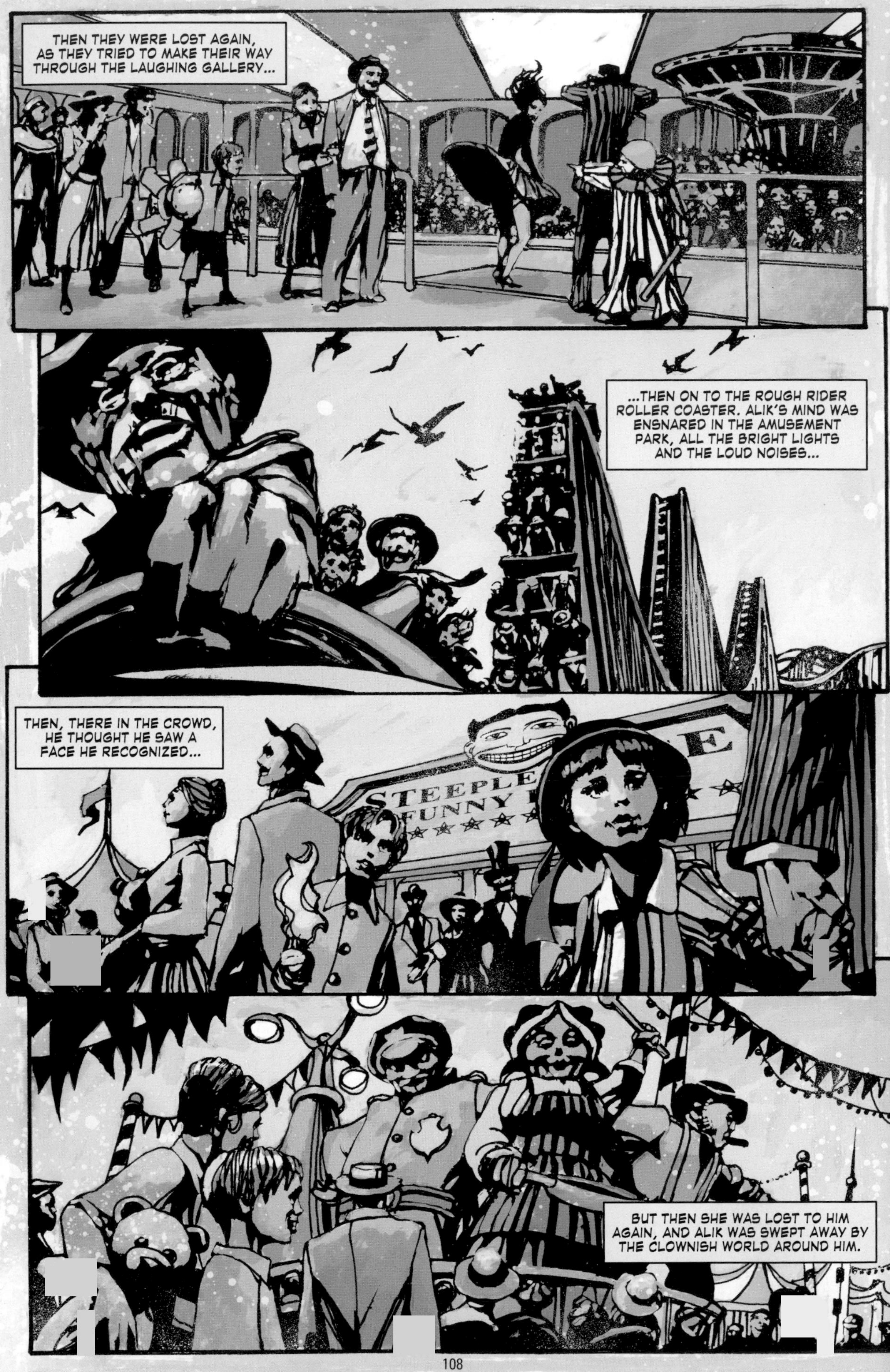
THEN THEY WERE LOST AGAIN, AS THEY TRIED TO MAKE THEIR WAY THROUGH THE LAUGHING GALLERY...
...THEN ON TO THE ROUGH RIDER ROLLER COASTER. ALIK'S MIND WAS ENSNARED IN THE AMUSEMENT PARK, ALL THE BRIGHT LIGHTS AND THE LOUD NOISES...
THEN, THERE IN THE CROWD, HE THOUGHT HE SAW A FACE HE RECOGNIZED...
BUT THEN SHE WAS LOST TO HIM AGAIN, AND ALIK WAS SWEPT AWAY BY THE CLOWNISH WORLD AROUND HIM.

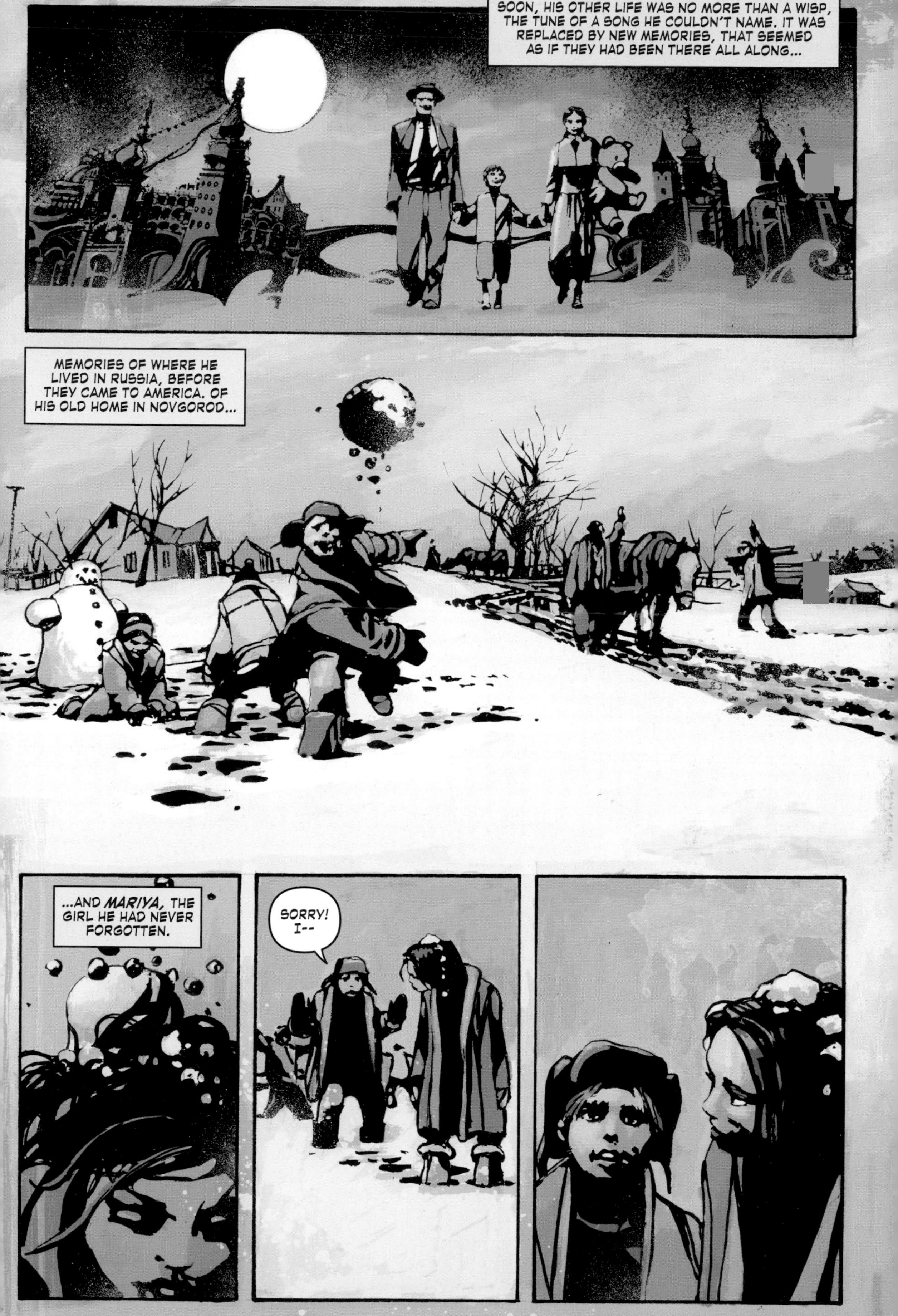
SOON, HIS OTHER LIFE WAS NO MORE THAN A WISP, THE TUNE OF A SONG HE COULDN'T NAME. IT WAS REPLACED BY NEW MEMORIES, THAT SEEMED AS IF THEY HAD BEEN THERE ALL ALONG...
MEMORIES OF WHERE HE LIVED IN RUSSIA, BEFORE THEY CAME TO AMERICA. OF HIS OLD HOME IN NOVGOROD...
...AND *MARIYA,* THE GIRL HE HAD NEVER FORGOTTEN.
SORRY! I--

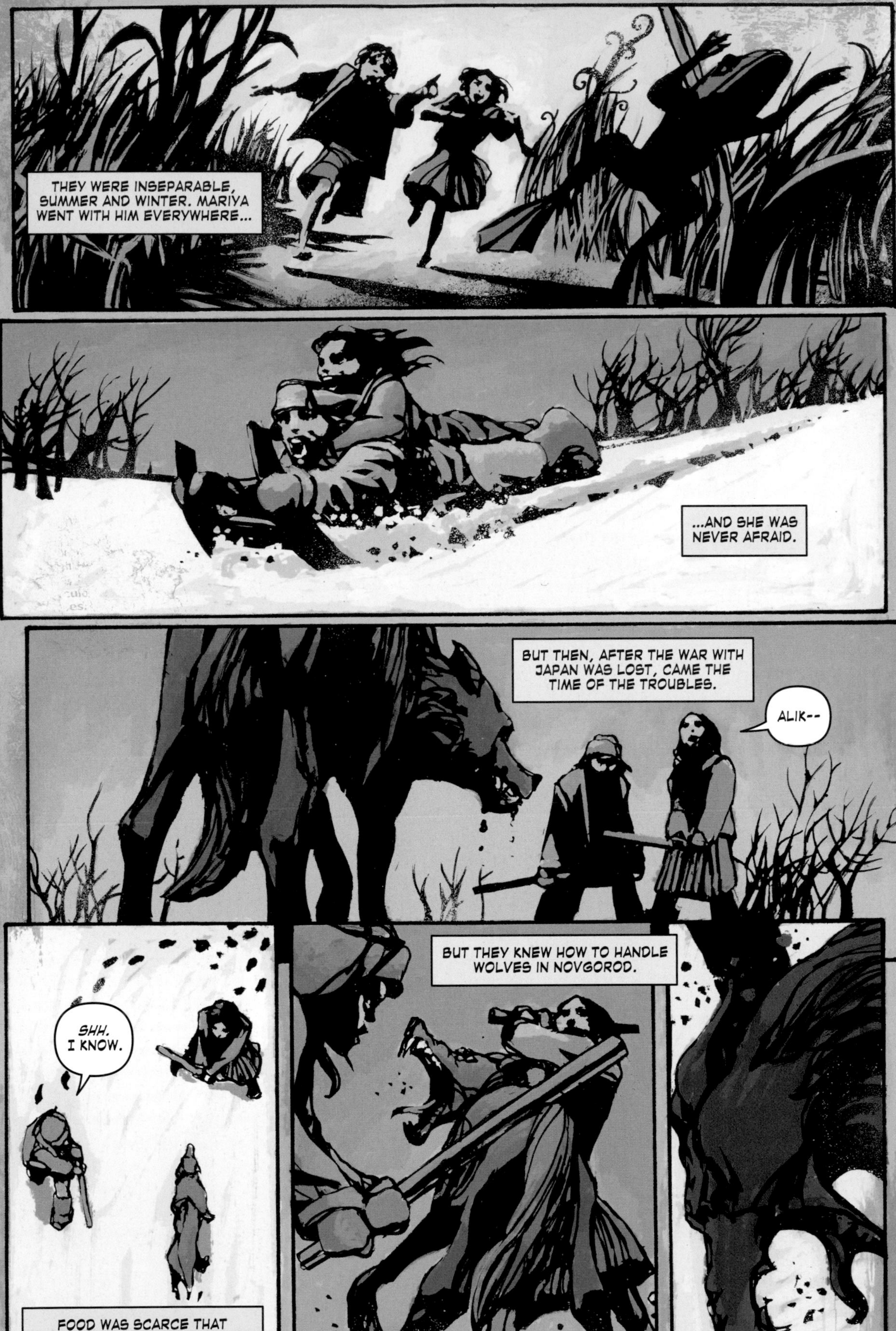
THEY WERE INSEPARABLE, SUMMER AND WINTER. MARIYA WENT WITH HIM EVERYWHERE...
...AND SHE WAS NEVER AFRAID.
BUT THEN, AFTER THE WAR WITH JAPAN WAS LOST, CAME THE TIME OF THE TROUBLES.
ALIK--
SHH. I KNOW.
FOOD WAS SCARCE THAT WINTER, AND WOLVES PROWLED AROUND THE VILLAGE.
BUT THEY KNEW HOW TO HANDLE WOLVES IN NOVGOROD.

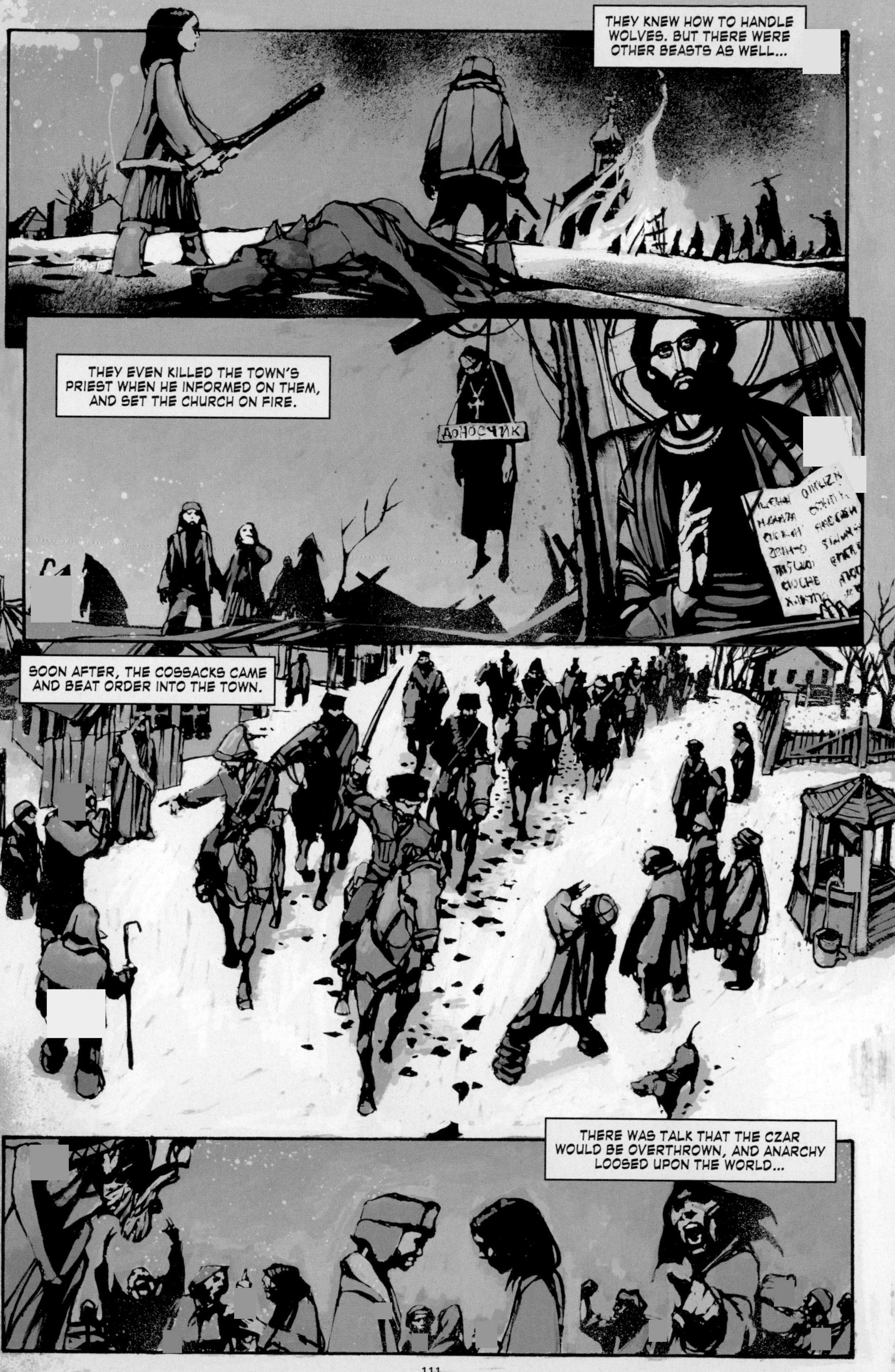
THEY KNEW HOW TO HANDLE WOLVES. BUT THERE WERE OTHER BEASTS AS WELL...
THEY EVEN KILLED THE TOWN'S PRIEST WHEN HE INFORMED ON THEM, AND SET THE CHURCH ON FIRE.
ДОНОСЧИК
SOON AFTER, THE COSSACKS CAME AND BEAT ORDER INTO THE TOWN.
THERE WAS TALK THAT THE CZAR WOULD BE OVERTHROWN, AND ANARCHY LOOSED UPON THE WORLD...

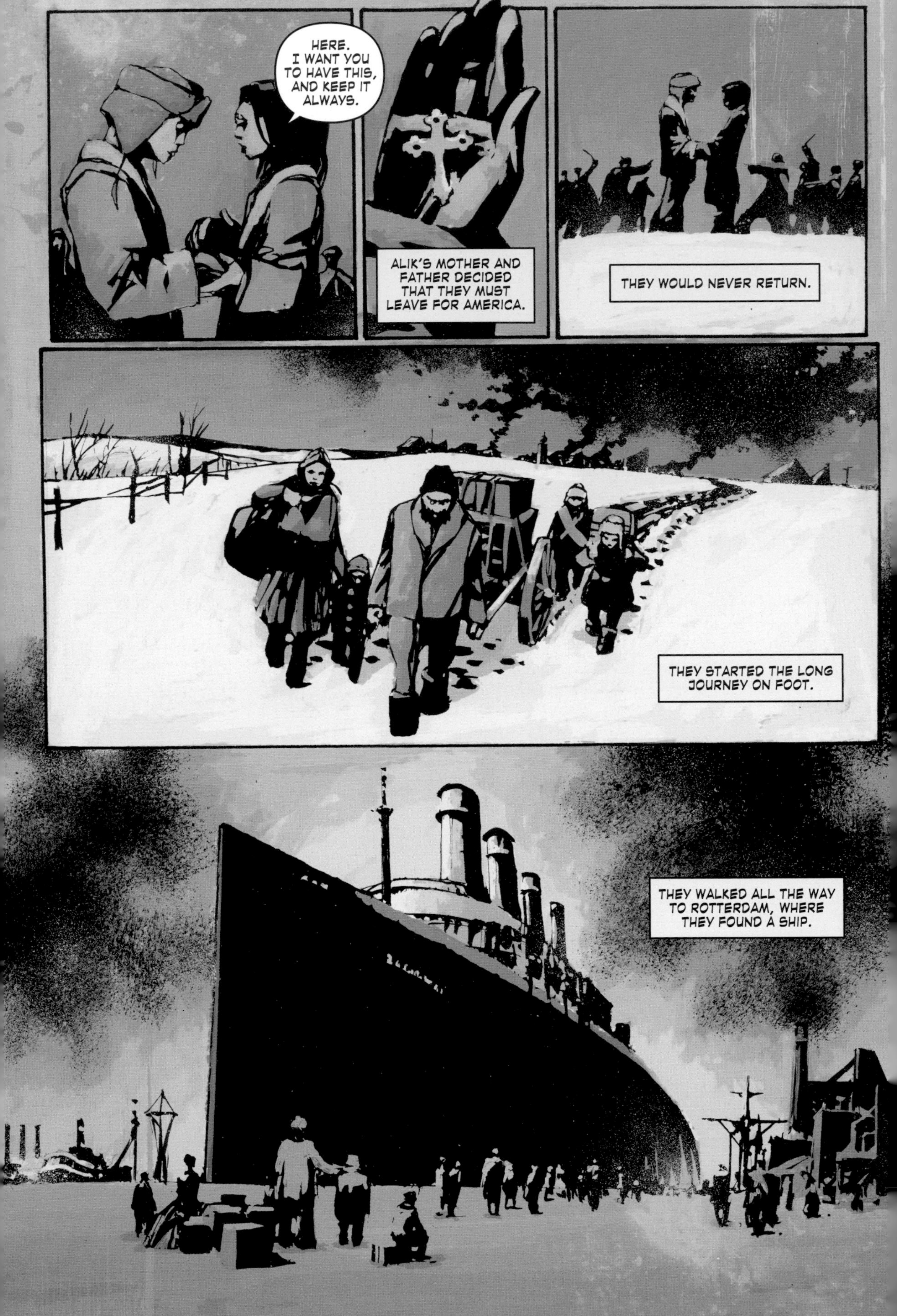
HERE. I WANT YOU TO HAVE THIS, AND KEEP IT ALWAYS.
ALIK'S MOTHER AND FATHER DECIDED THAT THEY MUST LEAVE FOR AMERICA.
THEY WOULD NEVER RETURN.
THEY STARTED THE LONG JOURNEY ON FOOT.
THEY WALKED ALL THE WAY TO ROTTERDAM, WHERE THEY FOUND A SHIP.

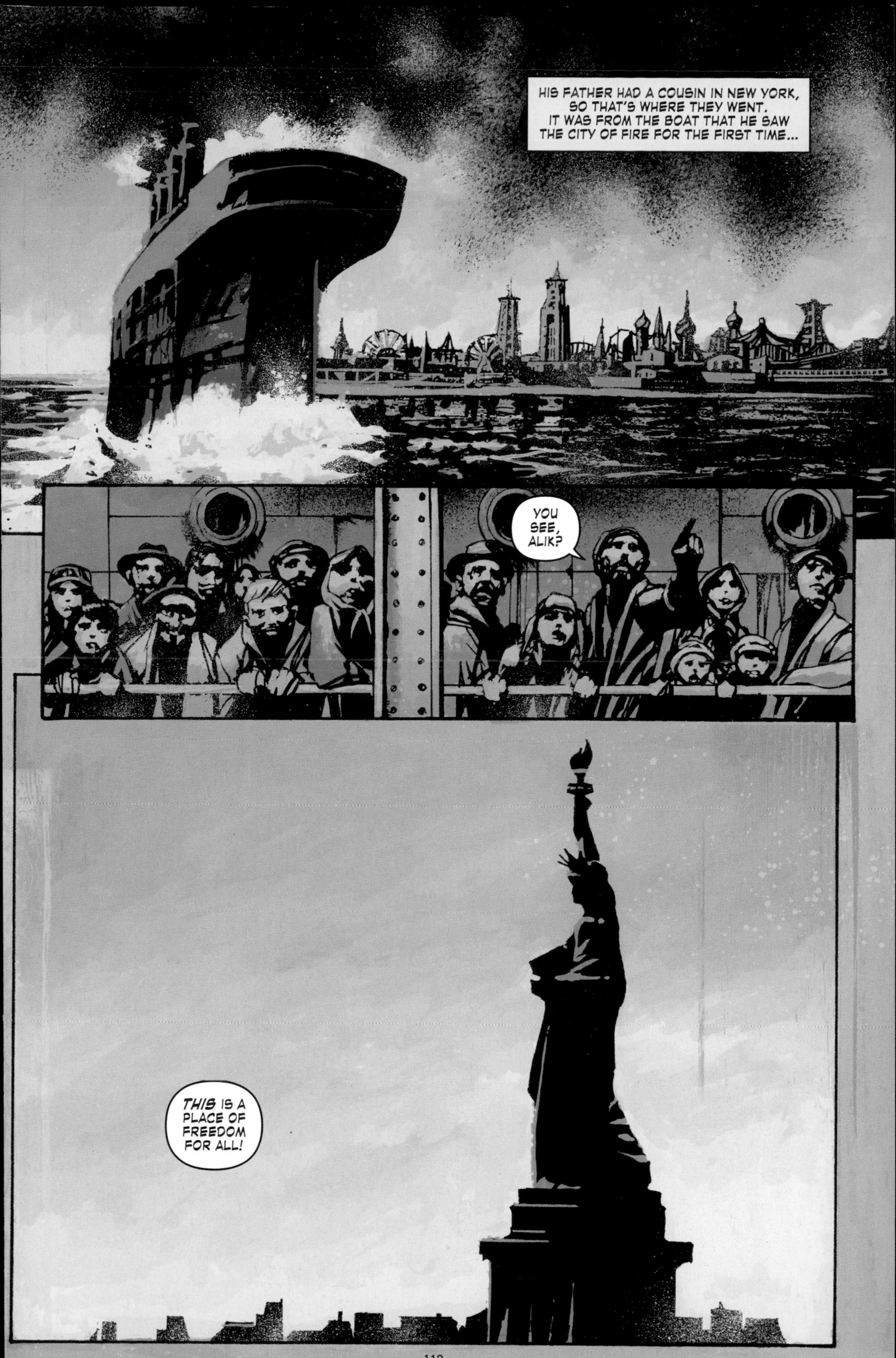
HIS FATHER HAD A COUSIN IN NEW YORK, SO THAT'S WHERE THEY WENT. IT WAS FROM THE BOAT THAT HE SAW THE CITY OF FIRE FOR THE FIRST TIME...
YOU SEE, ALIK?
*THIS* IS A PLACE OF FREEDOM FOR ALL!

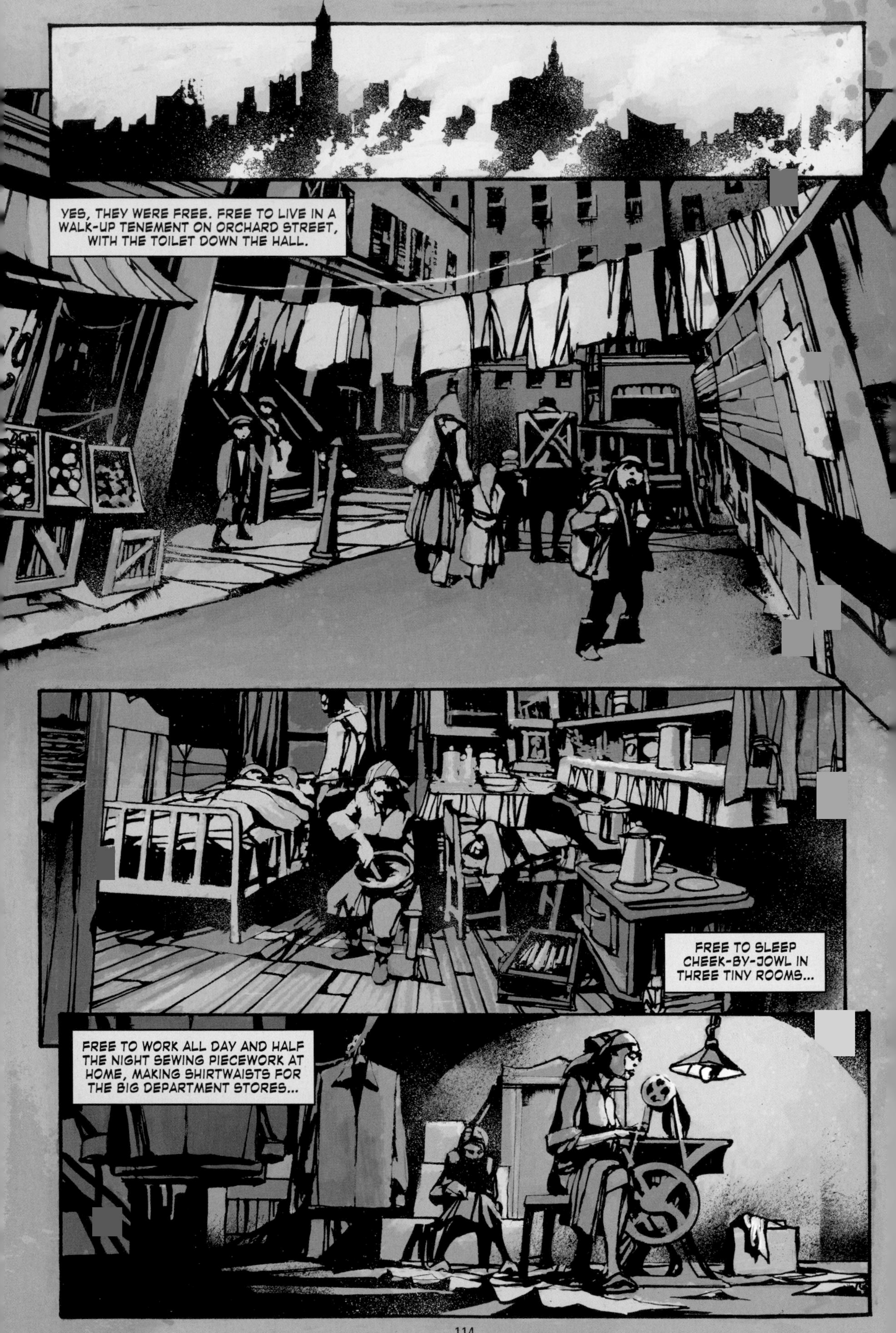
YES, THEY WERE FREE. FREE TO LIVE IN A WALK-UP TENEMENT ON ORCHARD STREET, WITH THE TOILET DOWN THE HALL.
FREE TO SLEEP CHEEK-BY-JOWL IN THREE TINY ROOMS...
FREE TO WORK ALL DAY AND HALF THE NIGHT SEWING PIECEWORK AT HOME, MAKING SHIRTWAISTS FOR THE BIG DEPARTMENT STORES...

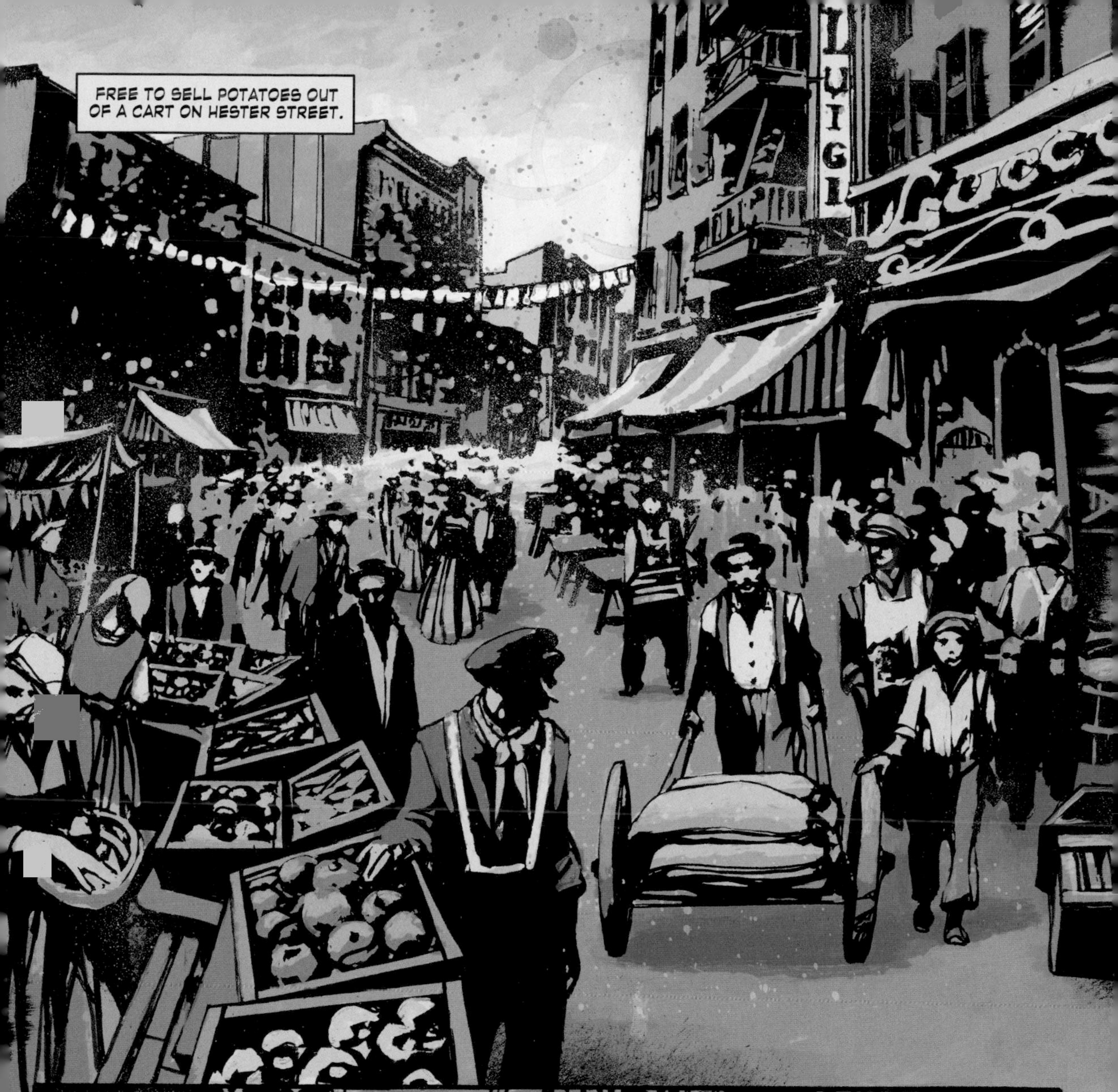
FREE TO SELL POTATOES OUT OF A CART ON HESTER STREET.
LUIGI

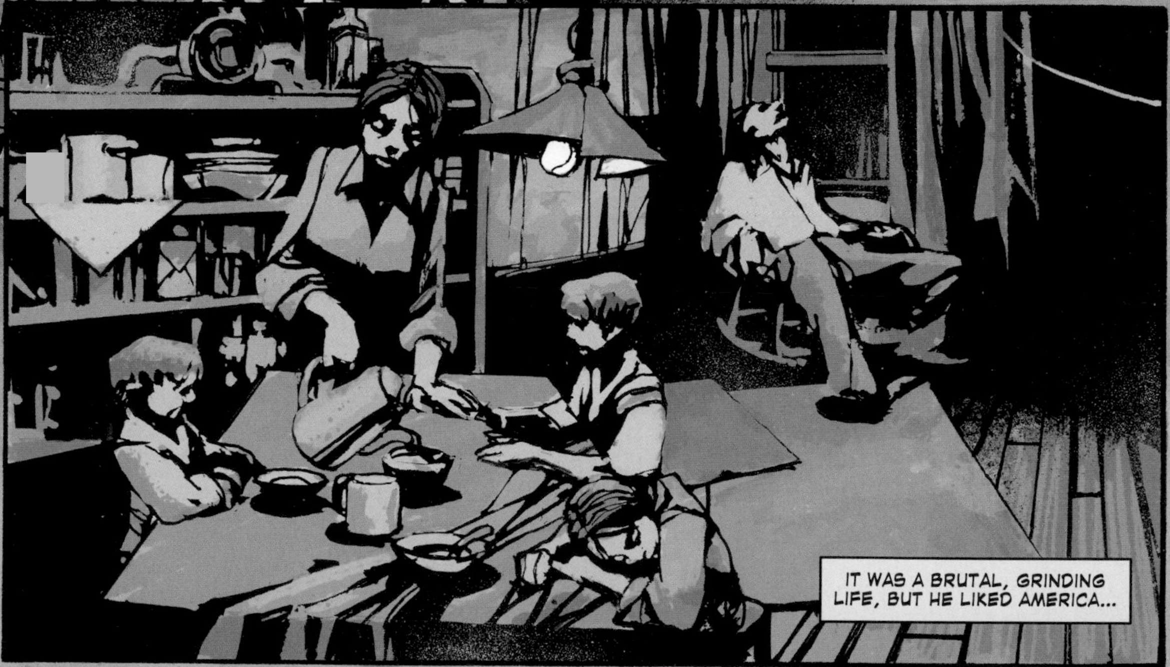
IT WAS A BRUTAL, GRINDING LIFE, BUT HE LIKED AMERICA...

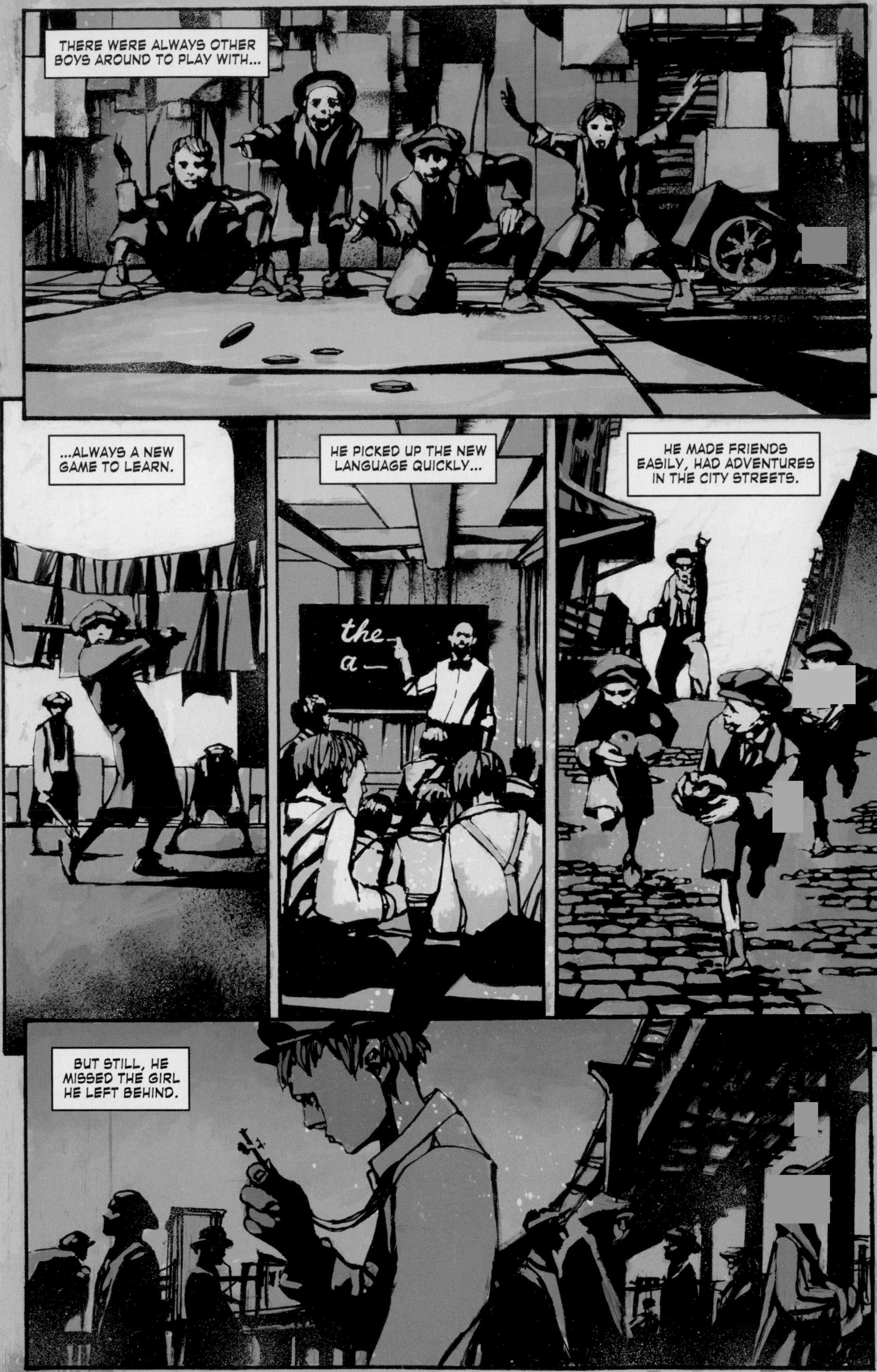
THERE WERE ALWAYS OTHER BOYS AROUND TO PLAY WITH...
...ALWAYS A NEW GAME TO LEARN.
HE PICKED UP THE NEW LANGUAGE QUICKLY...
the
a
HE MADE FRIENDS EASILY, HAD ADVENTURES IN THE CITY STREETS.
BUT STILL, HE MISSED THE GIRL HE LEFT BEHIND.

THEIR LIFE WAS NOT ALL WORK.

SOMETIMES HIS FATHER TOOK HIM ALL THE WAY UP TO THE POLO GROUNDS, TO WATCH THE GIANTS PLAY.

HE LIKED GOING TO DREAMLAND, AND STEALING LOOKS AT THE GIANT BREASTS OF THE ANGEL WHO GUARDED THE PARK'S ENTRANCE...

AND HE LIKED ALL THE WILD RIDES OVER AT STEEPLECHASE.

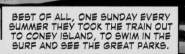

BEST OF ALL, ONE SUNDAY EVERY SUMMER THEY TOOK THE TRAIN OUT TO CONEY ISLAND, TO SWIM IN THE SURF AND SEE THE GREAT PARKS.

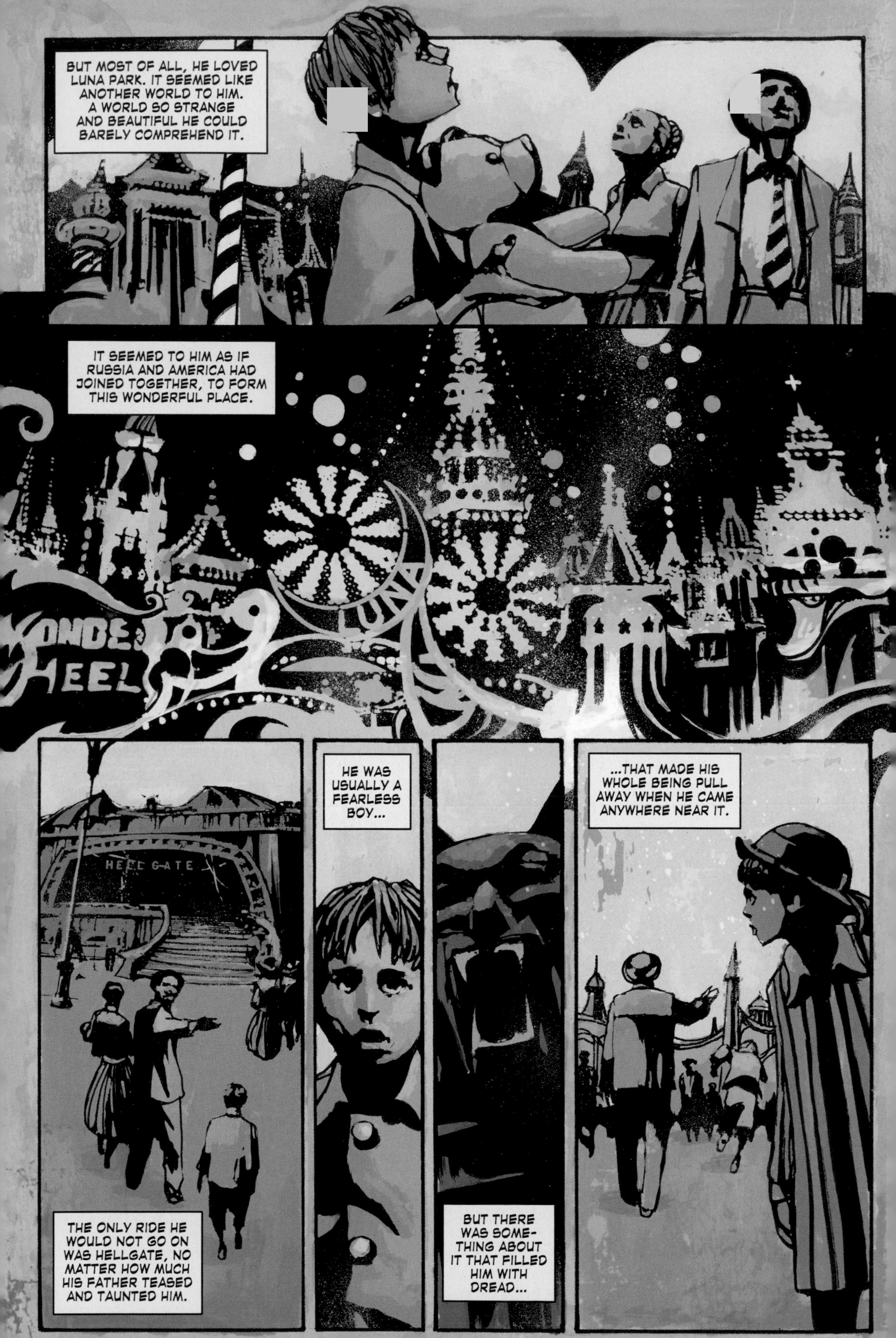
BUT MOST OF ALL, HE LOVED LUNA PARK. IT SEEMED LIKE ANOTHER WORLD TO HIM. A WORLD SO STRANGE AND BEAUTIFUL HE COULD BARELY COMPREHEND IT.
IT SEEMED TO HIM AS IF RUSSIA AND AMERICA HAD JOINED TOGETHER, TO FORM THIS WONDERFUL PLACE.
LUNA
HELLGATE
THE ONLY RIDE HE WOULD NOT GO ON WAS HELLGATE, NO MATTER HOW MUCH HIS FATHER TEASED AND TAUNTED HIM.
HE WAS USUALLY A FEARLESS BOY...
BUT THERE WAS SOME-THING ABOUT IT THAT FILLED HIM WITH DREAD...
...THAT MADE HIS WHOLE BEING PULL AWAY WHEN HE CAME ANYWHERE NEAR IT.

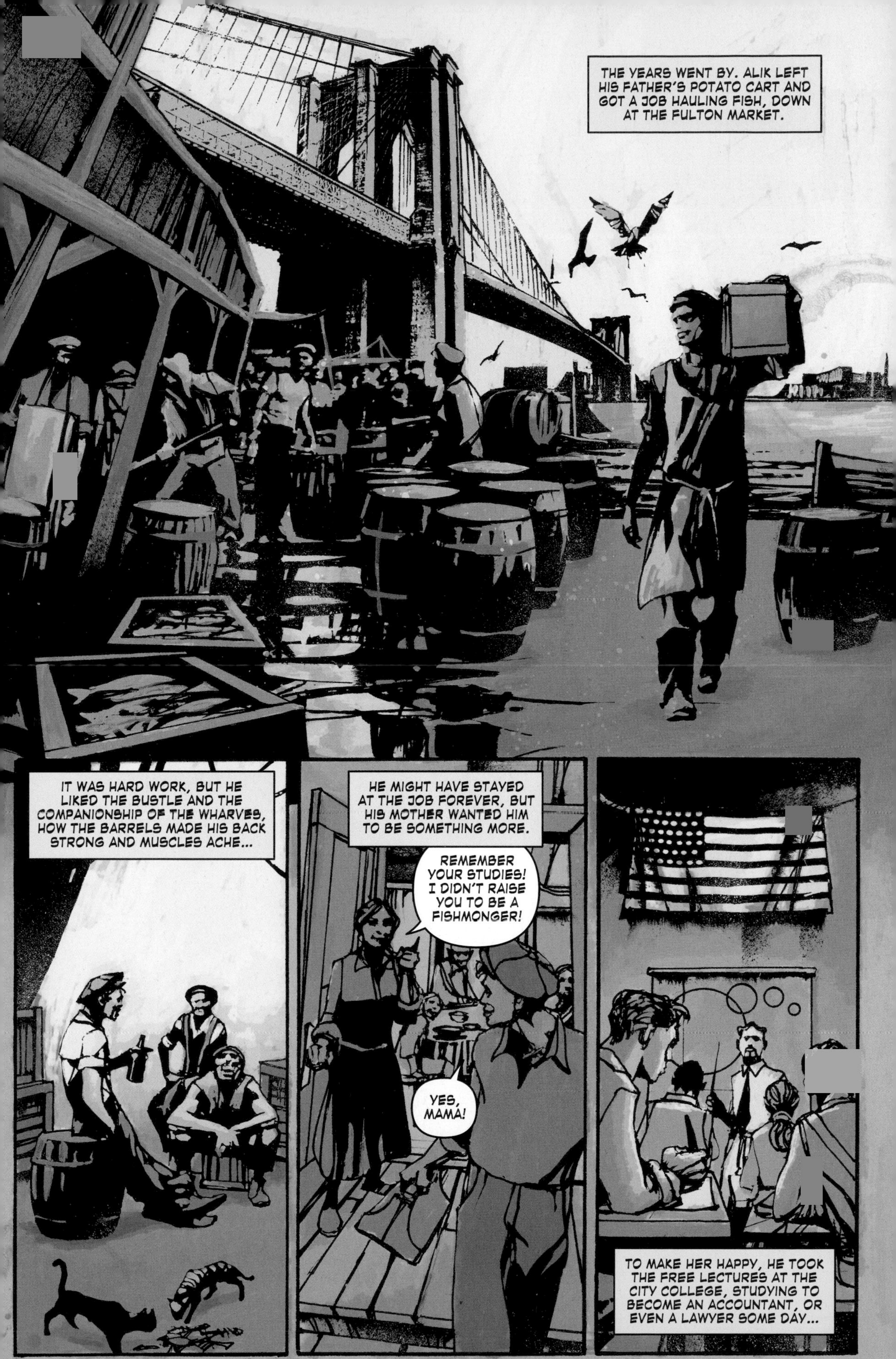
THE YEARS WENT BY. ALIK LEFT HIS FATHER'S POTATO CART AND GOT A JOB HAULING FISH, DOWN AT THE FULTON MARKET.
IT WAS HARD WORK, BUT HE LIKED THE BUSTLE AND THE COMPANIONSHIP OF THE WHARVES, HOW THE BARRELS MADE HIS BACK STRONG AND MUSCLES ACHE...
HE MIGHT HAVE STAYED AT THE JOB FOREVER, BUT HIS MOTHER WANTED HIM TO BE SOMETHING MORE.
REMEMBER YOUR STUDIES! I DIDN'T RAISE YOU TO BE A FISHMONGER!
YES, MAMA!
TO MAKE HER HAPPY, HE TOOK THE FREE LECTURES AT THE CITY COLLEGE, STUDYING TO BECOME AN ACCOUNTANT, OR EVEN A LAWYER SOME DAY...

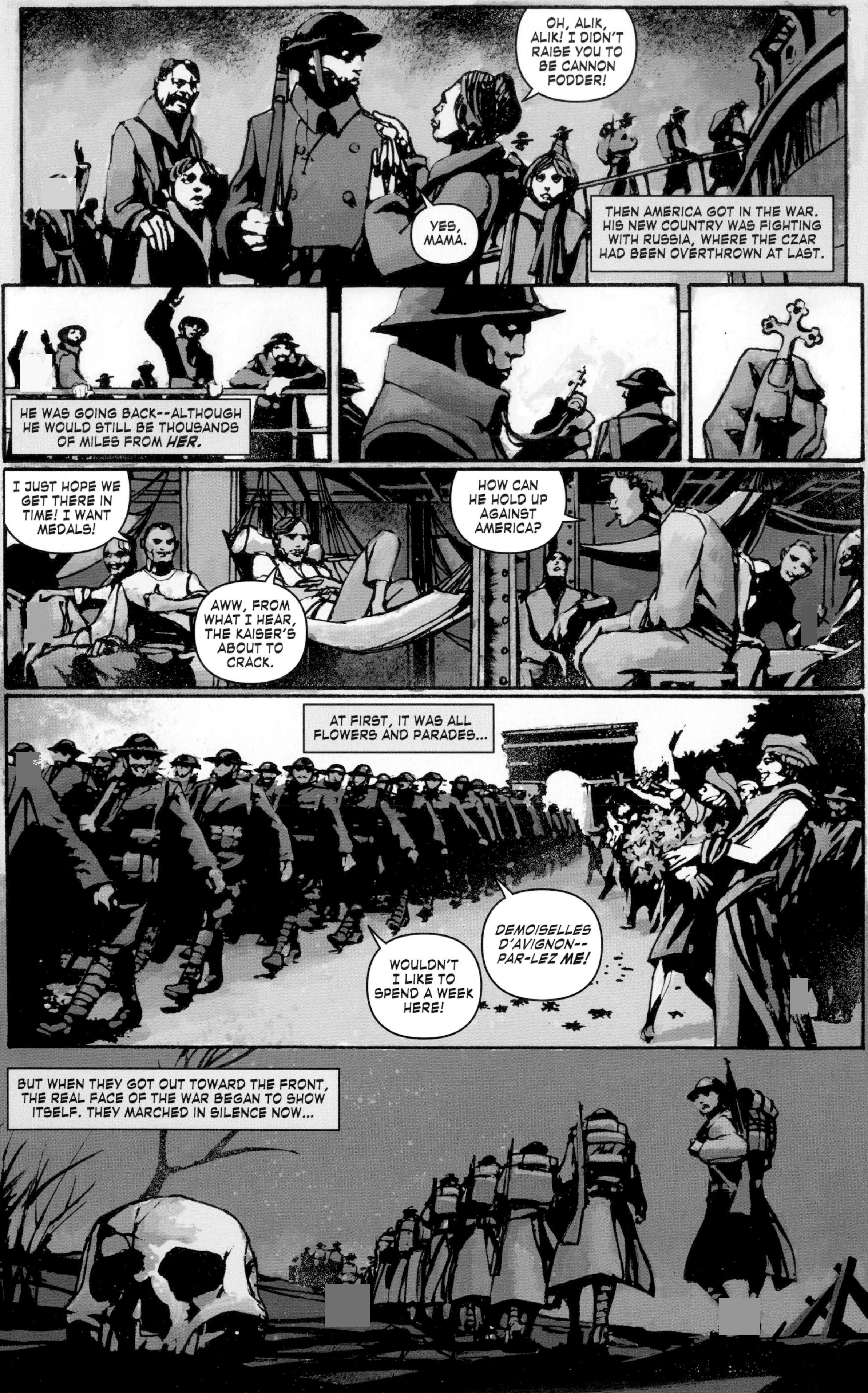
OH, ALIK, ALIK! I DIDN'T RAISE YOU TO BE CANNON FODDER!
YES, MAMA.
THEN AMERICA GOT IN THE WAR. HIS NEW COUNTRY WAS FIGHTING WITH RUSSIA, WHERE THE CZAR HAD BEEN OVERTHROWN AT LAST.
HE WAS GOING BACK--ALTHOUGH HE WOULD STILL BE THOUSANDS OF MILES FROM *HER.*
I JUST HOPE WE GET THERE IN TIME! I WANT MEDALS!
AWW, FROM WHAT I HEAR, THE KAISER'S ABOUT TO CRACK.
HOW CAN HE HOLD UP AGAINST AMERICA?
AT FIRST, IT WAS ALL FLOWERS AND PARADES...
*DEMOISELLES D'AVIGNON-- PAR-LEZ* ***ME!***
WOULDN'T I LIKE TO SPEND A WEEK HERE!
BUT WHEN THEY GOT OUT TOWARD THE FRONT, THE REAL FACE OF THE WAR BEGAN TO SHOW ITSELF. THEY MARCHED IN SILENCE NOW...

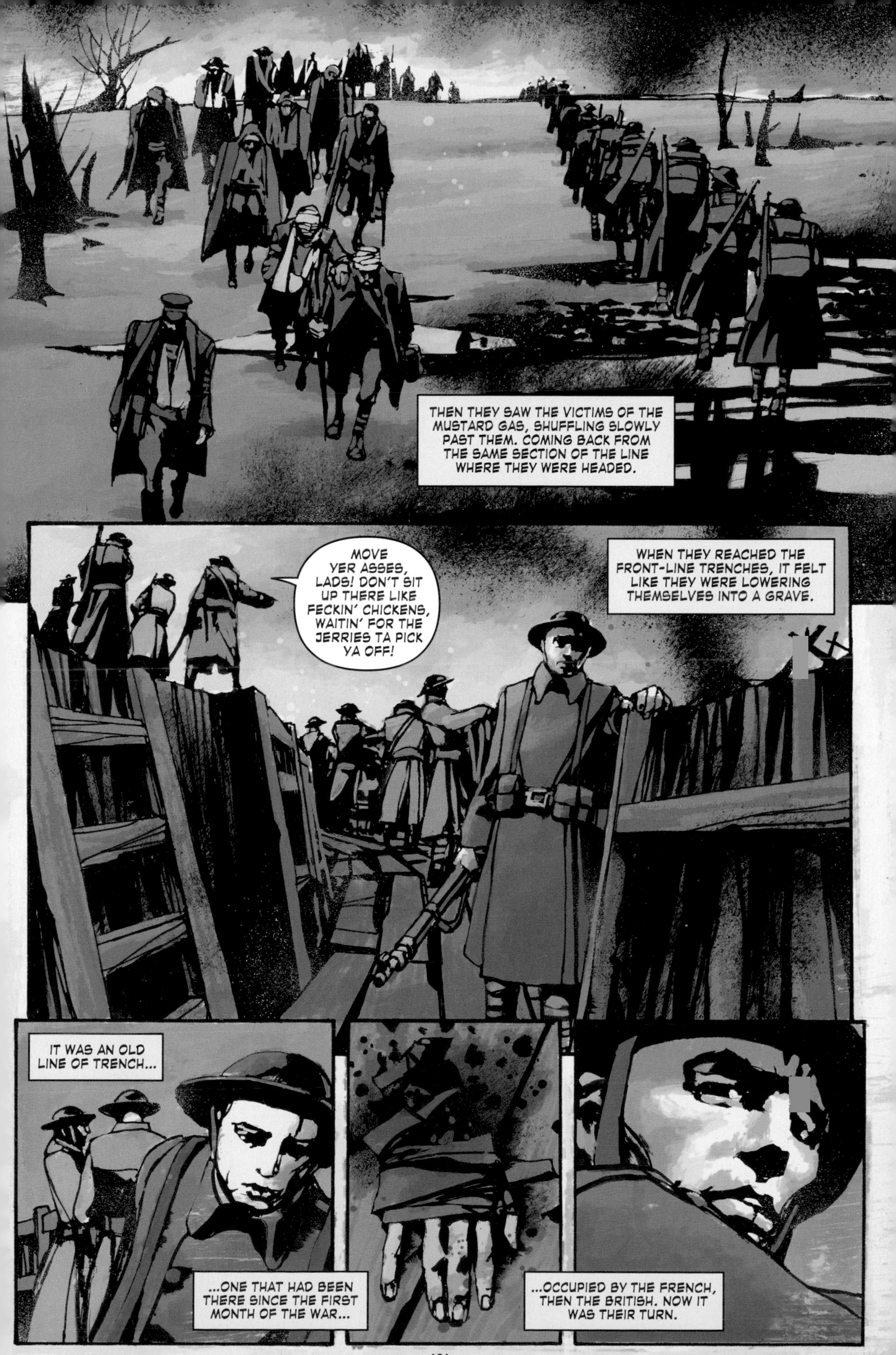
THEN THEY SAW THE VICTIMS OF THE MUSTARD GAS, SHUFFLING SLOWLY PAST THEM. COMING BACK FROM THE SAME SECTION OF THE LINE WHERE THEY WERE HEADED.
WHEN THEY REACHED THE FRONT-LINE TRENCHES, IT FELT LIKE THEY WERE LOWERING THEMSELVES INTO A GRAVE.
MOVE YER ASSES, LADS! DON'T SIT UP THERE LIKE FECKIN' CHICKENS, WAITIN' FOR THE JERRIES TA PICK YA OFF!
IT WAS AN OLD LINE OF TRENCH...
...ONE THAT HAD BEEN THERE SINCE THE FIRST MONTH OF THE WAR...
...OCCUPIED BY THE FRENCH, THEN THE BRITISH. NOW IT WAS THEIR TURN.

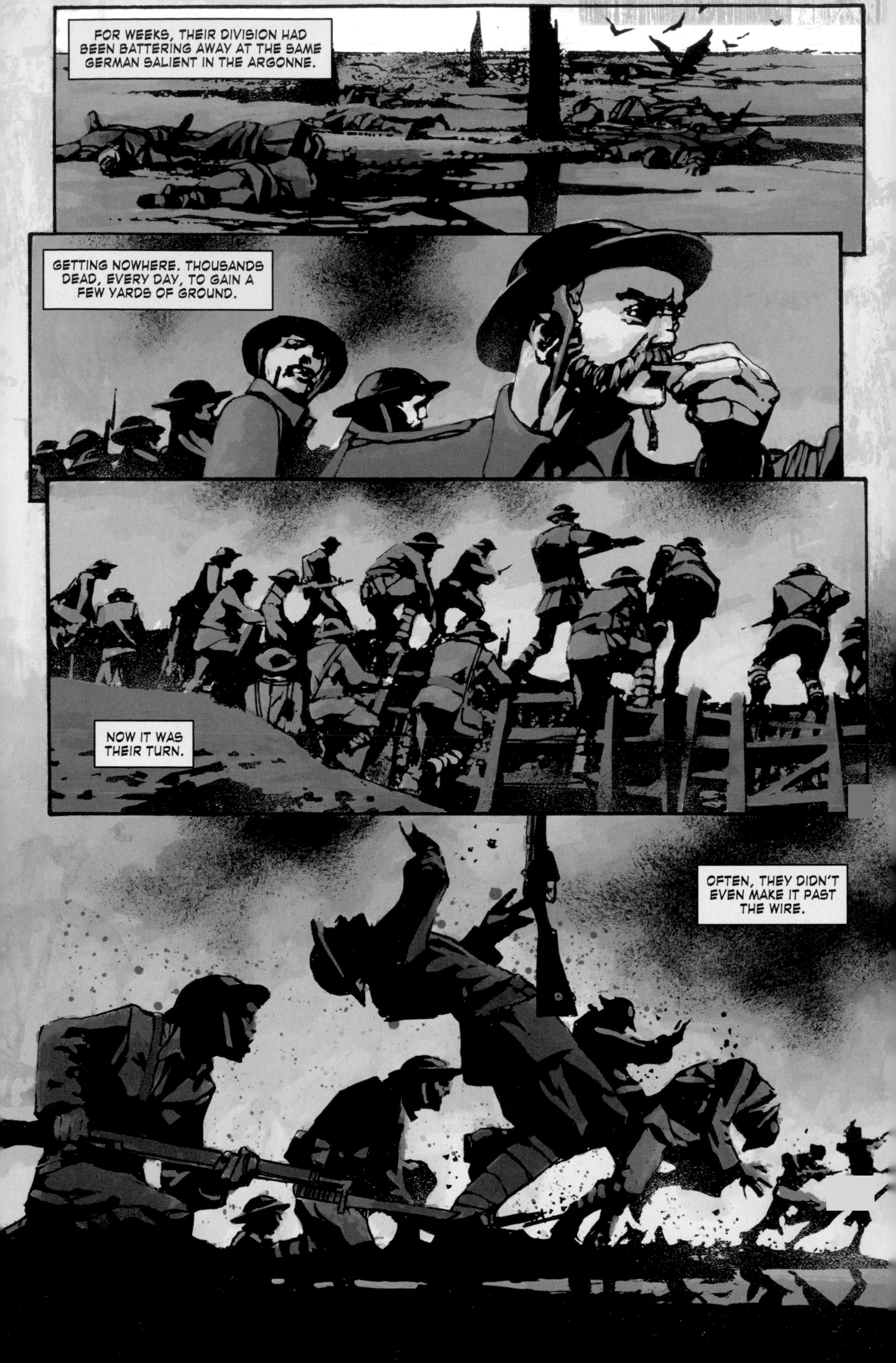
FOR WEEKS, THEIR DIVISION HAD BEEN BATTERING AWAY AT THE SAME GERMAN SALIENT IN THE ARGONNE.
GETTING NOWHERE. THOUSANDS DEAD, EVERY DAY, TO GAIN A FEW YARDS OF GROUND.
NOW IT WAS THEIR TURN.
OFTEN, THEY DIDN'T EVEN MAKE IT PAST THE WIRE.

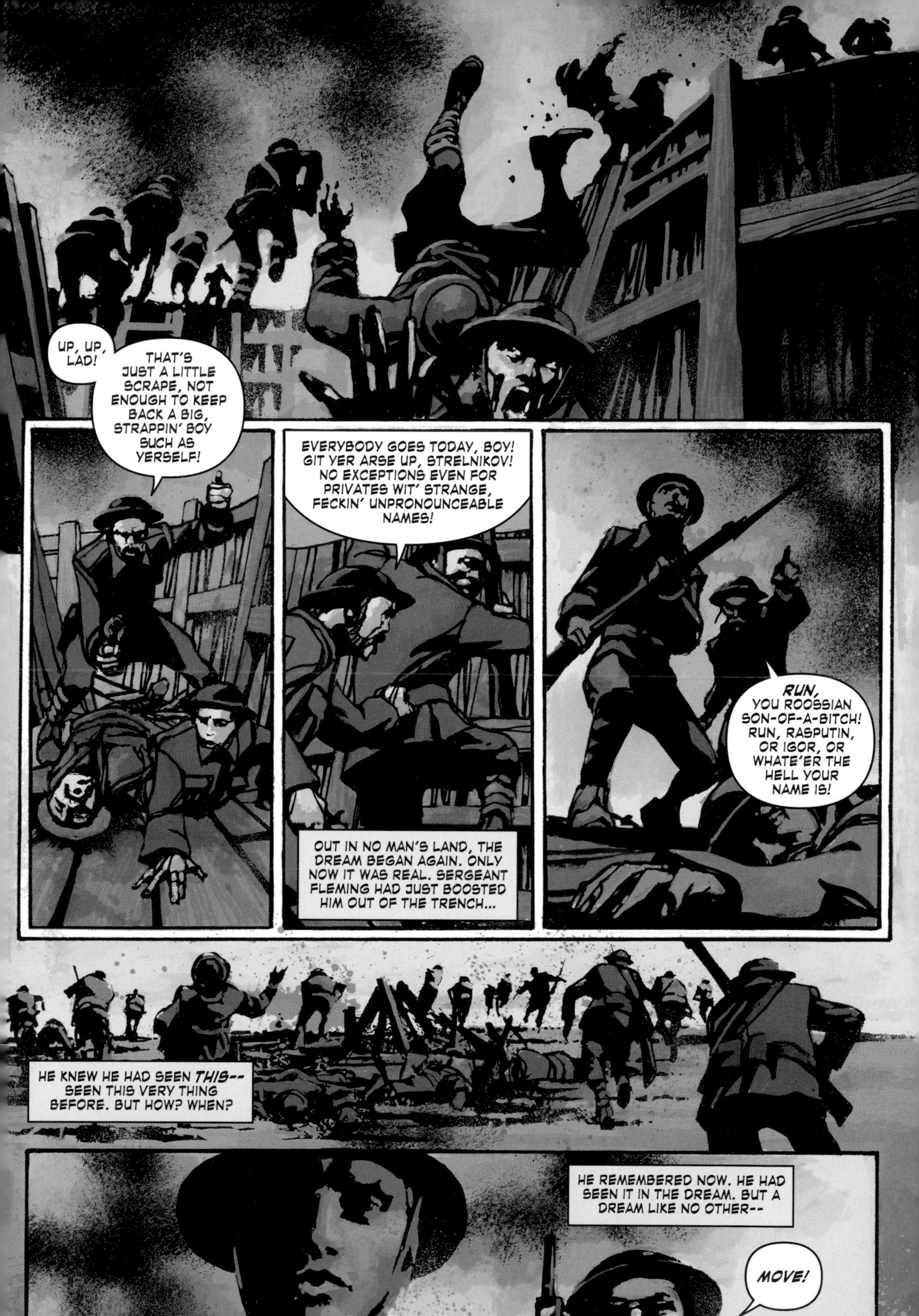
UP, UP, LAD!
THAT'S JUST A LITTLE SCRAPE, NOT ENOUGH TO KEEP BACK A BIG, STRAPPIN' BOY SUCH AS YERSELF!
EVERYBODY GOES TODAY, BOY! GIT YER ARSE UP, STRELNIKOV! NO EXCEPTIONS EVEN FOR PRIVATES WIT' STRANGE, FECKIN' UNPRONOUNCEABLE NAMES!
OUT IN NO MAN'S LAND, THE DREAM BEGAN AGAIN. ONLY NOW IT WAS REAL. SERGEANT FLEMING HAD JUST BOOSTED HIM OUT OF THE TRENCH...
RUN, YOU ROOSSIAN SON-OF-A-BITCH! RUN, RASPUTIN, OR IGOR, OR WHATE'ER THE HELL YOUR NAME IS!
HE KNEW HE HAD SEEN THIS-- SEEN THIS VERY THING BEFORE. BUT HOW? WHEN?
HE REMEMBERED NOW. HE HAD SEEN IT IN THE DREAM. BUT A DREAM LIKE NO OTHER--
MOVE!

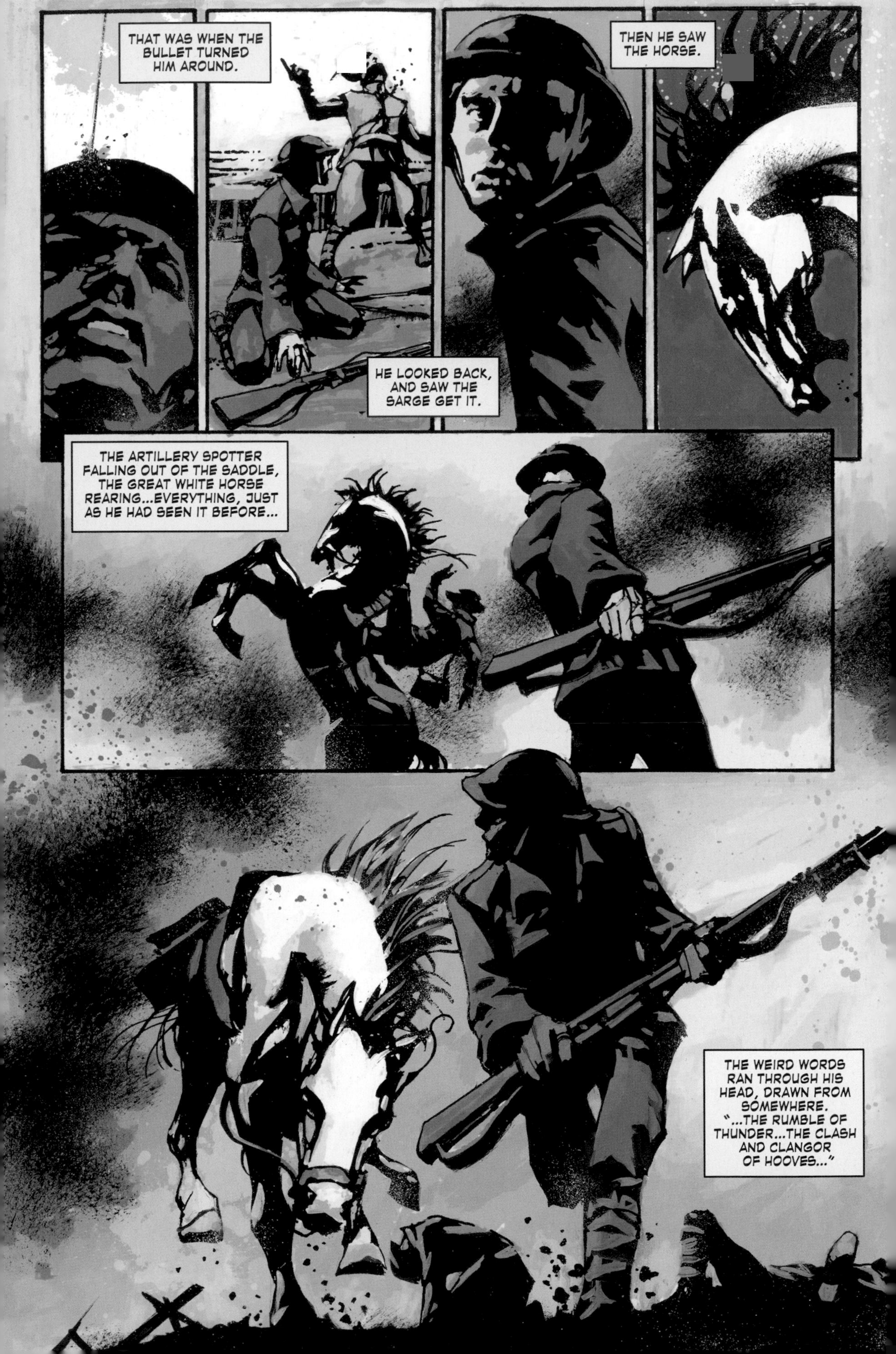
THAT WAS WHEN THE BULLET TURNED HIM AROUND.
HE LOOKED BACK, AND SAW THE SARGE GET IT.
THEN HE SAW THE HORSE.
THE ARTILLERY SPOTTER FALLING OUT OF THE SADDLE, THE GREAT WHITE HORSE REARING...EVERYTHING, JUST AS HE HAD SEEN IT BEFORE...
THE WEIRD WORDS RAN THROUGH HIS HEAD, DRAWN FROM SOMEWHERE. "...THE RUMBLE OF THUNDER...THE CLASH AND CLANGOR OF HOOVES..."

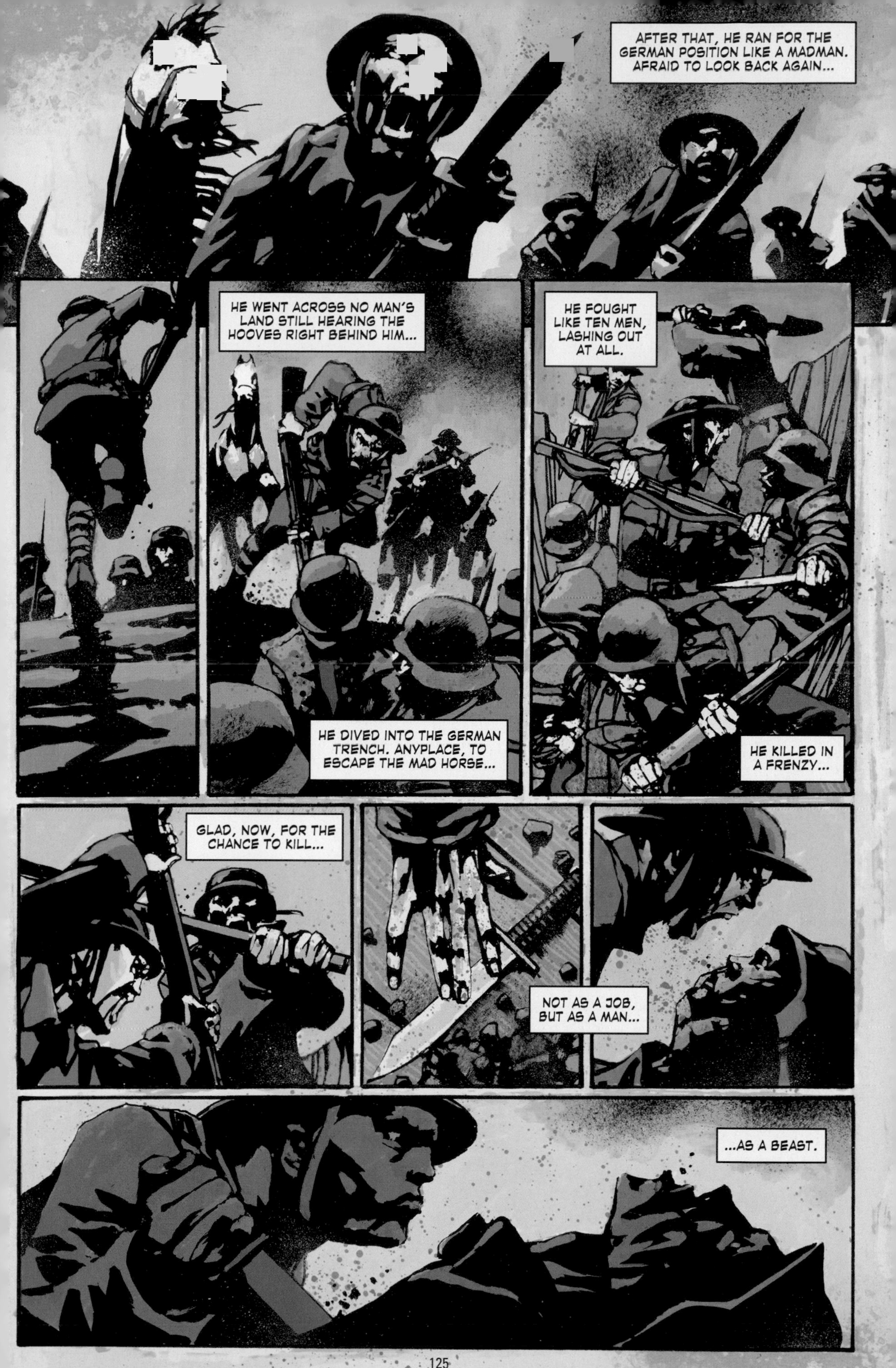
AFTER THAT, HE RAN FOR THE GERMAN POSITION LIKE A MADMAN. AFRAID TO LOOK BACK AGAIN...
HE WENT ACROSS NO MAN'S LAND STILL HEARING THE HOOVES RIGHT BEHIND HIM...
HE DIVED INTO THE GERMAN TRENCH. ANYPLACE, TO ESCAPE THE MAD HORSE...
HE FOUGHT LIKE TEN MEN, LASHING OUT AT ALL.
HE KILLED IN A FRENZY...
GLAD, NOW, FOR THE CHANCE TO KILL...
NOT AS A JOB, BUT AS A MAN...
...AS A BEAST.

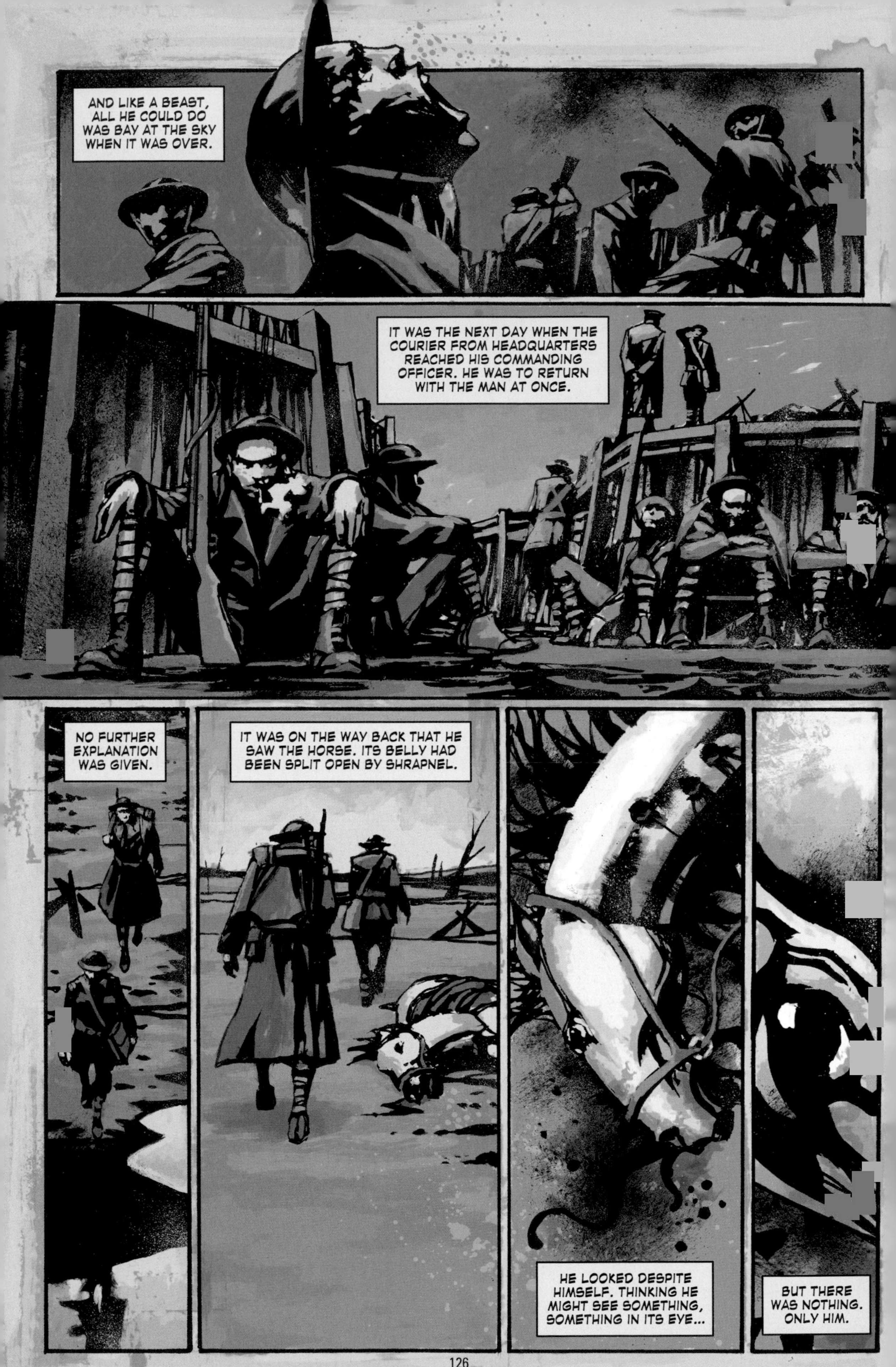
AND LIKE A BEAST, ALL HE COULD DO WAS BAY AT THE SKY WHEN IT WAS OVER.
IT WAS THE NEXT DAY WHEN THE COURIER FROM HEADQUARTERS REACHED HIS COMMANDING OFFICER. HE WAS TO RETURN WITH THE MAN AT ONCE.
NO FURTHER EXPLANATION WAS GIVEN.
IT WAS ON THE WAY BACK THAT HE SAW THE HORSE. ITS BELLY HAD BEEN SPLIT OPEN BY SHRAPNEL.
HE LOOKED DESPITE HIMSELF. THINKING HE MIGHT SEE SOMETHING, SOMETHING IN ITS EYE...
BUT THERE WAS NOTHING. ONLY HIM.

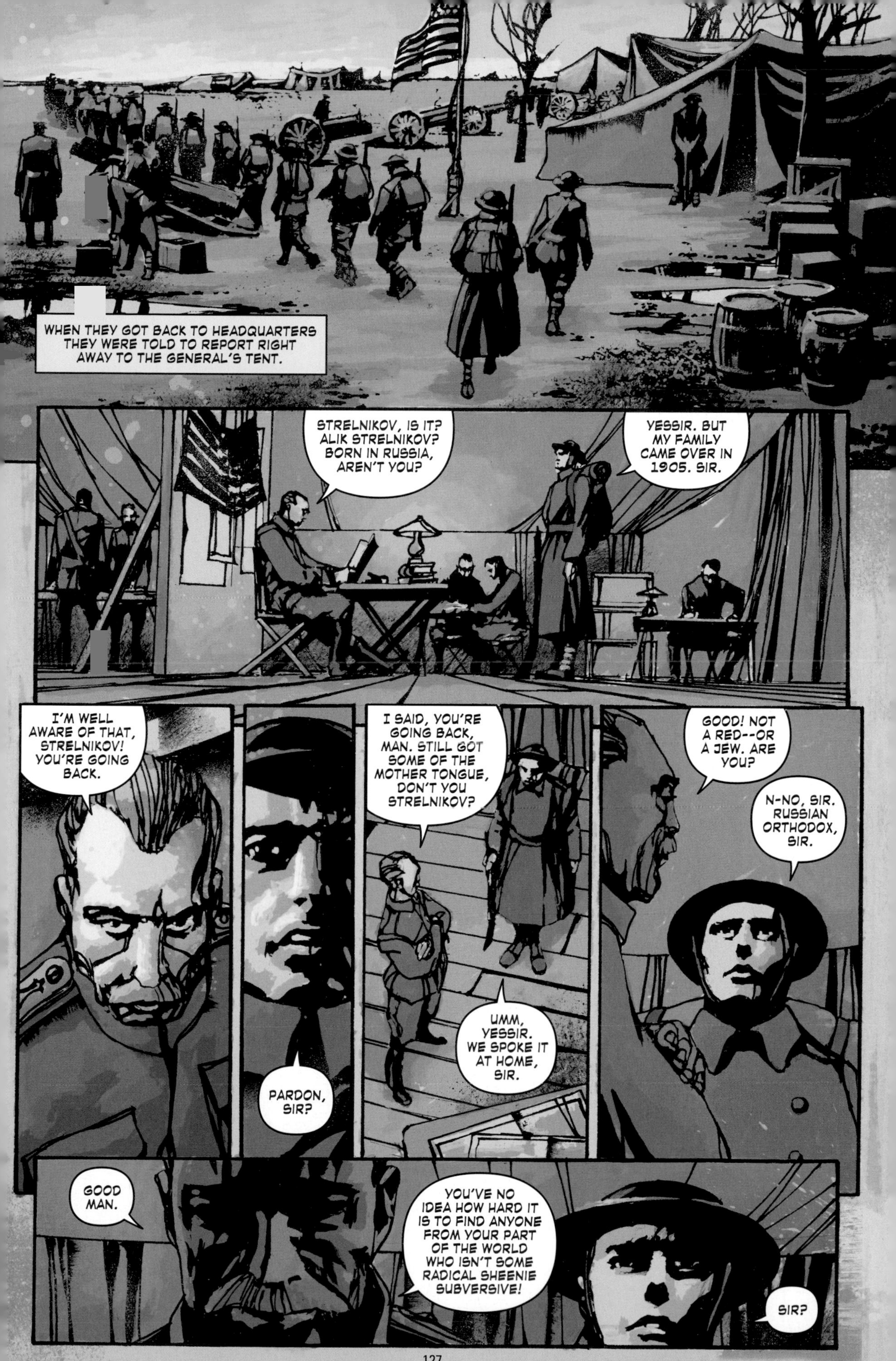
WHEN THEY GOT BACK TO HEADQUARTERS THEY WERE TOLD TO REPORT RIGHT AWAY TO THE GENERAL'S TENT.
STRELNIKOV, IS IT? ALIK STRELNIKOV? BORN IN RUSSIA, AREN'T YOU?
YESSIR. BUT MY FAMILY CAME OVER IN 1905. SIR.
I'M WELL AWARE OF THAT, STRELNIKOV! YOU'RE GOING BACK.
PARDON, SIR?
I SAID, YOU'RE GOING BACK, MAN. STILL GOT SOME OF THE MOTHER TONGUE, DON'T YOU STRELNIKOV?
UMM, YESSIR. WE SPOKE IT AT HOME, SIR.
GOOD! NOT A RED--OR A JEW. ARE YOU?
N-NO, SIR. RUSSIAN ORTHODOX, SIR.
GOOD MAN.
YOU'VE NO IDEA HOW HARD IT IS TO FIND ANYONE FROM YOUR PART OF THE WORLD WHO ISN'T SOME RADICAL SHEENIE SUBVERSIVE!
SIR?

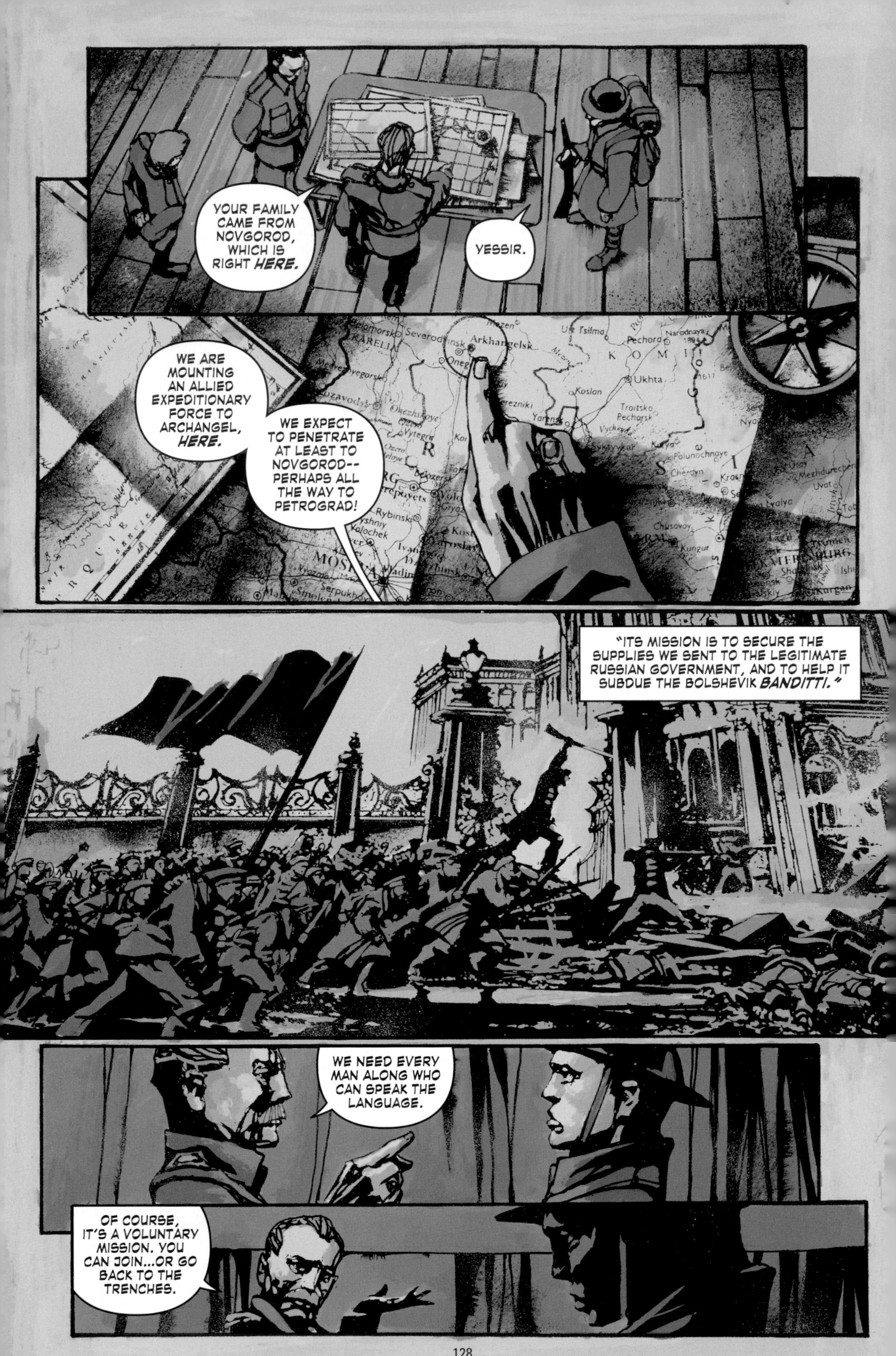
YOUR FAMILY CAME FROM NOVGOROD, WHICH IS RIGHT *HERE.*
YESSIR.
WE ARE MOUNTING AN ALLIED EXPEDITIONARY FORCE TO ARCHANGEL, *HERE.*
WE EXPECT TO PENETRATE AT LEAST TO NOVGOROD-- PERHAPS ALL THE WAY TO PETROGRAD!
"ITS MISSION IS TO SECURE THE SUPPLIES WE SENT TO THE LEGITIMATE RUSSIAN GOVERNMENT, AND TO HELP IT SUBDUE THE BOLSHEVIK *BANDITTI.*"
WE NEED EVERY MAN ALONG WHO CAN SPEAK THE LANGUAGE.
OF COURSE, IT'S A VOLUNTARY MISSION. YOU CAN JOIN...OR GO BACK TO THE TRENCHES.

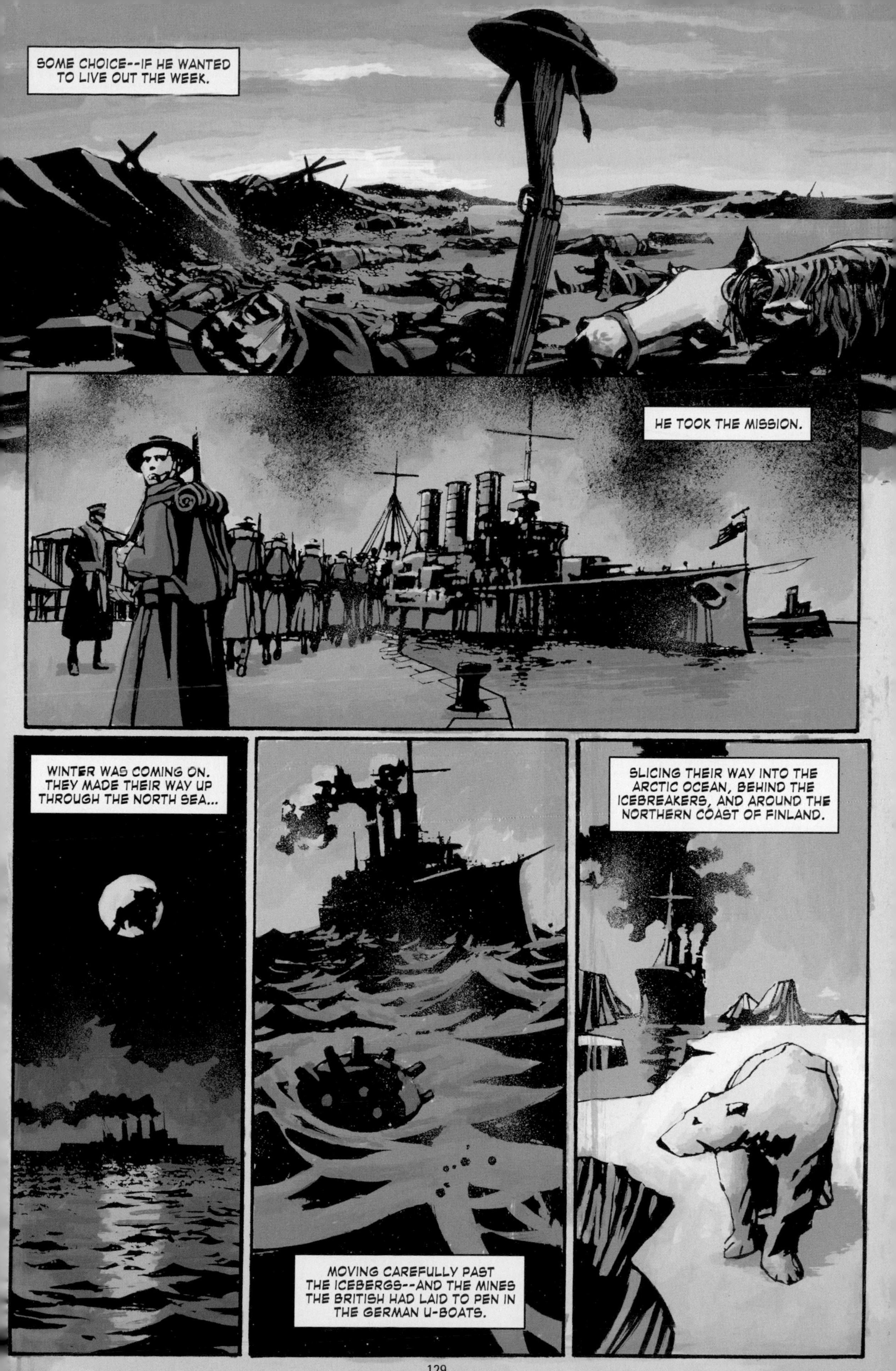
SOME CHOICE--IF HE WANTED TO LIVE OUT THE WEEK.
HE TOOK THE MISSION.
WINTER WAS COMING ON. THEY MADE THEIR WAY UP THROUGH THE NORTH SEA...
MOVING CAREFULLY PAST THE ICEBERGS--AND THE MINES THE BRITISH HAD LAID TO PEN IN THE GERMAN U-BOATS.
SLICING THEIR WAY INTO THE ARCTIC OCEAN, BEHIND THE ICEBREAKERS, AND AROUND THE NORTHERN COAST OF FINLAND.

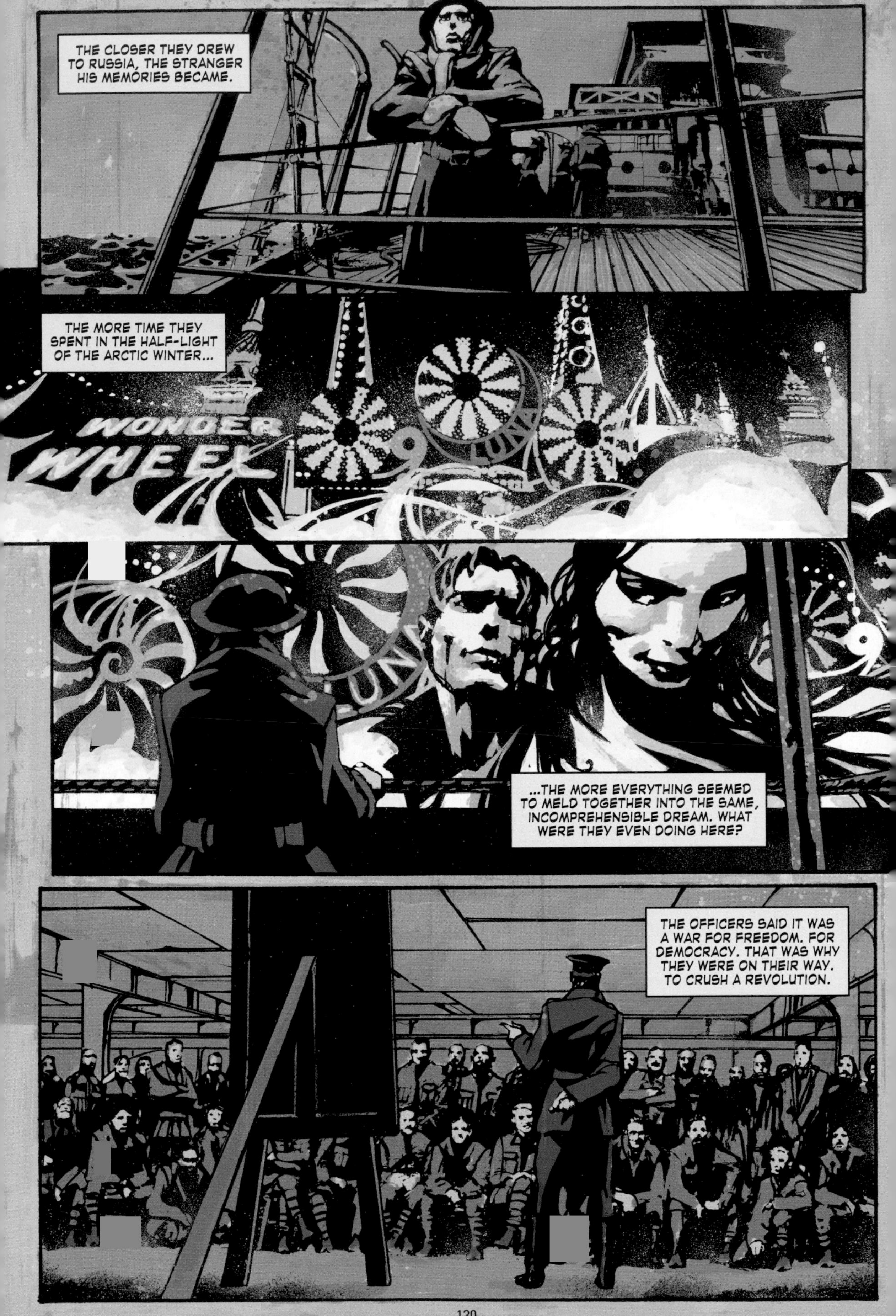
THE CLOSER THEY DREW TO RUSSIA, THE STRANGER HIS MEMORIES BECAME.
THE MORE TIME THEY SPENT IN THE HALF-LIGHT OF THE ARCTIC WINTER...
WONDER WHEEL
LUNA
...THE MORE EVERYTHING SEEMED TO MELD TOGETHER INTO THE SAME, INCOMPREHENSIBLE DREAM. WHAT WERE THEY EVEN DOING HERE?
THE OFFICERS SAID IT WAS A WAR FOR FREEDOM. FOR DEMOCRACY. THAT WAS WHY THEY WERE ON THEIR WAY. TO CRUSH A REVOLUTION.

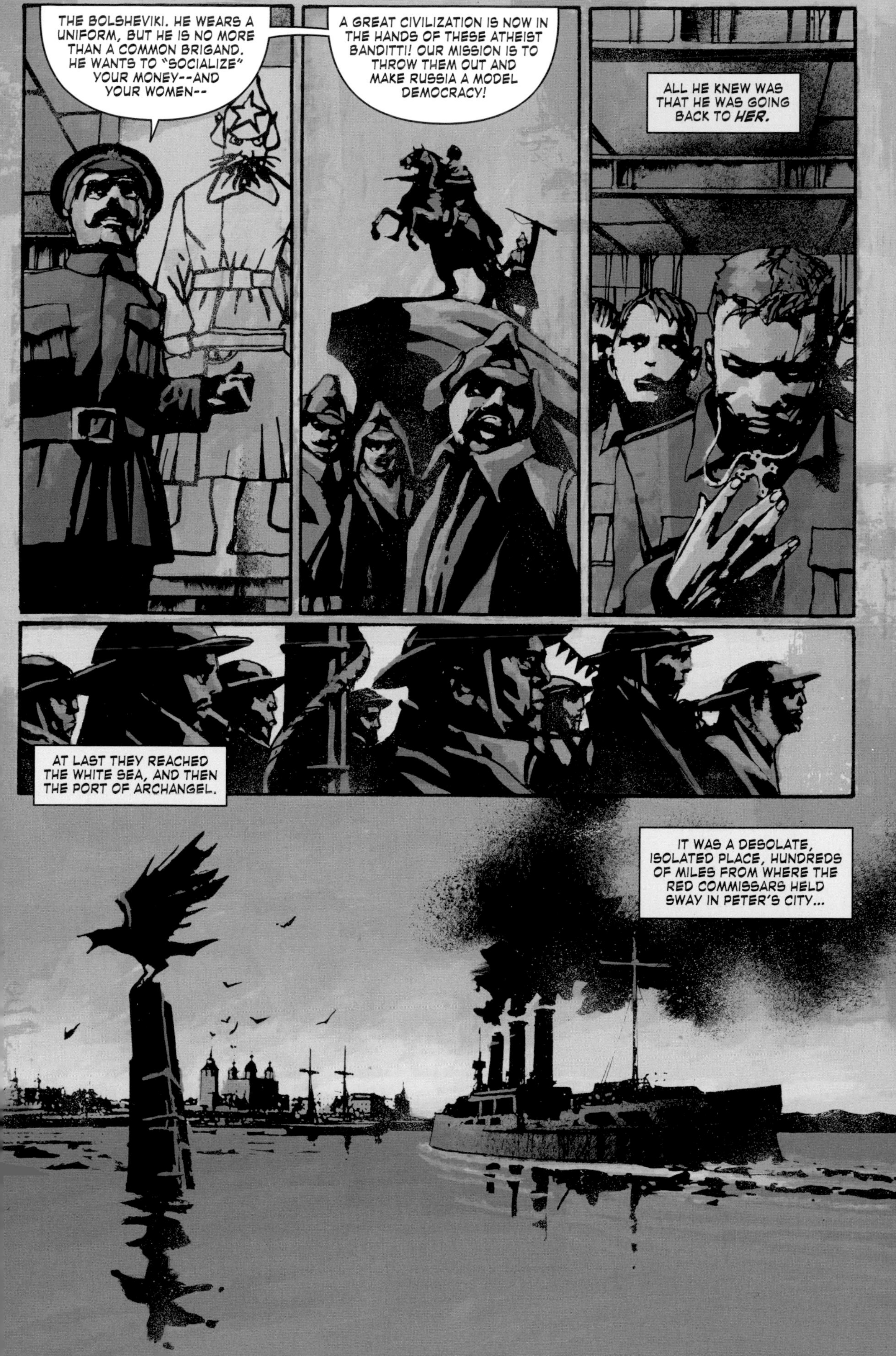
THE BOLSHEVIKI. HE WEARS A UNIFORM, BUT HE IS NO MORE THAN A COMMON BRIGAND. HE WANTS TO "SOCIALIZE" YOUR MONEY--AND YOUR WOMEN--
A GREAT CIVILIZATION IS NOW IN THE HANDS OF THESE ATHEIST BANDITTI! OUR MISSION IS TO THROW THEM OUT AND MAKE RUSSIA A MODEL DEMOCRACY!
ALL HE KNEW WAS THAT HE WAS GOING BACK TO HER.
AT LAST THEY REACHED THE WHITE SEA, AND THEN THE PORT OF ARCHANGEL.
IT WAS A DESOLATE, ISOLATED PLACE, HUNDREDS OF MILES FROM WHERE THE RED COMMISSARS HELD SWAY IN PETER'S CITY...

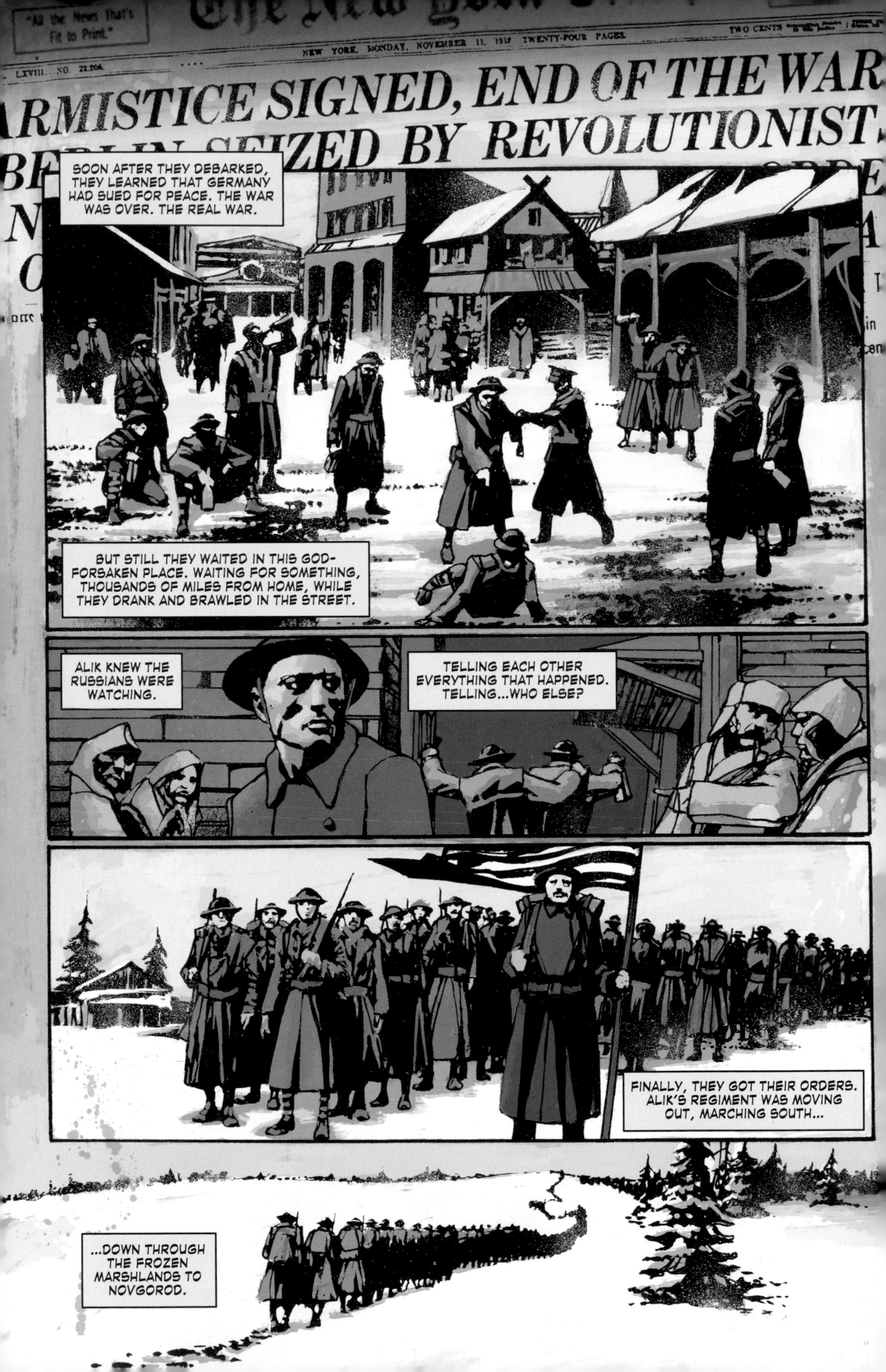
"All the News That's Fit to Print."
TWO CENTS
ARMISTICE SIGNED, END OF THE WAR
SEIZED BY REVOLUTIONIST
SOON AFTER THEY DEBARKED, THEY LEARNED THAT GERMANY HAD SUED FOR PEACE. THE WAR WAS OVER. THE REAL WAR.
BUT STILL THEY WAITED IN THIS GOD-FORSAKEN PLACE. WAITING FOR SOMETHING, THOUSANDS OF MILES FROM HOME, WHILE THEY DRANK AND BRAWLED IN THE STREET.
ALIK KNEW THE RUSSIANS WERE WATCHING.
TELLING EACH OTHER EVERYTHING THAT HAPPENED. TELLING...WHO ELSE?
FINALLY, THEY GOT THEIR ORDERS. ALIK'S REGIMENT WAS MOVING OUT, MARCHING SOUTH...
...DOWN THROUGH THE FROZEN MARSHLANDS TO NOVGOROD.

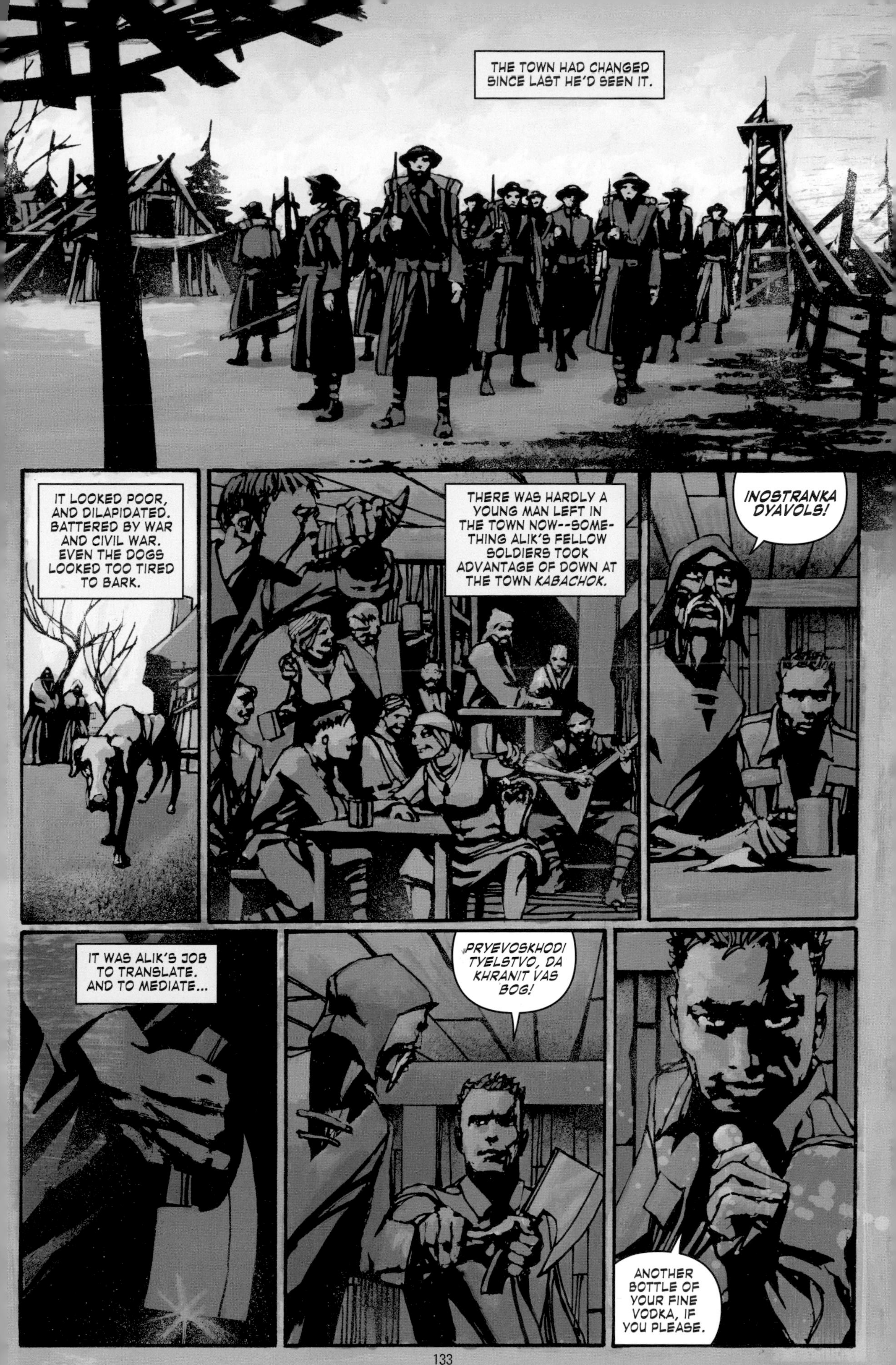
THE TOWN HAD CHANGED SINCE LAST HE'D SEEN IT.
IT LOOKED POOR, AND DILAPIDATED. BATTERED BY WAR AND CIVIL WAR. EVEN THE DOGS LOOKED TOO TIRED TO BARK.
THERE WAS HARDLY A YOUNG MAN LEFT IN THE TOWN NOW--SOMETHING ALIK'S FELLOW SOLDIERS TOOK ADVANTAGE OF DOWN AT THE TOWN *KABACHOK.*
*INOSTRANKA DYAVOLS!*
IT WAS ALIK'S JOB TO TRANSLATE. AND TO MEDIATE...
*PRYEVOSKHODI TYELSTVO, DA KHRANIT VAS BOG!*
ANOTHER BOTTLE OF YOUR FINE VODKA, IF YOU PLEASE.

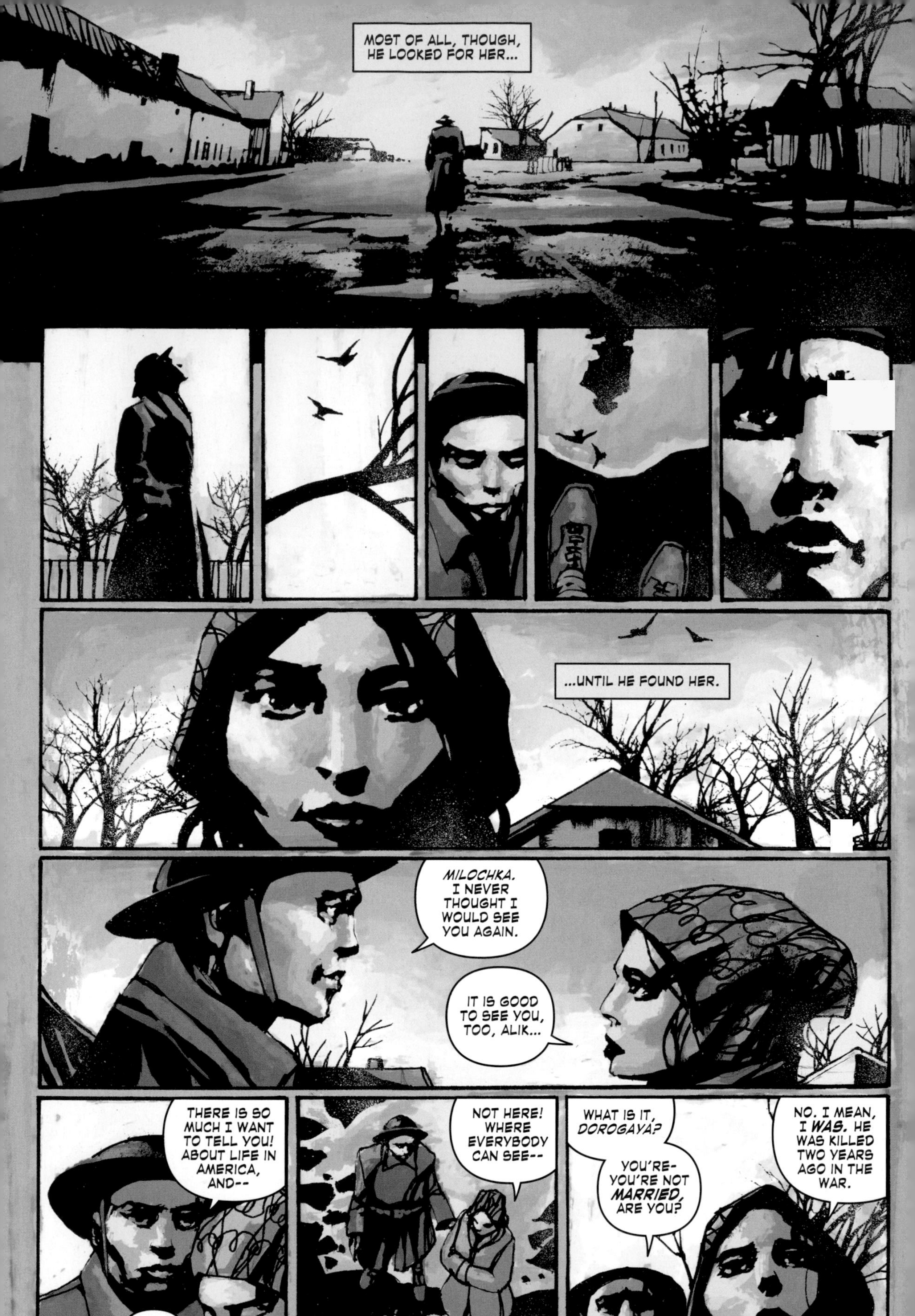
MOST OF ALL, THOUGH, HE LOOKED FOR HER...
...UNTIL HE FOUND HER.
*MILOCHKA.* I NEVER THOUGHT I WOULD SEE YOU AGAIN.
IT IS GOOD TO SEE YOU, TOO, ALIK...
THERE IS SO MUCH I WANT TO TELL YOU! ABOUT LIFE IN AMERICA, AND--
ALIK--
NOT HERE! WHERE EVERYBODY CAN SEE--
WHAT IS IT, *DOROGAYA?*
YOU'RE- YOU'RE NOT *MARRIED,* ARE YOU?
NO. I MEAN, I ***WAS.*** HE WAS KILLED TWO YEARS AGO IN THE WAR.

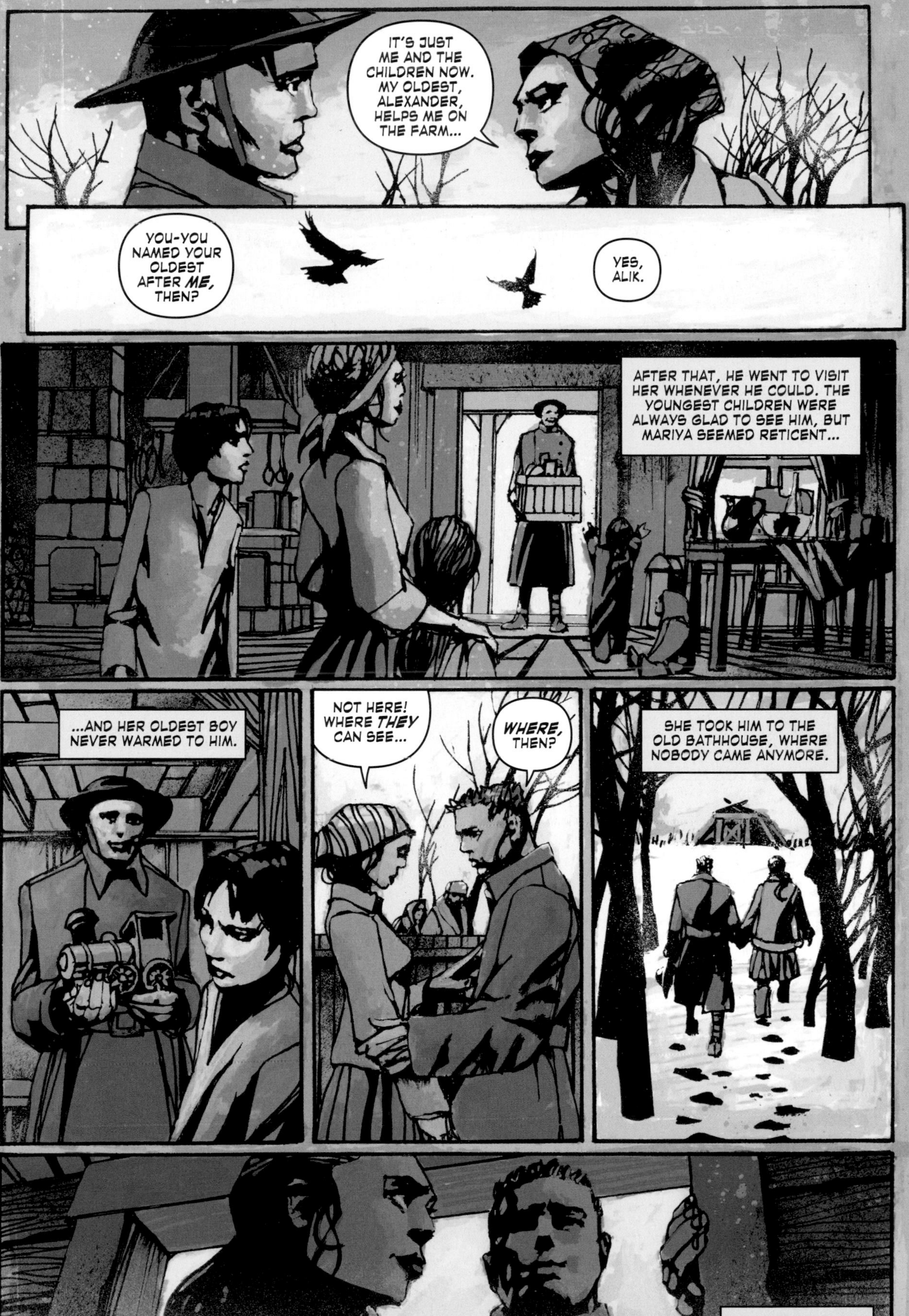
IT'S JUST ME AND THE CHILDREN NOW. MY OLDEST, ALEXANDER, HELPS ME ON THE FARM...
YOU-YOU NAMED YOUR OLDEST AFTER *ME*, THEN?
YES, ALIK.
AFTER THAT, HE WENT TO VISIT HER WHENEVER HE COULD. THE YOUNGEST CHILDREN WERE ALWAYS GLAD TO SEE HIM, BUT MARIYA SEEMED RETICENT...
...AND HER OLDEST BOY NEVER WARMED TO HIM.
NOT HERE! WHERE *THEY* CAN SEE...
*WHERE,* THEN?
SHE TOOK HIM TO THE OLD BATHHOUSE, WHERE NOBODY CAME ANYMORE.
THEY FIRED UP THE SAUNA AGAIN...

...AND INSIDE THEY MADE LOVE. SHE WAS WONDERFUL--PASSIONATE, SENSUOUS, NEEDY AND TENDER. EVERYTHING HE HAD DREAMED OF...

THROUGHOUT THAT STOLEN YEAR, HE MET HER AT THE STEAMBATH WHENEVER SHE COULD GET AWAY.

IN THE SUMMER THEY MADE LOVE OUTSIDE AND SWAM IN THE STREAMS HE REMEMBERED FROM HIS YOUTH.

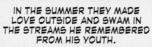

THE DAYS STRETCHED ON, GIDDY WITH PLEASURE.

NO, BE SERIOUS! I WANT A PICTURE I CAN SEND HOME TO MAMA!

YOUR MAMA WILL LOVE THIS!

NO ONE DISCOVERED THEIR SECRET. AT LEAST AS FAR AS THEY COULD TELL...

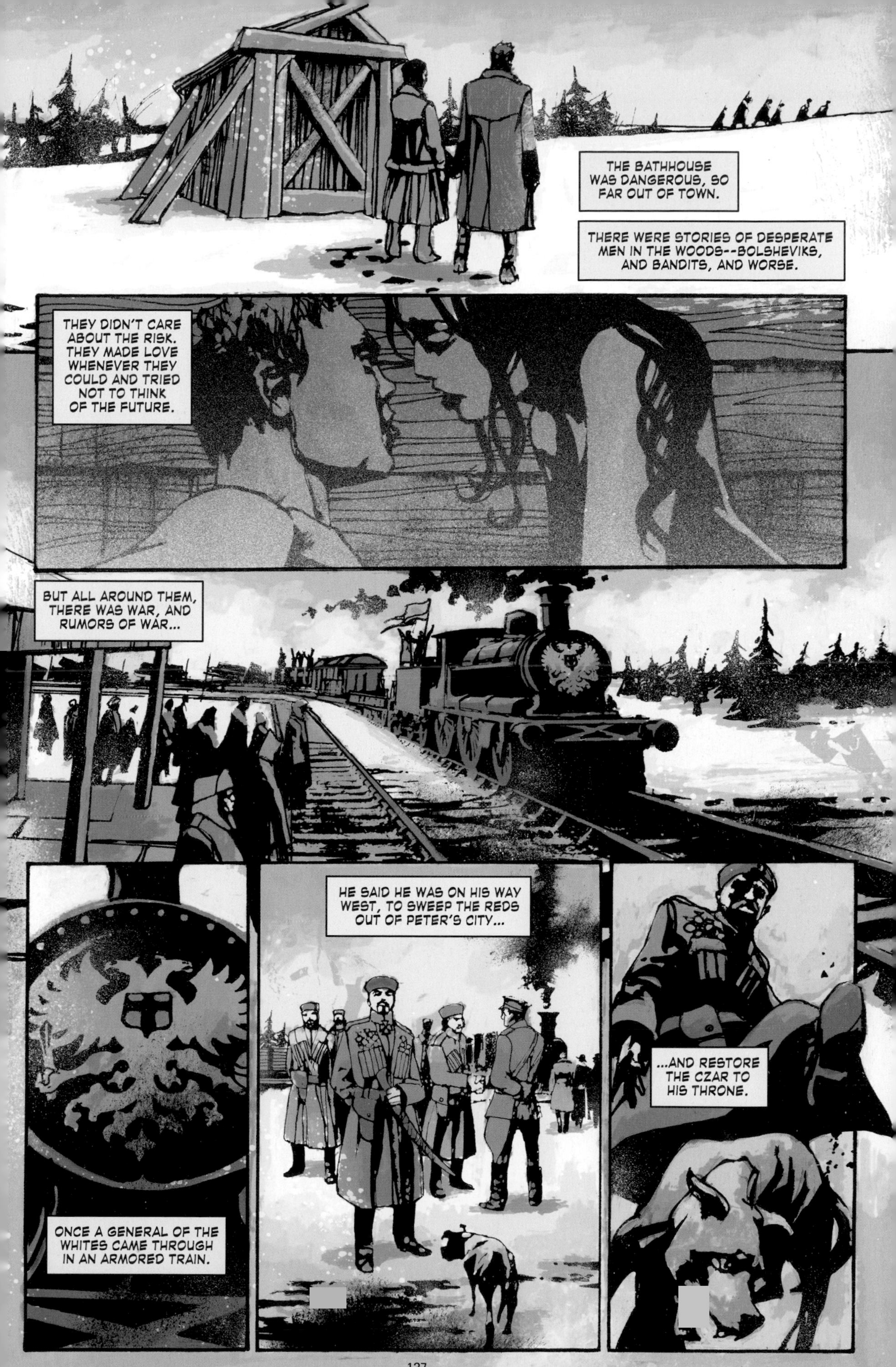
THE BATHHOUSE WAS DANGEROUS, SO FAR OUT OF TOWN.
THERE WERE STORIES OF DESPERATE MEN IN THE WOODS--BOLSHEVIKS, AND BANDITS, AND WORSE.
THEY DIDN'T CARE ABOUT THE RISK. THEY MADE LOVE WHENEVER THEY COULD AND TRIED NOT TO THINK OF THE FUTURE.
BUT ALL AROUND THEM, THERE WAS WAR, AND RUMORS OF WAR...
ONCE A GENERAL OF THE WHITES CAME THROUGH IN AN ARMORED TRAIN.
HE SAID HE WAS ON HIS WAY WEST, TO SWEEP THE REDS OUT OF PETER'S CITY...
...AND RESTORE THE CZAR TO HIS THRONE.

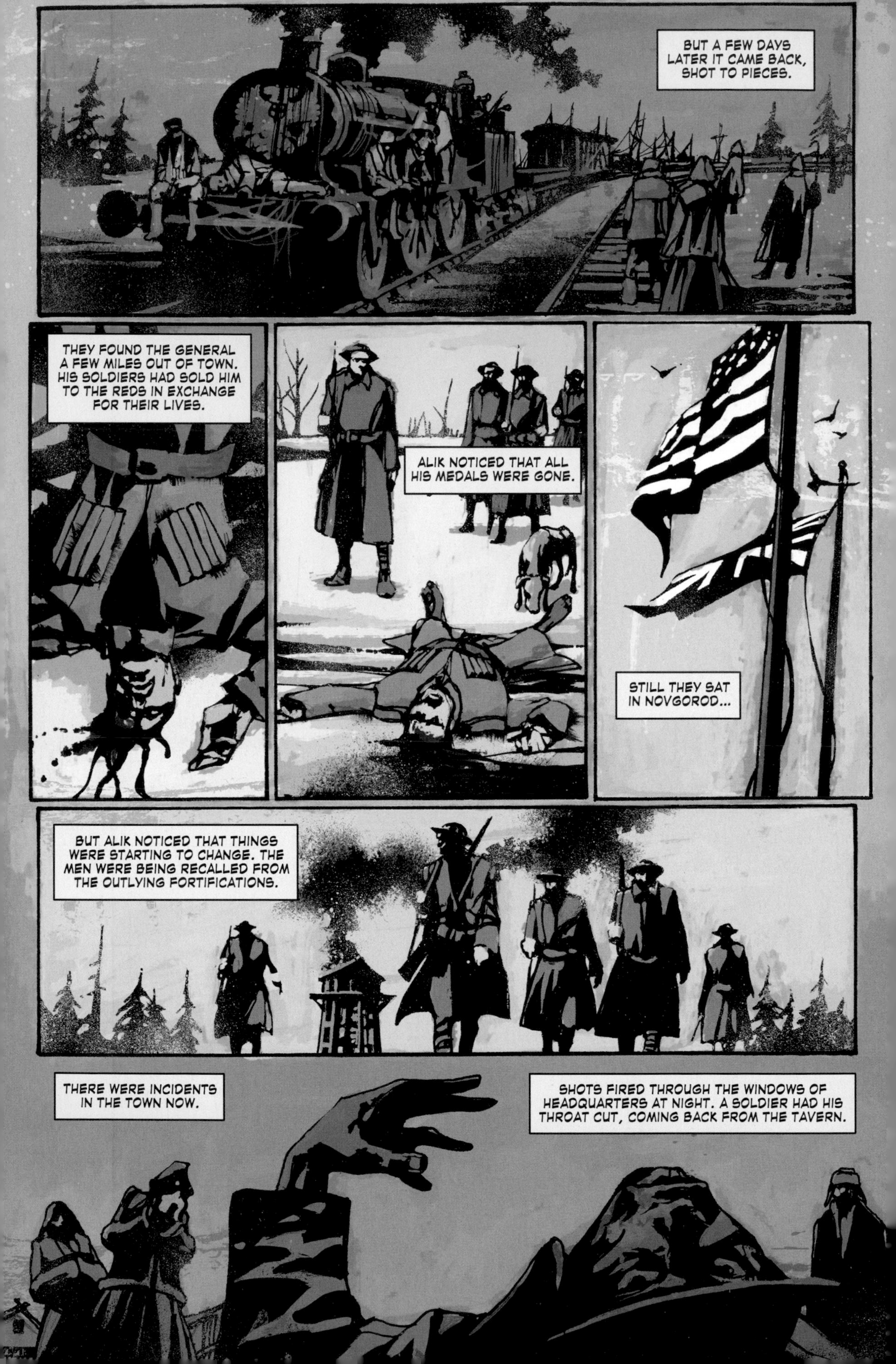
BUT A FEW DAYS LATER IT CAME BACK, SHOT TO PIECES.
THEY FOUND THE GENERAL A FEW MILES OUT OF TOWN. HIS SOLDIERS HAD SOLD HIM TO THE REDS IN EXCHANGE FOR THEIR LIVES.
ALIK NOTICED THAT ALL HIS MEDALS WERE GONE.
STILL THEY SAT IN NOVGOROD...
BUT ALIK NOTICED THAT THINGS WERE STARTING TO CHANGE. THE MEN WERE BEING RECALLED FROM THE OUTLYING FORTIFICATIONS.
THERE WERE INCIDENTS IN THE TOWN NOW.
SHOTS FIRED THROUGH THE WINDOWS OF HEADQUARTERS AT NIGHT. A SOLDIER HAD HIS THROAT CUT, COMING BACK FROM THE TAVERN.

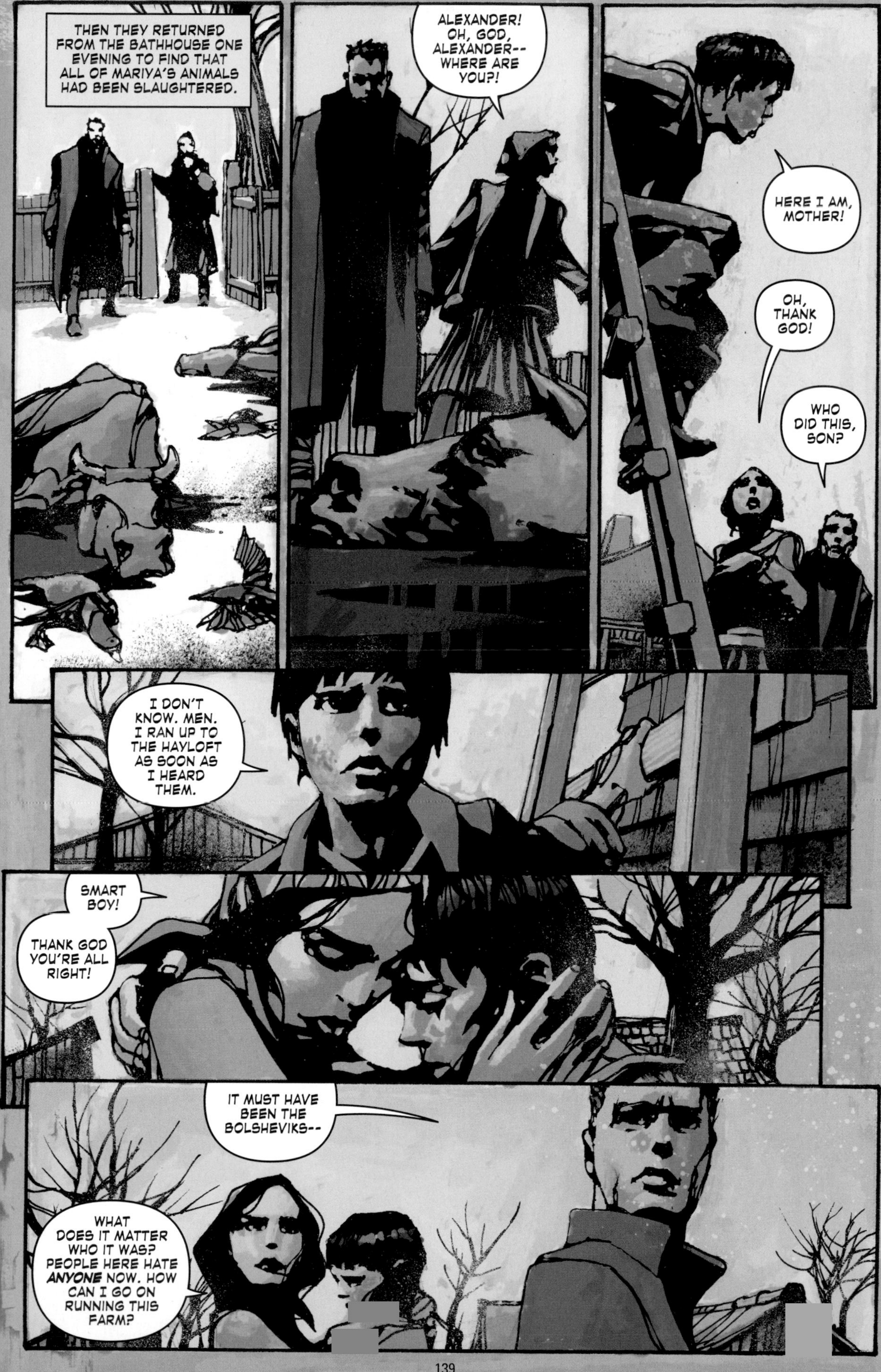

THEN THEY RETURNED FROM THE BATHHOUSE ONE EVENING TO FIND THAT ALL OF MARIYA'S ANIMALS HAD BEEN SLAUGHTERED.
ALEXANDER! OH, GOD, ALEXANDER-- WHERE ARE YOU?!
HERE I AM, MOTHER!
OH, THANK GOD!
WHO DID THIS, SON?
I DON'T KNOW. MEN. I RAN UP TO THE HAYLOFT AS SOON AS I HEARD THEM.
SMART BOY!
THANK GOD YOU'RE ALL RIGHT!
IT MUST HAVE BEEN THE BOLSHEVIKS--
WHAT DOES IT MATTER WHO IT WAS? PEOPLE HERE HATE ANYONE NOW. HOW CAN I GO ON RUNNING THIS FARM?

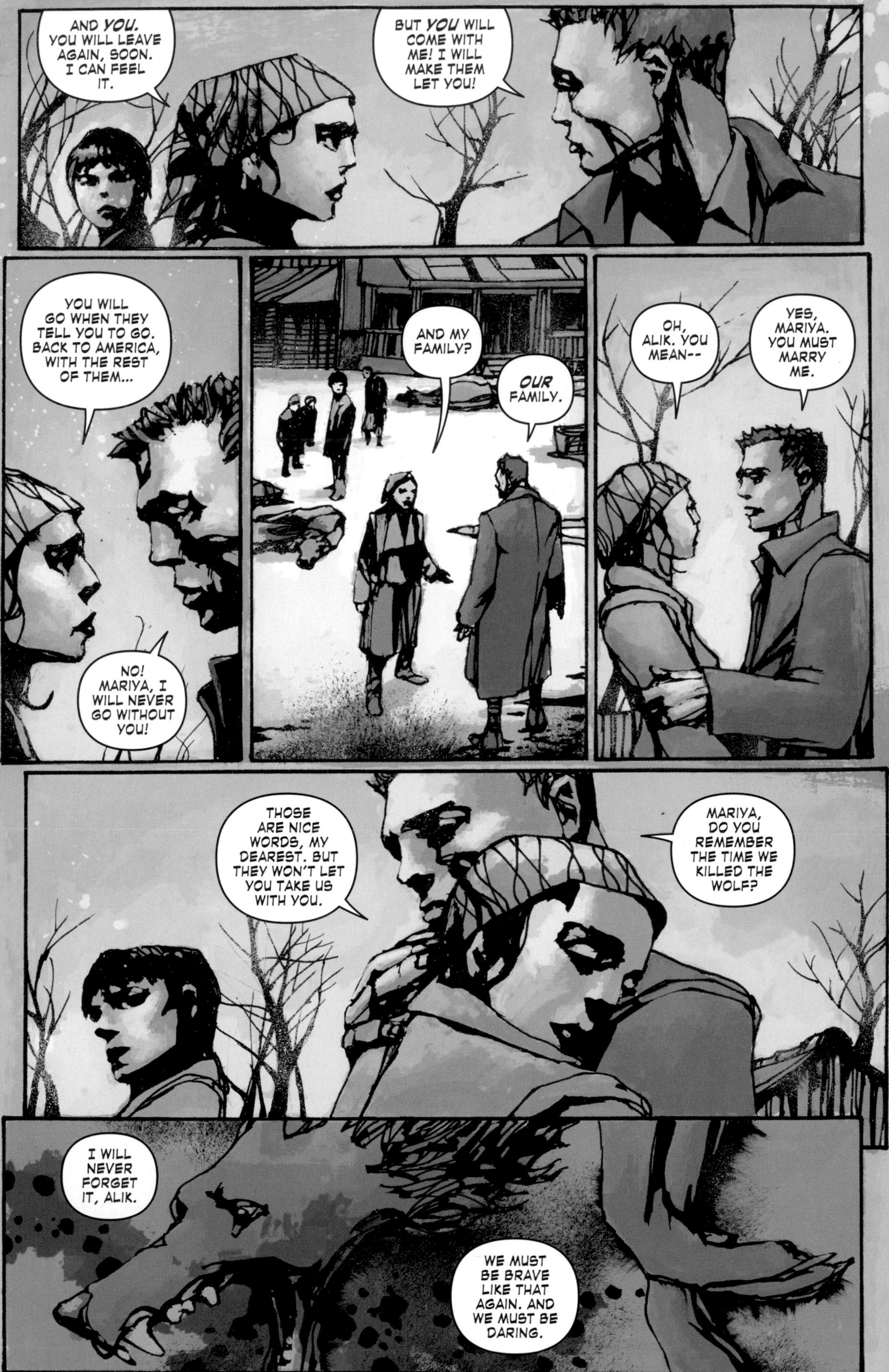
AND *YOU.* YOU WILL LEAVE AGAIN, SOON. I CAN FEEL IT.
BUT *YOU* WILL COME WITH ME! I WILL MAKE THEM LET YOU!
YOU WILL GO WHEN THEY TELL YOU TO GO. BACK TO AMERICA, WITH THE REST OF THEM...
NO! MARIYA, I WILL NEVER GO WITHOUT YOU!
AND MY FAMILY?
*OUR* FAMILY.
OH, ALIK. YOU MEAN--
YES, MARIYA. YOU MUST MARRY ME.
THOSE ARE NICE WORDS, MY DEAREST. BUT THEY WON'T LET YOU TAKE US WITH YOU.
MARIYA, DO YOU REMEMBER THE TIME WE KILLED THE WOLF?
I WILL NEVER FORGET IT, ALIK.
WE MUST BE BRAVE LIKE THAT AGAIN. AND WE MUST BE DARING.

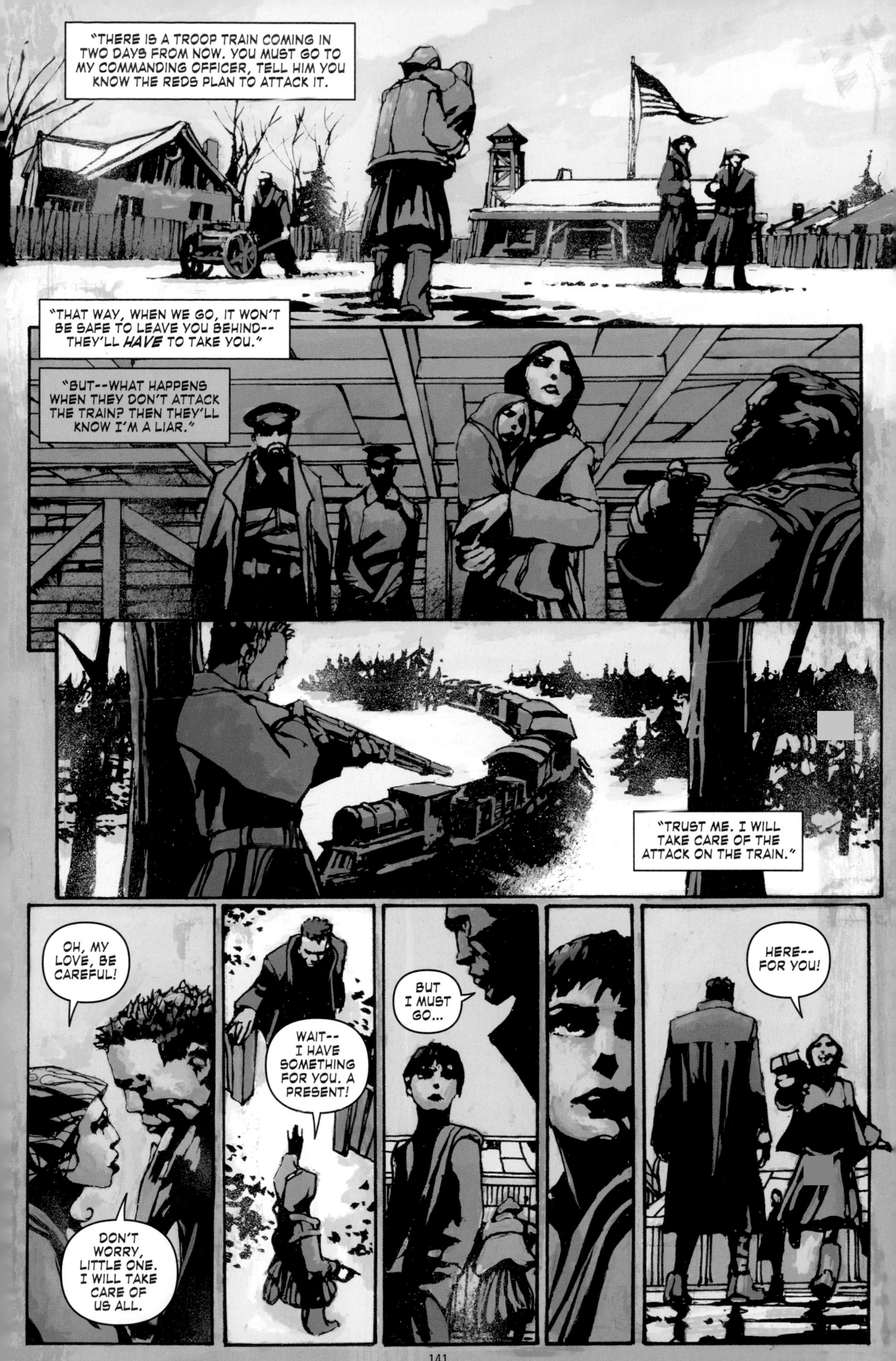
"THERE IS A TROOP TRAIN COMING IN TWO DAYS FROM NOW. YOU MUST GO TO MY COMMANDING OFFICER, TELL HIM YOU KNOW THE REDS PLAN TO ATTACK IT.
"THAT WAY, WHEN WE GO, IT WON'T BE SAFE TO LEAVE YOU BEHIND-- THEY'LL *HAVE* TO TAKE YOU."
"BUT--WHAT HAPPENS WHEN THEY DON'T ATTACK THE TRAIN? THEN THEY'LL KNOW I'M A LIAR."
"TRUST ME. I WILL TAKE CARE OF THE ATTACK ON THE TRAIN."
OH, MY LOVE, BE CAREFUL!
DON'T WORRY, LITTLE ONE. I WILL TAKE CARE OF US ALL.
WAIT-- I HAVE SOMETHING FOR YOU. A PRESENT!
BUT I MUST GO...
HERE-- FOR YOU!

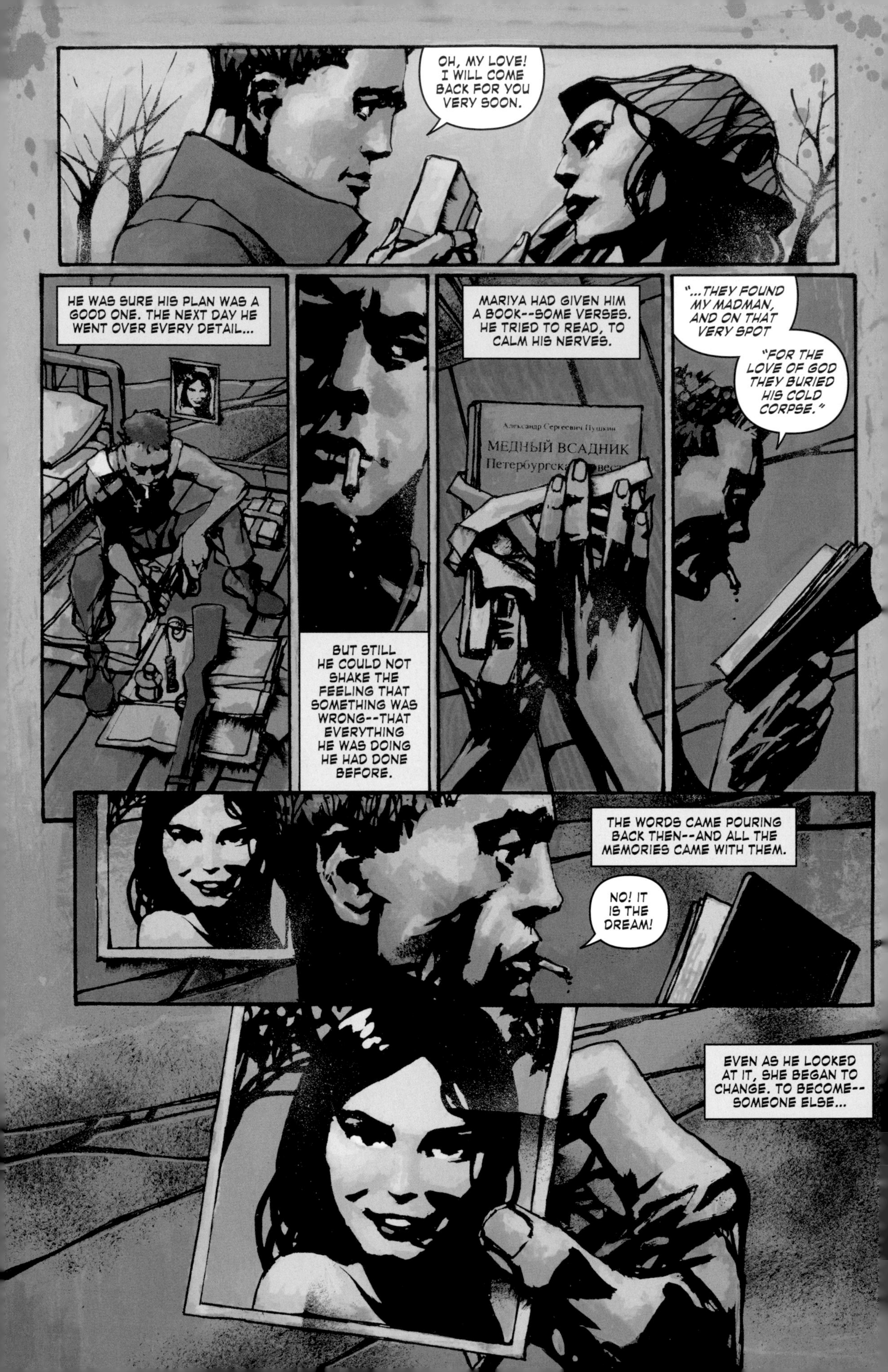
OH, MY LOVE! I WILL COME BACK FOR YOU VERY SOON.
HE WAS SURE HIS PLAN WAS A GOOD ONE. THE NEXT DAY HE WENT OVER EVERY DETAIL...
BUT STILL HE COULD NOT SHAKE THE FEELING THAT SOMETHING WAS WRONG--THAT EVERYTHING HE WAS DOING HE HAD DONE BEFORE.
MARIYA HAD GIVEN HIM A BOOK--SOME VERSES. HE TRIED TO READ, TO CALM HIS NERVES.
Александр Сергеевич Пушкин
МЕДНЫЙ ВСАДНИК
Петербургска
"...THEY FOUND MY MADMAN, AND ON THAT VERY SPOT
"FOR THE LOVE OF GOD THEY BURIED HIS COLD CORPSE."
THE WORDS CAME POURING BACK THEN--AND ALL THE MEMORIES CAME WITH THEM.
NO! IT IS THE DREAM!
EVEN AS HE LOOKED AT IT, SHE BEGAN TO CHANGE. TO BECOME--SOMEONE ELSE...

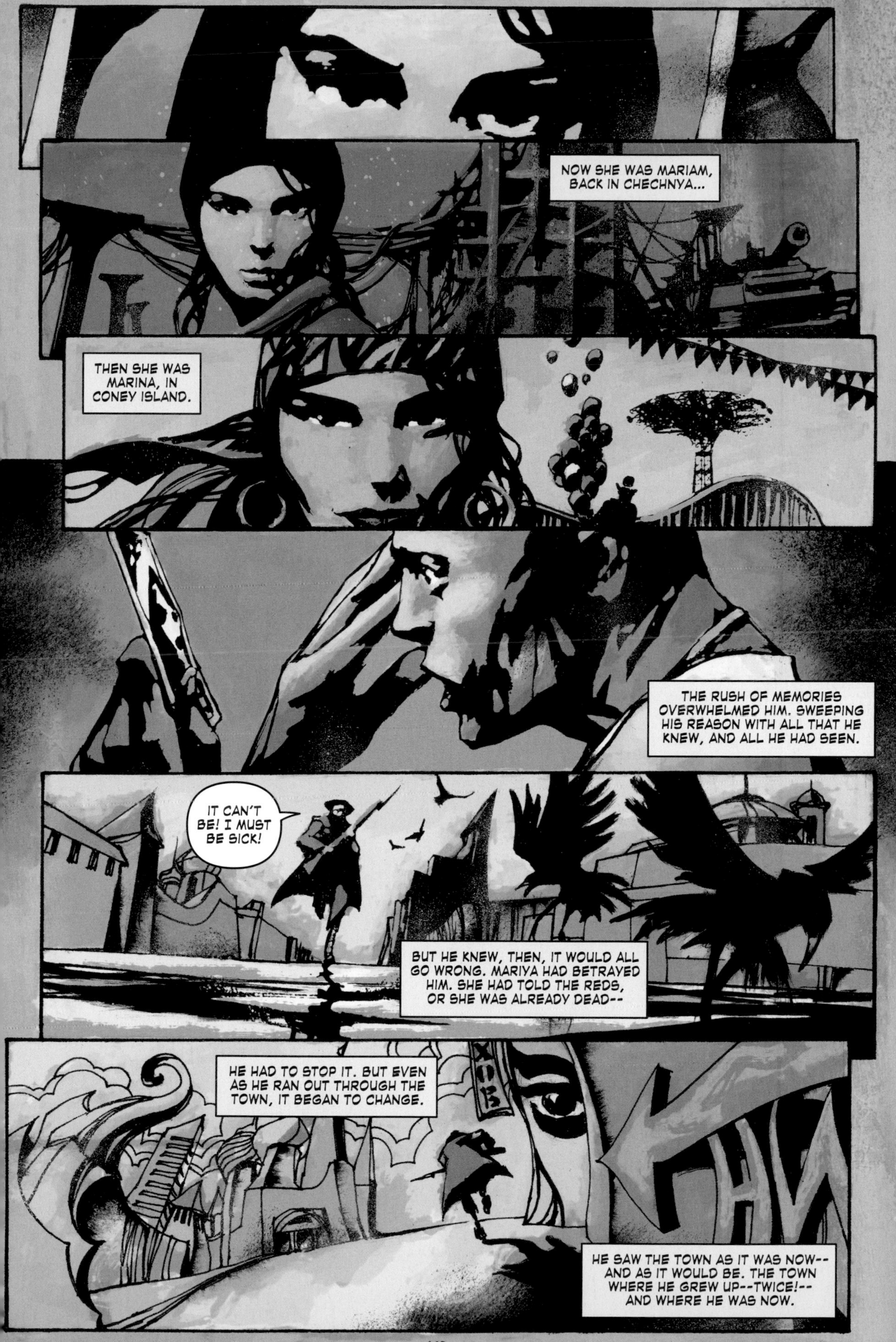
NOW SHE WAS MARIAM, BACK IN CHECHNYA...
THEN SHE WAS MARINA, IN CONEY ISLAND.
THE RUSH OF MEMORIES OVERWHELMED HIM. SWEEPING HIS REASON WITH ALL THAT HE KNEW, AND ALL HE HAD SEEN.
IT CAN'T BE! I MUST BE SICK!
BUT HE KNEW, THEN, IT WOULD ALL GO WRONG. MARIYA HAD BETRAYED HIM. SHE HAD TOLD THE REDS, OR SHE WAS ALREADY DEAD--
HE HAD TO STOP IT. BUT EVEN AS HE RAN OUT THROUGH THE TOWN, IT BEGAN TO CHANGE.
HE SAW THE TOWN AS IT WAS NOW-- AND AS IT WOULD BE. THE TOWN WHERE HE GREW UP--TWICE!-- AND WHERE HE WAS NOW.

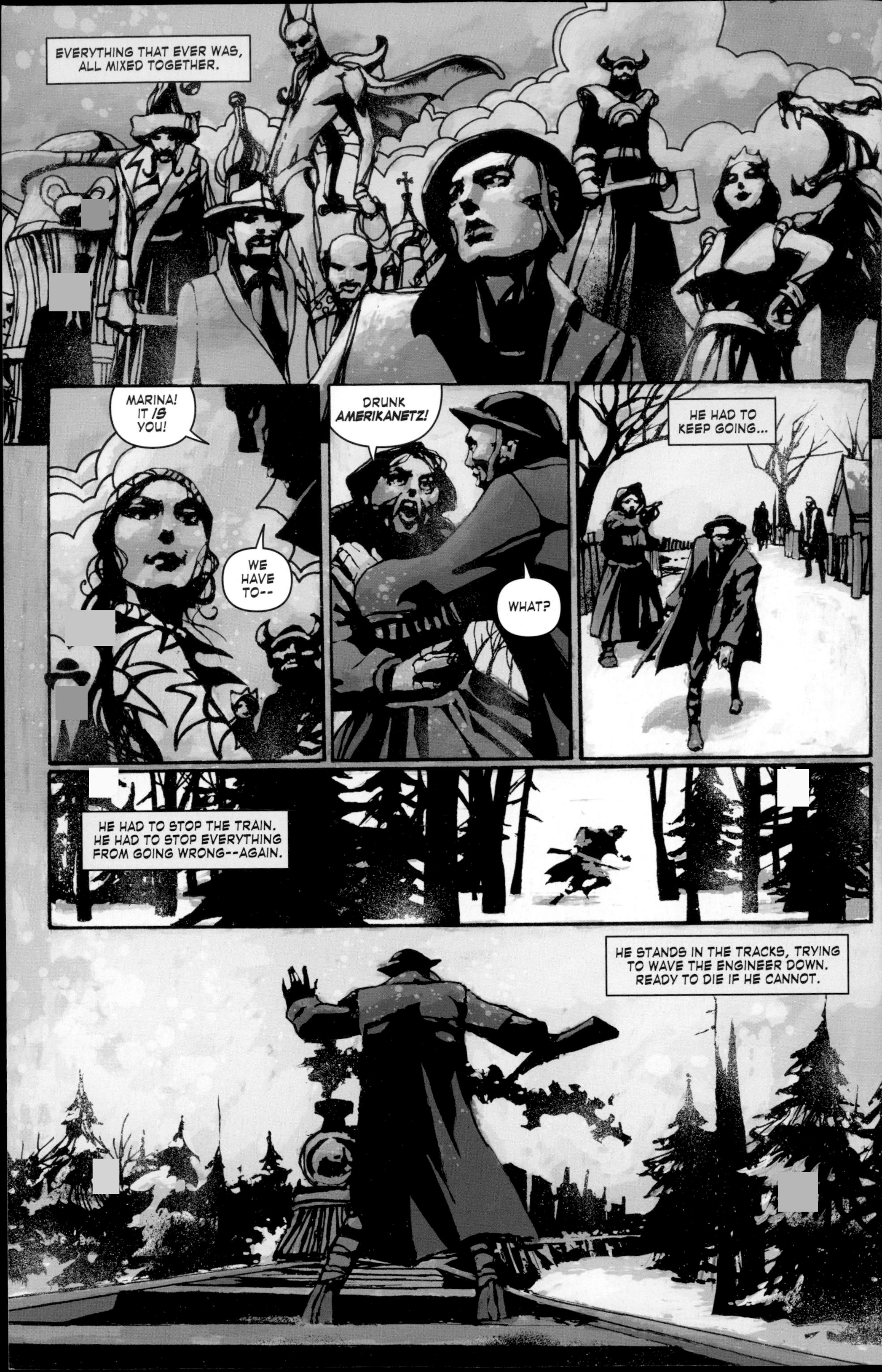
EVERYTHING THAT EVER WAS, ALL MIXED TOGETHER.
MARINA! IT IS YOU!
WE HAVE TO--
DRUNK AMERIKANETZ!
WHAT?
HE HAD TO KEEP GOING...
HE HAD TO STOP THE TRAIN. HE HAD TO STOP EVERYTHING FROM GOING WRONG--AGAIN.
HE STANDS IN THE TRACKS, TRYING TO WAVE THE ENGINEER DOWN. READY TO DIE IF HE CANNOT.

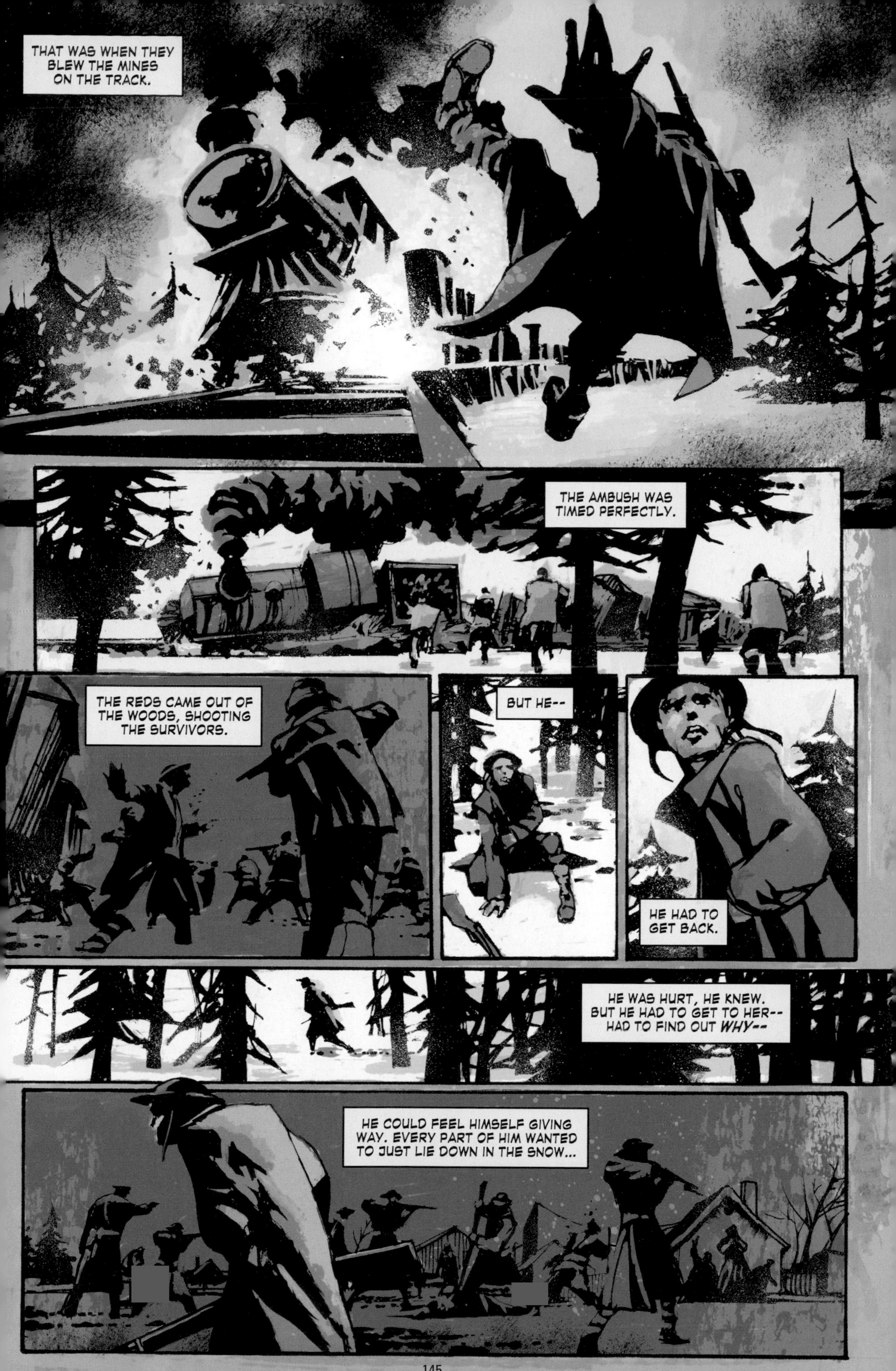
THAT WAS WHEN THEY BLEW THE MINES ON THE TRACK.
THE AMBUSH WAS TIMED PERFECTLY.
THE REDS CAME OUT OF THE WOODS, SHOOTING THE SURVIVORS.
BUT HE--
HE HAD TO GET BACK.
HE WAS HURT, HE KNEW. BUT HE HAD TO GET TO HER-- HAD TO FIND OUT *WHY*--
HE COULD FEEL HIMSELF GIVING WAY. EVERY PART OF HIM WANTED TO JUST LIE DOWN IN THE SNOW...

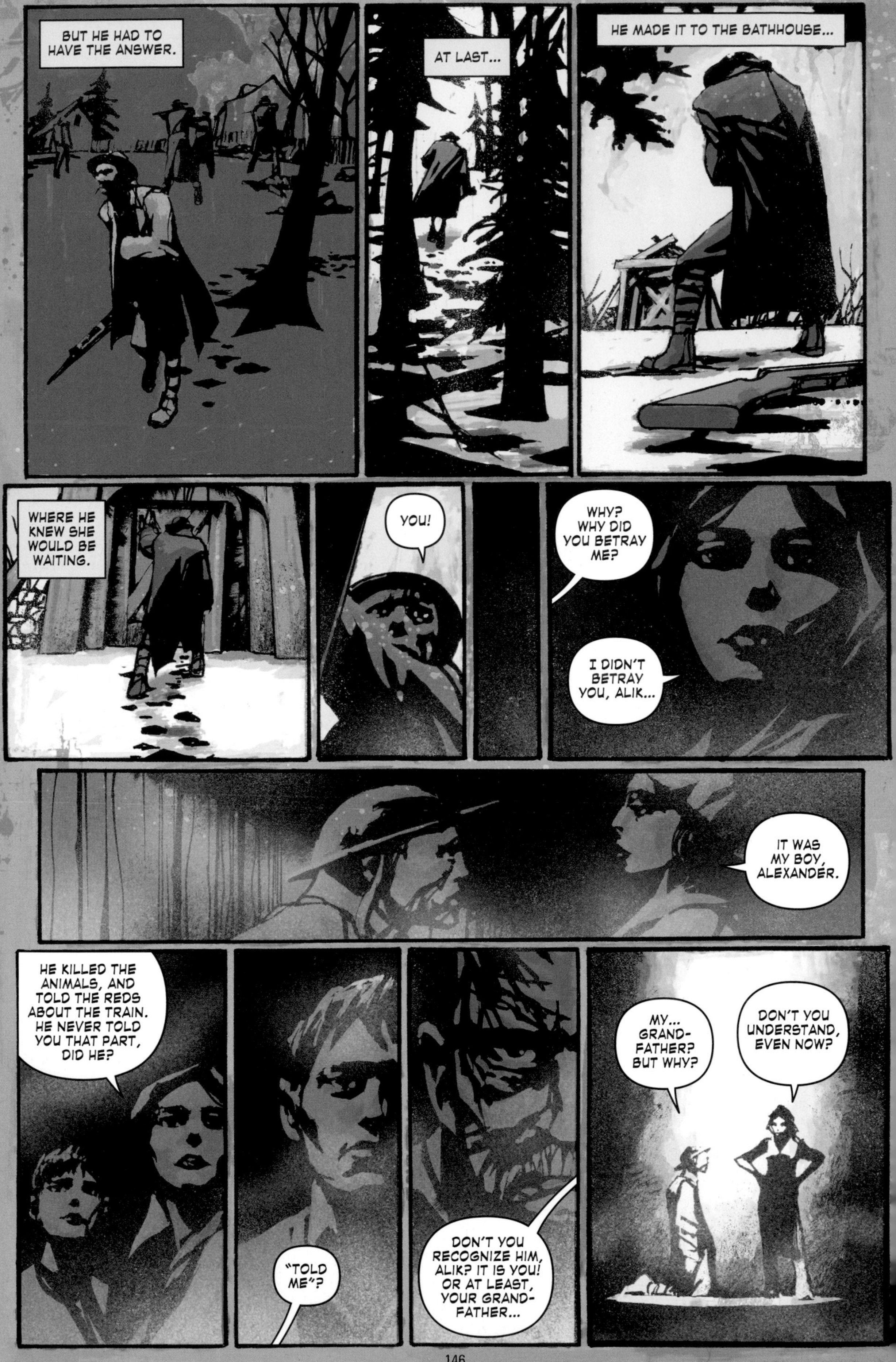

BUT HE HAD TO HAVE THE ANSWER.
AT LAST...
HE MADE IT TO THE BATHHOUSE...
WHERE HE KNEW SHE WOULD BE WAITING.
YOU!
WHY? WHY DID YOU BETRAY ME?
I DIDN'T BETRAY YOU, ALIK...
IT WAS MY BOY, ALEXANDÉR.
HE KILLED THE ANIMALS, AND TOLD THE REDS ABOUT THE TRAIN. HE NEVER TOLD YOU THAT PART, DID HE?
"TOLD ME"?
DON'T YOU RECOGNIZE HIM, ALIK? IT IS YOU! OR AT LEAST, YOUR GRAND-FATHER...
MY... GRAND-FATHER? BUT WHY?
DON'T YOU UNDERSTAND, EVEN NOW?

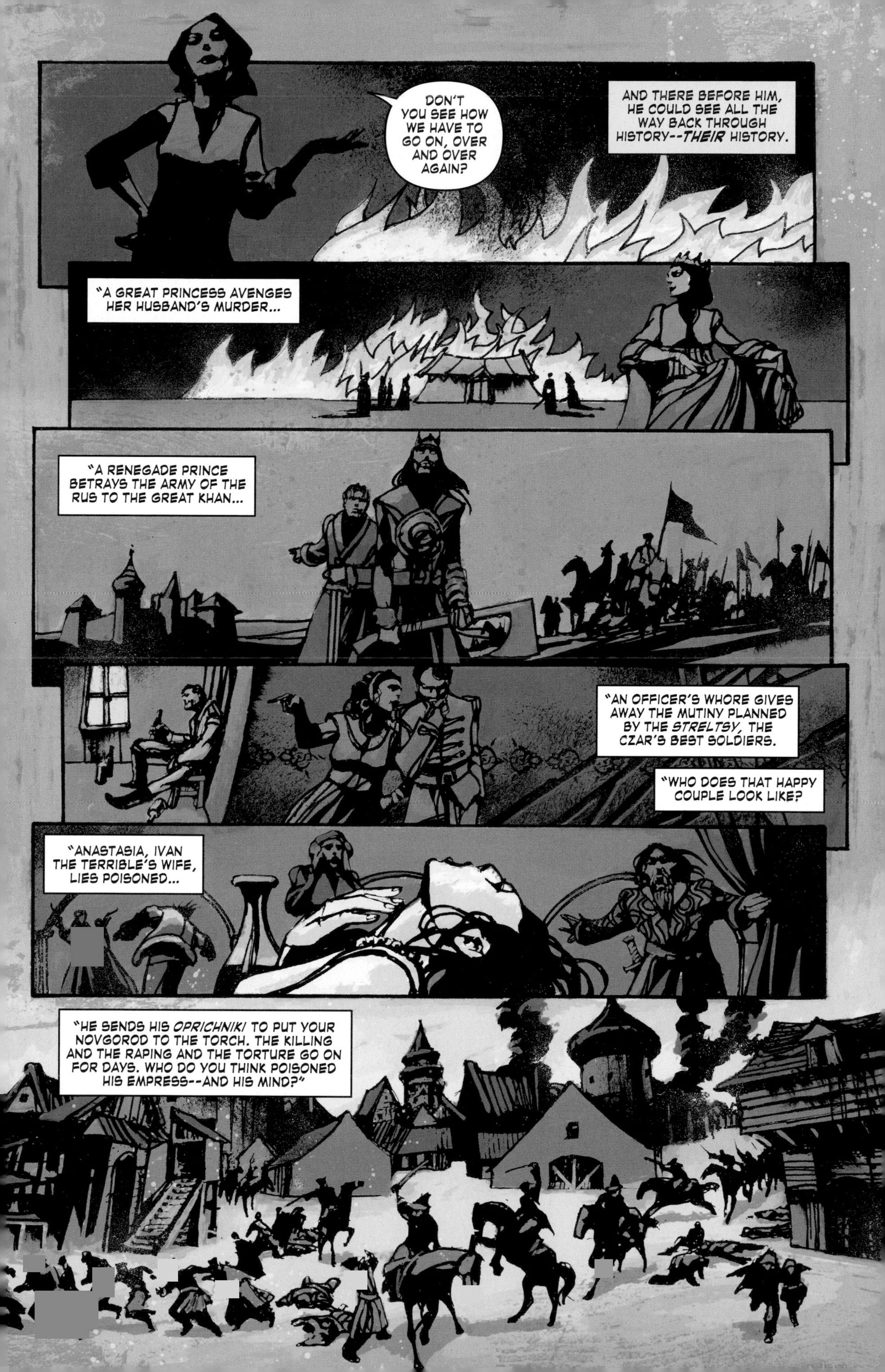
DON'T YOU SEE HOW WE HAVE TO GO ON, OVER AND OVER AGAIN?
AND THERE BEFORE HIM, HE COULD SEE ALL THE WAY BACK THROUGH HISTORY--*THEIR* HISTORY.
"A GREAT PRINCESS AVENGES HER HUSBAND'S MURDER...
"A RENEGADE PRINCE BETRAYS THE ARMY OF THE RUS TO THE GREAT KHAN...
"AN OFFICER'S WHORE GIVES AWAY THE MUTINY PLANNED BY THE *STRELTSY*, THE CZAR'S BEST SOLDIERS.
"WHO DOES THAT HAPPY COUPLE LOOK LIKE?
"ANASTASIA, IVAN THE TERRIBLE'S WIFE, LIES POISONED...
"HE SENDS HIS *OPRICHNIKI* TO PUT YOUR NOVGOROD TO THE TORCH. THE KILLING AND THE RAPING AND THE TORTURE GO ON FOR DAYS. WHO DO YOU THINK POISONED HIS EMPRESS--AND HIS MIND?"

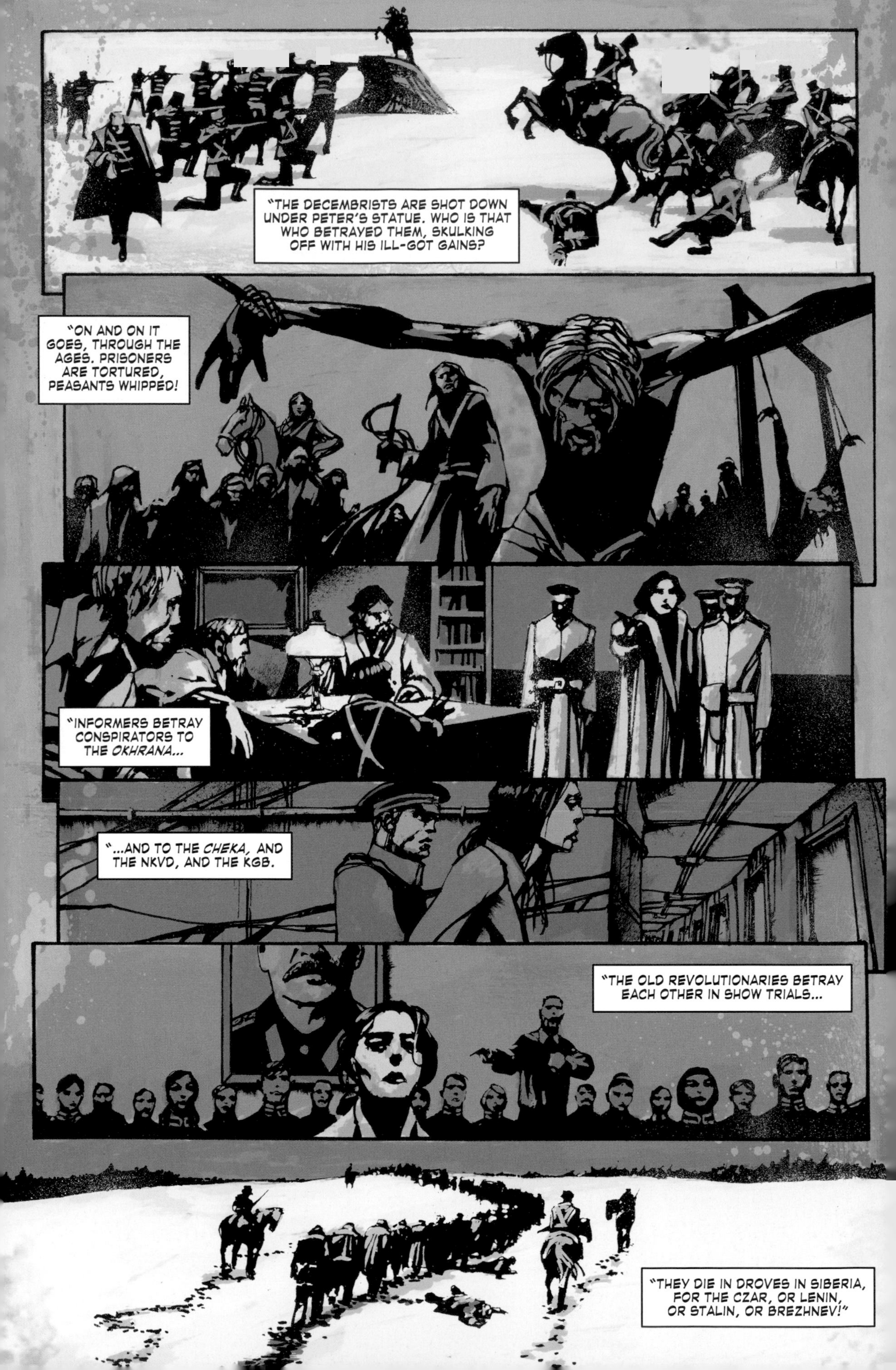
"THE DECEMBRISTS ARE SHOT DOWN UNDER PETER'S STATUE. WHO IS THAT WHO BETRAYED THEM, SKULKING OFF WITH HIS ILL-GOT GAINS?
"ON AND ON IT GOES, THROUGH THE AGES. PRISONERS ARE TORTURED, PEASANTS WHIPPED!
"INFORMERS BETRAY CONSPIRATORS TO THE *OKHRANA*...
"...AND TO THE *CHEKA,* AND THE NKVD, AND THE KGB.
"THE OLD REVOLUTIONARIES BETRAY EACH OTHER IN SHOW TRIALS...
"THEY DIE IN DROVES IN SIBERIA, FOR THE CZAR, OR LENIN, OR STALIN, OR BREZHNEV!"

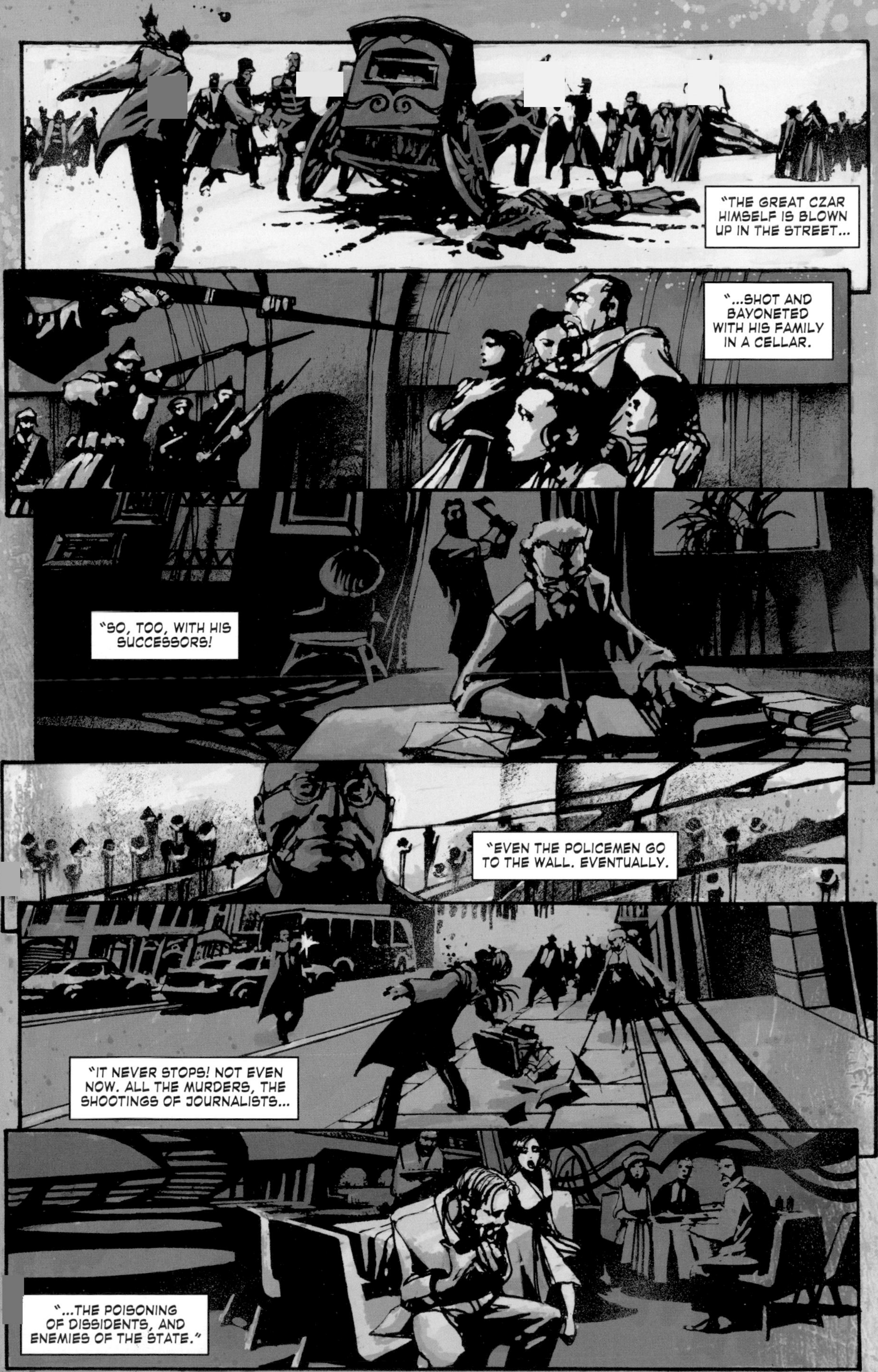
"THE GREAT CZAR HIMSELF IS BLOWN UP IN THE STREET...
"...SHOT AND BAYONETED WITH HIS FAMILY IN A CELLAR.
"SO, TOO, WITH HIS SUCCESSORS!
"EVEN THE POLICEMEN GO TO THE WALL. EVENTUALLY.
"IT NEVER STOPS! NOT EVEN NOW. ALL THE MURDERS, THE SHOOTINGS OF JOURNALISTS...
"...THE POISONING OF DISSIDENTS, AND ENEMIES OF THE STATE."

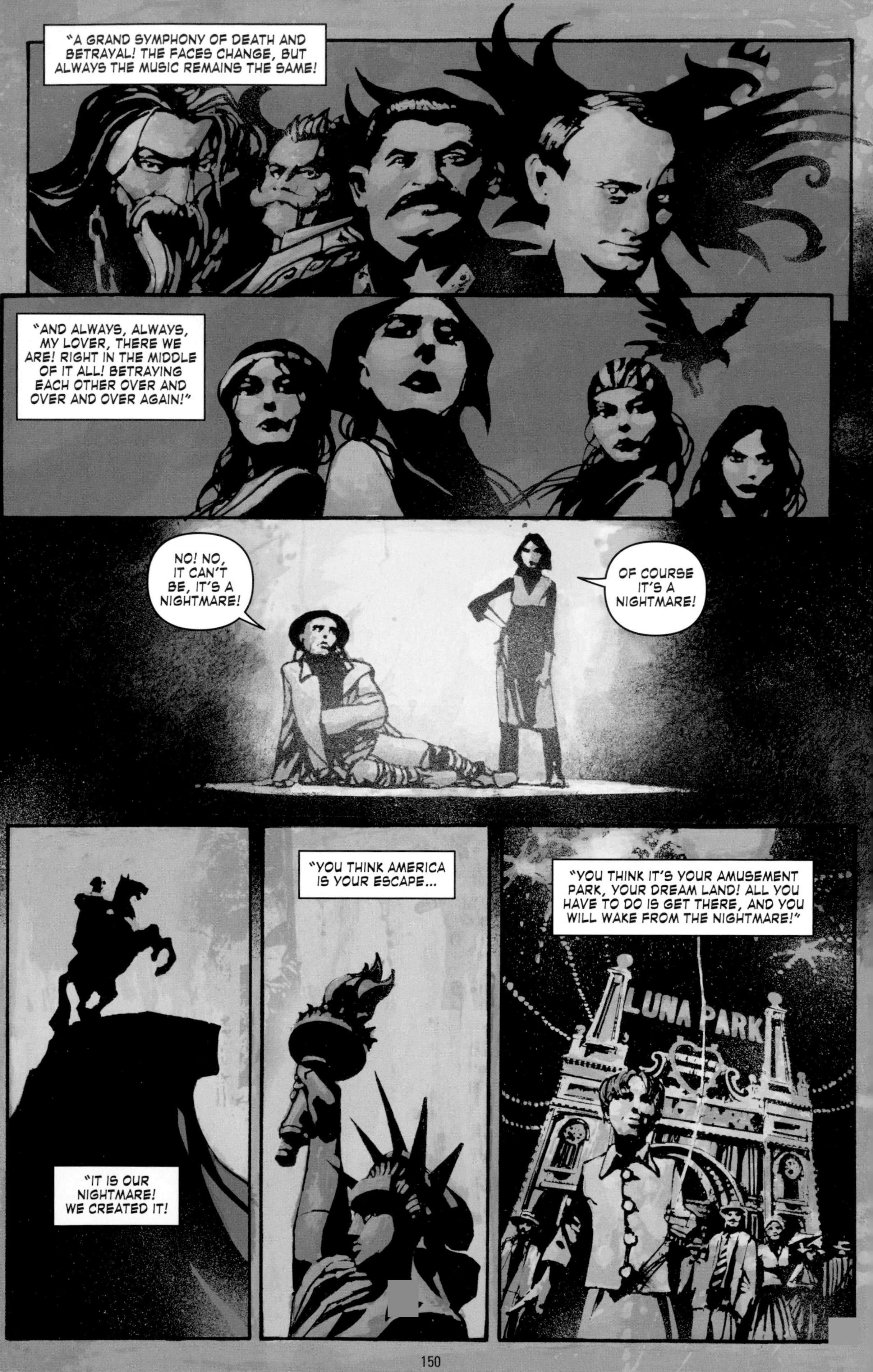
"A GRAND SYMPHONY OF DEATH AND BETRAYAL! THE FACES CHANGE, BUT ALWAYS THE MUSIC REMAINS THE SAME!
"AND ALWAYS, ALWAYS, MY LOVER, THERE WE ARE! RIGHT IN THE MIDDLE OF IT ALL! BETRAYING EACH OTHER OVER AND OVER AND OVER AGAIN!"
NO! NO, IT CAN'T BE, IT'S A NIGHTMARE!
OF COURSE IT'S A NIGHTMARE!
"IT IS OUR NIGHTMARE! WE CREATED IT!
"YOU THINK AMERICA IS YOUR ESCAPE...
"YOU THINK IT'S YOUR AMUSEMENT PARK, YOUR DREAM LAND! ALL YOU HAVE TO DO IS GET THERE, AND YOU WILL WAKE FROM THE NIGHTMARE!"
LUNA PARK

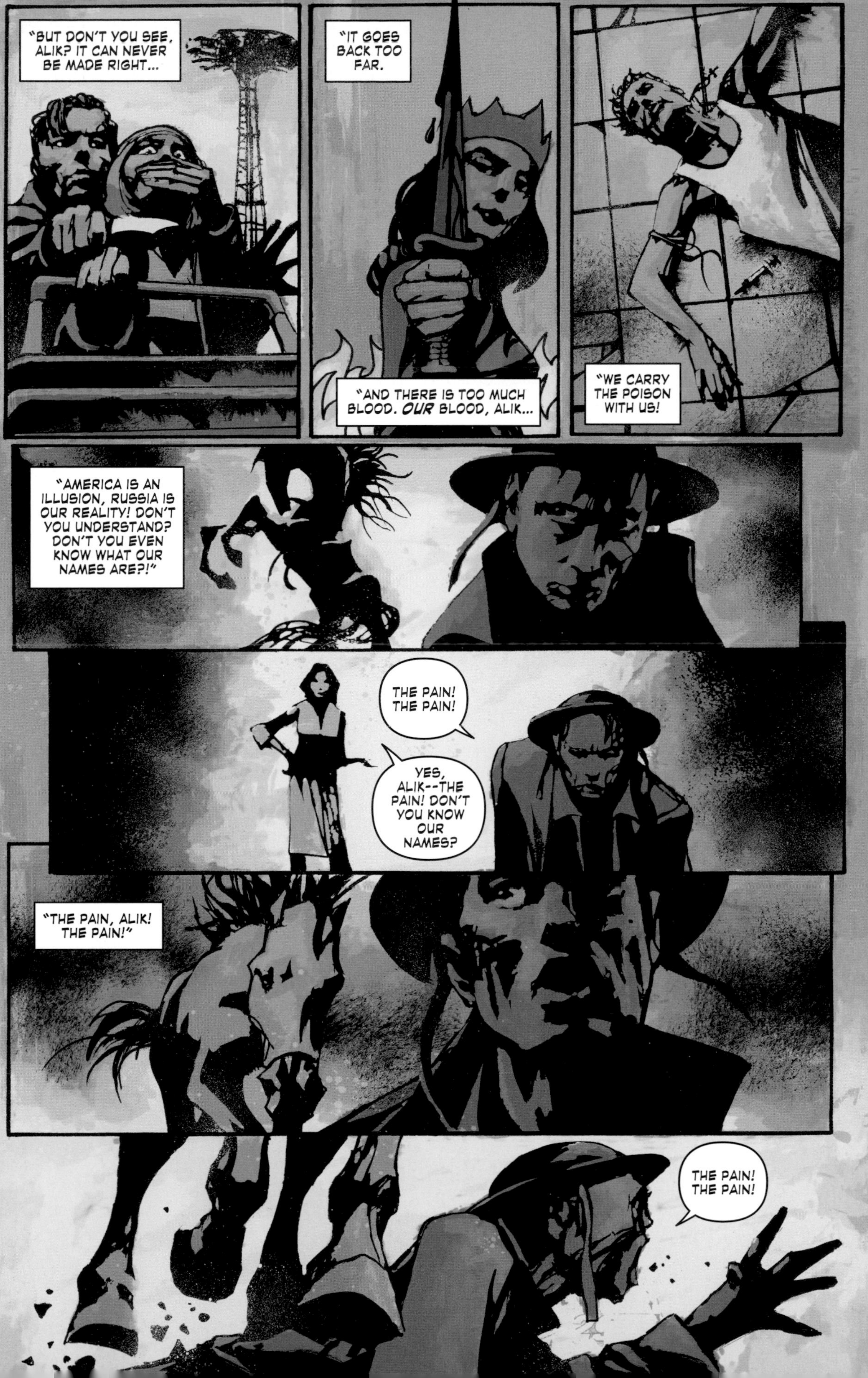
"BUT DON'T YOU SEE, ALIK? IT CAN NEVER BE MADE RIGHT...
"IT GOES BACK TOO FAR.
"AND THERE IS TOO MUCH BLOOD. OUR BLOOD, ALIK...
"WE CARRY THE POISON WITH US!
"AMERICA IS AN ILLUSION, RUSSIA IS OUR REALITY! DON'T YOU UNDERSTAND? DON'T YOU EVEN KNOW WHAT OUR NAMES ARE?!"
THE PAIN! THE PAIN!
YES, ALIK--THE PAIN! DON'T YOU KNOW OUR NAMES?
"THE PAIN, ALIK! THE PAIN!"
THE PAIN! THE PAIN!

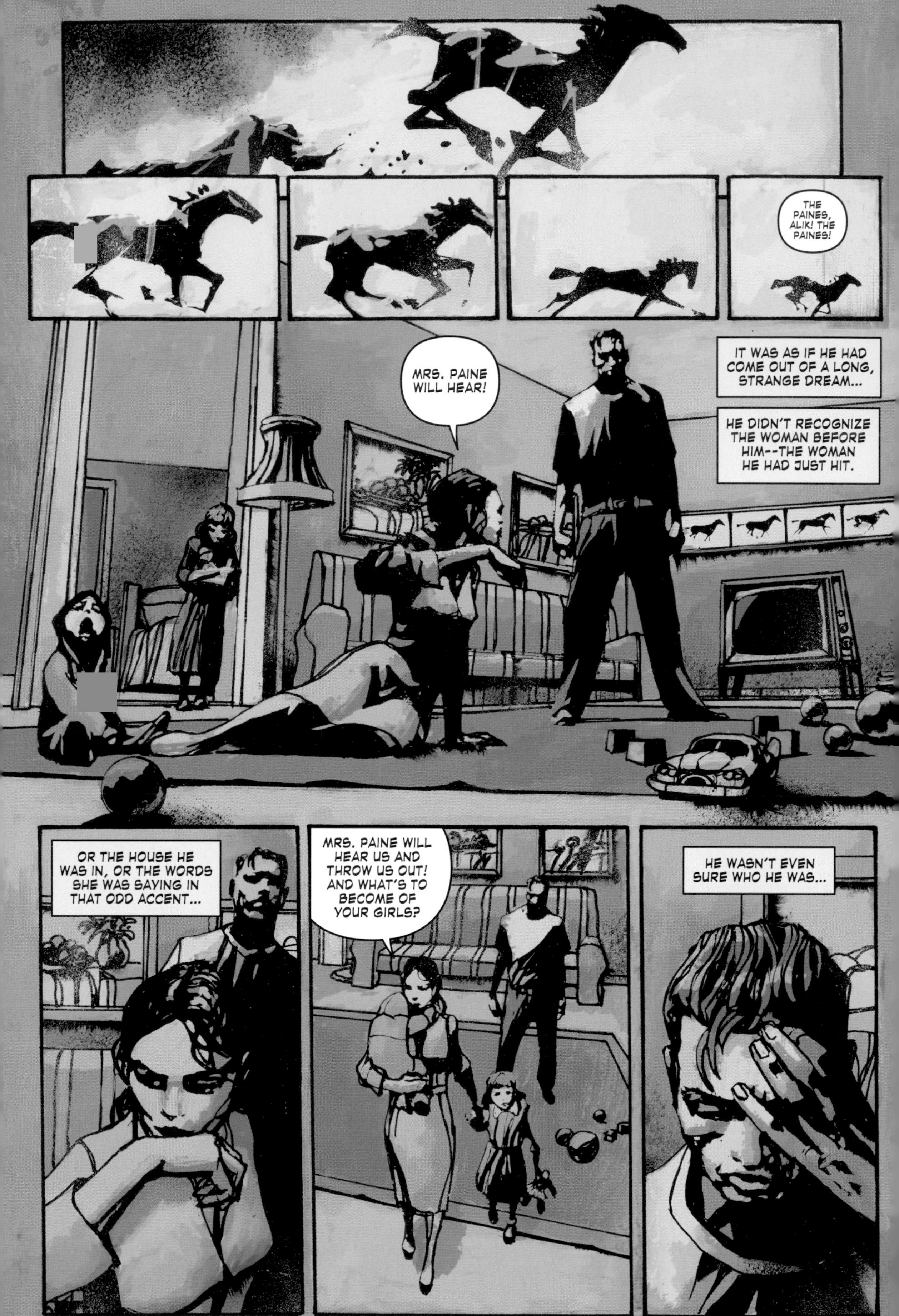
THE PAINES, ALIK! THE PAINES!
MRS. PAINE WILL HEAR!
IT WAS AS IF HE HAD COME OUT OF A LONG, STRANGE DREAM...
HE DIDN'T RECOGNIZE THE WOMAN BEFORE HIM--THE WOMAN HE HAD JUST HIT.
OR THE HOUSE HE WAS IN, OR THE WORDS SHE WAS SAYING IN THAT ODD ACCENT...
MRS. PAINE WILL HEAR US AND THROW US OUT! AND WHAT'S TO BECOME OF YOUR GIRLS?
HE WASN'T EVEN SURE WHO HE WAS...

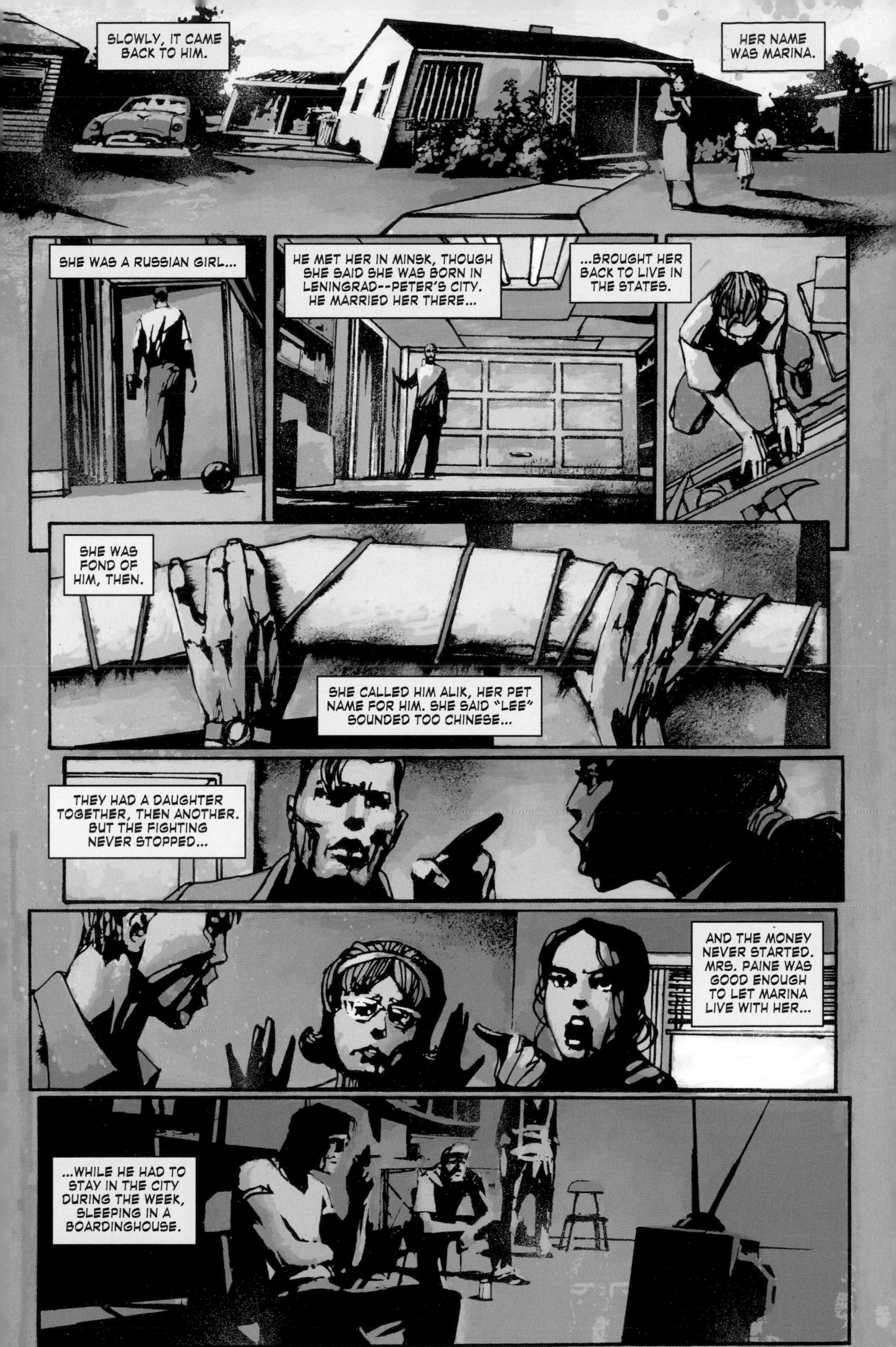
SLOWLY, IT CAME BACK TO HIM.
HER NAME WAS MARINA.
SHE WAS A RUSSIAN GIRL...
HE MET HER IN MINSK, THOUGH SHE SAID SHE WAS BORN IN LENINGRAD--PETER'S CITY. HE MARRIED HER THERE...
...BROUGHT HER BACK TO LIVE IN THE STATES.
SHE WAS FOND OF HIM, THEN.
SHE CALLED HIM ALIK, HER PET NAME FOR HIM. SHE SAID "LEE" SOUNDED TOO CHINESE...
THEY HAD A DAUGHTER TOGETHER, THEN ANOTHER. BUT THE FIGHTING NEVER STOPPED...
AND THE MONEY NEVER STARTED. MRS. PAINE WAS GOOD ENOUGH TO LET MARINA LIVE WITH HER...
...WHILE HE HAD TO STAY IN THE CITY DURING THE WEEK, SLEEPING IN A BOARDINGHOUSE.

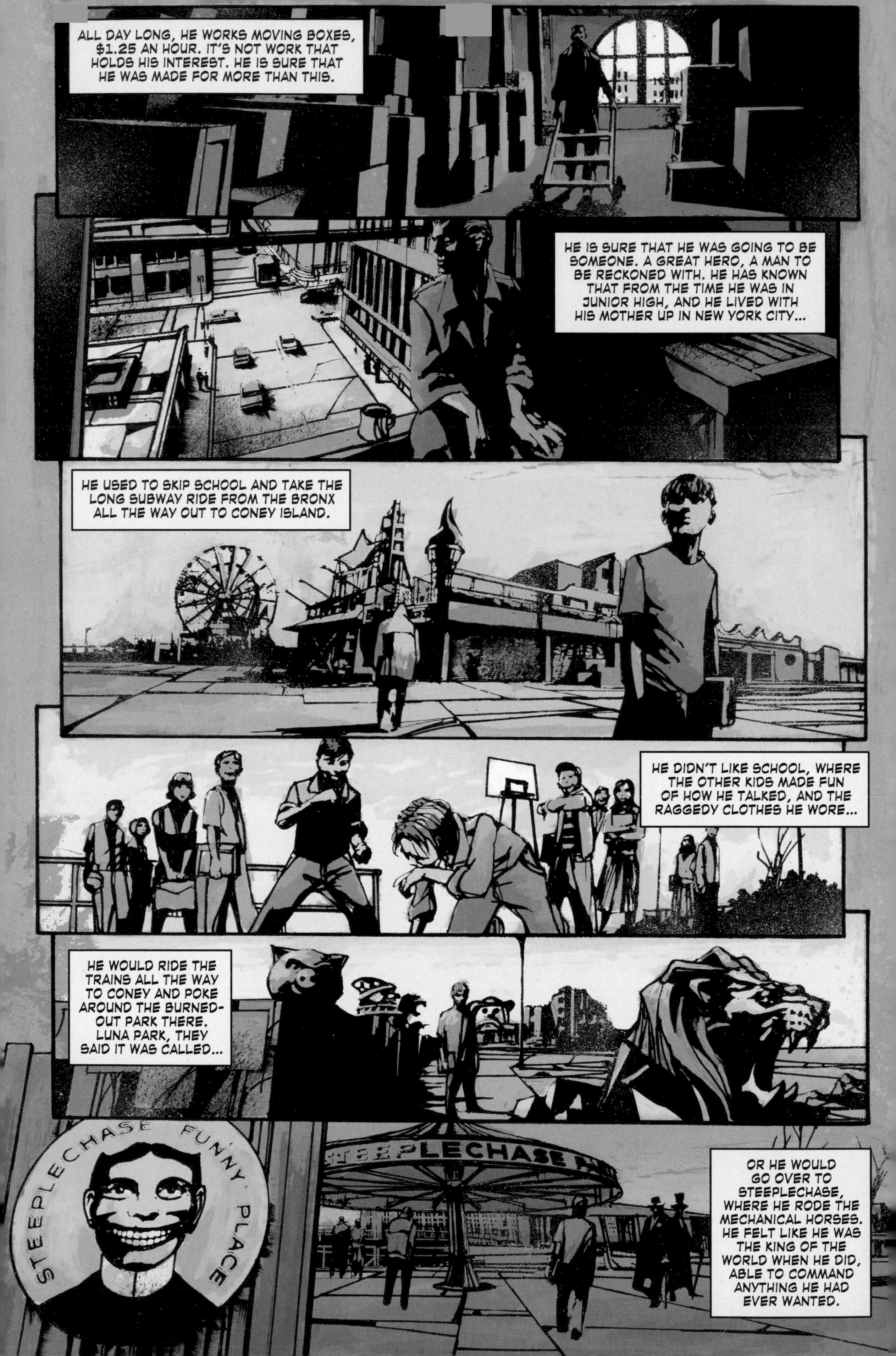
ALL DAY LONG, HE WORKS MOVING BOXES, $1.25 AN HOUR. IT'S NOT WORK THAT HOLDS HIS INTEREST. HE IS SURE THAT HE WAS MADE FOR MORE THAN THIS.
HE IS SURE THAT HE WAS GOING TO BE SOMEONE. A GREAT HERO, A MAN TO BE RECKONED WITH. HE HAS KNOWN THAT FROM THE TIME HE WAS IN JUNIOR HIGH, AND HE LIVED WITH HIS MOTHER UP IN NEW YORK CITY...
HE USED TO SKIP SCHOOL AND TAKE THE LONG SUBWAY RIDE FROM THE BRONX ALL THE WAY OUT TO CONEY ISLAND.
HE DIDN'T LIKE SCHOOL, WHERE THE OTHER KIDS MADE FUN OF HOW HE TALKED, AND THE RAGGEDY CLOTHES HE WORE...
HE WOULD RIDE THE TRAINS ALL THE WAY TO CONEY AND POKE AROUND THE BURNED-OUT PARK THERE. LUNA PARK, THEY SAID IT WAS CALLED...
STEEPLECHASE FUNNY PLACE
STEEPLECHASE
OR HE WOULD GO OVER TO STEEPLECHASE, WHERE HE RODE THE MECHANICAL HORSES. HE FELT LIKE HE WAS THE KING OF THE WORLD WHEN HE DID, ABLE TO COMMAND ANYTHING HE HAD EVER WANTED.

HE KNEW IT, THEN. HE WOULD BE A GREAT HERO, EVEN GREATER THAN HIS BROTHER, WHO WAS IN THE MARINES. HE WOULD BE MORE THAN JUST A LITTLE BASTARD WHOSE FATHER DIED BEFORE HE EVER SET EYES ON HIM...

BUT AT THE END OF THE DAY, HE ALWAYS HAD TO GO HOME.

HE DIDN'T LIKE BEING HOME, IN THEIR BASEMENT APARTMENT, WHERE HIS MOTHER WOULD FORGET TO BRING HOME DINNER. SHE DIDN'T GIVE A DAMN ABOUT HIM, HE KNEW. HIS OWN MOTHER. HE TRIED TO GET AWAY...

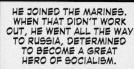

HE JOINED THE MARINES. WHEN THAT DIDN'T WORK OUT, HE WENT ALL THE WAY TO RUSSIA, DETERMINED TO BECOME A GREAT HERO OF SOCIALISM.

BUT THAT DIDN'T WORK, EITHER...

HE KNOWS MARINA BLAMES HIM, BUT SHE DOESN'T KNOW WHAT IT'S LIKE. WITH THE FBI BREATHING DOWN HIS NECK, SCARING AWAY JOBS...

BUT THAT'S ALREADY BEHIND HIM. HE HAS ANOTHER PLAN, ONE THAT HE'S ALREADY PUT INTO MOTION.

THAT NIGHT, HE LEAVES $170, ALL THE MONEY HE HAS IN THE WORLD, AND HIS WEDDING RING ON THE TOP OF THEIR DRESSER. *NOW* HE'S READY.

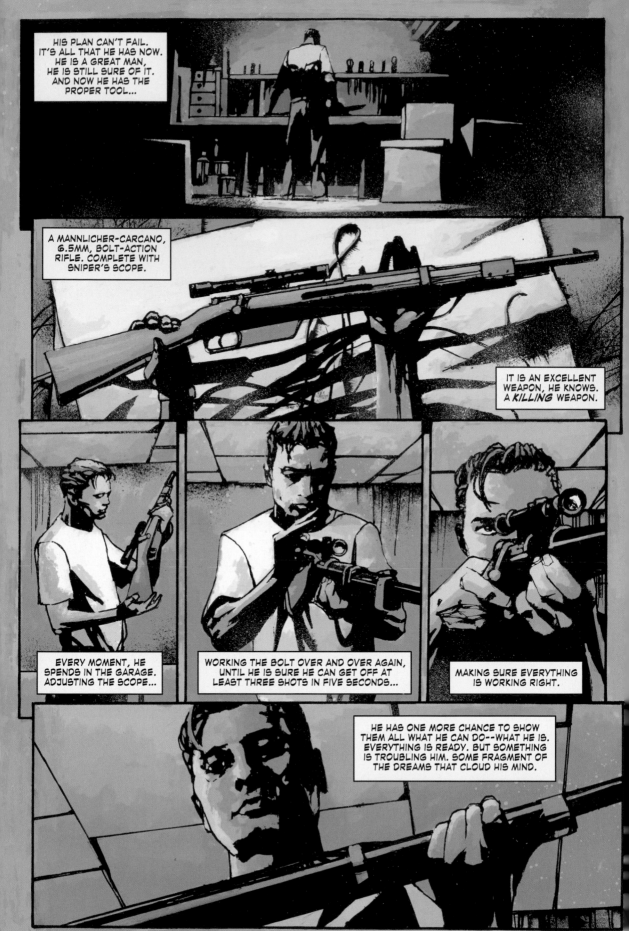

HIS PLAN CAN'T FAIL. IT'S ALL THAT HE HAS NOW. HE IS A GREAT MAN, HE IS STILL SURE OF IT. AND NOW HE HAS THE PROPER TOOL...

A MANNLICHER-CARCANO, 6.5MM, BOLT-ACTION RIFLE. COMPLETE WITH SNIPER'S SCOPE.

IT IS AN EXCELLENT WEAPON, HE KNOWS. A *KILLING* WEAPON.

EVERY MOMENT, HE SPENDS IN THE GARAGE. ADJUSTING THE SCOPE...

WORKING THE BOLT OVER AND OVER AGAIN, UNTIL HE IS SURE HE CAN GET OFF AT LEAST THREE SHOTS IN FIVE SECONDS...

MAKING SURE EVERYTHING IS WORKING RIGHT.

HE HAS ONE MORE CHANCE TO SHOW THEM ALL WHAT HE CAN DO--WHAT HE IS. EVERYTHING IS READY. BUT SOMETHING IS TROUBLING HIM. SOME FRAGMENT OF THE DREAMS THAT CLOUD HIS MIND.

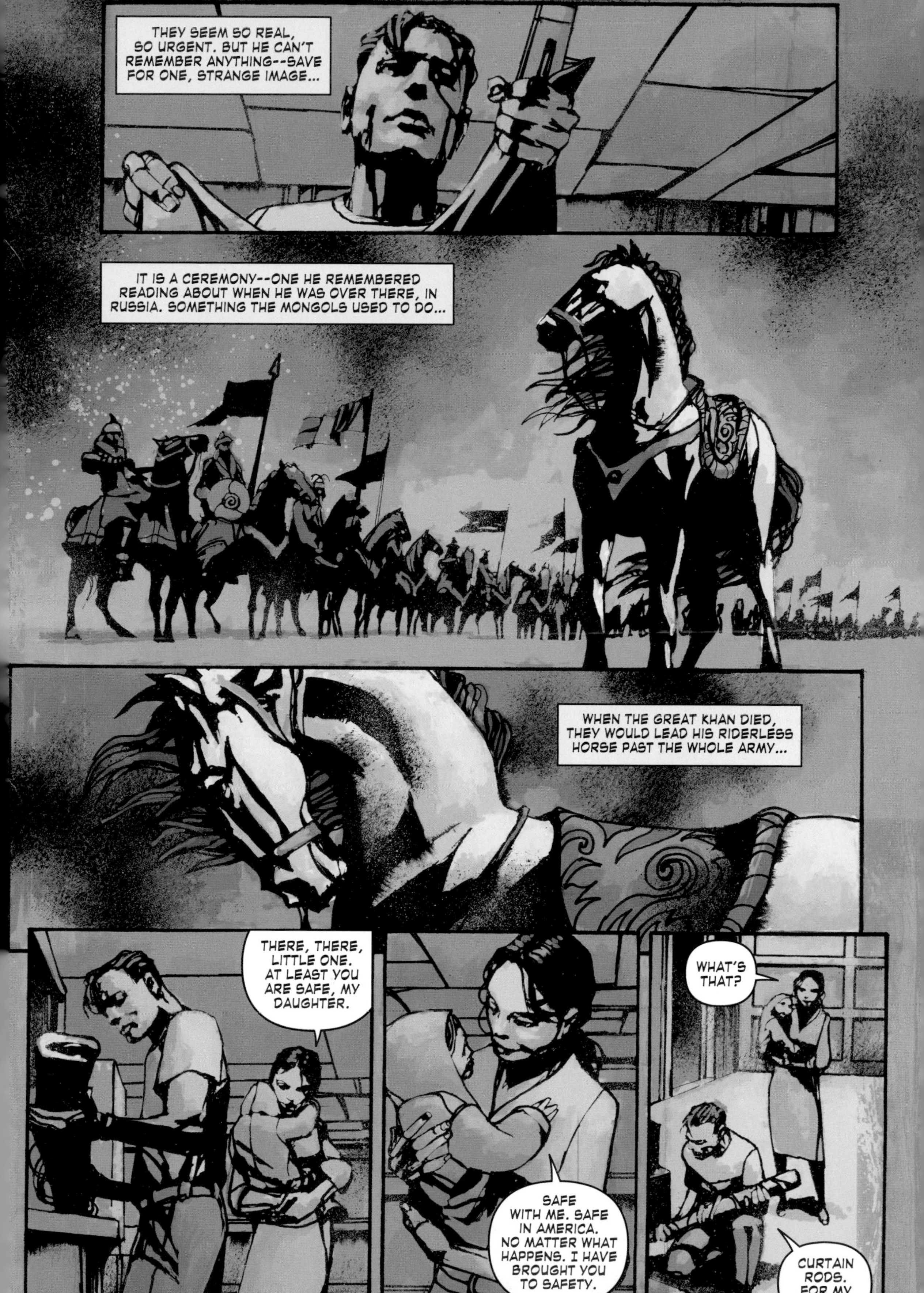
THEY SEEM SO REAL, SO URGENT. BUT HE CAN'T REMEMBER ANYTHING--SAVE FOR ONE, STRANGE IMAGE...
IT IS A CEREMONY--ONE HE REMEMBERED READING ABOUT WHEN HE WAS OVER THERE, IN RUSSIA. SOMETHING THE MONGOLS USED TO DO...
WHEN THE GREAT KHAN DIED, THEY WOULD LEAD HIS RIDERLESS HORSE PAST THE WHOLE ARMY...
THERE, THERE, LITTLE ONE. AT LEAST YOU ARE SAFE, MY DAUGHTER.
SAFE WITH ME. SAFE IN AMERICA. NO MATTER WHAT HAPPENS. I HAVE BROUGHT YOU TO SAFETY.
WHAT'S THAT?
CURTAIN RODS. FOR MY ROOM.

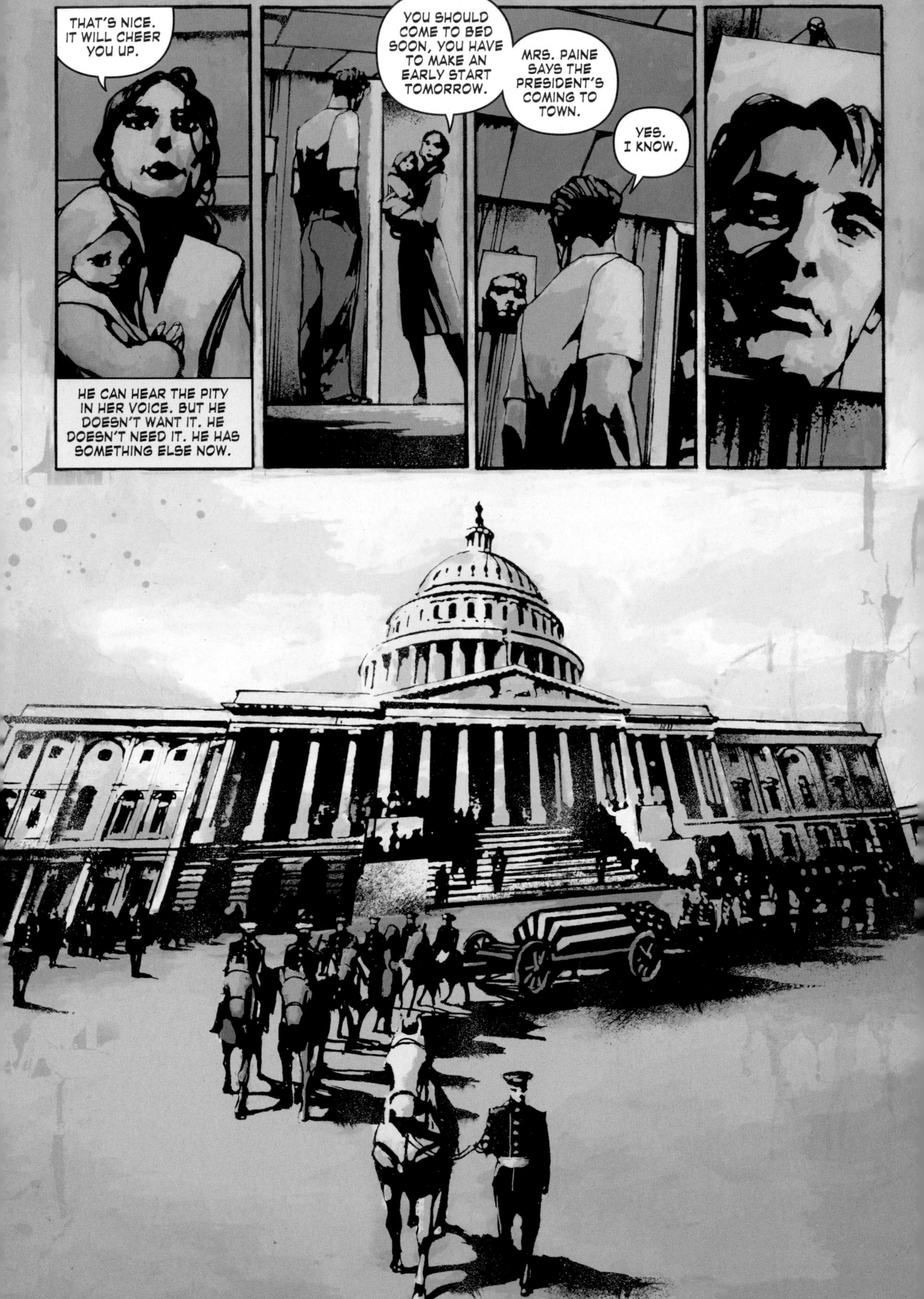
THAT'S NICE. IT WILL CHEER YOU UP.
HE CAN HEAR THE PITY IN HER VOICE. BUT HE DOESN'T WANT IT. HE DOESN'T NEED IT. HE HAS SOMETHING ELSE NOW.
YOU SHOULD COME TO BED SOON, YOU HAVE TO MAKE AN EARLY START TOMORROW.
MRS. PAINE SAYS THE PRESIDENT'S COMING TO TOWN.
YES. I KNOW.
THE END

KEVIN BAKER is the author of four novels, including the *City of Fire* trilogy: *Dreamland, Paradise Alley,* and *Strivers Row*. He is married and lives in New York City, and his website is www.kevinbaker.info.

DANIJEL ZEZELJ is a comic book artist, painter and illustrator and author of eighteen graphic novels. He studied classical painting, sculpting and printing at the Academy of Fine Arts in Zagreb, Croatia. His comics and illustrations have been published by DC Comics/ Vertigo, Marvel Comics, *The New York Times Book Review, Harper's Magazine, San Francisco Guardian, Editori del Grifo, Edizioni Charta,* etc. In 2001 in Zagreb, Croatia, he founded the publishing house and graphic workshop Petikat. He lives and works in Brooklyn, and his website is www.dzezelj.com.